Best Books for High School Readers

Best Books for High School Readers

GRADES 9–12

Supplement to the Second Edition

Catherine Barr

Children's and Young Adult Literature Reference

LIBRARIES UNLIMITED

AN IMPRINT OF ABC-CLIO, LLC
Santa Barbara, California • Denver, Colorado • Oxford, England

Library of Congress Cataloging-in-Publication Data

Barr, Catherine, 1951–
  Best books for high school readers : grades 9–12.
Supplement to the second edition / Catherine Barr.
      p. cm. — (Children's and young adult literature reference)
  Includes bibliographical references and indexes.
  ISBN 978-1-59884-785-7
 1. Young adult literature—Bibliography. 2. High school libraries—United States—Book lists.
3. Teenagers—Books and reading—United States. I. Title.
  Z1037.G4816 2009 Suppl.
  011.62—dc23   2011027353

ISBN: 978-1-59884-785-7

16 15 14 13 12   1 2 3 4 5

Libraries Unlimited
An Imprint of ABC-CLIO, LLC

ABC-CLIO, LLC
130 Cremona Drive, P.O. Box 1911
Santa Barbara, California 93116-1911

This book is printed on acid-free paper ∞
Manufactured in the United States of America

Contents

History and Geography

Philosophy and Religion

Society and the Individual

Guidance and Personal Development

Physical and Applied Sciences

Recreation and Sports

Major Subjects Arranged Alphabetically

Preface

Librarians and other specialists in children's literature have available, through print and online sources, a large number of bibliographies that recommend books suitable for young people. Unfortunately, these sources vary widely in quality and usefulness. The Best Books series was created to furnish authoritative, reliable, and comprehensive bibliographies for use in libraries that collect materials for readers from preschool through grade 12. The series now consists of three volumes: *Best Books for Children, Best Books for Middle School and Junior High Readers,* and *Best Books for High School Readers*.

Best Books for High School Readers supplies information on books recommended for readers in grades 9 through 12 or roughly ages 15 through 18. *Best Books for Children* contains books recommended for preschool through grade 6, and *Best Books for Middle School and Junior High Readers* covers grades 6 through 9.

As every librarian knows, reading levels are elastic. There is no such thing, for example, as a tenth-grade book. Instead there are only tenth-grade readers who, in their diversity, can represent a wide range of reading abilities and interests. This bibliography contains a liberal selection of entries that, one hopes, will accommodate readers in these grades and allow for their great range of tastes and reading competencies. By high school, a percentage of the books read should be at the adult level. Keeping this in mind, about one third of the entries in this volume are adult books suitable for young adult readers (these are designated by a reading level usually of 10–12 within the entries and by S–Adult in the subject index). At the other end of the spectrum, there are also many titles that are suitable for younger readers (these are indicated by grade level designations such as 5–10, 6–10, 7–10, and so forth).

Books that contain material that might be objectionable to some readers (scenes of graphic sex, for example), usually include a note in the annotation indicating that the book is suitable for mature readers, and many carry a grade level designation of 11–12.

In selecting books for inclusion, deciding on their arrangement, and collecting the information supplied on each, it was the editor's intention to reflect the current needs and interests of young readers while keeping in mind the latest trends and curricular emphases in today's schools.

General Scope and Criteria for Inclusion

This supplement covers a two-year period, picking up from the second edition of *Best Books for High School Readers*, which was published in 2009, and including recommended titles through early 2011. Of the 2,060 titles listed here, 1,986 are individually numbered entries and 74 are cited within the annotations as additional recommended titles by the same author (often these are titles that are part of an extensive series). It should be noted that some series are so extensive that, because of space limitations, only representative titles are included.

Excluded from this bibliography are general reference works, such as dictionaries and encyclopedias, except for a few single-volume works that are so heavily illustrated and attractive that they can also be used in the general circulation collection. Also excluded are professional books for librarians and teachers and mass market series books.

For most fiction and nonfiction, a minimum of two recommendations were required from the current reviewing sources consulted for a title to be considered for listing. However, there were a number of necessary exceptions. For example, in some reviewing journals only a few representative titles from extensive nonfiction series are reviewed even though others in the series will also be recommended. In such cases a single favorable review was enough for inclusion. This also held true for some of the adult titles suitable for young adult readers where, it has been found, reviewing journals tend to be less inclusive than with juvenile titles. Again, depending on the strength of the review, a single positive one was sufficient for inclusion. As well as favorable reviews, additional criteria such as availability, currency, accuracy, usefulness, and relevance were considered.

Sources Used

A number of current and retrospective sources were used in compiling this bibliography. Book reviewing journals consulted were *Booklist, Library Media Connection, School Library Journal*, and *VOYA (Voice of Youth Advocates)*. Other sources used include *Horn Book*.

Uses of This Book

Best Books for High School Readers was designed to help librarians and media specialists with four vital tasks: (1) evaluating the adequacy of existing collections; (2) building new collections or strengthening existing holdings; (3) providing reading guidance to young adults; and (4) preparing bibliographies and reading lists. To increase the book's usefulness, particularly in preparation of bibliographies or suggested reading lists, titles are arranged under broad areas of interest or, in the case of nonfiction works, by curriculum-oriented subjects rather than the Dewey Decimal classification (suggested Dewey classification numbers are nevertheless provided within nonfiction entries). The subject arrangement corresponds roughly to the one used in *Best Books for Children*, minus its large section on picture books.

Some arbitrary decisions were made concerning placement of books under specific subjects. For example, books of experiments and projects in general science are placed under "Physical and Applied Sciences — Experiments and Projects," whereas books of experiments and projects on a specific branch of science (e.g., physics) appear under that branch. It is hoped that use of the many "see" and "see also" references in the Subject/Grade Level Index will help guide the user in this regard.

With this edition, we have added symbols ♫ and **e** to indicate audio and ebook versions are available; we expect to see increasing use of these symbols with each new edition.

Arrangement

In the Table of Contents, subjects are arranged by the order in which they appear in the book. Following the Table of Contents is a listing of Major Subjects Arranged Alphabetically, which provides entry numbers as well as page numbers for easy access. Following the main body of the text, there are three indexes. The Author Index cites authors and editors, titles, and entry numbers (joint authors and editors are listed separately). The Title Index gives the book's entry number. Works of fiction in both of these indexes are indicated by (F) following the entry number. Finally, an extensive Subject/Grade Level Index lists entry numbers under hundreds of subject headings with specific grade level suitability given for each entry. The following codes are used to identify general grade levels:

JS   (Junior–Senior High) suitable for junior high and senior high grades (grades 7 and up)

S   (Senior High) suitable usually only for senior high grades (grades 10–12)

S-Adult (Senior High-Adult) written for an adult audience but suitable for high school collections (usually grades 10–12)

Entries

A typical entry contains the following information where applicable: (1) author, joint author, or editor; (2) title and subtitle; (3) specific grade levels given in parentheses; (4) adapter or translator; (5) indication of illustrations; (6) series title; (7) publication date; (8) publisher and price of hardbound edition (LB = library binding); (9) International Standard Book Number (ISBN) of hardbound edition; (10) paperback publisher (paper) and price (if no publisher is listed it is the same as the hardbound edition); (11) ISBN of paperback edition; (12) annotation; (13) indication that an audio version is available; (14) indication that an ebook version is available; (15) Lexile measure; (16) review citations; (17) Dewey Decimal classification number. For additional information on Lexile measures, visit www.lexile.com.

Review Citations

Review citations are given for books published and reviewed from July 2008 through early 2011. These citations can be used to find more detailed information about each of the books listed. The periodical sources identified are:

Booklist (BL)
Booklist Online (BLO)
Horn Book (HB)
Library Media Connection (LMC)
School Library Journal (SLJ)
VOYA (Voice of Youth Advocates) (VOYA)

Acknowledgments

Many thanks to Barbara Ittner of Libraries Unlimited and to Christine McNaull and Kristina Strain for their help with this volume.

Catherine Barr

Literary Forms

Fiction

Adventure and Survival Stories

1 Aguiar, Nadia. *The Lost Island of Tamarind* (7–10). 2008, Feiwel & Friends $17.95 (978-031238029-8). Part mystery, part fantasy, part survival story, this tale tells of 13-year-old Maya and her two young siblings who survive a storm aboard their parents' marine research boat and end up in a fantasy world full of danger and magic. **e** Lexile 880L (Rev: BLO 10/29/08; LMC 3–4/09; SLJ 10/1/08; VOYA 12/08)

2 Caveney, Philip. *Prince of Pirates* (7–10). Series: Sebastian Darke. 2009, Delacorte $16.99 (978-038573468-4); LB $19.99 (978-038590466-7). In the second book in the series, Sebastian Darke and his sidekicks try out the pirate life and sail off in search of treasure. Lexile 830L (Rev: BL 4/1/09; VOYA 10/09)

3 Gilman, David. *The Devil's Breath* (7–12). Series: Danger Zone. 2008, Delacorte $16.99 (978-038573560-5); LB $19.99 (978-038590546-6). In this action-packed adventure tale, 15-year-old Max Gordon embarks on a search for his missing father in the Namibian desert; the first installment in a series. ∩ (Rev: BL 11/1/08; SLJ 10/1/08)

4 Herlong, M. H. *The Great Wide Sea* (6–10). 2008, Viking $16.99 (978-067006330-7). Not long after their mother's death, three brothers find themselves stranded on an island in the Bahamas when their unpredictable father disappears in an ocean storm. Lexile 660L (Rev: BL 11/15/08; HB 1–2/09; SLJ 3/1/09)

5 Higson, Charlie. *The Enemy* (9–12). 2010, Hyperion $16.99 (978-1-4231-3175-5). In a new world where a virus has killed everyone over the age of 16, groups of teens struggle to survive and cooperate; an action-packed, thought-provoking novel. **e** Lexile HL590L (Rev: BL 5/15/10; LMC 10/10; SLJ 7/10)

6 Kessler, Cristina. *Trouble in Timbuktu* (7–12). 2009, Philomel $17.99 (978-039924451-3). The history and culture of the city of Timbuktu are an integral part of this novel about Malian twins Ahmed and Ayisha, who embark on a dangerous journey to foil the attempt of two American thieves trying to steal valuable ancient manuscripts. Lexile 900L (Rev: BL 12/15/08; LMC 8–9/09; SLJ 3/1/09; VOYA 6/09)

7 Meyer, L. A. *Rapture of the Deep: Being an Account of the Further Adventures of Jacky Faber, Soldier, Sailor, Mermaid, Spy* (7–12). Series: Bloody Jack Adventure. 2009, Harcourt $17 (978-0-15-206501-0). On her way to her wedding in 1806, Jacky is forced by the British Navy to head for the Caribbean to search for a sunken treasure ship. ∩ (Rev: BL 9/1/09; SLJ 12/09)

8 Neri, G. *Surf Mules* (10–12). 2009, Putnam $16.99 (978-039925086-6). Logan and Z-boy, Southern California high school seniors facing an uncertain future, unwisely decide to risk driving marijuana to Florida. (Rev: BL 6/1–15/09*; SLJ 6/1/09)

9 Schrefer, Eliot. *The School for Dangerous Girls* (8–11). 2009, Scholastic $16.99 (978-054503528-6). Angela, 15, uncovers what is happening to the "hopeless cases" at her Colorado reform school in this suspenseful novel about cruelty and punishment. (Rev: BL 2/1/09; LMC 5–6/09; SLJ 2/1/09)

10 Westerfeld, Scott. *Leviathan* (7–10). Illus. by Keith Thompson. 2009, Simon & Schuster $19.99 (978-1-4169-7173-3). An exciting steampunk adventure set in an alternate 1914 and featuring Prince Alek, son of the assassinated Archduke Ferdinand and a member of the technologically innovative Clankers, and Deryn, a girl from opposing Darwinist England masquerading as a boy in order to fly on the giant airship *Leviathan*. **e** Lexile 790L (Rev: BL 8/09; HB 11–12/09; SLJ 9/09)

11 Wild, K. *Firefight* (7–10). 2009, Scholastic $16.99 (978-043987176-1). Super-strong Freedom Smith must defeat an evil gang of kidnappers; world travel, action, the supernatural, and even romance combine in this exciting story, a sequel to *Fight Game* (2007). Lexile HL640L (Rev: BLO 3/24/09; SLJ 8/09)

Animal Stories

12 Brown, Paul. *Wolf Pack of the Winisk River* (6–12). 2009, Lobster paper $10.95 (978-189755010-6). Told in free verse from a wolf's point of view, this story takes the reader into the life of a wolf pack. (Rev: BL 4/15/09; LMC 10/09; SLJ 12/09)

13 Wilson, Susan. *One Good Dog* (9–12). 2010, St. Martin's $29.50 (978-031257125-2). The story of a man who has lost everything and finds himself caring for a mistreated pit bull named Chance is told from the points of view of both man and dog. ⏺ (Rev: BL 2/1/10)

Classics

Europe

GENERAL AND MISCELLANEOUS

14 Agard, John. *The Young Inferno* (9–12). Illus. by Satoshi Kitamura. 2009, Frances Lincoln $19.95 (978-1-84507-769-3). In this updated, heavily illustrated version of Dante's *Inferno*, the hoodie-wearing protagonist tours Hell with Aesop and meets a variety of sinners, many of whom will be familiar to today's readers. (Rev: LMC 11–12/09; SLJ 8/09)

GREAT BRITAIN AND IRELAND

15 Brontë, Charlotte, and Amy Corzine. *Jane Eyre, The Graphic Novel: Original Text* (7–10). Illus. by John M. Burns. Series: Classical Comics. 2009, Classical Comics paper $16.95 (978-190633247-1). Drawing directly from Brontë's text, this graphic-novel adaptation offers an appealing introduction to the story; back matter includes material on Brontë's life. (Rev: BL 3/1/09)

16 Chaucer, Geoffrey, and Peter Ackroyd. *The Canterbury Tales: A Retelling* (11–12). Illus. by Nick Bantock. 2009, Viking $35 (978-067002122-2). Author Peter Ackroyd recasts Chaucer's well-known tales in modern prose, retaining keeping much of the wit and bawdy humor; for advanced students. ℮ (Rev: BL 9/09)

17 Wilde, Oscar, and Ian Edginton. *The Picture of Dorian Gray* (8–12). Illus. by I. N. J. Culbard. 2009, Sterling paper $14.95 (978-141141593-5). This graphic-novel interpretation of the classic story will serve as an introduction for reluctant readers. (Rev: BL 4/1/09)

United States

18 Bradbury, Ray. *Fahrenheit 451: The Authorized Adaptation* (9–12). Illus. by Tim Hamilton. 2009, Farrar $30.00 (978-080905100-7); paper $16.95 (978-080905101-4). A faithful graphic-novel adaptation of the classic novel about censorship. (Rev: BL 7/09)

19 Lovecraft, H. P. *Nyarlathotep* (8–12). Illus. by Chuck BB. 2009, Boom! Studios $14.99 (978-193450665-3). A graphic and disturbing rendering of the horrifying 1920 prose poem. (Rev: BL 3/15/09; SLJ 7/09)

20 Sinclair, Upton, and Peter Kuper. *The Jungle* (7–12). Series: Classics Illustrated. 2010, Papercutz $9.99 (978-156163-404-0). Kuper's graphic-novel adaptation brings new life to Sinclair's 1906 classic about the meatpacking industry and the plight of immigrant workers. (Rev: BL 6/18/10; LMC 10/10)

Contemporary Life and Problems

General and Miscellaneous

21 Ahern, Cecelia. *The Gift* (9–12). 2009, Harper $19.99 (978-006170626-4). Businessman Lou Suffern is so focused on getting promoted that Christmas and family are the last thing on his mind, but his priorities are about to be challenged when the homeless man he hires to work in his company's mailroom invites himself into Lou's personal life. (Rev: BL 10/1/09)

22 Alenyikov, Michael. *Ivan and Misha* (11–12). 2010, Northwestern Univ. $18.95 (978-081012718-0). This insightful collection of short stories revolves around gay twin brothers who immigrated from Russia and now live in New York City; for mature readers. (Rev: BLO 9/15/10)

23 Alexander, Jill S. *The Sweetheart of Prosper County* (7–10). 2009, Feiwel & Friends $16.99 (978-0-312-54856-8). Funny characters populate this likable story about 15-year-old Austin, a girl who learns to look inward for the confidence to stand up to a boy who bullies her, and decides to enter a rooster in the local poultry competition. ⏺ Lexile 710L (Rev: BL 8/09; SLJ 9/09)

24 Anderson, Jodi Lynn. *Love and Peaches* (8–11). 2008, HarperTeen $16.99 (978-0-06-073311-7); LB $17.89 (978-0-06-073312-4). Friends Leeda, Murphy, and Birdie return to Darlington Orchard, where they face jilted boyfriends, inheritances, heartbreak, and goodbyes. (Rev: SLJ 4/1/09)

25 Anhalt, Ariela. *Freefall* (10–12). 2010, Harcourt $17 (978-0-15-206567-6). Submissive, weak-kneed boarding school student Luke goes along with his best friend's fencing team hazing plan, with disastrous results. **e** Lexile HL590L (Rev: BL 12/15/09; SLJ 1/10; VOYA 10/09)

26 Antieau, Kim. *Ruby's Imagine* (6–10). 2008, Houghton $16.00 (978-061899767-1). Ruby, 17, lives in New Orleans but is in tune with nature, and when Hurricane Katrina overwhelms the city Ruby heeds her grandmother rather than her instincts and ends up learning some family secrets. Lexile 540L (Rev: BL 11/15/08; LMC 3–4/09; SLJ 12/08)

27 Ayarbe, Heidi. *Freeze Frame* (9–12). 2008, HarperCollins $17.89 (978-006135174-7); LB $17.89 (978-006135174-7). A fatal shooting of which he cannot remember the details changes 15-year-old Kyle's life, leaving him filled with self-loathing as he tries to make sense of his actions. **e** Lexile 490L (Rev: BL 10/15/08; SLJ 2/1/09; VOYA 12/08)

28 Barron, Sandra Rodriguez. *Stay with Me* (10–12). 2010, Harper paper $14.99 (978-006165062-8). Five adults, bonded by a mysterious childhood event, reunite to try to discover their true identities in this mystery/romance novel. (Rev: BL 11/115/10)

29 Benway, Robin. *Audrey, Wait!* (8–11). 2008, Penguin $16.99 (978-159514191-0). Audrey's ex-boyfriend Even, a rock singer, writes a song about their breakup and she suddenly finds herself a reluctant celebrity. Lexile 760L (Rev: BL 8/08; SLJ 8/08)

30 Berwin, Margot. *Hothouse Flower and the Nine Plants of Desire* (11–12). 2009, Pantheon $24 (978-030737784-5). Ready for something new following her divorce, Lila Nova stumbles upon a unique Laundromat filled with exotic tropical plants and soon finds herself tangled in romance and adventure far from her Manhattan home; for mature readers. ∩ **e** (Rev: BL 5/1/09)

31 Bick, Ilsa J. *Draw the Dark* (9–12). 2010, Carolrhoda $16.95 (978-0-7613-5686-8). A multilayered story featuring 17-year-old Christian, who can paint others' thoughts and has nightmares about being a Jewish child in the 1940s. ∩ Lexile 790L (Rev: BL 10/1/10; LMC 11–12/10; SLJ 11/1/10; VOYA 12/10)

32 Bjorkman, Lauren. *My Invented Life* (10–12). 2009, Holt $17.99 (978-0-8050-8950-9). In order to re-establish the closeness she once shared with her sister, whom she suspects is gay, high school junior Roz Peterson pretends she herself is a lesbian, and this ruse prompts many unexpected revelations about her classmates as well as herself. **e** (Rev: BL 10/15/09; SLJ 12/09; VOYA 12/09)

33 Brande, Robin. *Fat Cat* (8–11). 2009, Knopf $16.99 (978-0-375-84449-2); LB $19.99 (978-0-375-94449-9). A science research project motivates overweight high school junior Cat to take on a prehistoric lifestyle and thereby lose pounds and for the first time attract male attention. ∩ **e** (Rev: BL 10/15/09; SLJ 1/10)

34 Brashares, Ann. *My Name Is Memory* (11–12). 2010, Riverhead $25.95 (978-159448758-3). Two lovers separated by chronological distance finally connect in this tantalizing, sometimes steamy novel reminiscent of Niffenegger's *The Time Traveler's Wife*; for mature teens. ∩ **e** (Rev: BL 3/15/10)

35 Buffie, Margaret. *Winter Shadows* (7–10). 2010, Tundra $19.95 (978-0-88776-968-9). High school senior Cass, unhappy and resentful of her stepmother, finds a diary written by Beatrice in the mid-19th century, who also is grappling with an unpleasant stepmother — and the two form a bond that transcends time. (Rev: BL 11/15/10; SLJ 12/1/10)

36 Cabot, Meg. *Being Nikki* (7–10). Series: Airhead. 2009, Scholastic $16.99 (978-054504056-3). Romance, suspense, and comedy (and a touch of science fiction) are intertwined in this second book about the ordinary teen whose brain has been transplanted into a famous model's body. ∩ Lexile 800L (Rev: BL 4/15/09; SLJ 1/10)

37 Cadnum, Michael. *Flash* (8–11). 2010, Farrar $16.99 (978-0-374-39911-5). On a tense day in Albany, California, five young people deal with various acute personal problems. (Rev: BL 5/1/10; HB 7–8/10; LMC 8–9/10; SLJ 6/10)

38 Calame, Don. *Beat the Band* (9–12). 2010, Candlewick $16.99 (978-0-7636-4633-2). Assigned to work with the dreaded "Hot Dog" Helen for a health class presentation on safe sex, 10th-grader Coop tries to recoup his rep by entering his musically challenged rock group in the "Battle of the Bands" competition. (Rev: BL 9/1/10; SLJ 12/1/10)

39 Caletti, Deb. *The Secret Life of Prince Charming* (8–11). 2009, Simon & Schuster $16.99 (978-141695940-3). Quinn, 17, and her sisters Sprout and Frances take a road trip to visit their father's former wives and girlfriends and to learn why men do the things they do. ∩ Lexile 760L (Rev: BL 4/1/09; HB 7–8/09; SLJ 6/1/09; VOYA 10/09)

40 Calloway, Cassidy. *Confessions of a First Daughter* (7–10). 2009, HarperTeen paper $8.99 (978-0-06-172439-8). Eighteen-year-old Morgan Abbott thinks that life as the First Daughter of the United States is trying enough as it is, but when her mother, the president, asks her to temporarily fill her shoes, Morgan finds that her life is about to get considerably more complicated. **e** (Rev: BL 7/09; SLJ 12/09; VOYA 8/09)

41 Calonita, Jen. *Paparazzi Princess* (6–10). Series: Secrets of My Hollywood Life. 2009, Little, Brown $16.99 (978-0-316-03064-9). Finding it difficult to cope with the impending end of her long-running show, teen TV star Kaitlin spends time with two publicity-hungry party girls until she finally realizes that their life is not satisfying. (Rev: SLJ 6/1/09; VOYA 6/09)

42 Calonita, Jen. *Reality Check* (7–10). 2010, Poppy $16.99 (978-0-316-04554-4). The friendship between four Long Island teenage girls does not survive when a media executive scout offers them their own reality TV show . ℰ Lexile HL690L (Rev: BL 4/15/10; SLJ 10/1/10; VOYA 8/10)

43 Calonita, Jen. *Sleepaway Girls* (7–10). 2009, Little, Brown $16.99 (978-031601717-6). Samantha has the time of her life at summer camp as a counselor in training. Lexile 710L (Rev: BL 5/1/09; SLJ 6/1/09)

44 Cameron, W. Bruce. *A Dog's Purpose* (10–12). 2010, Forge $22.99 (978-076532626-3). Narrated by clever, introspective Bailey, this charming, often humorous story charts the dog's diverse life changes — from stray to family dog, from K-9 rescue animal back to stray. ⌒ (Rev: BLO 7/10)

45 Campbell, Drusilla. *The Good Sister* (11–12). 2010, Grand Central paper $13.99 (978-044653578-6). Simone is on trial for attempting to murder her three children, and her sister Roxane tries, as always, to protect her in this novel that revisits the girls' difficult childhood and explores the tragedy of postpartum depression; for mature readers. ℰ (Rev: BLO 9/9/10)

46 Candela, Margo. *Good-bye to All That* (11–12). 2010, Touchstone paper $14 (978-141657135-3). Twenty-five-year-old marketing assistant Raquel copes with flirtation, family drama, and a seriously cutthroat work environment in Hollywood; for mature readers. (Rev: BL 6/1–15/10)

47 Carter, Ernessa T. *32 Candles* (11–12). 2010, Amistad $24.99 (978-006195784-0). Readers follow African American Davie Jones through her unhappy childhood in rural Mississippi to her career as a lounge singer in Los Angeles in this novel for mature readers about growth and first love. ⌒ ℰ (Rev: BL 7/10)

48 Castellucci, Cecil. *Rose Sees Red* (9–12). 2010, Scholastic $17.99 (978-0-545-06079-0). In 1980s New York City, teen ballet dancers Rose and her Russian neighbor Yrena overcome Cold War differences to enjoy a night of adventure. Lexile HL630L (Rev: BL 6/1/10; LMC 8–9/10; SLJ 9/1/10)

49 Castrovilla, Selene. *The Girl Next Door* (9–12). 2010, WestSide $16.95 (978-1-934813-15-7). Ever-successful Jesse, who should now be in his senior year, is instead battling lymphoma and, despite the grim survival rate, nurturing a bittersweet love affair with Samantha, the girl next door. (Rev: BL 7/15/10; SLJ 12/1/10)

50 Catton, Eleanor. *The Rehearsal* (11–12). 2010, Little, Brown $23.99 (978-031607433-9). In this inventive, intellectually challenging read, one girl's trauma — sexual abuse by her music teacher — becomes fodder for a nearby drama school's performance; for mature readers. ℰ (Rev: BL 4/15/10*)

51 Chandler, Ann. *Siena Summer* (7–10). 2009, Orca paper $12.95 (978-189658017-3). Angela spends a summer in Italy and rescues a doomed horse that she later rides in Siena's annual race. (Rev: BL 5/1/09)

52 Chiang, Ted. *The Lifecycle of Software Objects* (10–12). 2010, Subterranean $25 (978-159606317-4). Software tester Ana decides to train her capable, digital pet to live on its own in this novella that raises ethical questions about the role of artificial intelligence. (Rev: BL 7/10)

53 Cohen, Tish. *Little Black Lies* (8–12). 2009, Egmont USA $16.99 (978-1-60684-033-7); LB $19.99 (978-1-60684-046-7). When high school junior Sara Black allows her snobbish classmates to believe that she has just transferred to her upper-crust Boston school from London, England, this lie puts her father — the school's new janitor and obsessive-compulsive disorder victim — in a precarious position. and jeopardizes her relationship with him. ℰ (Rev: BL 11/1/09; SLJ 12/09; VOYA 12/09)

54 Cohn, Rachel. *Very LeFreak* (10–12). 2010, Knopf $16.99 (978-0-375-85758-4); LB $19.99 (978-0-375-95758-1). Very (short for Veronica) comes close to flunking out of Columbia because of her devotion to electronic media and her very active social and sexual life; an intervention sends her off to tech rehab. ⌒ ℰ (Rev: BL 11/1/09; HB 1–2/10; SLJ 1/10; VOYA 4/10)

55 Cohn, Rachel, and David Levithan. *Dash and Lily's Book of Dares* (9–12). 2010, Knopf $16.99 (978-0-375-86659-3); LB $19.99 (978-0-375-96659-0). Alone in Manhattan at Christmas time, lonely teens Dash and Lily carry on a kind of literary scavenger hunt/romance centered on the pages of a moleskin journal. ⌒ ℰ Lexile 860L (Rev: BL 11/1/10; HB 1–2/11; SLJ 10/1/10; VOYA 12/10)

56 Colasanti, Susane. *Take Me There* (7–10). 2008, Viking $17.99 (978-067006333-8). In this satisfying, often funny story delivered in alternating narratives, three teens describe their complicated relationships at home and at school. ℰ (Rev: BL 8/08; SLJ 9/1/08; VOYA 8/08)

57 Coleman, Rowan. *The Home for Broken Hearts* (11–12). 2010, Gallery paper $15 (978-143915685-8). When Ellen Wood's husband dies and she takes boarders to help make ends meet, her life and her relationships with her 11-year-old son and her sister begin to change; for mature readers. (Rev: BL 9/1/10)

58 Conrad, Lauren. *L.A. Candy* (9–12). 2009, Harper $17.99 (978-006176758-6). A frothy tale about two college-age teens who find themselves starring in a reality show as they settle into their lives in Los Angeles. ℰ (Rev: BLO 7/2/09; SLJ 10/09)

59 Crane, Dede. *Poster Boy* (8–12). 2009, Groundwood $17.95 (978-0-88899-855-2). When his younger sister is diagnosed with late-stage cancer, 16-year-old Gray Fallon's focus changes from parties and fun to an obsessive crusade against chemicals and toxins. Lexile 700L (Rev: BL 8/09; LMC 5–6/10; SLJ 12/09)

60 Cusick, John M. *Girl Parts* (9–12). 2010, Candlewick $16.99 (978-0-7636-4930-2). David's parents worry about their popular son's callous behavior and get him a special robot companion called Rose with unexpected results. ∩ Lexile HL590L (Rev: BLO 8/30/10; HB 9–10/10; LMC 10/10; SLJ 10/1/10; VOYA 10/10)

61 De Gramont, Nina. *Every Little Thing in the World* (8–11). 2010, Simon & Schuster $16.99 (978-1-4169-8013-1). Sent to a summer camp in Canada, 16-year-olds Sydney, who has just discovered she is pregnant, and her friend Natalia explore Sydney's options. ℮ Lexile 870L (Rev: BL 3/15/10; SLJ 4/10)

62 de la Cruz, Melissa. *Girl Stays in the Picture* (8–12). 2009, Simon & Schuster $16.99 (978-141696096-6). Gossip columns, news items, and parodies of real celebrities enliven this story of teens on a movie shoot in Saint-Tropez. (Rev: BL 7/09; SLJ 8/09)

63 De la Peña, Matt. *We Were Here* (7–12). 2009, Delacorte $17.99 (978-0-385-73667-1); LB $20.99 (978-0-385-90622-7). Thoughtful 16-year-old Miguel escapes from a California juvenile detention center with two other teens, and they become friends as they struggle to find a way to live. ℮ (Rev: BL 9/1/09; HB 11–12/09; SLJ 12/09; VOYA 12/09)

64 De Vigan, Delphine. *No and Me* (8–11). 2010, Bloomsbury $16.99 (978-1-59990-479-5). A moving book set in Paris about 13-year-old Lou's decision to invite a vagrant 18-year-old girl into her home, a home that has been unhappy since the death of Lou's younger sister. (Rev: BL 8/10; LMC 8–9/10; SLJ 7/10)

65 Dean, Zoey. *Hollywood Is Like High School with Money* (10–12). 2009, Grand Central paper $13.99 (978-044669719-4). A light novel about a young woman whose job as an assistant to a movie executive wakes her up to the dog-eat-dog world of Hollywood. ℮ (Rev: BL 7/09)

66 Delinsky, Barbara. *Not My Daughter* (11–12). 2010, Doubleday $25.95 (978-038552498-8). High-school principal Susan Tate is shocked to learn that her teenage daughter and friends have successfully made a pact to get pregnant; for mature readers. ∩ ℮ (Rev: BL 12/1/09)

67 Dessen, Sarah. *Along for the Ride* (9–12). 2009, Viking $19.99 (978-067001194-0). During her last summer before college, Auden learns about herself and falls in love while getting to know her father's new wife and baby. ∩ ℮ Lexile HL750L (Rev: BL 4/15/09; HB 5–6/09; SLJ 6/1/09*; VOYA 6/09)

68 Devillers, Julia. *Lynn Visible* (7–10). 2010, Dutton $16.99 (978-0-525-47691-7). Lynn's 9th-grade classmates mock her flamboyant clothes until she is chosen as the "It Girl" for an online magazine. Lexile HL560L (Rev: BL 3/1/10; SLJ 4/10)

69 Dexter, Pete. *Spooner* (10–12). 2009, Grand Central $26.99 (978-044654072-8). Irreverent and at times both funny and poignant, this faux-biography contains relationships that ring true, especially the one between difficult young protagonist Warren Spooner and his navy commander stepfather. ∩ ℮ (Rev: BL 7/09)

70 Diaz, Alexandra. *Of All the Stupid Things* (9–11). 2009, Egmont USA $16.99 (978-1-60684-034-4); LB $19.99 (978-1-60684-066-5). Tara, Whitney, and Pinkie, in their senior year at high school, find their longstanding friendship threatened when Tara is attracted to new-girl Riley. ℮ (Rev: BLO 2/17/10; SLJ 4/10)

71 Divakaruni, Chitra Banerjee. *One Amazing Thing* (11–12). 2010, Hyperion $23.99 (978-140134099-5). Trapped in an Indian consulate in an unnamed American city in the aftermath of an earthquake, nine diverse strangers each tell a story from their lives; for mature readers. ∩ (Rev: BL 1/1/10)

72 Draper, Sharon M. *Just Another Hero* (7–10). 2009, Simon & Schuster $16.99 (978-141690700-8). Bullying, family problems, drug addiction, thefts, and worries about school and college challenge the students introduced in *The Battle of Jericho* (2003) and *November Blues* (2007). ∩ (Rev: BL 6/1–15/09; SLJ 7/1/09)

73 Easton, Kelly. *To Be Mona* (8–11). 2008, Simon & Schuster $16.99 (978-141696940-2). Hampered by her life with a bipolar mother, 17-year-old Sage envies gorgeous class president Mona and overlooks friend Vern's devotion in favor of the attentions of the manipulative Roger; with an afterword about bipolar disorder and abusive relationships. ℮ (Rev: BL 11/15/08; LMC 3–4/09; SLJ 1/1/09)

74 Efaw, Amy. *After* (9–12). 2009, Viking $17.99 (978-0-670-01183-4). Fifteen-year-old Devon must face the fact that she has had a baby and left it to die. ∩ ℮ (Rev: BL 8/09; LMC 11–12/09; SLJ 9/09; VOYA 8/09)

75 Ehrenberg, Pamela. *Tillmon County Fire* (9–12). 2009, Eerdmans paper $9.00 (978-080285345-5). Who set the fire that destroyed a valuable home in a small Appalachian town? A number of teens give their perspectives on this incident. Lexile 1060L (Rev: BL 4/15/09; SLJ 4/1/09)

76 Elkeles, Simone. *How to Ruin Your Boyfriend's Reputation* (8–12). 2009, Flux paper $9.95 (978-0-7387-1897-8). Seventeen-year-old Amy's scheme to spend some face time with her long-distance boyfriend lands her in boot camp with the Israeli Defense Force. ℮ Lexile HL750L (Rev: SLJ 12/09; VOYA 2/10)

77 Ellsworth, Loretta. *In a Heartbeat* (8–12). 2010, Walker $16.99 (978-0-8027-2068-9). Figure skater Eagan, 16, dies in a fall and her heart is given to ailing 14-year-old Amelia, a procedure that affects both girls as they describe in alternating chapters. ℮ Lexile HL580L (Rev: BL 1/1/10; LMC 3–4/10; SLJ 2/10)

7

78 Epstein, Robin. *God Is in the Pancakes* (7–10). 2010, Dial $16.99 (978-0-803-73382-4). While working as a candy striper, 15-year-old Grace becomes friends with a man suffering from Lou Gehrig's disease, who eventually asks her to help him die. ∩ ℮ (Rev: LMC 10/10; SLJ 5/10; VOYA 8/10)

79 Eslami, Elizabeth. *Bone Worship* (11–12). 2010, Pegasus paper $15.95 (978-160598074-4). Iranian American college dropout Jasmine stalls her father's plans to have her marriage arranged and learns a few things about him, herself, and what she wants out of life; for mature readers. ℮ (Rev: BL 12/1/09)

80 Foley, John. *A Mighty Wall* (7–10). 2009, Flux paper $9.95 (978-073871448-6). Jordan's junior year in high school is all about rock climbing, friends, drinking, and sex—until an accident changes everything. ℮ (Rev: BL 3/1/09; SLJ 6/1/09)

81 Forman, Gayle. *If I Stay* (10–12). 2009, Dutton $16.99 (978-052542103-0). Seventeen-year-old Mia, critically injured in the crash that killed her parents, fights to survive, even as she reminisces, in first-person narrative, about people and events in her past, and wonders about her future in this fast-paced novel. ∩ Lexile 830L (Rev: BL 12/15/08*; HB 7–8/09; SLJ 5/1/09*; VOYA 2/09)

82 Franco, Betsy. *Metamorphosis: Junior Year* (7–10). Illus. by Tom Franco. 2009, Candlewick $16.99 (978-0-7636-3765-1). After the sudden departure of his drug-addicted sister, high school junior, poet, and artist Ovid finds himself the sole focus of his suddenly over-attentive parents in this contemporary novel that finds its inspiration in Roman mythology. ∩ Lexile HL740L (Rev: BL 9/1/09; SLJ 12/09; VOYA 2/10)

83 Freymann-Weyr, Garret. *After the Moment* (10–12). 2009, Houghton $16.00 (978-061860572-9). When 17-year-old Leigh moves to Maryland to live with his father, stepmother, and stepsister, he finds himself entranced by a disturbed girl named Maia; set against the backdrop of the U.S. invasion of Iraq. (Rev: BL 6/1–15/09*; LMC 8–9/09; SLJ 5/1/09)

84 Friend, Natasha. *For Keeps* (8–11). 2010, Viking $16.99 (978-0-670-01190-2). Josie's life is changing as she navigates her junior year — she has a serious boyfriend, and her mother also has found someone; and then the father she has never met comes back to town and shakes things up. ℮ (Rev: BL 1/1/10; HB 5–6/10; SLJ 4/10; VOYA 4/10)

85 Gabriele, Lisa. *The Almost Archer Sisters* (11–12). 2008, Simon & Schuster paper $14.00 (978-074325586-8). After catching her husband in bed with her glamorous sister Beth, quiet Peachy decides to go to New York City alone to seduce Beth's boyfriend; for mature teens. (Rev: BL 9/1/08)

86 George, Madeleine. *Looks* (7–10). 2008, Viking $16.99 (978-067006167-9). High school seniors Meghan, who is fat, and Aimee, who is razor thin, form

an unlikely alliance as they seek revenge against the popular and cruel Cara in this tense story. (Rev: BL 9/15/08*; HB 7–8/08; SLJ 5/08; VOYA 10/08)

87 Giles, Gail. *Dark Song* (7–11). 2010, Little, Brown $16.99 (978-0-316-06886-4). In this timely riches-to-rags story, well-heeled Ames's family lands on skid row, and the 15-year-old takes up with 22-year-old criminally inclined Marc. ℮ Lexile HL570L (Rev: BL 9/1/10; SLJ 10/1/10; VOYA 10/10)

88 Going, K. L. *King of the Screwups* (7–12). 2009, Harcourt $17.00 (978-015206258-3). Straight athlete Liam's love of fashion and fun irks his strict father, so Liam moves in with his cross-dressing uncle — "Aunt Pete" — and tries to fit in in his new environment. Lexile HL690L (Rev: BL 4/15/09; SLJ 4/1/09*)

89 Greene, Brian. *Icarus at the Edge of Time* (10–12). Illus. 2008, Knopf $19.95 (978-030726888-4). The tale of Icarus is told in a new futuristic setting of deep space — with black holes and gorgeous, mysterious galaxies shown in NASA and Hubble images; an inventive and appealing story presented on board rather than paper. (Rev: BL 9/1/08)

90 Griffin, Adele. *The Julian Game* (8–12). 2010, Penguin $16.99 (978-0-399-25460-4). Scholarship student Raye is eager to make friends at her elite school and agrees to help the popular Ella with Mandarin — and with an ill-advised Facebook attempt at revenge. ℮ Lexile HL700L (Rev: BL 8/10; SLJ 10/1/10; VOYA 10/10)

91 Griffin, Paul. *The Orange Houses* (10–12). 2009, Dial $16.99 (978-080373346-6). Three New York teenagers deal with different challenges—impaired hearing, illegal immigrant status, and postwar stress. Lexile HL610L (Rev: BL 5/1/09; SLJ 6/1/09; VOYA 10/09)

92 Gruen, Sara. *Ape House* (11–12). 2010, Spiegel & Grau $26 (978-038552321-9). Scientist Isabel would rather connect with her bonobo apes than most humans — until they escape and she has to deal with a motley assortment of her own kind, including an attractive but married reporter; for mature readers. ∩ ℮ (Rev: BL 8/10)

93 Hall, Barbara. *Tempo Change* (7–12). 2009, Delacorte $16.99 (978-038573607-7); LB $19.99 (978-038590585-5). High school sophomore Blanche hopes her band's gig at a music festival will help her meet her long-lost father. ℮ (Rev: BL 7/09; SLJ 10/09)

94 Halperin, David. *Journal of a UFO Investigator* (11–12). 2011, Viking $25.95 (978-067002245-8). This entertaining coming-of-age novel features a teen UFO investigator dealing with bickering parents, skeptical friends, romantic complications — and aliens — in a small Pennsylvania town in the 1960s; for mature readers. ∩ (Rev: BL 1/1/11)

95 Hand, Elizabeth. *Illyria* (10–12). 2010, Viking $15.99 (978-0-670-01212-1). In 1970s Yonkers teen cousins

Maddy and Rogan, who are involved in a sexual relationship, are chosen to play roles in *Twelfth Night* that expose the difficulties of this first love. e Lexile HL790L (Rev: BL 5/15/10*; HB 7–8/10; LMC 10/10; VOYA 8/10)

96 Harper, Suzanne. *The Juliet Club* (8–12). 2008, Greenwillow $16.99 (978-006136691-8); LB $17.89 (978-006136692-5). In this light, modern-day Shakespearean tale set in Verona, Italy, six teens — three American and three Italian — study and perform scenes from *Romeo and Juliet* — that mirror the events of their own lives. Lexile 830L (Rev: BL 8/08; SLJ 7/08; VOYA 6/08)

97 Harvey, Sarah N. *Plastic* (9–12). 2010, Orca $16.95 (978-1-55469-253-8). The focus on women's breasts will attract some reluctant readers to this story about 15-year-old Jack's concern about his friend who plans to have a "boob job." Lexile HL560L (Rev: BL 3/10; LMC 8–9/10; SLJ 7/10)

98 Hautman, Pete. *Blank Confession* (8–11). 2010, Simon & Schuster $16.99 (978-1-4169-1327-6). Bullying, drugs, and violence are themes in this story about a 16-year-old named Shayne who walks into a police station and confesses to murder. (Rev: BL 10/1/10; SLJ 12/1/10)

99 Haworth-Attard, Barbara. *My Life from Air-Bras to Zits* (8–10). 2009, Flux paper $9.95 (978-0-7387-1483-7). Tenth-grader Teresa chronicles her life in this entertaining diary-style narrative by taking readers on an A to Z trip through her myriad social and domestic challenges. (Rev: SLJ 3/1/09)

100 Haycak, Cara. *Living on Impulse* (9–12). 2009, Dutton $16.99 (978-0-525-42137-5). Forced by her mother to get a job after she's caught shoplifting, 15-year-old Mia Morrow soon realizes that employment is the one stable factor in her otherwise tumultuous life. e (Rev: BL 8/98; SLJ 12/09; VOYA 12/09)

101 Hernandez, David. *No More Us for You* (9–12). 2009, HarperTeen $16.99 (978-006117333-2). California 17-year-olds Carlos and Isabel fall for each other in the wake of tragedy. e (Rev: BL 1/1–15/09; SLJ 7/1/09; VOYA 2/09)

102 Hollings, Anastasia. *Beautiful World* (7–10). 2009, HarperTeen paper $8.99 (978-006143532-4). Amelia Warner wants a place in New York society and is determined to get it by hook or by crook in this first installment in a chick-lit series. e (Rev: BL 7/09)

103 Holmes, Gina. *Crossing Oceans* (11–12). 2010, Tyndale paper $13.99 (978-141433305-2). With only months to live, a single mother returns home to face up to her past — and let her former boyfriend know he has a 5-year-old daughter — in this thoughtful, faith-based novel. e (Rev: BL 5/15/10)

104 Hubbard, Jennifer R. *The Secret Year* (9–12). 2010, Viking $16.99 (978-0-670-01153-7). Sixteen-year-old

working-class Colt and rich Julia kept their affair a secret, which makes it hard for Colt to cope with his grief when she is killed in a crash. Lexile HL650L (Rev: BL 12/1/09; SLJ 2/10)

105 Huntley, Amy. *The Everafter* (8–11). 2009, HarperCollins $16.99 (978-0-06-177679-3); LB $17.89 (978-0-06-177680-9). Working from the afterlife, 17-year-old Maddy Stanton attempts to unravel the mystery of how she met her untimely demise. ⌒ e Lexile HL680L (Rev: BL 8/09; SLJ 12/09; VOYA 12/09)

106 Hutchinson, Shaun David. *The Deathday Letter* (10–12). 2010, Simon & Schuster paper $9.99 (978-1-4169-9608-8). After receiving a letter notifying him that he will die within 24 hours, 15-year-old Ollie and his two friends decide to try to fulfill his last wishes, some of which include driving, drugs, and sex. e Lexile HL700L (Rev: BL 6/1/10; LMC 8–9/10; SLJ 11/1/10)

107 Jackson, Joshilyn. *Backseat Saints* (11–12). 2010, Grand Central $24.99 (978-044658234-6). When an airport gypsy tells troubled Rose to leave her abusive husband — or risk death — Rose listens, setting off a string of tense events; for mature readers. ⌒ e (Rev: BL 4/15/10*)

108 Jacobs, Kate. *Knit the Season* (9–12). Series: Friday Night Knitting Club. 2009, Putnam $24.95 (978-039915638-0). Set during the Christmas season, this heartwarming third installment follows the familiar, multigenerational characters as they deal with an impending marriage, a stalled romance, and life-changing decisions. ⌒ (Rev: BL 10/1/09)

109 James, Rebecca. *Beautiful Malice* (11–12). 2010, Bantam $25 (978-055380805-6). When grief-stricken, shy Katherine is befriended by emotionally troubled Alice, she slowly gains self-confidence — and a fresh perspective on her friend; for mature readers. (Rev: BL 6/1–15/10)

110 Jenkins, Jerry B. *Riven* (10–12). 2008, Tyndale $24.99 (978-1-4143-0904-0). In this Christian tale of reconciliation and redemption, troubled teenage Brady and failed preacher Thomas Carey come to rely on each other as their lives become increasingly chaotic. ⌒ e (Rev: BL 6/1–15/08)

111 Johnson, Maureen. *Scarlett Fever* (8–10). 2010, Scholastic $16.99 (978-0-439-89928-4). In this follow-up to 2008's *Suite Scarlett,* life at the Hopewell Hotel has reverted to its usual humdrum pace, and 15-year-old Scarlett is desperate for something to break the ennui even as she handles various crises. ⌒ e Lexile 710L (Rev: BLO 12/8/09; HB 3–4/10; SLJ 1/10; VOYA 8/10)

112 Jones, Carrie. *Girl, Hero* (7–10). 2008, Flux $16.95 (978-0-7387-1051-8). High school freshman Lili writes letters to John Wayne, confiding to this hero her worries about her perhaps-gay father, her mother's new boyfriend who likes to drink, her own romantic interests, school challenges, and so forth. Lexile HL700L (Rev: BLO 9/15/08; SLJ 1/1/09)

113 Jones, Patrick. *Stolen Car* (8–12). 2008, Walker $16.99 (978-080279700-1). Enraged by the shabby behavior of the older boy for whom she neglected her friends,15-year-old Danielle steals his car and takes off on a road trip with BFF Ashley. **e** (Rev: BL 11/15/08; LMC 1–2/09; SLJ 12/08; VOYA 2/09)

114 Juby, Susan. *Getting the Girl: A Guide to Private Investigation, Surveillance, and Cookery* (8–10). 2008, HarperTeen $16.99 (978-006076525-5); LB $17.89 (978-006076527-9). Goodhearted Sherman Mack sets out to protect the reputations of girls in his school through a combination of sleuthing, persuasion, and ultimately standing up for his beliefs in this quirky first-person story. **e** (Rev: BL 10/1/08; HB 9–10/08; SLJ 11/1/08)

115 Kate, Lauren. *The Betrayal of Natalie Hargrove* (9–12). 2009, Penguin paper $9.99 (978-1-595-14265-8). Palmetto Princess shoo-in Natalie and her boyfriend Mike cook up a scheme to ensure that Mike, not the much-disliked Justin, is crowned Prince; naturally, the prank goes awry and Natalie and Mike find themselves embroiled in an increasingly dangerous coverup. (Rev: BL 9/15/09; LMC 11–12/09; VOYA 4/10)

116 Key, Watt. *Dirt Road Home* (7–10). 2010, Farrar $16.99 (978-0-374-30863-6). Eager to get out of the state home for juvenile delinquents, 14-year-old Hal tries to behave amid the pervasive gang violence and hopes that his father will quit drinking. **e** Lexile HL540L (Rev: BL 6/1/10; HB 9–10/10; LMC 11–12/10; SLJ 11/1/10; VOYA 12/10)

117 Kiernan, Kristy. *Matters of Faith* (11–12). 2008, Berkley paper $14.00 (978-042522179-2). Eighteen-year-old Marshall's zealous girlfriend attempts to "cure" his sister of her life-threatening food allergy, with disastrous results. **e** (Rev: BL 7/08)

118 King, A. S. *Please Ignore Vera Dietz* (10–12). 2010, Knopf $16.99 (978-0-375-86586-2); LB $19.99 (978-0-375-96586-9). High school senior Vera Dietz trusted her friend Charlie, but he betrayed her and then died; now his ghost is asking her to clear his name. ⋂ **e** (Rev: BL 11/15/10; SLJ 12/1/10)

119 Koertge, Ron. *Deadville* (9–12). 2008, Candlewick $16.99 (978-076363580-0). Ryan is compelled to re-evaluate the drug-riddled, isolated life he chose after his sister's death two years ago when he visits his comatose classmate Charlotte in the hospital. Lexile HL560L (Rev: BL 11/15/08; LMC 3–4/09; SLJ 11/1/08; VOYA 12/08)

120 Konigsberg, Bill. *Out of the Pocket* (9–12). 2008, Dutton $16.99 (978-052547996-3). High school quarterback Bobby Framingham's homosexuality is suddenly revealed and the teen faces a range of reactions while also dealing with his father's cancer diagnosis. **e** Lexile HL710L (Rev: BL 9/1/08; SLJ 9/1/08)

121 Kraus, Daniel. *The Monster Variations* (8–12). 2009, Delacorte $16.99 (978-038573733-3); LB $19.99 (978-038590659-3). James remembers the summer he was 12 and the wave of violence that swept his small town, terrifying him and his friends. (Rev: BLO 6/1–15/09; LMC 10/09; SLJ 11/09)

122 Kraut, Julie. *Slept Away* (7–10). 2009, LB $11.99 (978-038590661-6); paper $8.99 (978-038573737-1). Very urban Laney Parker, 15, has a hard time adapting when she is sent to a summer camp in the Pennsylvania countryside. (Rev: BL 7/09; SLJ 8/09)

123 Kuehnert, Stephanie. *I Wanna Be Your Joey Ramone* (11–12). 2008, Pocket/MTV paper $13.00 (978-141656269-6). Punk rocker's daughter Emily starts her own band and finds instant success in this fast-paced story of teenage rebellion, search for a missing mother, and redemption; for mature readers. **e** (Rev: BL 6/1–15/08)

124 Laxer, Mark. *The Monkey Bible: A Modern Allegory* (11–12). Illus. 2010, Outer Rim $25 (978-096381080-9). A spiritual college student faces a crisis of faith and identity when he discovers he is half-man, half-ape in this thought-provoking novel. (Rev: BL 9/15/10)

125 Lennon, Stella, and Melissa Kantor. *Invisible I* (7–10). Series: The Amanda Project. 2009, HarperCollins $16.99 (978-0-06-174212-5). Callie is facing enough problems at home when she finds herself implicated in defacing the vice principal's car. She is sure her friend Amanda was the perpetrator, but where is Amanda now? ⋂ **e** (Rev: BL 8/09; LMC 1–2/10; SLJ 9/09)

126 Lerangis, Peter. *wtf* (9–12). 2009, Simon & Schuster paper $8.99 (978-1-4169-1360-3). In alternate narratives, six teens describe an eventful and tense night in New York City where a drug deal gets complicated. **e** (Rev: BL 10/15/09; SLJ 2/10; VOYA 12/09)

127 Lodato, Victor. *Mathilda Savitch* (10–12). 2009, Farrar $25 (978-0-374-20400-6). Grief-stricken after the death of her beloved 16-year-old sister, Mathilda sets out to confront the man she believes is responsible; however, the man she finds is not the heartless murderer that she expected in this often humorous novel. (Rev: BL 8/09; SLJ 2/10)

128 Lodge, Hillary Manton. *Plain Jayne* (10–12). 2010, Harvest paper $13.99 (978-073692698-0). After the death of her father, journalist Jayne is forced to regroup and turns to the nearby Amish community for a new perspective on life; there she also finds a new love. **e** (Rev: BL 11/15/09)

129 McDonald, Abby. *Sophomore Switch* (9–12). 2009, Candlewick $17.99 (978-076363936-5). British Emily and California girl Tasha do a student exchange and try out each other's lifestyles in this entertaining and insightful novel. ℮ Lexile HL780L (Rev: BL 2/15/09; LMC 8–9/09; SLJ 6/1/09)

130 Mackler, Carolyn. *Tangled* (9–12). 2010, Harper-Teen $16.99 (978-0-06-173104-4). On vacation in the Caribbean teens Jena (inferiority complex) and Skye (beautiful but depressed) have complex interactions with brothers Dakota (an overconfident drinker) and Owen (insecure geek); told in alternating first-person narratives. ℮ Lexile HL750L (Rev: BL 1/1/10; SLJ 1/10; VOYA 2/10)

131 McLaughlin, Emma, and Nicola Kraus. *The Real Real* (9–12). 2009, HarperTeen $16.99 (978-0-06-172040-6). In this fast-paced page-turner, high school senior Jesse accepts a role on a new reality TV series — trading all semblance of "normal life" for a $40 K scholarship — and ends up more servant than star, compromising her integrity for the sake of her career. (Rev: SLJ 7/1/09; VOYA 8/09)

132 McNeal, Laura. *Dark Water* (8–12). 2010, Knopf $16.99 (978-0-375-84973-2); LB $19.99 (978-0-375-94973-9). Troubled 15-year-old Pearl seduces a mute migrant worker and faces difficult choices when wild-fires approach her California town and threaten her uncle's ranch. ℮ (Rev: HB 1–2/11; SLJ 10/1/10; VOYA 12/10)

133 Madigan, L. K. *Flash Burnout* (9–12). 2009, Houghton $16 (978-0-547-19489-9). Blake, 15, navigates high school with a feeling of optimism but has trouble when trying to juggle his new girlfriend Shannon and his best friend Marissa, who shares his love of photography. ∩ ℮ Lexile HL570L (Rev: BL 9/15/09*; SLJ 11/09)

134 Mancusi, Marianne. *Gamer Girl* (6–10). 2008, Dutton $16.99 (978-052547995-6). Manga drawing and the online game Fields of Fantasy help Maddy cope with her parents' divorce, unpopularity in her new school, and rejection by boys, but she eventually finds the courage to reach out to others. Lexile HL660L (Rev: BL 11/15/08; SLJ 1/1/09)

135 Mapson, Jo-Ann. *Solomon's Oak* (11–12). 2010, Bloomsbury $25 (978-160819330-1). A widow fostering a surly 14-year-old girl whose sister has disappeared receives help from a world-weary ex-cop with problems of his own in this novel about second chances; for mature readers. ∩ ℮ (Rev: BL 9/1/10)

136 Marsden, John. *Hamlet* (9–12). 2009, Candlewick $16.99 (978-0-7636-4451-2). This modernized version of the story emphasizes Hamlet's youth and typical teen anxieties. Lexile HL760L (Rev: SLJ 8/09; VOYA 12/09)

137 Martin, C. K. Kelly. *I Know It's Over* (9–12). 2008, Random $16.99 (978-037584566-6); LB $19.99 (978-037594566-3). Starting with the bombshell of his ex-girlfriend's pregnancy and working backward, this story explores 16-year-old Nick's emotions and the various tensions he must deal with — including a gay

best friend and divorced parents. ℮ (Rev: BL 11/15/08; SLJ 11/1/08)

138 Matlock, Curtiss Ann. *Little Town, Great Big Life* (11–12). 2010, MIRA paper $13.95 (978-077832788-2). In this conclusion to the Valentine series, reluctantly pregnant Belinda's family — and their pharmacy, an institution — prepare for their small town's centennial celebration.; for mature readers (Rev: BL 6/1–15/10)

139 Maynard, Joyce. *Labor Day* (11–12). 2009, Morrow $24.99 (978-006184340-2). An escaped convict charms his way into the lives of a 13-year-old boy and his emotionally vulnerable mother in this suspense-filled novel written from the perspective of young Henry; for mature readers. (Rev: BL 7/09)

140 Meister, Ellen. *The Smart One* (10–12). 2008, Avon paper $13.95 (978-006112962-9). Bev Bloomrosen, the smart sister, house-sits for her parents over the summer and winds up involved in her sisters' troubles, unexpected romance, and a murder mystery in this entertaining novel. (Rev: BL 8/08)

141 Monroe, Mary Alice. *Time Is a River* (11–12). 2008, Pocket $25.00 (978-141654436-4). Affronted by her adulterous husband, breast cancer survivor Mia heads to a secluded mountain cabin for some fly fishing, reflection, self-affirmation, and eventual healing; for mature readers. (Rev: BL 7/08)

142 Morris, Keith Lee. *The Dart League King* (11–12). 2008, Tin House $14.95 (978-097941988-1). Drugs and darts combine in this suspenseful novel about five interconnected characters who come together for a dart contest in their small town; for mature readers. (Rev: BL 9/15/08*)

143 Murray, Yxta Maya. *Good Girl's Guide to Getting Kidnapped* (9–12). 2010, Penguin $16.99 (978-1-595-14272-6). Michelle was known as Princess P when she lived with her Mexican American gangster father; now with a foster parent she is succeeding academically and athletically — until the gang kidnaps her and a friend for ransom money; with street language and realistic violence. ℮ (Rev: BL 12/1/09; LMC 1–2/10; SLJ 2/10)

144 Myers, Edward. *Far from Gringo Land* (7–10). 2010, Clarion $17 (978-0-547-05630-2). Rick, a teenager from Colorado, gets more than he bargained for when he moves to Mexico for a summer job and experiences culture shock. ℮ Lexile 990 (Rev: BL 11/15/09; LMC 1–2/10; SLJ 12/09)

145 Nadol, Jen. *The Mark* (9–12). 2010, Bloomsbury $16.99 (978-1-59990-431-3). Cassie, 16, can tell if a person is about to die within the next 24 hours, a "gift" that she questions as she falls in love with a handsome philosophy student. ℮ Lexile 700L (Rev: BL 12/15/09; HB 5–6/10; LMC 3–4/10; SLJ 2/10)

146 Nunez, Sigrid. *Salvation City* (10–12). 2010, Riverhead $25.95 (978-159448766-8). Young Cole finds himself orphaned by a flu pandemic, transplanted to a super-religious settlement in near-future postapocalyptic America, and grappling with guns, sexuality, and a lust for knowledge. ∩ ℮ (Rev: BL 8/10)

147 Oaks, J. Adams. *Why I Fight* (8–12). 2009, Simon & Schuster $16.99 (978-141691177-7). Since the age of 12, Wyatt has been traveling with his drifter uncle named Spade and earning money with his fists. Lexile 770L (Rev: BL 4/15/09*; SLJ 7/1/09; VOYA 6/09)

148 Oliver, Lauren. *Before I Fall* (9–12). 2010, HarperCollins $17.99 (978-0-06-172680-4). As she relives — seven times — the day of her death in a car accident, high school senior Samantha gains insight into her life and the mistakes she has made. ∩ ℮ Lexile 860L (Rev: BL 10/15/09; LMC 1–2/10; SLJ 4/10)

149 Oppel, Kenneth. *Half Brother* (7–10). 2010, Scholastic $17.99 (978-0-545-22925-8). In 1970s Canada 13-year-old Ben's psychologist father brings home a young chimp that will be raised as a member of the family. ∩ ℮ Lexile 680L (Rev: BL 9/1/10; HB 9–10/10; LMC 11–12/10; SLJ 9/1/10*; VOYA 12/10)

150 Ostow, Micol. *So Punk Rock (and Other Ways to Disappoint Your Mother)* (8–12). Illus. by David Ostow. 2009, Flux paper $9.95 (978-073871471-4). This is a funny and affecting story about four New Jersey Jewish teens and the ways in which their band's success affects their lives. (Rev: BL 6/1–15/09*; SLJ 11/09)

151 Papademetriou, Lisa. *Drop* (7–12). 2008, Knopf $15.99 (978-037584244-3); LB $18.99 (978-037594244-0). Three Las Vegas teens band together to try to beat the system at the roulette tables, one to pay off gambling debts, one to escape family problems, and one to prove her mathematical theories in this tense, fast-paced novel. Lexile 690L (Rev: BL 12/1/08; LMC 3–4/09; SLJ 12/08; VOYA 4/09)

152 Pattillo, Beth. *Mr. Darcy Broke My Heart* (10–12). 2010, Guideposts paper $14.99 (978-082494793-4). Charged with presenting a paper at a Jane Austen seminar, Claire feels overwhelmed until an elderly Harriet Dalrymple presents her with a revelatory early draft of *Pride and Prejudice* and Claire comes to recognize some truths about her own romantic relationships. (Rev: BLO 1/8/10)

153 Picardie, Justine. *Daphne* (10–12). 2008, Bloomsbury $24.95 (978-159691341-7). Part literary mystery, part biography of Daphne du Maurier and Branwell Brontë (brother of the famed Brontë sisters), this engrossing story includes a modern-day plotline that mirrors the gothic, suspenseful tone of du Maurier's work. ℮ (Rev: BL 7/08)

154 Picoult, Jodi. *House Rules* (11–12). 2010, Atria $28 (978-074329643-4). Told from multiple viewpoints, this story features Jacob Hunt, a teen with Asperger's syndrome who is accused of murder; for mature readers. ∩ (Rev: BL 12/15/09)

155 Picoult, Jodi. *Sing You Home* (11–12). 2011, Atria $28 (978-143910272-5). Before they divorced, Zoe and Max stored embryos for future use and now Zoe, who just married her new love Vanessa, wants to use them to become a mother, but Max, backed by his church, sues her for custody of the embryos; for mature readers. ∩ ℮ (Rev: BL 1/1/11)

156 Pierson, D. C. *The Boy Who Couldn't Sleep and Never Had To* (10–12). 2010, Vintage paper $14 (978-030747461-2). Darren and his best friend Eric, who never sleeps, become embroiled in an adventure that parallels the science fiction epic they are working on, in this entertaining coming-of-age story. (Rev: BL 12/15/09)

157 Potter, Ryan. *Exit Strategy* (9–12). 2010, Flux paper $9.95 (978-0-73871-573-5). Zach aims to leave his depressed Detroit suburb (and his unhappy family) as soon as he can, but in the meantime the high schooler realizes that his friend Tank's wired behavior is due to steroids provided by the coach and that he is attracted to Tank's sister; a gritty novel with mature themes. ℮ Lexile HL790L (Rev: BL 2/1/10; LMC 5–6/10)

158 Prinz, Yvonne. *The Vinyl Princess* (7–11). 2010, HarperCollins $16.99 (978-0-06-171583-9). Allie, 16, blogs about music, collects vinyl, and works in a record store while dreaming of romance, which proves rocky. ℮ Lexile 850L (Rev: BL 11/1/09; LMC 3–4/10; SLJ 2/10)

159 Resau, Laura. *The Indigo Notebook* (7–10). 2009, Delacorte $16.99 (978-0-385-73652-7); LB $19.99 (978-0-385-90614-2). It's move number 15 (to Ecuador), and 15-year-old Zeeta is heartily tired of their itinerant life; helping an American teenager find his birth parents brings her interest as she becomes involved in a mysterious adventure that involves magical realism. (Rev: BL 11/1/09; SLJ 12/09)

160 Rich, Naomi. *Alis* (9–12). 2009, Viking $16.99 (978-067001125-4). Set in a fictional historical time period, 14-year-old Alis, member of a conservative religious group called "The Community of the Book," runs away after she is ordered to marry a much older man, finding herself in even more peril outside of her community. ℮ Lexile 730L (Rev: BL 12/15/08; LMC 3–4/09; SLJ 3/1/09)

161 Roesch, Mattox. *Sometimes We're Always Real Same-Same* (11–12). 2009, Unbridled Bks paper $15.95 (978-1-932961-87-4). Seventeen-year-old Cesar, a tough Los Angeles gang member, must come to grips with his relocation to remote Unalakleet, Alaska, where his cousin Go-Boy helps him acclimate to his new community and lifestyle; for mature readers. (Rev: BL 9/15/09; SLJ 11/09)

162 Roth, Matthue. *Losers* (9–12). 2008, Scholastic paper $8.99 (978-054506893-2). Russian immigrant Jupiter Glazer struggles to find himself — and escape the rampant bullying in his new high school — as he bonds over music with an unlikely new friend. **e** Lexile 930L (Rev: BL 11/1/08*; LMC 3–4/09; SLJ 1/1/09)

163 Rottman, S. L. *Out of the Blue* (8–11). 2009, Peachtree $16.95 (978-1-56145-499-0). Newly moved to Minot Air Force Base in North Dakota, 15-year-old Stu Ballentyne is compelled to act when he witnesses child abuse first hand, and the experience draws him out of his loneliness and isolation. Lexile 660L (Rev: BL 12/1/09; SLJ 10/09)

164 Sales, Leila. *Mostly Good Girls* (8–12). 2010, Simon & Schuster $16.99 (978-1-4424-0679-7). Witty, sometimes whiny Violet narrates this story of two private-school friends growing apart as they contend with boys, PSATs, and school politicking. **e** Lexile 820L (Rev: BL 10/15/10; SLJ 10/1/10*)

165 Shreve, Anita. *Testimony* (11–12). 2008, Little, Brown $25.99 (978-031605986-2). *Testimony* tells the story of a shocking prep school sex scandal, the events that preceded it, and the many lives that are ruined by the disastrous fallout; for mature readers. ∩ **e** (Rev: BL 9/1/08*)

166 Sittenfeld, Curtis. *American Wife* (10–12). 2008, Random $26.00 (978-140006475-5). Based on the life of First Lady Laura Bush, this first-person fictional memoir captures a Wisconsin girl's unlikely rise to the White House and her struggle to come to grips with her husband's intimidating family and contentious politics. ∩ **e** (Rev: BL 7/08*)

167 Smith, Andrew. *Ghost Medicine* (8–12). 2008, Feiwel & Friends $17.95 (978-0-312-37557-7). Following the death of his brother and then of his mother, 16-year-old Troy finds comfort in a camping trip, spending time with his friends, and practicing "ghost medicine," but also must deal with the bullying son of the sheriff. (Rev: LMC 3–4/09; SLJ 9/1/08)

168 Standiford, Natalie. *How to Say Goodbye in Robot* (9–12). 2009, Scholastic $17.99 (978-0-545-10708-2). High school senior Bea Szabo has adopted the cold persona of "Robot Girl" to cope with family drama, but she is slowly drawn out of her isolation by her new friend Jonas, the issues facing him, and a late-night radio show they enjoy together. ∩ **e** Lexile HL560L (Rev: BL 11/1/09; HB 1–2/10; LMC 11/09; SLJ 10/09)

169 Stork, Francisco X. *Last Summer of the Death Warriors* (8–12). 2010, Scholastic $17.99 (978-0-545-15133-7). This complex tale features 17-year-olds Pancho, who seeks to avenge his sister's death, and D.Q., who is dying of brain cancer, as they contemplate the meaning of being a "Death Warrior." ∩ **e** Lexile HL640L (Rev: BL 2/1/10*; HB 3–4/10; LMC 3–4/10; SLJ 3/10)

170 Supplee, Suzanne. *Somebody Everybody Listens To* (8–11). 2010, Dutton $16.99 (978-0-525-42242-6). Plucky country-star wannabe Retta heads for Nashville and succeeds despite having to sleep in her car at first. **e** Lexile 830L (Rev: BL 6/1/10; SLJ 10/1/10)

171 Tashjian, Janet. *Larry and the Meaning of Life* (8–12). 2008, Henry Holt $16.95 (978-080507735-3). In this third book in the series, Josh/Larry falls in with a mysterious guru named Gus and finds himself having a series of bizarre adventures. ∩ Lexile 760L (Rev: BL 9/1/08; SLJ 12/08; VOYA 2/09)

172 Teller, Janne. *Nothing* (7–12). 2010, Simon & Schuster $16.99 (978-1-4169-8579-2). A group of 7th-grade students struggle to defuse a classmate's existential crisis in this compelling novel translated from Danish. ∩ **e** (Rev: BL 12/1/09*; LMC 3–4/10; SLJ 4/10)

173 Trigiani, Adriana. *Viola in Reel Life* (7–10). 2009, HarperTeen $16.99 (978-0-06-145102-7). Ninth-grader Viola feels neglected after her parents, documentary filmmakers, send her to a boarding school while they film in Afghanistan; but after making friends and getting involved in activities, she warms to her new school and finds a potential new romantic interest. **e** Lexile 820L (Rev: BL 8/09; SLJ 9/09; VOYA 12/09)

174 van de Ruit, John. *Spud — The Madness Continues . . .* (8–12). 2008, Penguin $16.99 (978-159514190-3). In this humorous sequel to *Spud* (2007), Spud is still at his South African boarding school and dealing with puberty, a changing voice, racism, and particularly useless adults. (Rev: BLO 10/1/08; LMC 3/08)

175 Walls, Jeannette. *Half Broke Horses* (11–12). 2009, Scribner $25 (978-141658628-9). In this "true-life novel" the author of *The Glass Castle* (2005) tells the story of her maternal grandmother, an impressive character who trained horses at a young age, taught school, and ran a large ranch during hard times in the Southwest; for mature readers. ∩ (Rev: BL 9/09*)

176 Watson, Sasha. *Vidalia in Paris* (9–12). 2008, Viking $16.99 (978-067001094-3). Studying art in Paris, Vidalia Sloane is beguiled by wily, smooth-talking Marco, a wannabe art dealer who isn't afraid to bend the rules to get what he wants. **e** Lexile HL710L (Rev: BL 11/15/08; SLJ 4/1/09; VOYA 12/08)

177 Weiner, Jennifer. *Best Friends Forever* (10–12). 2009, Atria $26.95 (978-074329429-4). This story of a high school reunion gone awry includes many flashbacks to friends Val and Addie's younger lives. ∩ (Rev: BL 7/09*)

178 Weingarten, Lynn. *Wherever Nina Lies* (8–12). 2009, Scholastic $16.99 (978-054506631-0). Ellie, 16, sets out on a road trip to find her missing older sister and encounters romance and mystery in this compelling read. Lexile HL780L (Rev: BL 2/15/09; SLJ 8/09)

179 Willey, Margaret. *A Summer of Silk Moths* (7–10). 2009, Flux paper $9.95 (978-0-7387-1540-7). Seventeen-year-old Pete and Nora overcome their initial animosity as they realize sobering truths about their pasts in this contemplative story with a nature preserve setting. (Rev: BLO 11/16/09; LMC 11–12/09; SLJ 1/10)

180 Wingate, Lisa. *Never Say Never* (11–12). 2010, Bethany paper $14.99 (978-076420492-0). A motley crew of hurricane evacuees, from 69-year-old Donetta to 27-year-old Kai, wind up in Daily, Texas, where they find new experiences; a quirky Christian adventure story with a dollop of romance. (Rev: BL 2/15/10)

181 Wiseman, Rosalind. *Boys, Girls and Other Hazardous Materials* (7–10). 2010, Putnam $17.99 (978-0-399-24796-5). Freshman Charlie finds new and old friends in high school and learns about romance and social pressure while navigating bullies and cliques. **℮** Lexile HL660L (Rev: BL 12/15/09; SLJ 1/10; VOYA 4/10)

182 Wizner, Jake. *Castration Celebration* (11–12). 2009, Random $16.99 (978-037585215-2); LB $19.99 (978-037595215-9). Olivia has a wild summer (including sex and drugs) at a Yale drama camp, culminating in a production of her musical about castration; this lighthearted book is full of entertaining references. (Rev: BL 4/15/09; SLJ 4/1/09)

183 Wroblewski, David. *The Story of Edgar Sawtelle* (11–12). 2008, Ecco $26.95 (978-006137422-7). When mute teen Edgar Sawtelle's father is murdered by his uncle, Edgar turns to the dogs on his small Wisconsin farm — as well as his own wits and a Shakespeare-style apparition of his dead father — to understand the crime; suitable for mature readers. ∩ **℮** (Rev: BL 6/1–15/08)

184 Zarr, Sara. *Once Was Lost* (8–10). 2009, Little, Brown $16.99 (978-0-316-03604-7). A 13-year-old girl is missing and 15-year-old Samara begins to question her faith. ∩ **℮** (Rev: BL 11/15/09*; SLJ 11/09)

185 Zemser, Amy Bronwen. *Dear Julia* (7–10). 2008, Greenwillow $16.99 (978-006029458-8); LB $17.89 (978-006029459-5). Two unlikely young women — Elaine, 16, and Lucinda — forge a friendship built on shared family quirks and their separate quests for fulfillment and renown in this lighthearted exploration of feminist themes. Lexile 780L (Rev: BL 9/1/08; SLJ 1/1/09; VOYA 2/09)

Ethnic Groups and Problems

186 Abdel-Fattah, Randa. *Ten Things I Hate About Me* (7–10). 2009, Scholastic $16.99 (978-054505055-5). In this humorous story about fitting in and finding who you really are, 16-year-old Jamilah — known as Jamie at school — is a Lebanese Australian Muslim who isn't comfortable telling her friends who she really is and hides her identity by dying her hair blond and wearing blue contact lenses. Lexile HL720L (Rev: BL 12/1/08; SLJ 2/1/09; VOYA 6/09)

187 Acosta, Belinda. *Sisters, Strangers, and Starting Over* (11–12). 2010, Grand Central paper $13.99 (978-044654052-0). Planning Celeste's quinceañera celebration keeps her extended family together in spite of rapidly changing dynamics and turmoil, as well as questions about her mother's murder; for mature readers. (Rev: BL 6/1–15/10)

188 Adler, Emily, and Alex Echevarria. *Sweet 15* (7–10). 2010, Marshall Cavendish $16.99 (978-0-7614-5584-4). Destiny Lozada is not sure she wants to have a quinceañera but she also does not want to disappoint her Puerto Rican family. (Rev: BLO 3/4/10; LMC 8–9/10; SLJ 7/10)

189 Asim, Jabari. *A Taste of Honey* (11–12). 2010, Broadway paper $13 (978-076791978-4). In this collection of vivid, fast-paced stories, Asim weaves a rich tapestry of life in the fictional Midwest town of Gateway City, where a black family is grappling with racial limitation and family dynamics in 1967; for mature readers. (Rev: BL 3/1/10)

190 Baca, Jimmy Santiago. *A Glass of Water* (11–12). 2009, Grove $23 (978-080211922-3). Baca's novel about two immigrant brothers illustrates the tragic circumstances of life on the U.S./Mexico border; suitable for mature readers. (Rev: BL 9/09)

191 Carlson, Lori Marie, ed. *Voices in First Person: Reflections on Latino Identity* (7–12). Illus. by Flavio Morais. 2008, Simon & Schuster $16.99 (978-141696212-0). This book explores the experiences of Latinos in America through a variety of fictional monologues, poems, and short stories focusing on themes of heartbreak, prejudice, identity, and pride. **℮** (Rev: BL 10/1/08; HB 7–8/08; LMC 11–12/08; SLJ 8/08; VOYA 8/08)

192 Gonzalez, Christina Diaz. *The Red Umbrella* (6–10). 2010, Knopf $16.99 (978-0-375-86190-1). Lucia and her brother are uprooted from their comfortable life in Cuba and sent to live in Nebraska during the Communist revolution of the 1960s. (Rev: BLO 7/15/10; LMC 8–9/10; SLJ 5/10; VOYA 6/10)

193 Hijuelos, Oscar. *Dark Dude* (9–12). 2008, Simon & Schuster $16.99 (978-141694804-9). Cuban American teen Rico runs away from his troubled Harlem life to a midwestern hippie farm. ∩ **℮** Lexile 980L (Rev: BL 11/1/08; LMC 1–2/09; SLJ 11/1/08; VOYA 10/08)

194 Jimenez, Francisco. *Reaching Out* (7–12). 2008, Houghton $16 (978-061803851-0). In this fictionalized autobiography young Jimenez struggles to rise beyond his immigrant migrant farm family and succeed in college. **℮** Lexile 910L (Rev: BL 8/08*; LMC 1–2/09; SLJ 12/08; VOYA 10/08)

195 Jordan, Dream. *Hot Girl* (7–10). 2008, St. Martin's paper $9.95 (978-031238284-1). Troubled 14-year-old African American Kate's resolve to stick with her new foster family is threatened when smooth-talking Naleejah takes her in, gives her a makeover, and teaches her how to win her crush's affection. **℮** Lexile HL660L (Rev: BLO 11/19/08; SLJ 4/1/09; VOYA 12/08)

196 Karim, Sheba. *Skunk Girl* (7–10). 2009, Farrar $16.95 (978-037437011-4). Muslim Nina, 16, comes from the only Pakistani American family in town, and struggles with her parents' strict rules and expectations and her own hairiness. Lexile 840L (Rev: BL 4/15/09; SLJ 4/1/09; VOYA 4/10)

197 Kwok, Jean. *Girl in Translation* (11–12). 2010, Riverhead $25.95 (978-159448756-9). In this immigrant coming-of-age story, Kwok tells the story — loosely based on her own experience — of Kim, who arrives in Brooklyn from Hong Kong, helps her mother at the sweatshops, and faces down hostility and discrimination at every turn; for mature readers. ☊ ℮ (Rev: BL 4/1/10)

198 Lynch, Janet Nichols. *Messed Up* (7–10). 2009, Holiday $17.95 (978-082342185-5). Part Cheyenne, part Mexican R.D. tries to make it on his own when the only reliable adult in his life dies and he must navigate life in an unstable school and a violent neighborhood. Lexile 780L (Rev: BL 4/1/09; SLJ 8/09; VOYA 8/09)

199 McMullan, Margaret. *Cashay* (7–10). 2009, Houghton $15.00 (978-054707656-0). Cashay's younger sister is killed in gang-related violence in their housing project, and Cashay is helped by a white mentor as her mother returns to drug taking. ℮ Lexile 700L (Rev: BLO 5/27/09; SLJ 8/09)

200 Meminger, Neesha. *Shine, Coconut Moon* (7–10). 2009, Simon & Schuster $16.99 (978-141695495-8). An Indian American girl realizes how vital her heritage is to her in the months following 9/11. Lexile HL740L (Rev: BL 2/15/09; SLJ 4/1/09)

201 Pellegrino, Marge. *Journey of Dreams* (6–10). 2009, Frances Lincoln $15.95 (978-1-84780-061-9). Eleven-year-old Tomasa's family is reunited in Arizona after escaping violent persecution in their Mayan village. Lexile 740L (Rev: BL 8/09; SLJ 8/09)

202 Perkins, Mitali. *Secret Keeper* (7–12). 2009, Delacorte $16.99 (978-038573340-3); LB $19.99 (978-038590356-1). In the mid -1970s, 16-year-old Asha Gupta and her family make a difficult move from India to the United States, where Indian tradition and Asha's dreams for herself clash when she meets the boy next door, and attempts to rescue her older sister from a horrible arranged marriage. ℮ Lexile 800L (Rev: BL 12/15/08; SLJ 3/1/09)

203 Wu, Fan. *Beautiful as Yesterday* (11–12). 2009, Atria $24 (978-141659889-3). Chinese American Mary Chang tries to make peace with her younger sister and her family history when her mother arrives from China; for mature readers. ℮ (Rev: BL 7/09)

204 Yee, Paul. *Learning to Fly* (6–10). 2008, Orca $16.95 (978-155143955-6); paper $9.95 (978-155143953-2). Chinese immigrant Jason, 17, bonds with Native American "Chief"— and falls in with a pot-smoking crowd — to escape prejudice and feeling like an outsider in his small Canadian town. ℮ Lexile HL540L (Rev: BL 10/1/08; LMC 3–4/09; SLJ 3/1/09; VOYA 10/08)

205 Yunis, Alia. *The Night Counter* (10–12). 2009, Crown $24 (978-030745362-4). Original, heartwarming, and funny, this novel about a Lebanese grandmother who believes she is about to die is full of twists and surprises. ℮ (Rev: BL 7/09)

Family Life and Problems

206 Avasthi, Swati. *Split* (9–12). 2010, Knopf/Borzoi $16.99 (978-0-375-86340-0); LB $19.99 (978-0-375-96340-7). Sixteen-year-old Jace is thrown out by his abusive father and hopes to live with his older brother — who fled the violent situation five years earlier; both young men struggle to make a life together while worrying about what's happening to their mother in their absence. ℮ Lexile HL610L (Rev: HB 5–6/10; SLJ 3/10)

207 Barkley, Brad, and Heather Hepler. *Jars of Glass* (7–10). 2008, Dutton $16.99 (978-052547911-6). Sisters Chloe, 15, and Shana, 15, react differently when their artist mother is suddenly committed to a mental institution and their father turns to alcohol to cope. ℮ (Rev: BLO 12/11/08; SLJ 12/08; VOYA 12/08)

208 Barnes, John. *Tales of the Madman Underground* (9–12). 2009, Viking $18.99 (978-067006081-8). Six days in the life of a teenager in a small Ohio town in the 1970s. Karl comes from a dysfunctional home and has a collection of dysfunctional friends from his therapy group, yet he manages to get by with humor. Lexile 1040L (Rev: BL 5/1/09; HB 9–10/09; SLJ 7/1/09*; VOYA 6/09)

209 Baron, Kathi. *Shattered* (8–10). 2009, WestSide $16.95 (978-1-934813-08-9). When Cassie's father, in a fit of rage at his own father, shatters her vintage violin on the day of her debut performance with the Chicago Youth Orchestra, the 14-year-old virtuoso heads for her grandfather's house and uncovers the disturbing genesis of her father's fury. Lexile HL660L (Rev: BLO 8/20/09; SLJ 12/09)

210 Bauman, Beth Ann. *Rosie and Skate* (9–12). 2009, Random $15.99 (978-038573735-7). Rosie and Skate, sisters who attend high school in New Jersey, deal with their father's alcoholism and incarceration in different ways. Lexile HL590L (Rev: BL 10/1/09*; SLJ 11/09)

211 Booth, Coe. *Kendra* (10–12). 2008, Scholastic $16.99 (978-043992536-5). Fifteen-year-old Kendra turns to sex to fight the sting of her mother's abandonment. ℮ Lexile 770L (Rev: BL 11/1/08*; HB 11–12/08; SLJ 10/1/08*; VOYA 10/08)

212 Braff, Joshua. *Peep Show* (11–12). 2010, Algonquin paper $13.95 (978-156512508-7). Caught between two worlds, child of divorce David, 16, sides with his father, who owns a porn theater, failing to anticipate the difficulty of being separated from his mother, now a strict Hasidic Jew; for mature readers. **e** (Rev: BL 5/15/10*)

213 Brew-Hammond, Nana Ekua. *Powder Necklace* (10–12). 2010, Washington Square paper $15 (978-143912610-3). Fifteen-year-old Lila struggles to adapt as she is shipped first from her mother's home in London to a provincial boarding school in her parents' homeland of Ghana and then to Manhattan to stay with her father and his family. (Rev: BL 2/15/10)

214 Briant, Ed. *Choppy Socky Blues* (8–11). 2010, Flux paper $9.95 (978-0-73871-897-2). Fourteen-year-old Jason's interest in a girl fascinated with karate prompts him to approach his father, a martial arts teacher whom he has not seen since his parents' difficult divorce; set in England. (Rev: BL 4/15/110; LMC 8–9/10; SLJ 5/10; VOYA 10/10)

215 Chaltas, Thalia. *Because I Am Furniture* (8–12). 2009, Viking $16.99 (978-0-670-06298-0). This novel in verse tracks the development of 14-year-old Anke, the only one of the three siblings in her family to escape her father's abuse, as she gains sufficient confidence to challenge him. (Rev: LMC 8–9/09; SLJ 6/1/09; VOYA 4/09)

216 Cheng, Andrea. *Brushing Mom's Hair* (7–10). Illus. by Nicole Wong. 2009, Boyds Mills $17.95 (978-1-59078-599-7). This novel in verse follows 15-year-old dancer Ann through her mother's ultimately successful battle with breast cancer. (Rev: BL 9/1/09; SLJ 10/09)

217 Cohen, Tish. *The Truth About Delilah Blue* (10–12). 2010, Harper paper $13.99 (978-006187597-7). Twenty-year-old Lila, living in Los Angeles and hoping to become a model, struggles to forge a new identity for herself as she copes with new information from her mother about her now-ill father. **e** (Rev: BL 4/15/10)

218 Colebank, Susan. *Cashing In* (9–12). 2009, Dutton $16.99 (978-0-525-42151-1). After the death of her father, 18-year-old Reggie grapples with her mother's gambling addiction and her own reluctance to interfere. **e** Lexile 720L (Rev: BLO 12/8/09; SLJ 1/10)

219 Connelly, Neil. *The Miracle Stealer* (9–12). 2010, Scholastic $17.99 (978-0-545-13195-7). Andi, 19, tries to protect her 6-year-old brother Daniel, who was miraculously rescued from a well and is now being touted as a miracle worker in his own right. **e** Lexile 910L (Rev: BL 11/1/10; HB 11–12/10; LMC 11–12/10; SLJ 12/1/10; VOYA 12/10)

220 Cook, Gloria. *Leaving Shades* (11–12). 2010, Severn $28.95 (978-072786905-0). Eager to avenge her long-ago abandonment, self-righteous Beth finally meets her mother — and realizes she must prove herself to win the affection of her new family in this story set in Cornwall. (Rev: BLO 7/10)

221 De Goldi, Kate. *The 10 p.m. Question* (7–12). 2010, Candlewick $15.99 (978-0-7636-4939-5). Frankie, 12, worries about many things until free-thinking Sydney,

veteran of 22 schools, makes him question his priorities; set in New Zealand. ⌒ Lexile 830L (Rev: BL 8/10*; HB 11–12/10; LMC 1–2/11; SLJ 9/1/10; VOYA 12/10)

222 Dellasega, Cheryl. *Sistrsic92 (Meg)* (7–10). Illus. by Tyler Beauford. 2009, Marshall Cavendish $16.99 (978-0-7614-5456-4). When Meg's older, perfect sister Cara develops an eating disorder, plain, average Meg feels even more isolated from her family and confides her woes to her blog. (Rev: BL 10/1/09; SLJ 1/10; VOYA 2/10)

223 Dowd, Siobhan. *Solace of the Road* (8–12). 2009, Random $17.99 (978-0-375-84971-8); LB $20.99 (978-0-375-94971-5). Holly Hogan, 14, assumes an alter-ego and escapes from her London foster home to reunite with her mother in Ireland, learning a valuable lesson about herself along the way. ⌒ **e** Lexile HL650L (Rev: BL 10/1/09*; SLJ 10/09)

224 Durrow, Heidi W. *The Girl Who Fell from the Sky* (11–12). 2010, Algonquin $22.95 (978-156512680-0). After a tragedy involving her Danish mother and her siblings, young Rachel finds herself living with her African American grandmother in a black neighborhood in Portland, Oregon, where she faces new challenges; for mature readers. ⌒ (Rev: BL 2/1/10)

225 Galante, Cecilia. *The Sweetness of Salt* (9–12). 2010, Bloomsbury $16.99 (978-1-59990-512-9). High school graduate Julia has her immediate future mapped out until her estranged older sister Sophie turns up and reveals family secrets that force Julia to reassess. **e** Lexile 630L (Rev: LMC 10/10; SLJ 12/1/10; VOYA 12/10)

226 Garsee, Jeannine. *Say the Word* (9–12). 2009, Bloomsbury $16.99 (978-159990333-0). Seventeen-year-old Shawna's life is turned upside-down when she learns that her lesbian mother—who abandoned the family years ago—is ill and that her father is bitter and cold-hearted. Lexile HL580L (Rev: BL 4/1/09; SLJ 6/1/09; VOYA 6/09)

227 Glover, Bonnie J. *Going Down South* (11–12). 2008, Oneworld paper $14.00 (978-034548091-0). When Daisy's 15-year-old daughter gets pregnant in 1960s Brooklyn, the family leaves its black middle-class neighborhood for Alabama, where Daisy's mother puts the family back together with sass and compassion. **e** (Rev: BL 6/1–15/08; SLJ 10/08)

228 Grant, Vicki. *Comeback* (6–10). 2010, Orca LB $16.95 (978-1-55469-311-5); paper $9.95 (978-1-55469-310-8). Upset when her father's plane goes down, Ria runs away from her mother's home with her 5-year-old brother and faces many challenges; for reluctant readers. **e** Lexile HL550L (Rev: BL 4/15/10; SLJ 4/10)

229 Haigh, Jennifer. *The Condition* (11–12). 2008, HarperCollins $25.95 (978-006075578-2). In this family drama for mature readers that spreads across 20 years,

16

siblings Billy, Scott, and Gwen cope with their parents' inattention (and impending divorce), as well as Gwen's genetic disorder. ∩ ℮ (Rev: BL 6/1–15/08)

230 Hamilton, Ruth. *A Parallel Life* (11–12). 2010, Severn $28.95 (978-072786886-2). Emotionally complex Harrie, 21, struggles to carry the weight of a dysfunctional family on her shoulders as she aspires to become a jeweler; for mature readers. (Rev: BL 6/1–15/10)

231 Hopkins, Ellen. *Fallout* (9–12). 2010, Simon & Schuster $18.99 (978-1-4169-5009-7). This sequel to *Crank* (2004) and *Glass* (2007) focuses on Kristina's oldest children and the problems they face resulting from her addiction to crystal meth. ℮ (Rev: LMC 11–12/10*; SLJ 9/1/10; VOYA 10/10)

232 Howrey, Meg. *Blind Sight* (10–12). 2011, Pantheon $24.95 (978-030737916-0). Seventeen-year-old Luke spends the summer in Los Angeles with the TV-star father he just met, and uses his college application essay to examine their relationship. (Rev: BL 3/1/11)

233 Huston, Nancy. *Fault Lines* (11–12). 2008, Grove paper $14.00 (978-080217051-4). Four generations of one family are affected by an ugly secret that slowly comes to light through four young narrators, beginning in contemporary California and reeling backward to World War II Germany; for mature readers. ∩ (Rev: BL 8/08*)

234 James, Brian. *The Heights* (8–12). 2009, Feiwel & Friends $16.99 (978-031236853-1). Privileged Catherine and her stepbrother Henry, a Mexican orphan, share a doomed passion for each other in this contemporary retelling of *Wuthering Heights* set in San Francisco. Lexile 900L (Rev: BL 5/1/09; HB 5–6/09; LMC 8–9/09; SLJ 7/1/09)

235 James, Tania. *Atlas of Unknowns* (10–12). 2009, Knopf $24.95 (978-030726890-7). This novel describes the lives of two bright Indian sisters whose bond is stronger than the separation, deceptions, pain, and success they meet; set in both India and the United States, this is suitable for mature students. ℮ (Rev: BL 4/15/09)

236 Kiernan, Kristy. *Between Friends* (11–12). 2010, Berkley paper $15 (978-042523347-4). Single career woman Cora donates an egg to her barren friend Ali; fourteen years later she's coping with the possibility that she passed a hereditary disease onto the child in this complex family drama; for mature readers. (Rev: BL 3/15/10)

237 King, Lily. *Father of the Rain* (11–12). 2010, Atlantic Monthly $24 (978-080211949-0). Daughter-of-divorce Daley, 11, copes with her father's disastrous new affair, drinking problem, and seemingly sudden lack of morals in this compelling portrait of a dysfunctional family; for mature readers. ℮ (Rev: BL 4/15/10)

238 Kneale, Matthew. *When We Were Romans* (10–12). 2008, Doubleday $23.95 (978-038552625-8). Nine-year-old Lawrence tells the story of his mother's flight from London (and her imagined stalker) to Rome as he witnesses the slow undoing of his family. ℮ (Rev: BL 7/08*; SLJ 9/08)

239 Kring, Sandra. *Thank You for All Things* (11–12). 2008, Bantam paper $12.00 (978-038534120-2). Bright 11-year-old Lucy, who is curious about her missing father, dredges up some unpleasant family history; for mature teens. ℮ (Rev: BL 8/08)

240 Kwasney, Michelle D. *Blue Plate Special* (9–12). 2010, Chronicle $16.99 (978-0-8118-6780-1). An absorbing story of three generations of young women, told in alternating narratives. (Rev: BL 10/15/09; LMC 1–2/10; SLJ 12/09)

241 Lancaster, Craig. *The Summer Son* (11–12). 2011, AmazonEncore paper $14.95 (978-193559724-7). An angry, 40-something man suffering a midlife crisis recalls his difficult youth when he returns to Montana to confront his violent, estranged father in this book best suited to mature readers. (Rev: BL 1/1/11)

242 London, Julia. *Summer of Two Wishes* (11–12). 2009, Pocket paper $7.99 (978-141654708-2). Macy, who is newly married to Wyatt, finds out that her beloved first husband Finn was not killed by the Taliban years ago but has been found alive and is on his way home; for mature readers. ∩ (Rev: BL 9/09)

243 Lynch, Chris. *The Big Game of Everything* (7–10). 2008, HarperTeen $16.99 (978-006074034-4); LB $17.89 (978-006074035-1). Jock and his younger brother Egon spend a summer working at their grandfather's golf course and learn the importance of integrity versus material gain. Lexile 830L (Rev: BL 9/1/08; HB 9–10/08; SLJ 10/1/08; VOYA 8/08)

244 Mitchell, Mary E. *Americans in Space* (11–12). 2009, St. Martin's $24.99 (978-031237245-3). Still reeling two years after the death of her husband, high school guidance counselor Kate Cavanaugh finds it a struggle to simply get through her day; to complicate matters, her 14-year-old daughter is exhibiting some disconcerting behavior; for mature readers. (Rev: BL 10/1/09)

245 Murray, Martine. *How to Make a Bird* (8–12). 2010, Scholastic $16.99 (978-0-439-66951-1). Manon, 17, travels from the Australian countryside to Melbourne, where she hopes to come to terms with family tragedies. ℮ (Rev: BL 4/15/10; LMC 8–9/10; SLJ 8/10)

246 Myracle, Lauren. *Peace, Love, and Baby Ducks* (8–12). 2009, Dutton $16.99 (978-052547743-3). Privileged Atlanta teen sisters Anna and Carly deal with boys, looks, and emerging belief systems as they navigate family and school life. ∩ Lexile HL630L (Rev: BL 4/15/09; HB 7–8/09; SLJ 8/09; VOYA 8/09)

247 Nelson, Jandy. *The Sky Is Everywhere* (8–11). 2010, Dial $17.99 (978-0-8037-3495-1). When Lennie's popular older sister suddenly dies, the 17-year-old struggles to fill her shoes — which include a fiancé and the lead role in Romeo and Juliet. ☊ ✇ (Rev: BL 1/1/10; HB 3–4/10; SLJ 3/10; VOYA 8/10)

248 O'Dell, Tawni. *Fragile Beasts* (11–12). 2010, Crown $25 (978-030735168-5). After their father is killed in an accident, two teenaged boys are taken in by a wealthy town matriarch with a melancholy past and thereby avoid returning to the mother who abandoned them; this arresting tale suitable for mature readers is set in a western Pennsylvania coal town. (Rev: BL 2/15/10)

249 Omololu, C. J. *Dirty Little Secrets* (7–10). 2010, Walker $16.99 (978-0-8027-8660-9). High school sophomore Lucy is determined to hide the fact that her mother is a hoarder, and when she finds her mother dead from an asthma attack amid the stacks of junk, Lucy decides to take drastic action. ☊ ✇ Lexile 890L (Rev: BL 10/1509; LMC 3–4/10; SLJ 2/10)

250 Puchner, Eric. *Model Home* (11–12). 2010, Scribner $26 (978-074327048-9). Warren moves his endearing yet dysfunctional family to California, where a series of mishaps — from his own real estate foible to his daughter's rocky relationship — draws them deeper and deeper into crazy, though amusing, chaos. ☊ (Rev: BL 1/1/10*)

251 Quindlen, Anna. *Every Last One* (11–12). 2010, Random $26 (978-140006574-5). Mary Beth copes with tragedy — and the task of rebuilding her likable family — in this engrossing novel suitable for mature readers. ☊ (Rev: BL 3/15/10)

252 Reinhardt, Dana. *The Things a Brother Knows* (9–12). 2010, Random $16.99 (978-0-375-84455-3); LB $19.99 (978-0-375-94455-0). Former marine Boaz has returned from combat a changed young man, and 17-year-old Levi is sufficiently concerned about his behavior to follow him when he leaves home and sets out on a walking trip. ✇ (Rev: BL 10/1/10*; SLJ 12/1/10*)

253 Reynolds, Marilyn. *Shut Up!* (8–12). 2008, Morning Glory $15.96 (978-193253893-9); paper $9.95 (978-193253888-5). Seventeen-year-old Mario desperately attempts to get help when he finds his brother is being abused by his aunt's boyfriend in this inspiring story of a strong family coping with conflict. ✇ (Rev: BL 11/15/08; SLJ 2/1/09; VOYA 12/08)

254 Rice, Luanne. *The Deep Blue Sea for Beginners* (11–12). 2009, Bantam $26 (978-055380514-7). A multilayered story for mature readers about how a daughter tracks down her estranged mother on the island of Capri; this tale includes characters from *The Geometry of Sisters* (2009. ☊ (Rev: BL 7/09)

255 Sachar, Louis. *The Cardturner* (9–12). 2010, Delacorte $17.99 (978-0-385-73662-6). Alton, 17, volunteers to help his rich, blind uncle with his games of bridge and learns the game and a lot more; optional passages allow non-bridge players to skip details of the game. ☊ ✇ Lexile HL720L (Rev: BL 5/15/10*; HB 5–6/10; LMC 11–12/10; SLJ 6/10)

256 Schumacher, Julie. *Black Box* (9–12). 2008, Delacorte $15.99 (978-038573542-1); LB $18.99 (978-038590523-7). When stoic high school freshman Elena's older sister Dora is hospitalized for depression, Elena takes it upon herself to look after Dora even as her family falls to pieces around her. ✇ Lexile NC600L (Rev: BL 11/1/08; SLJ 8/08*; VOYA 12/08)

257 Seigel, Andrea. *The Kid Table* (10–12). 2010, Bloomsbury $16.99 (978-1-59990-480-1). Ingrid, 16, and her five teenage cousins bring their various problems to the "kid table" at family gatherings; Ingrid's observations are perceptive about herself, her cousins, and the adults in this dysfunctional yet tight-knit group. ✇ Lexile 950L (Rev: LMC 10/10; SLJ 11/1/10; VOYA 12/10)

258 Shreve, Anita. *Rescue* (10–12). 2010, Little, Brown $26.99 (978-031602072-5). EMT Pete Webster seeks out the alcoholic wife who left him years ago so she can help him save their daughter, Rowan, who has fallen into the same self-destructive behaviors. ☊ ✇ (Rev: BL 9/15/10)

259 Shreve, Porter. *When the White House Was Ours* (11–12). 2008, Houghton paper $12.95 (978-061872210-5). His father continues to lose teaching jobs and 12-year-old Daniel Truitt's life has been in constant flux; now his delusional parents are dragging him to Washington, D.C., in hopes of starting a progressive school; an entertaining read for mature teens, this is set in 1976. (Rev: BL 8/08)

260 Stevenson, Robin. *A Thousand Shades of Blue* (9–11). 2008, Orca paper $12.95 (978-155143921-1). Sixteen-year-old Rachel's troubled family spends a year sailing through the Caribbean, where Rachel learns about secrets, trust, and sexuality. ✇ Lexile NC600L (Rev: BL 1/1–15/09; SLJ 3/1/09; VOYA 12/08)

261 Trollope, Joanna. *The Other Family* (11–12). 2010, Touchstone paper $15 (978-143912983-8). Chrissie is overwhelmed when her partner Richie dies and leaves key items to his long-estranged wife rather than to her and their three daughters; for mature readers. (Rev: BL 2/15/10)

262 Valentine, Jenny. *Broken Soup* (9–12). 2009, HarperTeen $16.99 (978-006085071-5). Following her older brother's death, Rowan discovers things about his life that lead to growth and healing. Lexile HL730L (Rev: BL 2/15/09; HB 5–6/09; SLJ 4/1/09)

263 Wallace, Rich. *Perpetual Check* (8–11). 2009, Knopf $15.99 (978-037584058-6); LB $18.99 (978-037594058-3). Brothers Zeke and Randy face off against each other in chess while growing closer and making important discoveries about life. ℮ Lexile 750L (Rev: BL 1/1–15/09; SLJ 2/1/09; VOYA 6/09)

264 Warman, Jessica. *Breathless* (9–12). 2009, Walker $16.99 (978-0-8027-9849-7). Fifteen-year-old Katie's schizophrenic older brother overshadows her life even when she goes away to boarding school. (Rev: BL 7/09; SLJ 11/09)

265 Williams, Carol Lynch. *Glimpse* (8–11). 2010, Simon & Schuster $16.99 (978-1-4169-9730-6). In free verse, Williams tells the story of two sisters who together face the difficulties of living with an alcoholic, prostitute mother; when Lizzie attempts suicide, the younger Hope plumbs her memories of abuse. ℮ Lexile 630L (Rev: BL 4/15/10; LMC 10/10; SLJ 8/10)

266 Williams, Suzanne Morgan. *Bull Rider* (7–10). 2009, Simon & Schuster $16.99 (978-141696130-7). Fourteen-year-old Cam enters a bull-riding competition to win prize money to help with his brother's rehabilitation from injuries suffered in Iraq. ℮ (Rev: BL 1/1–15/09; SLJ 4/1/09)

Physical and Emotional Problems

267 Anderson, Laurie Halse. *Wintergirls* (9–12). 2009, Viking $17.99 (978-067001110-0). In an intense first-person narrative, 18-year-old Lia describes her feelings as she slides further into the depths of anorexia after her former best friend dies of another eating disorder. ∩ (Rev: BL 12/15/08*; HB 3–40/09; LMC 8–9/09; SLJ 2/1/09*; VOYA 4/09)

268 Ayarbe, Heidi. *Compulsion* (10–12). 2011, Harper-Collins $16.99 (978-006199386-2). Soccer star Jake, 17, tries to hide his obsessive compulsive disorder in this compelling novel that clearly describes the difficulties of living with this problem. (Rev: BL 3/15/11*; SLJ 6/11; VOYA 8/11)

269 Borris, Albert. *Crash into Me* (8–12). 2009, Simon & Schuster $16.99 (978-141697435-2). Four suicidal teenagers set off on a road trip planning to kill themselves when they reach their destination, but things change along the way. Lexile HL530L (Rev: BL 5/15/09; SLJ 8/09; VOYA 12/09)

270 Coffelt, Nancy. *Listen* (8–11). 2009, WestSide $16.95 (978-1-934813-07-2). In alternating narratives, this compelling, fast-paced novel introduces 18-year-old orphan Will, whose lonely life intersects with those of troubled 14-year-old Kurt and middle-aged schizophrenic Carrie. Lexile HL770L (Rev: BL 9/1/09; SLJ 12/09)

271 Crutcher, Chris. *Angry Management* (9–12). 2009, Greenwillow $16.99 (978-0-06-050247-8); LB $17.89 (978-0-06-050246-1). Anger is at the center of these three stories featuring "angry management" classes

held by Mr. Nak (of *Ironman*) and starring other familiar Crutcher characters. ℮ Lexile HL730L (Rev: HB 11–12/09; SLJ 9/09; VOYA 8/09)

272 Cummings, Priscilla. *Blindsided* (6–10). 2010, Dutton $16.99 (978-0-525-42161-0). Natalie, 14, is losing her eyesight and struggles to accept this reality and learn special skills at her new school for the blind. ℮ Lexile 710L (Rev: BL 6/1/10; LMC 10/10; SLJ 7/10; VOYA 8/10)

273 Davidson, Andrew. *The Gargoyle* (11–12). 2008, Doubleday $25.95 (978-038552494-0). In this tale of excess, pain, and self-loathing, a former porn star who is planning suicide gets an unexpected chance at love and redemption when an unlikely woman enters his life with a tale of reincarnation; for mature readers only. ∩ ℮ (Rev: BL 9/1/08)

274 Denman, K. L. *Me, Myself and Ike* (7–10). 2009, Orca paper $12.95 (978-1-55469-086-2). Encouraged to commit suicide by his antagonistic companion Ike, who is in reality the result of a schizophrenia-induced hallucination, 17-year-old Kit, once popular and even-tempered, becomes increasingly insular and paranoid. ℮ (Rev: BL 11/1/09; SLJ 12/09; VOYA 12/09)

275 Dorfman, Joaquin. *The Long Wait for Tomorrow* (9–12). 2009, Random $16.99 (978-037584694-6); LB $19.99 (978-037594694-3). Star quarterback Kelly confounds his friends by suddenly changing his personality and claiming to have time-traveled from a mental institution. ℮ (Rev: BL 7/09; SLJ 12/09)

276 Geus, Mireille. *Piggy* (6–10). Trans. by Nancy Forest-Flier. 2008, Front Street $14.95 (978-159078636-9). Told in the first-person voice of 12-year-old Lizzy, who has autism, this story recounts the constant teasing Lizzy faces everyday until she forms an unlikely friendship with Peggy, which leads to complications of its own. Lexile HL390L (Rev: BLO 11/19/08; HB 1–2/09; LMC 1–2/09; SLJ 1/1/09)

277 Gonzalez, Ann. *Running for My Life* (8–10). 2009, WestSide $16.95 (978-193481300-3). Andrea turns to running as a way to cope with her mother's schizophrenia, but still suffers from anxiety and nightmares. Lexile HL520L (Rev: BL 5/1/09; SLJ 7/1/09)

278 Halpin, Brendan. *Forever Changes* (8–11). 2008, Farrar $16.95 (978-037432436-0). Cystic fibrosis sufferer Brianna ponders the meaning of life, and the futility of planning a future she likely won't live to see. Lexile 890L (Rev: BL 10/15/08; SLJ 11/1/08; VOYA 6/08)

279 Headley, Justina Chen. *North of Beautiful* (9–12). 2009, Little, Brown $16.99 (978-031602505-8). Friendship with Jacob, a Goth Chinese boy with a cleft lip scar, helps 16-year-old Terra, who feels flawed because of a birthmark on her cheek. Lexile 850L (Rev: BL 2/15/09; SLJ 2/1/09; VOYA 6/09)

280 Hyde, Catherine Ryan. *Diary of a Witness* (7–10). 2009, Knopf $16.99 (978-037585684-6). Will gets pushed to the breaking point by school bullies and the death of his younger brother. The story is told through entries in Will's friend Ernie's diary. Lexile HL510L (Rev: BLO 5/27/09; SLJ 9/09)

281 John, Antony. *Five Flavors of Dumb* (9–12). 2010, Dial $16.99 (978-0-8037-3433-3). Eighteen-year-old Piper, who is profoundly hearing impaired and whose younger sister requires expensive cochlear implants, becomes the manager of the school's popular rock band, Dumb. ℮ (Rev: SLJ 12/1/10; VOYA 2/11)

282 Littman, Sarah Darer. *Purge* (7–10). 2009, Scholastic $16.99 (978-054505235-1). Janie, 16, confronts her bulimia as well as other psychological problems while at a rehab facility for eating disorders. Lexile 950L (Rev: BLO 2/9/09; LMC 5–6/09; SLJ 7/1/09)

283 McDaniel, Lurlene. *Breathless* (7–10). 2009, Delacorte $10.99 (978-038573459-2); LB $13.99 (978-038590458-2). This moving story about a champion diver who learns he has bone cancer is told from his perspective and from those of three other teens who all struggle with Travis's desire for assisted suicide. (Rev: BL 7/09; SLJ 4/1/09)

284 Moskowitz, Hannah. *Break* (9–12). 2009, Simon & Schuster paper $8.99 (978-141698275-3). Jonah, 17, responds to the problems of his dysfunctional family with self-destructive risk taking. (Rev: BL 6/1–15/09*; SLJ 1/10)

285 Nolan, Han. *Crazy* (7–10). 2010, Houghton $17 (978-0-15-205109-9). Fifteen-year-old Jason's mother has died and he must cope alone with his mentally ill father; fear of his father and for his own sanity are alleviated when his predicament is discovered and he is sent to foster care. (Rev: BL 8/10*; HB 11–12/10; SLJ 9/1/10)

286 Rapp, Adam. *Punkzilla* (10–12). 2009, Candlewick $16.99 (978-076363031-7). Jamie, known as "Punkzilla," runs away from military school and decides to hitchhike across-country to visit his dying older brother; sexual encounters, crime, drugs, danger, and loneliness are all part of his journey. Lexile 1300L (Rev: BL 4/15/09*; LMC 10/09; SLJ 7/09)

287 Ryan, Darlene. *Five Minutes More* (7–10). 2009, Orca paper $12.95 (978-155469006-0). D'Arcy has trouble adjusting after the death of her father, who suffered from ALS; the idea that he killed himself makes everything worse. Lexile HL570L (Rev: BLO 4/14/09; VOYA 6/09)

288 Sanchez, Alex. *Bait* (7–10). 2009, Simon & Schuster $16.99 (978-141693772-2). When Diego ends up in juvenile court, his parole officer helps him get to the source of his anger problems—namely, being sexually abused by his stepfather. Lexile HL630L (Rev: BL 5/15/09; SLJ 7/1/09*; VOYA 8/09)

289 Sandell, Lisa Ann. *A Map of the Known World* (7–10). 2009, Scholastic $16.99 (978-054506970-0). After her brother Nate dies in a car crash, 14-year-old Cora becomes close to Nate's best friend, who survived the crash, and learns that there was an artistic, thoughtful side to Nate that she had never seen. Lexile 800L (Rev: BL 4/1/09; SLJ 6/1/09)

290 Schindler, Holly. *A Blue So Dark* (8–11). 2010, Flux paper $9.95 (978-0-73871-926-9). When 15-year-old Aura's mentally ill mother finally enters a catatonic state of schizophrenia, Aura realizes she can't care for her on her own. ℮ (Rev: BL 5/1/10*; LMC 8–9/10; SLJ 6/10)

291 Scott, Elizabeth. *Love You Hate You Miss You* (9–12). 2009, HarperTeen $16.99 (978-006112283-5); LB $17.89 (978-006112284-2). Through therapy and journal entries, wayward teen Amy comes to terms with the death of her friend Julia and the destructiveness of her own behavior. (Rev: BL 4/1/09; HB 7–8/09; SLJ 6/1/09; VOYA 10/09)

292 Sheinmel, Courtney. *Positively* (6–10). 2009, Simon & Schuster $15.99 (978-141697169-6). This is 13-year-old Emmy's first-person account of coming to accept living with AIDS. (Rev: BL 7/09; SLJ 1/10)

293 Stork, Francisco X. *Marcelo in the Real World* (9–12). 2009, Scholastic $17.99 (978-054505474-4). Marcelo, a 17-year-old with Asperger's syndrome, is thrown into the "real world" when he takes a job in the mailroom at his father's law firm and must make ethical decisions. ⌂ Lexile HL700L (Rev: BL 4/1/09; LMC 5–6/09; SLJ 3/09)

294 Tullson, Diane. *Riley Park* (7–12). 2009, LB $16.95 (978-155469124-1); paper $9.95 (978-155469123-4). After a night of partying and fighting, friends Darius and Corbin are attacked in a park. Darius dies and Corbin is seriously injured. A suspenseful offering for reluctant readers. Lexile HL480L (Rev: BL 5/1/09; SLJ 10/09)

295 Waldorf, Heather. *Tripping* (8–12). 2009, Red Deer paper $12.95 (978-088995426-7). Rainey, who has a prosthetic leg, sets off on an Outward Bound-type trip across Canada and learns about herself, her mother, and her fellow travelers. Lexile HL780L (Rev: BL 5/1/09; SLJ 5/1/09)

296 Wieringa, Tommy. *Joe Speedboat* (10–12). 2010, Black Cat paper $14.95 (978-080217072-9). Wheelchair-bound Frankie becomes an arm-wrestling champ under the management of the energetic, eccentric young Joe Speedboat. (Rev: BL 3/1/10)

297 Wolfson, Jill. *Cold Hands, Warm Heart* (8–10). 2009, Holt $17.95 (978-080508282-1). When a 14-year-old gymnast dies, her organs are transplanted, affecting many people in profound ways. Lexile HL760L (Rev: BL 3/15/09; SLJ 5/1/09; VOYA 6/09)

Personal Problems and Growing into Maturity

298 Baskin, Nora Raleigh. *All We Know of Love* (7–10). 2008, Candlewick $16.99 (978-076363623-4). Sixteen-year-old Natalie Gordon sets off on a bus trip from Connecticut to Florida to find the mother who abandoned her four years ago, and learns lessons about herself, and about love, along the way. Lexile NC660L (Rev: BL 10/15/08; SLJ 9/1/08; VOYA 8/08)

299 Beam, Matt. *Last December* (9–12). 2009, Front Street $18.95 (978-1-59078-651-2). Steven is a troubled 15-year-old who struggles with and eventually learns to weather multiple stresses in his life; the book is told in notes to his unborn sister. Lexile NC1750L (Rev: BL 10/15/09; LMC 1–2/10)

300 Bloss, Josie. *Albatross* (8–11). Series: Band Geek. 2010, Flux paper $9.95 (978-0-73871-476-9). Tess, a 16-year-old French horn player lacking in self-confidence, falls for pianist Micah despite his abusive and manipulative behavior. Lexile HL680L (Rev: BLO 1/8/10; LMC 5–6/10; SLJ 3/10)

301 Bognanni, Peter. *The House of Tomorrow* (10–12). 2010, Putnam $24.95 (978-039915609-0). Sheltered, home-schooled Sebastian must leave his isolated bubble when his grandmother suffers a stroke; and with the help of the Whitcomb family he discovers a totally new world. ∩ ℯ (Rev: BL 3/1/10)

302 Brashares, Ann. *3 Willows: The Sisterhood Grows* (6–10). Series: Sisterhood. 2009, Delacorte $18.99 (978-038573676-3); LB $21.99 (978-038590628-9). The author of *The Sisterhood of the Traveling Pants* introduces Ama, Jo, and Polly, who are about to enter high school and face different but typical challenges. ∩ ℯ Lexile 700L (Rev: BL 2/15/09; HB 3–4/09; LMC 5–6/09; SLJ 1/1/09)

303 Bryant, Jen. *The Fortune of Carmen Navarro* (9–12). 2010, Knopf $16.99 (978-0-375-85759-1); LB $19.99 (978-0-375-95759-8). In this modern retelling of the opera set in Valley Forge, Pennsylvania, Carmen is a high school dropout hoping to become a famous singer and Ryan is a military cadet; the pair's friends seek to protect them when their mutual passion becomes evident. ℯ (Rev: BL 12/1/10; SLJ 12/1/10)

304 Burd, Nick. *The Vast Fields of Ordinary* (9–12). 2009, Dial $16.99 (978-080373340-4). Dade, a gay teenager watching his parents move toward divorce, learns to be honest about his sexuality during the summer after his high school graduation. Lexile HL730L (Rev: BL 5/15/09; SLJ 6/1/09*; VOYA 10/09)

305 Burgess, Melvin. *Nicholas Dane* (9–12). 2010, Holt $17.99 (978-0-8050-9203-5). When his mother dies of a heroin overdose, 14-year-old Nick ends up in an English boys' home where he experiences all kinds of horrors and abuse. (Rev: BL 11/1/10; SLJ 12/1/10)

306 Calame, Don. *Swim the Fly* (9–12). 2009, Candlewick $16.99 (978-076364157-3). See a naked girl: This is the summer's goal for 15-year-old Matt and his friends Sean and Coop in this light and funny story that involves a lot of swimming. ∩ ℯ Lexile HL620L (Rev: BL 3/15/09; SLJ 4/1/09; VOYA 8/09)

307 Cart, Michael, ed. *How Beautiful the Ordinary: Twelve Stories of Identity* (11–12). 2009, HarperTeen $16.99 (978-0-06-115498-0). Twelve stories — by well-known authors including Ron Koertge, Francesca Lia Block, and Eric Shanower — explore diverse aspects of gay, lesbian, and transgender youth. (Rev: BL 10/15/09; SLJ 9/09; VOYA 12/09)

308 Carter, Scott William. *The Last Great Getaway of the Water Balloon Boys* (8–11). 2010, Simon & Schuster $16.99 (978-1-4169-7156-6). Charlie, 16, unwisely renews a friendship with the wayward Jake and the two embark on a series of unfortunate adventures that involve theft, car racing, drug use, and violence. (Rev: BLO 4/12/10; LMC 5–6/10; SLJ 4/10)

309 Collins, B. R. *The Traitor Game* (9–12). 2008, Bloomsbury $16.95 (978-159990261-6). When insecure underdog Michael's secret fantasy world is exposed to ridicule, he immediately blames his new friend, Francis, in this story that explores betrayal, bullying, and the paranoia of the bullied. Lexile 650L (Rev: BL 10/15/08*; LMC 8–9/08; SLJ 8/08; VOYA 10/08)

310 de la Peña, Matt. *Mexican WhiteBoy* (9–12). 2008, Delacorte $15.99 (978-038573310-6); LB $18.99 (978-038590329-5). Baseball helps biracial 16-year-old Danny Lopez to escape his troubled family, feelings of isolation, and tendency toward self-injury. ℯ Lexile 680L (Rev: BL 8/08; HB 9–10/08; SLJ 9/1/08; VOYA 10/08)

311 Emond, Stephen. *Happyface* (7–10). Illus. by author. 2010, Little, Brown $16.99 (978-0-316-04100-3). In this quirky journal-style offering, awkward, talented teen Happyface records his life — his painful past, his determination to make a fresh start, and the smile he wears to hide the truth. (Rev: LMC 11–12/09; SLJ 3/10; VOYA 6/10)

312 Fehlbaum, Beth. *Courage in Patience* (11–12). 2008, Kunati $14.95 (978-160164156-4). Young teenager Ashley Asher narrates this distressing story of surviving sexual abuse; for mature teens. (Rev: BL 8/08)

313 Ferrell, Monica. *The Answer Is Always Yes* (11–12). 2008, Dial $24.00 (978-0-385-33929-2). Underdog Matt suddenly and surprisingly becomes King of Club

Kids when he's hired as a promoter in 1990s New York in this novel for mature teens. (Rev: BL 6/1–15/08*)

314 Ford, Michael Thomas. *Suicide Notes* (10–12). 2008, HarperTeen $16.99 (978-006073755-9); LB $17.89 (978-006073756-6). Sarcastic, flippant 15-year-old Jeff is forced out of denial about his sexuality after a suicide attempt lands him in a psychiatric hospital. **e** Lexile HL670L (Rev: BL 10/1/08; LMC 3–4/09; SLJ 2/1/09)

315 Gibson, Tanya Egan. *How to Buy a Love of Reading* (11–12). 2009, Dutton $25.95 (978-052595114-8). Set in an extremely competitive and wealthy community, this novel centers on stressed-out and "intellectually impoverished" 15-year-old Carley, whose parents decide to hire a live-in author to write a book for Carley; for mature readers. ⌒ (Rev: BL 4/15/09)

316 Goldman, Steven. *Two Parties, One Tux, and a Very Short Film About The Grapes of Wrath* (9–12). 2008, Bloomsbury $16.99 (978-1-59990-271-5). Realistic yet wildly funny, this is the story of high school student Mitchell and his friends and family. Lexile HL770L (Rev: SLJ 10/1/08*; VOYA 10/08)

317 Goodman, Shawn. *Something Like Hope* (9–12). 2010, Delacorte $16.99 (978-0-385-73939-9); LB $19.99 (978-0-385-90786-6). African American Shavonne, 17, will soon be released from juvenile lock-up and must conquer her anger at her grim past and her current situation in order to succeed in the future. **e** (Rev: BL 12/15/10; SLJ 12/1/10)

318 Green, John, and David Levithan. *Will Grayson, Will Grayson* (9–12). 2010, Dutton $17.99 (978-0-525-42158-0). The lives of two Will Graysons — one straight and one gay — intersect in this quirky and compelling novel that deals frankly with teen attractions and includes graphic language. ⌒ **e** Lexile 930L (Rev: BL 1/1/10*; HB 5=6/10; LMC 3–4/10; SLJ 3/10)

319 Halpern, Julie. *Into the Wild Nerd Yonder* (9–12). 2009, Feiwel & Friends $16.99 (978-0-312-38252-0). With her old friends dabbling in partying and punk rock, Jess finds she has more in common with the "nerds," learning that true friendship transcends stereotypes. **e** (Rev: BL 11/15/09; HB 11–12/09; SLJ 9/09)

320 Hardy, Mark. *Nothing Pink* (10–12). 2008, Front Street $16.95 (978-193242524-6). Son of a Baptist minister, closeted gay Vincent, 15, finds himself between a rock and hard place when he falls in love with Robert. (Rev: BL 10/1/08; LMC 1–2/09; SLJ 3/1/09)

321 Harmon, Michael. *Brutal* (9–12). 2009, Knopf $16.99 (978-037584099-9); LB $19.99 (978-037594099-6). Rebellious Poe, 16, is sent to live with a father she barely knows and makes friends with the outcasts at her new school. ⌒ **e** Lexile HL620L (Rev: BL 1/1–15/09; SLJ 6/1/09)

322 Hills, Lia. *The Beginner's Guide to Living* (9–12). 2010, Farrar $16.99 (978-0-374-30659-5). Over-

whelmed by his mother's death in an accident, 17-year-old Will feels isolated from his father and brother and is amazed to find himself falling hard for a girl called Taryn, who he met at the funeral. (Rev: BL 10/15/10; SLJ 12/1/10)

323 Hopkins, Ellen. *Tricks* (10–12). 2009, Simon & Schuster $18.99 (978-1-4169-5007-3). Five unhappy teens, now prostitutes, grapple with their pasts and their identities as they navigate the high-stakes underbelly of Las Vegas; told in separate verse narratives. Lexile HL590L (Rev: BL 8/09; SLJ 10/09; VOYA 4/10)

324 Hrdlitschka, Shelley. *Sister Wife* (9–12). 2008, Orca paper $12.95 (978-155143927-3). A 15-year-old girl born into a polygamist sect faces her impending arranged marriage to an older man as she struggles with her faith and typical teen desires. (Rev: BL 12/15/08; LMC 5–6/09; SLJ 4/1/09)

325 Jacoby, M. Ann. *Life After Genius* (11–12). 2008, Grand Central $24.99 (978-044619971-1). Math genius Mead is about graduate from college at the age of 18 when he decides not to continue and struggles to find life's meaning. (Rev: BL 9/15/08)

326 Johnson, Angela. *Sweet, Hereafter* (8–11). 2010, Simon & Schuster $16.95 (978-0-689-87385-0). African American teen Shoogy (Sweet) has left her home and moved into a cabin with Curtis when the army summons him for another tour in Iraq, a prospect he cannot face; the final volume in the trilogy that began with *Heaven* (1998) and *The First Part Last* (2003). **e** Lexile 750L (Rev: BL 12/1/09; HB 3–4/10; LMC 5–6/10; SLJ 1/10)

327 Johnson, LouAnne. *Muchacho* (8–12). 2009, Knopf $15.99 (978-0-375-86117-8); LB $18.99 (978-0-375-96117-5). A serious girlfriend and his love of reading are two major factors in stopping Mexican American high school junior Eddie Corazon's slide into juvenile delinquency. Lexile 1250L (Rev: LMC 11–12/09; SLJ 9/09; VOYA 12/09)

328 Johnson, Varian. *Saving Maddie* (10–12). 2010, Delacorte LB $19.99 (978-0-385-90708-8). College-age preacher's kid Maddie returns to her southern hometown where her rebellious ways and provocative clothes do not make her popular, but her childhood friend Joshua, son of a preacher, recognizes her unhappiness and stands by her. **e** Lexile HL590L (Rev: BL 4/15/10; LMC 5–6/10; SLJ 2/10)

329 Katcher, Brian. *Almost Perfect* (9–12). 2009, Delacorte $17.99 (978-0-385-73664-0); LB $20.99 (978-0-385-90620-3). Eighteen-year-old high school senior Logan is devastated when he learns that the new classmate to whom he is attracted is actually a transgendered male who is in transition to become a female. **e** Lexile HL620L (Rev: BLO 12/8/09; SLJ 12/09; VOYA 2/10)

330 Knowles, Jo. *Jumping Off Swings* (9–12). 2009, Candlewick $16.99 (978-076363949-5). In alternating narratives, this novel describes the repercussions of a single sexual encounter that leaves Ellie pregnant. (Rev: BL 7/09; SLJ 8/09)

331 Koja, Kathe. *Headlong* (9–12). 2008, Farrar $16.95 (978-037432912-9). When punk rocker Hazel transfers to Lily's upscale, preppy boarding school, it forces Lily to see her school — and her life of privilege — in a new light. Lexile 920L (Rev: BL 11/15/08; SLJ 11/1/08; VOYA 8/08)

332 Korman, Gordon. *The Juvie Three* (7–10). 2008, Hyperion $15.99 (978-142310158-1). Troubled kids Terence, Arjay, and Gecko are given a second chance by a kindhearted social worker named Doug; when Doug ends up comatose the three band together to conceal his absence from the authorities. ∩ Lexile NC730L (Rev: BL 11/15/08*; LMC 1–2/09; SLJ 12/08; VOYA 10/08)

333 Kramon, Justin. *Finny* (10–12). 2010, Random paper $15 (978-081298023-3). In this plucky coming-of-age story, we follow willful, independent Delphine (aka Finny) from age 14 to her mid-30s, watching episodes in her life — sometimes happy, sometimes hard — unfold. ℮ (Rev: BL 4/15/10)

334 Kuehnert, Stephanie. *Ballads of Suburbia* (11–12). 2009, Pocket/MTV paper $13 (978-143910282-4). Troubled teens find solace in drugs, alcohol, self-abuse, music, and each other in this gripping and realistic novel suitable for mature readers. ℮ (Rev: BL 7/09)

335 LaCour, Nina. *Hold Still* (9–12). 2009, Dutton $17.99 (978-0-525-42155-9). After her best friend commits suicide, Caitlin comes to terms with this devastating act through reading her friend's diary and finding comfort in new friends. ∩ ℮ Lexile HL770L (Rev: BL 10/15/09; LMC 1–2/10; SLJ 12/09)

336 Lamott, Anne. *Imperfect Birds* (11–12). 2010, Riverhead $25.95 (978-159448751-4). In this stirring novel of redemption and unconditional love, 17-year-old Rosie Ferguson lives in a world of sex, lies, and substance abuse until she hits rock bottom and both she and her parents must face the fact that Rosie needs serious help. ∩ ℮ (Rev: BL 2/1/10)

337 Leveen, Tom. *Party* (9–12). 2010, Random $16.99 (978-0-375-86436-0); LB $19.99 (978-0-375-96436-7). In multiple narratives, 11 teens describe their experiences at an end-of-the-year party that involves drinking, sex, a fight, and generally wild behavior. ℮ (Rev: BL 5/1/10; SLJ 4/10; VOYA 8/10)

338 Lieberman, Leanne. *Gravity* (10–12). 2008, Orca paper $12.95 (978-155469049-7). Fifteen-year-old Orthodox Jew Ellie struggles with faith, family dysfunction, and her growing attraction to Lindsay in this coming-of-age story. ℮ Lexile 680L (Rev: BL 10/1/08; SLJ 4/1/09; VOYA 12/08)

339 Lockhart, E. *The Treasure Map of Boys* (9–12). 2009, Delacorte $15.99 (978-038573426-4); LB $18.99 (978-038590437-7). Ruby Oliver, who appeared in the humorous *The Boyfriend List* (2005) and *The Boy Book* (2006), has boy troubles again; the Seattle 16-year-old also deals with her mother, therapy, and running a school bake sale. ∩ Lexile 790L (Rev: BLO 4/24/09; SLJ 9/09; VOYA 10/09)

340 Logsted, Greg. *Something Happened* (9–12). 2008, Simon & Schuster paper $8.99 (978-141696561-9). After the death of his father, 13-year-old Billy finds solace in his warm, empathetic 8th-grade teacher, Miss Gale, but their relationship quickly evolves into something less appropriate. (Rev: BL 11/15/08; SLJ 3/1/09; VOYA 4/09)

341 McBride, Susan. *The Debs: Love, Lies, and Texas Dips* (9–12). 2009, Delacorte $12.99 (978-038590509-1); paper $9.99 (978-038573520-9). The Houston debutantes first seen in *The Debs* (2008) face a variety of problems involving rivalry and jealousy among themselves as they attend etiquette classes. ℮ (Rev: BLO 6/16/09)

342 McCaffrey, Kate. *In Ecstasy* (9–12). 2009, Annick $21.95 (978-1-55451-175-4); paper $12.95 (978-1-55451-174-7). Best friends Sophie and Mia head down diverging paths after an experience with Ecstasy yields lessons one friend heeds and the other ignores. Lexile HL630L (Rev: BL 12/1/09; SLJ 1/10; VOYA 609)

343 McVoy, Terra Elan. *Pure* (8–11). 2009, Simon & Schuster $16.99 (978-141697872-5). When one girl in their group of friends breaks the promise symbolized by her purity ring, 15-year-old Tabitha is shocked and forced to examine her friendship and her faith. Lexile 970L (Rev: BL 4/1/09; SLJ 9/09)

344 Martin, C. K. Kelly. *The Lighter Side of Life and Death* (9–12). 2010, Random $16.99 (978-0-375-84588-8); LB $19.99 (978-0-375-95588-4). Mason and Kat are best friends until they have sex after a drunken party; Kat becomes distant while Mason, 16, starts a relationship with an older woman. (Rev: BL 3/15/10*; SLJ 8/10)

345 Mitchell, Todd. *The Secret to Lying* (9–12). 2010, Candlewick $17.99 (978-0-7636-4084-2). Fifteen-year-old James transfers to a boarding school for gifted students and decides to reinvent himself, a plan that is initially successful but also involves lying, cutting himself, and self-destructive behavior. Lexile HL730L (Rev: BL 6/1/10; LMC 8–9/10; SLJ 6/10)

346 Moore, Lorrie. *A Gate at the Stairs* (11–12). 2009, Knopf $25 (978-037540928-8). A wide-ranging and compelling novel about college student Tassie as she navigates through a year of school and personal growth during which she also cares for a biracial adoptee. ∩ ℮ (Rev: BL 7/09*)

347 Moyer, Kermit. *The Chester Chronicles* (9–12). 2010, Permanent Press $28 (978-157962194-0). Sixteen episodes relate coming-of-age experiences of Chet

Patterson, an Army brat used to constant moves; set in the late 1950s and early 1960s. ℮ (Rev: BL 12/15/09*)

348 Munson, Sam. *The November Criminals* (11–12). 2010, Doubleday $23.95 (978-038553227-3). The novel's protagonist, a disaffected high school pot dealer, struggles with problems both mundane (filling out college applications, keeping a girlfriend at arm's length) and extraordinary (trying to solve a classmate's murder) in this book suitable for older teens. (Rev: BL 2/15/10)

349 Murdock, Catherine Gilbert. *Front and Center* (7–10). Series: Dairy Queen. 2009, Houghton $16 (978-0-618-95982-2). Now in her junior year, basketball star D.J. is pressured by adults to choose the "right" college and navigates a tricky social life in this well-written, final volume in the trilogy. ∩ ℮ Lexile 980L (Rev: BL 10/1/09; HB 9–10/09; SLJ 9/09; VOYA 12/09)

350 Myers, Walter Dean. *Dope Sick* (9–12). 2009, HarperTeen $16.99 (978-006121477-6); LB $17.89 (978-006121478-3). Seventeen-year-old African American Lil J encounters a mysterious old man who makes him question his chosen life of drugs, crime, and chaos. ∩ ℮ Lexile HL720L (Rev: BL 11/15/08; HB 3–4/09; LMC 8–9/09; SLJ 4/1/09*; VOYA 4/09)

351 Myers, Walter Dean. *Lockdown* (7–10). 2010, Amistad $16.99 (978-0-06-121480-6); LB $17.89 (978-0-06-121481-3). Determined not to sink deeper into a criminal life, 14-year-old African American Reese tries to control his behavior during his time at a juvenile corrections facility. ∩ Lexile 730L (Rev: BL 12/1/09; HB 3–4/10; SLJ 2/10; VOYA 2/10)

352 Naylor, Phyllis Reynolds. *Intensely Alice* (9–12). Series: Alice. 2009, Simon & Schuster $16.99 (978-141697551-9). In this installment in the long series, Alice is 17 and facing the end of high school, the possibility of sex with her college-age boyfriend, and even the death of a friend. Lexile HL770L (Rev: BL 5/1/09; HB 7–8/09; VOYA 6/09)

353 Nelson, Blake. *Destroy All Cars* (8–11). 2009, Scholastic $17.99 (978-054510474-6). Following 17-year-old James through his junior year, this novel describes his early obsessions with environmental threats and base consumerism (and his ex-girlfriend) and his gradual development of a less austere attitude. (Rev: BL 6/1–15/09)

354 Nelson, R. A. *Days of Little Texas* (8–10). 2009, Knopf $16.99 (978-037585593-1); LB $19.99 (978-037595593-8). Ronald Earl, a 16-year-old evangelist, begins to question his faith as he becomes obsessed by the ghost of a girl he failed to cure in this well-written, thought-provoking novel. ∩ (Rev: BL 6/1–15/09; SLJ 10/09)

355 Pearson, Mary E. *The Miles Between* (9–12). 2009, Holt $16.99 (978-080508828-1). Unhappy 17-year-old Destiny and three classmates from the exclusive Hedge-

row Academy set off on a quest to find "one fair day," a day of justification. ∩ (Rev: BL 7/09; SLJ 9/09)

356 Peck, Dale. *Sprout* (10–12). 2009, Bloomsbury $16.99 (978-159990160-2). Sixteen-year-old Sprout, cynical, green-haired gay son of a drunk father, prepares for an essay contest and deals humorously with challenges at school and at home. Lexile 1060L (Rev: BL 5/15/09; HB 7–8/09; SLJ 6/1/09; VOYA 6/09)

357 Petrucha, Stefan. *Split* (7–10). 2010, Walker $16.99 (978-0-8027-9372-0). Wade has trouble dealing with the death of his mother, and as a high school senior develops two quite different and separate personalities; the serious Wade is skilled with computers while the wayward Wade is a musician who gets in debt to gangsters. Lexile HL610L (Rev: BL 2/15/10; LMC 5–6/10; SLJ 3/10)

358 Piper, Steffan. *Greyhound* (11–12). 2010, Amazon Encore paper $13.95 (978-098255509-5). On a cross-country bus trip from California to his grandparents' Pennsylvania town, 11-year-old Sebastien mulls over his recent abandonment and unhappy childhood, and encounters memorable characters along the way in this road trip bildungsroman; for mature readers. ℮ (Rev: BL 5/15/10)

359 Prose, Francine. *Touch* (10–12). 2009, HarperTeen $16.99 (978-006137517-0); LB $17.89 (978-006137518-7). Maisie is conflicted about an incident on the school bus that some are calling sexual harassment and others are saying was all her idea. Lexile 820L (Rev: BL 4/15/09*; SLJ 6/1/09; VOYA 6/09)

360 Quigley, Sarah. *TMI* (7–10). 2009, Dutton $16.99 (978-052547908-6). Becca, 15, learns the hard way that blogs are not private and that gossip can hurt people deeply. (Rev: BL 4/1/09; VOYA 12/09)

361 Quintero, Sofia. *Efrain's Secret* (8–11). 2010, Knopf $16.99 (978-0-375-84706-6). Latino star student Efrain, 17, turns to dealing drugs to earn tuition money for an Ivy League college. Lexile 780L (Rev: BL 3/1/10*; LMC 8–9/10; SLJ 6/10)

362 Rainfield, Cheryl. *Scars* (8–11). 2010, WestSide $16.95 (978-1-93481332-4.). Kendra, now 15 and hiding her habit of cutting herself, was sexually abused when she was younger and is sure her attacker is following her; her deepening relationship with classmate Meghan gives her support. Lexile HL560L (Rev: BL 3/1/10; LMC 10/10; SLJ 5/10; VOYA 4/10)

363 Robar, Serena. *Giving Up the V* (10–12). 2009, Simon & Schuster paper $8.99 (978-1-4169-7558-8). Does she want to lose her virginity? And if so, who with? Spencer, 16, has birth control pills but is uncertain about her desires in this frank story. ℮ (Rev: BL 8/09; SLJ 7/1/09)

364 Roche, Lorcan. *The Companion* (11–12). 2010, Europa paper $15 (978-193337284-6). Loquacious Irishman Trevor uses his talent for storytelling as he cares for — and inspires — a young man with muscular dystrophy in this funny, irreverent coming-of-age story for mature readers. (Rev: BL 6/1–15/10)

365 Ruby, Laura. *Bad Apple* (8–12). 2009, HarperTeen $16.99 (978-0-06-124330-1). Tola (Cenerentola) Riley, a high school junior, struggles to tell the truth when she and her art teacher are accused of having an affair. (Rev: BL 11/15/09; LMC 11–12/09; SLJ 12/09)

366 Runyon, Brent. *Surface Tension: A Novel in Four Summers* (8–11). 2009, Knopf $16.99 (978-037584446-1); LB $19.99 (978-037594446-8). This novel records how Luke changes over the summers he spends at his family's lake cabin from the ages of 13 to 16. Lexile HL720L (Rev: BL 2/15/09; SLJ 4/1/09)

367 Ryan, P. E. *In Mike We Trust* (8–12). 2009, HarperTeen $16.99 (978-006085813-1). Gay-but-closeted Garth, 15, tries to free himself from the complications created by lies cooked up by his exploitative Uncle Mike. Lexile HL690L (Rev: BL 2/15/09; SLJ 3/1/09)

368 Sáenz, Benjamin Alire. *Last Night I Sang to the Monster* (9–12). 2009, Cinco Puntos $19.95 (978-1-933693-58-3). Zach, an 18-year-old alcoholic from a dysfunctional family, ends up in residential rehab facility and begins the slow path towards healing aided by art, writing, and his middle-aged roommate Rafael. ◓ e Lexile HL490L (Rev: BL 9/15/09; HB 1–2/10; LMC 3–4/10; SLJ 10/09; VOYA 12/09)

369 Sanchez, Alex. *Boyfriends with Girlfriends* (9–12). 2011, Simon & Schuster $16.99 (978-141693773-9). Lance is gay and Sergio is bisexual, and heterosexual Allie finds herself attracted to Sergio's lesbian friend Kimiko in this novel about teens exploring their sexual identities. e Lexile HL620L (Rev: BL 3/1/11*; SLJ 4/11; VOYA 4/11)

370 Scott, Elizabeth. *Living Dead Girl* (10–12). 2008, Simon & Schuster $16.99 (978-141696059-1). A courageous 15-year-old girl describes the horrors of her five years as a captive, undergoing sexual and emotional abuse at the hands of a man called Ray who will then discard her as too old; a compelling and distressing story. ◓ e Lexile 870L (Rev: BL 10/15/08*; HB 11–12/08; LMC 1–2/09; SLJ 10/1/08; VOYA 2/09)

371 Scott, Elizabeth. *Something, Maybe* (8–11). 2009, Simon & Schuster $16.99 (978-141697865-7). Hannah — the child of a famous playboy and an Internet sex celebrity — is unsure about romance and about her relationship with her father. Lexile HL760L (Rev: BL 2/15/09; SLJ 5/1/09)

372 Shulman, Mark. *Scrawl* (7–10). 2010, Roaring Brook $16.99 (978-1-59643-417-2). Todd, an 8th-grade bully, gets caught vandalizing school property and is sentenced to detention and writing journal entries — which proves quite revealing. e Lexile 650L

(Rev: BLO 8/30/10; LMC 11–12/10*; SLJ 11/1/10; VOYA 10/10)

373 Skovron, Jon. *Struts and Frets* (9–12). 2009, Abrams $16.95 (978-0-8109-4174-8). In this funny novel, Sammy, 17, is preoccupied with his band — is it good enough to enter that recording competition? — and with his girlfriend, who seems to be interested in getting physical. Lexile HL670L (Rev: BLO 10/9/09; SLJ 1/10; VOYA 2/10)

374 Smith, Jennifer E. *You Are Here* (8–11). 2009, Simon & Schuster $15.99 (978-141696799-6). Sixteen-year-old Emma, who has always felt detached from her family, discovers she had a twin brother who died when they were newly born; she and a friend Peter set off on a road trip to visit her brother's grave and learn about each other on the way. (Rev: BL 6/1–15/09; SLJ 8/09)

375 Soehnlein, K. M. *Robin and Ruby* (11–12). 2010, Kensington $24 (978-075823218-2). Robin, the protagonist of *The World of Normal Boys* (2000), returns to save his sister from a troubled boyfriend who's recently resurfaced, and explore his deepening affections for his best friend George, in this novel set against the high-stakes backdrop of 1980s AIDS paranoia; for mature readers. (Rev: BL 3/15/10)

376 Spencer, Katherine. *More Than Friends* (7–10). 2008, Harcourt paper $6.95 (978-015205746-6). Teenage Grace is determined to overcome the self-destructive behavior she adopted after her brother's death in this story with a romantic twist; a sequel to *Saving Grace* (2006). (Rev: BL 8/08; VOYA 4/08)

377 Stevenson, Robin. *Inferno* (9–12). 2009, Orca paper $12.95 (978-155469077-0). A move from the city to a suburban high school leaves lesbian Dante dissatisfied and she struggles to find her balance when a new friend leaves town and a dropout's unconventional life seems attractive. (Rev: BL 6/1–15/09)

378 Stinson, Loretta. *Little Green* (11–12). 2010, Hawthorne paper $15.95 (978-097901881-7). When troubled 16-year-old Janie hooks up with Paul, a drug-dealing biker, at an Oregon bar, she slowly comes to understand the peril of their relationship and the changes she must make in order to protect herself.; set in the 1970s this book is suitable for mature readers. (Rev: BL 6/1–15/10)

379 Stone, Heather Duffy. *This Is What I Want to Tell You* (9–12). 2009, Flux paper $9.95 (978-073871450-9). Teenage twins Nadio and Noelle deal with romantic relationships and shifting friendships. e (Rev: BL 1/1–15/09)

380 Strasnick, Lauren. *Nothing Like You* (8–10). 2009, Simon & Schuster paper $16.99 (978-1-4169-8264-7). After her mother's death, high school senior Holly Hirsch puts her self-worth aside to seek acceptance in the arms of a popular, handsome guy who hides their relationship from everyone he knows. **e** (Rev: BL 9/15/09; SLJ 10/09)

381 Sullivan, J. Courtney. *Commencement* (11–12). 2009, Knopf $24 (978-030727074-0). Four girls meet at Smith College and though they have different personalities and goals, they form bonds that last until well after graduation; for mature readers. ∩ **e** (Rev: BL 5/1/09)

382 Tharp, Tim. *The Spectacular Now* (8–12). 2008, Knopf $16.99 (978-037585179-7); LB $19.99 (978-037595179-4). Part comedic, part poignant, this novel explores the often reckless life of Sutter, a high school party boy, and the hurt and denial driving him. ∩ **e** Lexile HL790L (Rev: BL 11/15/08; SLJ 12/08)

383 Todd, Pamela. *The Blind Faith Hotel* (8–12). 2008, Simon & Schuster $16.99 (978-141695494-1). After getting caught shoplifting, defiant 14-year-old Zoe is assigned community service at a nature center and finally comes to appreciate her new surroundings in the rural Midwest, aided by a budding romance with fellow miscreant Todd. **e** Lexile 780L (Rev: BL 10/15/08; SLJ 12/08; VOYA 2/09)

384 Vail, Rachel. *Gorgeous* (7–10). Series: Avery Sisters Trilogy. 2009, HarperTeen $16.99 (978-0-06-089046-9). Ninth-grader Allison longs to be attractive and is stunned when she becomes a finalist in a teen magazine model contest. **e** Lexile 740L (Rev: BL 8/09; HB 7–8/09; SLJ 7/1/09; VOYA 8/09)

385 Vivian, Siobhan. *Same Difference* (8–11). 2009, Scholastic $16.99 (978-054500407-7). Sixteen-year-old Emily takes a summer art course in Philadelphia and finds many differences from — and similarities to — her life in privileged suburbia. Lexile HL740L (Rev: BL 5/1/09; SLJ 5/1/09; VOYA 6/09)

386 Vlautin, Willy. *Lean on Pete* (10–12). 2010, Harper-Perennial paper $13.99 (978-006145653-4). Homeless 15-year-old Charley finds a friend in an aging racehorse, and relays the story of his troubled life as he and the horse travel together searching for a safe haven. **e** (Rev: BL 4/15/10*)

387 Volponi, Paul. *Homestretch* (7–10). 2009, Simon & Schuster $16.99 (978-1-4169-3987-0). When his father's behavior becomes unbearable after his mother is killed in an accident, high school senior Gas runs away and finds work at a horse track with the help of young Mexicans, a group his bigoted father blamed for his mother's death. (Rev: BL 9/15/09; SLJ 12/09)

388 Volponi, Paul. *Rikers High* (8–11). 2010, Viking $16.99 (978-0-670-011070-). Martin attends high school at Rikers Island while he is waiting for his trial date; this book gives a good description of life in jail and will appeal to male reluctant readers. **e** Lexile 790L (Rev: BL 12/1/09; LMC 3–4/10; SLJ 1/10)

389 White, Michael J. *Weeping Underwater Looks a Lot Like Laughter* (10–12). 2009, Putnam $24.95 (978-039915590-1). Seventeen-year-old George struggles to navigate his status as the new kid in an Iowa high school, his first crush on a beautiful girl, and the crush that girl's sister has on him in this humorous, emotional story. **e** (Rev: BL 2/1/10)

390 Wilkins, Ebony Joy. *Sellout* (7–10). 2010, Scholastic $17.99 (978-0-545-10928-4). Socially uncertain African American NaTasha's parents have moved her to a privileged high school in New Jersey, but a summer with her grandmother in Harlem and volunteering at a crisis center in the Bronx help her adjust her preconceptions. **e** Lexile 720L (Rev: BL 9/1/10; LMC 10/10; SLJ 8/10)

391 Williams-Garcia, Rita. *Jumped* (9–12). 2009, HarperTeen $16.99 (978-006076091-5); LB $17.89 (978-006076092-2). Leticia is unsure whether to speak up about Dominique's plans to "jump" another girl after school in this story about high school tensions and violence. ∩ **e** Lexile HL600L (Rev: BL 2/1/09*; HB 3–4/09; LMC 8–9/09; SLJ 3/1/09)

392 Wilson, Jacqueline. *Kiss* (7–10). 2010, Roaring Brook $16.99 (978-1-59643-242-0). At age 14, Sylvie has always assumed that she will eventually marry her best friend Carl, but with high school things change and Carl appears to be more interested in his new friend Paul. ∩ **e** Lexile HL680L (Rev: BL 2/1/10; HB 3–4/10; LMC 5–6/10; SLJ 3/10)

393 Wilson, Martin. *What They Always Tell Us* (9–12). 2008, Delacorte $15.99 (978-038573507-0); LB $18.99 (978-038590500-8). In Tuscaloosa, Alabama, two brothers — James, a successful senior hoping to be accepted to Duke, and Alex, a junior who is recovering from a foolish, perhaps suicidal act with the help of Nathen — navigate their daily lives. **e** (Rev: BL 11/15/08; HB 9–10/08; LMC 10/08; SLJ 9/1/08; VOYA 12/08)

394 Wyatt, Melissa. *Funny How Things Change* (9–12). 2009, Farrar $16.95 (978-037430233-7). After high school 17-year-old Remy must decide whether to accompany his girlfriend to Pennsylvania, where she will attend college, or stay in West Virginia and work in a garage; additional factors are his love for his mountain town and his interest in a visiting artist. Lexile HL690L (Rev: BL 3/15/09; SLJ 4/1/09; VOYA 6/09)

395 Yang, J. A. *Exclusively Chloe* (6–10). 2009, Penguin paper $7.99 (978-014241226-8). A "makeunder" allows 16-year-old Chinese American Chloe to escape the constant attention her adoptive parents' celebrity has imposed on her. (Rev: BL 7/09)

396 Yee, Lisa. *Absolutely Maybe* (7–10). 2009, Scholastic $16.99 (978-043983844-3). This is a mostly humorous tale about high school junior Maybe (short for Maybelline, her mother's favorite mascara), who leaves her soon-to-be-married-again mother's home and heads for California to search for her biological father. **e** Lexile HL570L (Rev: BL 12/1/08; HB 3–4/09)

397 Young-Stone, Michele. *The Handbook for Lightning Strike Survivors* (11–12). 2010, Crown $24 (978-030746447-7). Lightning strikes — which hit Becca at the age of 8 and kill Buckley's mother when he is 13 — have profound impacts on these young people's lives; for mature readers. (Rev: BL 3/1/10)

398 Zeller, Florian. *Julien Parme* (10–12). Trans. by William Rodarmor. 2008, Other $23.95 (978-159051280-7). Dramatic, disaffected Julien runs away from home in this compelling French coming-of-age story with a Salingeresque flavor. (Rev: BL 6/1–15/08)

399 Zulkey, Claire. *An Off Year* (9–12). 2009, Dutton $16.99 (978-0-525-42159-7). Arriving at college for the first time, 18-year-old Cecily decides she's not ready and heads back home to spend a year reviewing her options. **e** (Rev: BL 8/1/09; SLJ 11/09)

World Affairs and Contemporary Problems

400 Akinti, Peter. *Forest Gate* (11–12). 2010, Free Press paper $14 (978-143917217-9). In this gripping novel set in the London slums, teens James and Meina — who saw her parents tortured and murdered in her native Somalia — seek to overcome their violent backgrounds and find stability in their love for each other; for mature readers. (Rev: BL 1/1/10)

401 Brown, Jennifer. *Hate List* (9–12). 2009, Little, Brown $16.99 (978-0-316-04144-7). Valerie and her boyfriend Nick created a list of classmates' names to vent frustration about school bullying, but in the aftermath of her boyfriend's attack on the school, their list is turned against Val as she grapples with her own guilt and grief. **e** Lexile HL760L (Rev: BL 9/1/09; SLJ 10/09; VOYA 12/09)

402 Cowan, Jennifer. *Earthgirl* (8–11). 2009, Groundwood $17.95 (978-088899889-7); paper $12.95 (978-088899890-3). A fast-food lunch tossed out a window spurs 16-year-old Sabine to environmental activism and she starts a successful blog and becomes involved in a relationship with Vray, a passionate eco-warrior. (Rev: BL 6/1–15/09; SLJ 6/1/09*)

403 Dixon, Peter. *Hunting the Dragon* (8–12). 2010, Hyperion $15.99 (978-1-4231-2498-6). Eighteen-year-old Billy becomes a passionate defender of the rights of dolphins after working on a tuna boat. (Rev: LMC 8–9/10; SLJ 6/10)

404 Gomez, Iris. *Try to Remember* (11–12). 2010, Grand Central paper $13.99 (978-044655619-4). In 1970s Miami Gabriela's family worries constantly about deportation back to Colombia while Papi's mental illness gets worse, Mami despairs about her menial work, and

Gabriela's movements are limited; for mature readers. **e** (Rev: BL 4/1/10)

405 Guest, Jacqueline. *War Games* (7–10). 2009, Orca $16.95 (978-155277036-8); paper $9.95 (978-155277035-1). His strict soldier father is in Afghanistan, and 15-year-old Ryan enjoys a freer life and ample access to computer war games while at the same time recognizing the dangers his father faces. (Rev: BL 6/1–15/09; SLJ 12/09)

406 Henry, April. *Torched* (8–11). 2009, Putnam $16.99 (978-039924645-6). Ellie, 16, is recruited by the FBI to infiltrate and report on an ecoterrorism group, the Mother Earth Defenders; action, romance, and an environmental message combine for an exciting read. Lexile HL710L (Rev: BL 2/15/09; SLJ 4/1/09)

407 Kilbourne, Christina. *They Called Me Red* (8–12). 2008, Lobster $10.95 (978-189707388-9). This is a dark story about human trafficking in which an American teen is sold by his Vietnamese stepmother into a Cambodian brothel after his father dies. (Rev: BLO 12/30/08)

408 Levithan, David. *Love Is the Higher Law* (8–12). 2009, Knopf $15.99 (978-037583468-4); LB $18.99 (978-037593468-1). Three New York City teens—Claire, Peter, and Peter's potential boyfriend Jasper—witness the events of September 11, 2001, and become close as they deal with the experience. (Rev: BL 6/1–15/09; LMC 11–12/09; SLJ 9/09)

409 Liggett, Cathy. *Beaded Hope* (10–12). 2010, Tyndale paper $12.99 (978-141433212-3). Three women and a pregnant teen, each with recent troubles on their minds, travel on a mission trip to South Africa where they meet a single mother with AIDS and are moved to help the community by selling their beaded jewelry in the United States. (Rev: BL 2/15/10)

410 McCormick, Patricia. *Purple Heart* (9–12). 2009, HarperTeen $16.99 (978-006173090-0); LB $17.89 (978-006173091-7). In Iraq Private Matt Duffy must cope with both his own traumatic brain injury and his suspicion that the Army is covering something up. ☊ (Rev: BL 7/09; LMC 11–12/09; SLJ 11/09)

411 Miller-Lachmann, Lyn. *Gringolandia* (9–12). 2009, Curbstone $16.95 (978-193189649-8). When 17-year-old Daniel's father is released by Pinochet in 1986 and travels from Chile to Wisconsin to join his family, the repercussions of his years of torture affect his health and the lives of Daniel and his activist girlfriend Courtney. (Rev: BL 7/09; HB 11–12/09; LMC 10/09; SLJ 4/1/09)

412 Naqvi, H. M. *Home Boy* (11–12). 2009, Crown $23 (978-030740910-2). In this story of immigration and identity, three young Pakistani men take an unwise roadtrip right after 9/11 and find themselves locked up in the Metropolitan Detention Center; for mature teens. (Rev: BL 9/09)

413 Strasser, Todd. *If I Grow Up* (7–10). 2009, Simon & Schuster $16.99 (978-141692523-1). This story follows DeShawn's life in the projects from the ages of 12 to 28, and his efforts to resist the lure of gangs. ℮ Lexile 650L (Rev: BL 1/1–15/09; LMC 8–9/09; SLJ 2/1/09; VOYA 12/08)

414 Stratton, Allan. *Borderline* (8–11). 2010, Harper-Teen $16.99 (978-0-06-145111-9); LB $17.89 (978-0-06-145112-6). In this culturally charged thriller, young Muslim Sami copes with faith-based bullying at school and his father's increasingly cold behavior, until his family is groundlessly accused of terrorism by the FBI. ℮ Lexile HL560L (Rev: BL 1/1/10; SLJ 3/10)

415 Wilson, Edward O. *Anthill* (11–12). 2010, Norton $24.95 (978-039307119-1). Raff Cody explores the lush Alabama woods as a boy and fights for that same land as a young lawyer. (Rev: BL 2/15/10)

Fantasy

416 Aaron, Rachel. *The Spirit Eater* (10–12). Series: The Legend of Eli Monpress. 2011, Orbit paper $13.99 (978-031606908-3). This third installment in the fast-paced series has master thief Eli and his party traveling to the far north in search of Storn, the wizard who made Nico's coat. ∩ ℮ (Rev: BL 1/1/11)

417 Aaron, Rachel. *Spirit Rebellion* (10–12). Series: Legend of Eli Monpress. 2010, Orbit paper $7.99 (978-031606911-3). This follow-up to *The Spirit Thief* (2010) finds Miranda heading for a mysterious kingdom to prevent Eli from stealing a legendary artifact. (Rev: BLO 11/17/10)

418 Aaron, Rachel. *The Spirit Thief* (10–12). Series: Legend of Eli Monpress. 2010, Orbit paper $7.99 (978-031606905-2). In his quest to steal $1 million in gold, master thief and magician Eli Monpress kidnaps the king of Mellinor, and is pursued by the sorceress Miranda; the first installment of a fantasy trilogy. (Rev: BLO 11/16/10)

419 Abbott, Ellen Jensen. *Watersmeet* (7–10). 2009, Marshall Cavendish $16.99 (978-076145536-3). Abisina, 14, learns to love those who are different from her when she travels to Watersmeet, a more diverse environment than her home of Vranille. (Rev: BLO 3/11/09; LMC 8–9/09; SLJ 8/09; VOYA 8/09)

420 Alexander, Alma. *Cybermage* (7–10). Series: Worldweavers. 2009, Eos $17.99 (978-006083961-1). Thea tackles new challenges at Wandless Academy, including new powers, old friends, and mysteries; the third volume in the trilogy. ℮ (Rev: BLO 2/2/09; SLJ 8/09)

421 Allen, Justin. *Year of the Horse* (9–12). 2009, Overlook paper $12.95 (978-1-59020-273-9). A diverse, multiethnic group faces a perilous journey as they band together to avenge a nefarious deed perpetrated decades earlier by an unearthly bandit in this action-packed fantasy set in the Old West. (Rev: BL 9/15/09; SLJ 12/09)

422 Anderson, R. J. *Faery Rebels: Spell Hunter* (7–10). 2009, HarperCollins $16.99 (978-006155474-2). The fairy world of Oakenwyld is dying and a hunter named Knife sets out to save the Oakenfolk, involving herself with humans in the process. (Rev: BL 7/09; SLJ 8/09; VOYA 8/09)

423 Armstrong, Kelley. *The Awakening* (7–10). Series: Darkest Powers. 2009, HarperCollins $17.99 (978-006166276-8); LB $18.89 (978-006166280-5). This sequel to *The Summoning* (2008) finds Chloe on the run and enlisting the help of other teens who have supernatural powers. ∩ ℮ Lexile HL630L (Rev: BL 4/1/09; SLJ 9/09; VOYA 8/09)

424 Ashby, Amanda. *Zombie Queen of Newbury High* (8–12). 2009, Penguin paper $7.99 (978-014241256-5). Mia accidentally turns her fellow high school students into flesh-eating zombies and escapes only with the help of handsome Chase, who works for the Department of Paranormal Containment. ℮ Lexile HL810L (Rev: BL 4/1/09; SLJ 6/09; VOYA 2/09)

425 Augarde, Steve. *Winter Wood* (7–10). Series: The Touchstone Trilogy. 2009, Random $17.99 (978-038575074-5); LB $20.99 (978-038575075-2). Midge moves to Mill Farm and finally meets her great-aunt Celandine, who holds the key to the fate of the Various, a race of tiny winged people; the final volume in the trilogy, following *The Various* (2004) and *Celandine* (2006). Lexile 750L (Rev: BL 4/1/09; SLJ 6/1/09; VOYA 8/09)

426 Augarde, Steve. *X Isle* (7–10). 2010, Random $17.99 (978-0-385-75193-3). After rising sea levels flood the mainland, their parents send Baz and Ray to an island that is supposed to be a haven; when the boys find that it's little more than a labor camp run by a religious fanatic they start a rebellion. ℮ (Rev: BL 6/1/10; LMC 10/10)

427 Baker, E. D. *The Wide-Awake Princess* (7–10). 2010, Bloomsbury $16.99 (978-1-59990-487-0). Annie, Sleeping Beauty's little sister, is left wide awake when the rest of the castle falls into its 100-year slumber, so it's up to her to save the day. Lexile 890L (Rev: BLO 4/22/10; LMC 8–9/10; SLJ 6/10)

428 Baker, Kage. *The Bird of the River* (10–12). 2010, Tor $25.99 (978-076532296-8). When half-siblings Eliss and Alder climb aboard a river maintenance barge, their paths quickly diverge: Alder jumps ship, while Eliss becomes an indispensable lookout for a young assassin. (Rev: BL 7/10)

429 Baker, Kage. *The House of the Stag* (10–12). 2008, Tor $24.95 (978-076531745-2). Gard fights against the enslavement of his people and eventually becomes a powerful, vicious ruler who surprisingly chooses good in the end; for strong readers. **℮** (Rev: BL 9/15/08)

430 Balog, Cyn. *Fairy Tale* (7–10). 2009, Delacorte $16.99 (978-038573706-7); LB $19.99 (978-038590644-9). Morgan learns that her long-term boyfriend is a fairy changeling and does not belong in her world. (Rev: BL 5/15/09; LMC 10/09; SLJ 12/09)

431 Balog, Cyn. *Sleepless* (7–10). 2010, Delacorte $16.99 (978-0-385-73848-4). Romance and fantasy blend in this novel about a Sandman called Eron whose contract is up and who must return to human form; he is reluctant to hand over care of his beloved Julia's nightly sleep to Griffin, her recently deceased boyfriend. **℮** (Rev: LMC 10/10; SLJ 8/10)

432 Barrett, Tracy. *King of Ithaka* (7–10). 2010, Henry Holt $16.99 (978-0-8050-8969-1). At the age of 16, Telemachos sets off from Ithaka to find his long-departed father Odysseus in this action-packed novel. **℮** Lexile 830L (Rev: BL 10/1/10; LMC 11–12/10; SLJ 11/1/10; VOYA 12/10)

433 Barron, T. A. *Merlin's Dragon* (7–10). Series: Merlin's Dragon Trilogy. 2008, Philomel $19.99 (978-039924750-7). Basil, a lizard-like creature with magical powers, sets off to track down Merlin and warn him of impending doom and, at the same time, find others like himself in this latest installment in Barron's Merlin saga. The second volume is *Doomraga's Revenge* (2009). Lexile 820L (Rev: BL 9/1/08; SLJ 9/1/08; VOYA 8/08)

434 Beagle, Peter S., ed. *The Secret History of Fantasy* (10–12). 2010, Tachyon paper $15.95 (978-189239199-5). Stephen King, T. C. Boyle, Terry Bisson, and Francesca Lia Block are among the writers featured in this anthology. (Rev: BL 9/15/10)

435 Bell, Hilari. *Trickster's Girl* (7–10). 2010, Houghton $16 (978-0-547-19620-6). Humans have caused untold damage to the ecosystem and terrorism is rife, so in the year 2098, 15-year-old Kelsa hopes to use her magic to heal these ills. (Rev: BL 12/15/10; SLJ 12/1/10)

436 Bemis, John Claude. *The Wolf Tree* (7–10). Series: Clockwork Dark. 2010, Random $16.99 (978-0-375-85566-5); LB $19.99 (978-0-375-95566-2). A Darkness is spreading over the land and Ray Cobb and the remaining Ramblers must cross into the Gloaming and try to stop the Gog's evil machine; the second book in the series. **℮** (Rev: BL 10/1/10; SLJ 12/1/10)

437 Bennett, Holly. *Shapeshifter* (7–10). 2010, Orca paper $12.95 (978-1-55469-158-6). Sive uses her shapeshifting ability to become a deer in the mortal world and escape from the evil Far Doirche, who seeks to exploit her magical voice; a fantasy based on an ancient Irish legend. Lexile 910L (Rev: BL 6/1/10; LMC 11–12/10; SLJ 10/1/10; VOYA 8/10)

438 Bernobich, Beth. *Passion Play* (11–12). 2010, Tor $24.99 (978-076532217-3). Fifteen-year-old Ilse runs away from home when she learns her father plans to marry her to an older man, but when she arrives in the city of Tiralien she ends up in even deeper trouble; for mature readers. **℮** (Rev: BL 9/1/10)

439 Bertagna, Julie. *Zenith* (6–10). 2009, Walker $16.99 (978-080279803-9). In a world nearly obliterated by global warming, Mara seeks out higher ground with a group of refugees; a sequel to *Exodus* (2008). Lexile 820L (Rev: BL 2/15/09; SLJ 7/1/09)

440 Black, Holly. *The Poison Eaters and Other Stories* (9–12). 2010, Big Mouth $17.99 (978-1-931520-63-8). Vampires, fairies, unicorns, romance, and magic are all found in this collection of 12 dark stories. **℮** Lexile HL760L (Rev: BLO 12/15/09; HB 5–6/10; SLJ 2/10; VOYA 4/10)

441 Black, Holly. *White Cat* (7–10). Series: The Curse Workers. 2010, Simon & Schuster $17.99 (978-1-4169-6396-7). Cassel is a member of a family of curse workers — illegal practitioners who can change fate — but have they now turned on him? The first installment in a series. **℮** Lexile HL700L (Rev: BL 4/1/10; LMC 10/10; SLJ 10/10)

442 Black, Holly, and Justine Larbalestier, eds. *Zombies vs. Unicorns* (9–12). 2010, Simon & Schuster $16.99 (978-1-4169-8953-0). Which is better — zombies or unicorns? Twelve entertaining stories fuel this important debate in a well-designed anthology. ∩ **℮** Lexile 860L (Rev: BL 9/1/10; LMC 1–2/11; SLJ 10/1/10*)

443 Blubaugh, Penny. *Serendipity Market* (6–10). 2009, HarperCollins $16.99 (978-006146875-9); LB $17.89 (978-006146876-6). Mama Inez calls on storytellers from all over the world to tell their tales and get the earth back on track. **℮** (Rev: BL 3/15/09; SLJ 4/1/09; VOYA 8/09)

444 Bracken, Alexandra. *Brightly Woven* (7–10). 2010, Egmont USA $16.99 (978-1-60684-038-2). A wizard named Wayland whisks 16-year-old weaver Sydelle off on an action-packed effort to stop a war in this fantasy that features magic, romance, and danger. **℮** Lexile HL760L (Rev: BL 3/15/10; LMC 10/10; SLJ 4/10)

445 Bray, Libba. *Going Bovine* (8–12). 2009, Delacorte $17.99 (978-0-385-73397-7); LB $20.99 (978-0-385-90411-7). After Cameron, 16, is diagnosed with "mad cow" disease, he finds himself transported by an angel of kinds who sends him on a quest to save mankind; similarities to Don Quixote will amuse readers who know the story. ∩ Lexile HL680L (Rev: BL 8/09*; HB 9–10/09; SLJ 9/09; VOYA 8/09)

446 Brennan, Sarah Rees. *The Demon's Lexicon* (9–12). 2009, Simon & Schuster $17.99 (978-141696379-0). The first book in a series about two brothers who have been on guard against demons and evil magicians since their father's mysterious death. The sequel is *The Demon's Covenant* (2010). Lexile HL830L (Rev: BL 4/15/09; HB 9–10/09; SLJ 7/1/09*; VOYA 4/10)

447 Briceland, V. *The Buccaneer's Apprentice* (7–11). Series: The Cassaforte Chronicles. 2010, Flux paper $9.95 (978-0-73871895-8.). Escaping servitude, 17-year-old Nic has many adventures at sea in his quest to save the city of Cassaforte. Lexile 880L (Rev: BLO 3/4/10; LMC 8–9/10; SLJ 7/10)

448 Briceland, V. *The Glass Maker's Daughter* (7–11). Series: The Cassaforte Chronicles. 2009, Flux paper $9.95 (978-073871424-0). Risa struggles to find her place in the medieval city of Cassaforte when she is not chosen to learn valuable enchantment secrets. Lexile 840L (Rev: BL 4/15/09; SLJ 7/1/09)

449 Brom. *The Child Thief* (11–12). Illus. 2009, Eos $26.99 (978-006167133-3). Egocentric Peter Pan is back in this reimagined scenario that explains young Peter's origins and why, about a thousand or so years later, he is gathering lost children from New York City to help him defeat the evil captain; for mature readers. (Rev: BL 9/09*)

450 Brooks, Terry. *Bearers of the Black Staff* (10–12). Series: Legends of Shannara. 2010, Del Rey $27 (978-034548417-8). Centuries after the apocalyptic end to the Genesis of Shannara trilogy, elves and humans are using their magic to restore peace to their homeland in the face of menacing outside threats. **e** (Rev: BL 8/10)

451 Brooks, Terry. *The Gypsy Morph* (9–12). Series: Genesis of Shannara. 2008, Del Rey $27.00 (978-0-345-48414-7). In the conclusion to the trilogy, magical powers promise to aid the survivors of the horrors of a world gone mad. ◓ (Rev: BL 6/1–15/08*)

452 Brooks, Terry. *A Princess of Landover* (10–12). 2009, Del Rey $26 (978-0-345-45852-0). This sequel to *Witches' Brew* (1995) finds 15-year-old heroine Mistaya returning home and, with the help of her magical allies, fending off an evil magician's plan to unleash demons on the magical kingdom of Landover. (Rev: BL 6/1–15/09; SLJ 12/09)

453 Bullen, Allexandra. *Wish* (8–11). 2010, Scholastic $17.99 (978-0-545-13905-2). Three magical dresses aid — and complicate — Olivia's efforts to recover from the death of her twin sister Violet. **e** Lexile 1150 (Rev: BL 12/109; LMC 3–4/10; SLJ 1/10)

454 Bunce, Elizabeth C. *Star Crossed* (8–11). 2010, Scholastic $17.99 (978-0-545-13605-1). Fleeing after a job goes wrong, teen thief Digger takes on the persona of Celyn, a lady's maid, in this intricate fantasy full of political intrigue and magic. Lexile 820L (Rev: BL 11/15/10; LMC 11–12/10; VOYA 2/11)

455 Cabot, Meg. *Insatiable* (11–12). 2010, Morrow $22.99 (978-006173506-6). Young soap opera writer Meena can see how people will die, but she does not realize that her new lover is a vampire. ◓ **e** (Rev: BL 5/15/10)

456 Cann, Kate. *Possessed* (9–12). 2010, Scholastic $16.99 (978-0-545-12812-4). Sixteen-year-old Rayne escapes from her unsatisfactory mother and boyfriend in London and takes a job at a manor house only to find that she's in an even worse environment. Lexile 740L (Rev: BL 12/15/09; LMC 3–4/10; SLJ 2/10)

457 Card, Orson Scott. *Stonefather* (10–12). Illus. 2008, Subterranean $35.00 (978-159606194-1). An honest young man finds himself in a large city, realizes that he has magical powers, and navigates the world of unscrupulous characters who want to use him. (Rev: BL 8/08)

458 Carey, Janet Lee. *Stealing Death* (7–10). 2009, Egmont USA $16.99 (978-1-60684-009-2); LB $19.99 (978-1-60684-045-0). After a tragic fire that kills his parents and brother, 17-year-old Kipp is on a mission to steal the sack in which the Gwali collects souls of the dead, hoping to keep his other loved ones from dying. Lexile 710L (Rev: BL 9/15/09; SLJ 9/09; VOYA 10/09)

459 Carmody, Isobelle. *Alyzon Whitestarr* (7–10). 2009, Random $17.99 (978-037583938-2); LB $20.99 (978-037593938-9). A concussion endows Alyzon Whitestarr with amazing abilities that will perhaps enable her to save her unusual family from disaster; set in Australia, this is a multilayered story full of mystery and romance. (Rev: BL 6/1–15/09; SLJ 11/09)

460 Cashore, Kristin. *Fire* (8–12). 2009, Dial $17.99 (978-0-8037-3461-6). A prequel to *Graceling*, this book focuses on the beautiful Fire, who, like the other inhabitants of the Dells, is part monster and has supernatural powers. **e** Lexile 870L (Rev: BL 9/15/09*; HB 9–10/09; LMC 11–12/09; SLJ 8/09)

461 Cashore, Kristin. *Graceling* (9–12). 2008, Harcourt $17.00 (978-015206396-2). Prince Po convinces Katsa — a talented fighter who's been subserviently using her powers on the brutal king's disloyal subjects — to stand up for herself in this exciting, romance-tinged story. ◓ Lexile 730L (Rev: BL 10/1/08*; HB 11–12/08; LMC 3–4/09; SLJ 10/1/08*)

462 Charlton, Blake. *Spellwright* (10–12). 2010, Tor $24.99 (978-076531727-8). Dyslexic young wizard Nico struggles to discover his purpose in life as he fends off evil as well as the suspicions of his peers in this first installment in a series. (Rev: BL 2/15/10)

463 Childs, Tera Lynn. *Goddess Boot Camp* (7–10). 2009, Dutton $16.99 (978-052542134-4). Teenage Phoebe is a real goddess — a descendant of Nike — who first appeared in *Oh. My. Gods* (2008). Here she suffers through goddess boot camp on a Greek island. Lexile 710L (Rev: BLO 4/23/09; SLJ 7/1/09)

464 Chima, Cinda Williams. *The Demon King* (6–10). Series: Seven Realms. 2009, Hyperion $17.99 (978-1-4231-1823-7). A rich and varied fantasy featuring one-time thief Han Alister, owner of magic silver cuffs, and Princess Raisa, who rebels against many aspects of the royal court; their lives intersect as they face danger and challenge; the first installment in the series. ∩ ℮ Lexile 760L (Rev: HB 1–2/10; LMC 1–2/10; SLJ 12/09)

465 Clare, Cassandra. *City of Glass* (8–11). Series: Mortal Instruments. 2009, Simon & Schuster $17.99 (978-141691430-3). Clary uncovers secrets about her family as she continues to seek a cure for her mother in this multilayered story; the third installment in the series. ∩ ℮ Lexile 760L (Rev: BL 3/1/09; SLJ 7/1/09; VOYA 4/09)

466 Clare, Cassandra. *Clockwork Angel* (8–12). Series: The Infernal Devices. 2010, Simon & Schuster $19.99 (978-1-4169-7586-1). In Victorian England, 16-year-old Tessa Gray is kidnapped by the sinister Dark Sisters, who want to use her powers for their own diabolical purposes. ℮ Lexile HL780L (Rev: BL 8/10; LMC 1-2/11; SLJ 10/1/10; VOYA 8/10)

467 Clement-Moore, Rosemary. *Highway to Hell* (8–10). Series: Maggie Quinn: Girl vs. Evil. 2009, Delacorte $16.99 (978-038573463-9); LB $19.99 (978-038590462-9). Magic, legends, and religion mix while Maggie and Lisa are on vacation in south Texas. (Rev: BL 3/15/09; SLJ 4/1/09; VOYA 2/09)

468 Collins, Suzanne. *Mockingjay* (6–12). Series: Hunger Games. 2010, Scholastic $17.99 (978-1-439-02351-1). Katniss has survived the Hunger Games and is now being asked to serve as a kind of poster girl for the rebels hoping to oust the evil President Snow. ∩ ℮ Lexile 800L (Rev: BLO 8/25/10*; HB 11–12/10; SLJ 10/1/10)

469 Condie, Ally. *Matched* (9–12). 2010, Dutton $17.99 (978-0-525-42364-5). The Society decides everything in Cassia's life — even her future husband — so why does her neighbor Ky also turn up on her match disk? (Rev: BL 9/15/10; SLJ 12/1/10)

470 Cremer, Andrea. *Nightshade* (7–11). 2010, Philomel $17.99 (978-0-399-25482-6). Werewolves Calla and Ren, both pack leaders, plan to marry, but when Shay, a human, arrives on the scene, Calla falls for him and risks everything. (Rev: BL 8/10; SLJ 12/1/10)

471 Croggon, Alison. *The Singing* (7–12). Series: Pellinor. 2009, Candlewick $19.99 (978-076363665-4). Maerad and her brother Hem combine their powers to retrieve the Treesong and conquer evil in this compelling final installment in the quartet. ∩ ℮ Lexile 900L (Rev: BL 3/1/09; SLJ 5/1/09)

472 Cross, Sarah. *Dull Boy* (7–10). 2009, Dutton $16.99 (978-052542133-7). Avery discovers he has superpowers and that there are others like him. Will they use their abilities for good or evil? Lexile 770L (Rev: BLO 4/14/09; SLJ 8/09)

473 Dann, Jack, ed. *The Dragon Book* (9–12). 2009, Ace $24.95 (978-044101764-5). A collection of 19 unique, atmospheric tales by contemporary fantasy writers including Garth Nix, Harry Turtledove, Bruce Coville, and Tanith Lee. (Rev: BL 11/15/09)

474 Datlow, Ellen, and Terri Windling, eds. *The Beastly Bride: Tales of the Animal People* (10–12). Illus. by Charles Vess. 2010, Viking $19.99 (978-0-670-01145-2). Shape-changers are the focus of this collection of short stories featuring bears, deer, rats, fish, werewolves, and so forth. ℮ (Rev: BLO 3/4/10; LMC 3–4/10; SLJ 5/10)

475 Davidson, Jenny. *The Explosionist* (8–12). 2008, HarperTeen $17.99 (978-0-06-123975-5); LB $18.89 (978-0-06-123976-2). Set in 1938 in an alternate Scotland (Napoleon won at Waterloo and spiritualists work with scientists), this is the story of Sophie, a 15-year-old girl whose message from a psychic medium sends her into a political firestorm. ℮ Lexile 1010L (Rev: SLJ 10/1/08)

476 de Alcantara, Pedro. *Backtracked* (8–11). 2009, Delacorte $15.99 (978-038573419-6); LB $18.99 (978-038590433-9). Tommy, a teenage drifter, travels through time while staying in New York City, experiencing the flu epidemic of 1918, the Depression, and World War II. ℮ Lexile HL570L (Rev: BL 1/1–15/09; SLJ 6/1/09)

477 de Lint, Charles. *Eyes Like Leaves* (10–12). 2009, Subterranean $35 (978-159606282-5). Gods clash and humans suffer the consequences in this fantasy set in the Green Isles. (Rev: BL 10/15/09)

478 de Lint, Charles. *The Painted Boy* (7–12). 2010, Viking $18.99 (978-0-670-01191-9). Now a member of the Yellow Dragon Clan, part-dragon high-schooler Jay Li finds an Arizona barrio where he can do good work. (Rev: BL 12/8/10; SLJ 12/1/10)

479 Delany, Shannon. *13 to Life* (7–10). 2010, St. Martin's paper $9.99 (978-0-312-60914-6). High school junior Jessica is still dealing with her mother's death in a car accident when strange events start happening in her town and she finds herself drawn to Pietr, the new guy at school, with whom she seems to share some kind of connection. ℮ (Rev: BL 6/1/10; SLJ 10/1/10)

480 Dixon, Heather. *Entwined* (7–10). 2011, Greenwillow $17.99 (978-006200103-0). In this dark version of a Grimm tale, Princess Azalea and her eleven sisters dance all night despite their mother's death, able to do so through the Keeper, whose intentions may not be kindly. ∩ ℮ Lexile 740L (Rev: BL 2/1/11*; HB 5–6/11; SLJ 5/11; VOYA 4/11)

481 Dolamore, Jaclyn. *Magic Under Glass* (7–10). 2010, Bloomsbury Children's Books $16.99 (978-1-59990-430-6). Seventeen-year-old Nimira discovers that an automaton is in fact a trapped fairy prince and sets out to rescue him from the handsome sorcerer Hollin Parry. ℮ Lexile HL680L (Rev: BL 10/15/09*; LMC 3–4/10; SLJ 3/10)

482 Drake, David. *The Legions of Fire* (10–12). 2010, Tor $25.99 (978-076532078-0). In this action fantasy set in the world of Carce, two young men and two young women discover ominous clues that seem to foretell disaster for their city, which resembles an early Roman Empire. € (Rev: BL 5/15/10)

483 Durst, Sarah Beth. *Enchanted Ivy* (7–12). 2010, Simon & Schuster $16.99 (978-1-4169-8645-4). Sixteen-year-old Lily's special admission test for Princeton University, engineered by her alumnus grandfather, in fact qualifies her to enter a parallel world full of magical creatures. € (Rev: BLO 12/7/10; SLJ 12/1/10)

484 Durst, Sarah Beth. *Ice* (7–10). 2009, Simon & Schuster $16.99 (978-1-4169-8643-0). The daughter of a scientist who studies polar bears in the Arctic, Cassie was raised believing that her mother was taken away by trolls; consequently, she agrees to marry the Polar Bear King if he will return her mother to her in this romantic fantasy. € (Rev: BL 9/1/09; LMC 11–12/09; SLJ 12/09)

485 Ellis, Helen. *What Curiosity Kills* (8–11). Series: The Turning. 2010, Sourcebooks $14.99 (978-1-4022-3861-1). As 16-year-old Mary gradually turns into a cat she discovers that there are many cat people out at night and battles are looming between the domestic cats and the strays of New York City. € Lexile HL700L (Rev: BL 5/15/10; LMC 10/10)

486 Fantaskey, Beth. *Jessica's Guide to Dating on the Dark Side* (8–12). 2009, Harcourt $17.00 (978-015206384-9). Jessica learns she is a vampire princess when the Romanian boy to whom she was betrothed at birth shows up at her high school. ∩ € Lexile 700L (Rev: BL 3/1/09; SLJ 3/1/09; VOYA 6/09)

487 Fforde, Jasper. *Shades of Grey: The Road to High Saffron* (10–12). 2010, Viking $25.95 (978-067001963-2). Eddie fully accepts that color is king in his society until he moves to East Carmine and falls in love with a Grey named Jane and has some amazing adventures. € (Rev: BL 12/15/09*)

488 Finnin, Ann. *The Sorcerer of Sainte Felice* (7–10). 2010, Flux paper $9.95 (978-0-73872070-8.). Rescued from the stake by a Benedictine abbot, 15-year-old Michael de Lorraine becomes a wizard's apprentice in this novel set in turbulent 15th-century France. € (Rev: BL 6/1/10; LMC 10/10; SLJ 9/1/10; VOYA 6/10)

489 Fisher, Catherine. *Incarceron* (8–12). 2010, Dial $17.99 (978-0-803-73396-1). In a future world, the daughter of the warden of a prison called Incarceron joins forces with an escaping prisoner in a tense adventure. ∩ € Lexile HL600L (Rev: BL 1/1/10*; HB 1–2/10*; LMC 1–2/10; SLJ 2/10)

490 Fisher, Catherine. *Sapphique* (9–12). 2010, Dial $17.99 (978-080373397-8). Finn faces an uncertain future in the months after his escape from Incarceron, wondering if he will in fact be king of the Realm. ∩ Lexile HL570L (Rev: BL 10/1/10*; HB 1–2/11; SLJ 12/1/10)

491 Fitzpatrick, Becca. *Hush, Hush* (9–12). 2009, Simon & Schuster $17.99 (978-1-4169-8941-7). High school sophomore Nora ignores her inner unease and warnings from others when she becomes attracted to Patch, who turns out to be a fallen angel who wants to become human. ∩ € Lexile HL640L (Rev: BL 10/15/09; LMC 1–2/10; SLJ 12/09)

492 Flinn, Alex. *A Kiss in Time* (7–10). 2009, HarperTeen $16.99 (978-006087419-3); LB $17.89 (978-006087420-9). A fractured and lively Sleeping Beauty tale in which Princess Talia of Euphrasia is awakened after 300 years by young American Jack. ∩ (Rev: BL 5/15/09; HB 7–8/09; SLJ 8/09; VOYA 6/09)

493 Francis, Melissa. *Bite Me!* (9–12). 2009, HarperTeen paper $8.99 (978-0-06-143098-5). Mississippi high school senior AJ Ashe is trying her hardest to hide the fact that she is a vampire, but her efforts are complicated when she realizes that she may have inadvertently turned a classmate into a malevolent vampire during a drunken escapade. € (Rev: BL 10/1/09; SLJ 12/09)

494 Funke, Cornelia. *Inkdeath* (8–12). 2008, Scholastic $24.99 (978-043986628-6). An old bookbinder brings characters both benevolent and evil to life in this plot-driven conclusion to Funke's popular trilogy. ∩ Lexile 830L (Rev: BL 11/1/08*; HB 1–2/09; SLJ 12/08; VOYA 12/08)

495 Gaiman, Neil. *The Graveyard Book* (6–10). Illus. by Dave McKean. 2008, HarperCollins $17.99 (978-006053092-1); LB $18.89 (978-006053093-8). After the murder of his family, a toddler wanders out of his house into a graveyard, where the residents agree to raise him and protect him from the killer. ∩ (Rev: BL 9/15/08*; HB 11–12/08; SLJ 10/1/08)

496 Garcia, Kami, and Margaret Stohl. *Beautiful Creatures* (9–12). 2009, Little, Brown $17.99 (978-0-316-04267-3). High school sophomore Ethan Wate's burning desire to escape his mundane southern hometown is dampened when spell caster Lena Duchannes and her peculiar family arrive on the scene in this contemporary romance with a gothic twist. ∩ € Lexile HL670L (Rev: BL 11/1/09; SLJ 12/09; VOYA 12/09)

497 Gee, Maurice. *Salt* (7–10). 2009, Orca $18 (978-1-55469-209-5). This gripping, dark fantasy features Hari, a 17-year-old telepath who fights the oppressive ruling class that kidnapped his father; the first in a trilogy. Lexile 700L (Rev: LMC 1–2/10; SLJ 11/09)

498 George, Jessica Day. *Princess of the Midnight Ball* (6–10). 2009, Bloomsbury $16.99 (978-159990322-4). Galen, a young soldier at the end of a long war in a fictional 19th century, falls in love with a princess and saves her and her 11 dancing sisters by using his talent for knitting. € Lexile 830L (Rev: BL 1/1–15/09; SLJ 4/1/09; VOYA 6/09)

499 Goodman, Alison. *Eon: Dragoneye Reborn* (7–10). 2008, Viking $19.99 (978-067006227-0). A hypnotic tale about a 12-year-old girl who poses as a boy to compete to become the next apprentice to a dragon tamer, and who is pulled into the dangerous intrigues and political machinations of the Asian-inspired fantasy world in which the story takes place. (Rev: BL 12/15/08*; LMC 5–6/09; SLJ 1/1/09)

500 Goto, Hiromi. *Half World* (8–10). Illus. by Jillian Tamaki. 2010, Viking $16.99 (978-0-670-01220-6). Looking for her mother, 14-year-old Melanie Tamaki enters the Half World and finds herself in a gruesome realm of souls caught between life and death. **℮** Lexile 710L (Rev: BL 3/1/10; HB 7–8/10; LMC 3–4/10; SLJ 4/10)

501 Gourley, Susan. *The Keepers of Sulbreth* (10–12). 2010, Medallion paper $7.95 (978-160542065-3). Two young heroes attempt to restore order to Fuhark — where elves and humans once lived in harmony — in this multifaceted fantasy. (Rev: BL 1/1/10)

502 Grant, K. M. *White Heat* (7–10). Series: The Perfect Fire. 2009, Walker $16.99 (978-0-8027-9695-0). In 13th-century France Raimon struggles to protect the mythical Blue Flame even as he worries about the fate of his love, Yolanda; the sequel to *Blue Flame* (2008). Lexile 820L (Rev: BL 3/15/10; HB 11–12/09; SLJ 1/10)

503 Gray, Claudia. *Hourglass* (9–12). Series: Evernight. 2010, HarperTeen $16.99 (978-0-06-128441-0). Teen vampire Bianca and her unlikely vampire-hunting love interest Lucas attempt to disguise the truth as they fight together in Manhattan's war between vampires and mortals; the third installment in the series. **℮** Lexile 700L (Rev: BL 2/1/10; SLJ 3/10; VOYA 12/10)

504 Hale, Shannon. *Forest Born* (7–10). Series: Books of Bayern. 2009, Bloomsbury $17.99 (978-1-59990-167-1). An engaging addition to the series, this stand-alone volume follows a girl named Rin who comes to understand the value of her own special gifts as she and others struggle to defeat the evil Selia. **℮** Lexile 800L (Rev: BL 12/15/09; HB 9–10/09; LMC 10/09; SLJ 9/09)

505 Hamilton, Kersten. *Tyger Tyger* (7–10). 2010, Clarion $17 (978-0-547-33008-2). The lives of Teagan Wylltson and her disabled brother change dramatically when their cousin Finn Mac Cumhaill arrives in Chicago and the three are drawn into a dangerous mission. (Rev: BL 11/1/10; SLJ 12/1/10*)

506 Hardinge, Frances. *The Lost Conspiracy* (6–10). 2009, HarperCollins $16.99 (978-006088041-5); LB $17.89 (978-006088042-2). In the strange world of Gullstruck Island, Hathin and her sister Arilou are on the run from a mysterious force killing off the Lost people. Lexile 970L (Rev: BL 5/15/09; HB 9–10/09; LMC 3–4/10; SLJ 9/09)

507 Harrison, Mette Ivie. *The Princess and the Bear* (7–10). 2009, HarperTeen $17.99 (978-0-06-155314-1).

This unlikely love story is told from the points of view of King Richon and Chala, human/animal shape-shifters whose bond grows as they try to end war in their kingdom. **℮** Lexile 790L (Rev: SLJ 9/09; VOYA 8/09)

508 Hartnett, Sonya. *The Ghost's Child* (8–12). 2008, Candlewick $16.99 (978-076363964-8). In this melancholic fantasy, elderly Matilda recounts the ill-fated romance of her youth to a mysterious young boy who turns out to have a connection to her past. ♫ Lexile 900L (Rev: BL 11/1/08*; LMC 3–4/09; SLJ 1/1/09; VOYA 2/09)

509 Healey, Karen. *Guardian of the Dead* (9–12). 2010, Little, Brown $17.99 (978-0-316-04430-1). At boarding school in New Zealand 17-year-old Ellie finds herself embroiled in a battle involving ancient Maori beings. ♫ **℮** Lexile HL790L (Rev: BL 3/15/10; HB 7–8/10; LMC 10/10; SLJ 5/10; VOYA 6/10)

510 Hobb, Robin. *Dragon Haven* (11–12). Series: Rain Wilds Chronicles. 2010, Eos $26.99 (978-006193141-3). Trouble stalks the Dragon Keepers as they desperately try to understand why their dragon hatchlings fail to thrive; the second installment in this series for mature readers. ♫ **℮** (Rev: BL 5/15/10*)

511 Hobb, Robin. *Dragon Keeper* (11–12). Series: Rain Wilds Chronicles. 2010, Eos $26.99 (978-006156162-7). A rich woman and a tribal girl grow close during their adventures sending endangered dragons to a better habitat; for mature readers. ♫ **℮** (Rev: BL 12/1/09*)

512 Hoffman, Alice. *Green Witch* (7–12). 2010, Scholastic $17.99 (978-0-545-14195-6). Seventeen-year-old Green — first seen in *Green Angel* (2003) — is tending her garden and listening to stories of other survivors of her ruined civilization while she hopes to find her lost love. **℮** Lexile 740L (Rev: BL 1/1/10; LMC 3–4/10; SLJ 5/10)

513 Holder, Nancy, and Debbie Viguié. *Resurrection* (9–12). Illus. Series: Wicked. 2009, Simon & Schuster paper $9.99 (978-141697227-3). Witches Holly, Nicole, and Amanda tackle an evil threat in this fifth and final installment in the series. ♫ (Rev: BL 7/09; SLJ 10/09)

514 Horowitz, Anthony. *Necropolis* (7–12). Series: Gatekeepers. 2009, Scholastic $17.99 (978-043968003-5). Fifteen-year-old Scarlet joins the other four teens struggling to defeat the Old Ones. ♫ (Rev: BLO 6/16/09)

515 Hubbard, Mandy. *Prada and Prejudice* (7–10). 2009, Penguin paper $8.99 (978-159514260-3). On a class trip to England, bumbling Callie has a bad fall and wakes up in the year 1815. She makes friends with Emily, a girl about to be forced into an unfortunate marriage, and gains the affections of a young duke. (Rev: BL 5/15/09; SLJ 7/1/09)

516 Hughes, Mark Peter. *A Crack in the Sky* (6–10). 2010, Delacorte $16.99 (978-0-385-73708-1). Eli, a 13-year-old with special powers, notices problems with his dome-city but his worries are ignored and his continuing investigations lead to him being sent for reeducation. ℮ Lexile 740L (Rev: BL 7/10; LMC 11–12/10; SLJ 10/1/10)

517 Jinks, Catherine. *The Reformed Vampire Support Group* (8–12). 2009, Houghton $17.00 (978-015206609-3). Nina's support group for vampires is thrown for a loop when one member is killed by a stake through the heart; a funny take on the modern vampire genre. ⌒ ℮ Lexile 750L (Rev: BL 1/1–15/09; HB 5–6/09; SLJ 3/1/09; VOYA 10/09)

518 Johnson, Christine. *Claire de Lune* (8–10). 2010, Simon & Schuster $16.99 (978-1-4169-9182-3). Claire discovers that she is destined to become a werewolf and face terrible danger in this fast-paced fantasy. ℮ (Rev: BL 5/15/10; LMC 8–9/10; SLJ 4/10)

519 Jolin, Paula. *Three Witches* (9–12). 2009, Roaring Brook $17.99 (978-1-59643-353-3). Three girls from different cultural and religious backgrounds join together in hope of contacting their friend Trevor, who died in a car accident. ℮ (Rev: BL 8/09; SLJ 10/09)

520 Jones, Frewin. *Warrior Princess* (7–10). Series: Warrior Princess. 2009, Eos $16.99 (978-006087143-7). Branwen must choose between the pampered life of a princess and the dangerous life of a warrior in this action-paced story set in medieval Britain; the first in a series. Lexile 780L (Rev: BL 2/15/09; SLJ 2/1/09)

521 Jones, Patrick. *The Tear Collector* (9–12). 2009, Walker $16.99 (978-0-8027-8710-1). In contemporary Michigan, 17-year-old Cassandra collects tears and brings them to the head of her vampire-like family that thrives on human suffering; but her loyalty to this way of life is threatened when she falls in love with human Scott and must make a difficult choice. Lexile HL670L (Rev: BL 9/1/09; SLJ 12/09; VOYA 12/09)

522 Kaye, Marilyn. *Demon Chick* (9–12). 2009, Holt $16.99 (978-0-8050-8880-9). When Jessica, 16, realizes her mother has sold her to a demon named Brad in exchange for political gain, she plots to bring down her mother's plans for world domination— and to escape from Hell. ℮ (Rev: BL 8/09; HB 9–10/09; LMC 11–12/09; SLJ 10/09)

523 Kincy, Karen. *Other* (9–12). 2010, Flux paper $9.95 (978-0-7387-1919-1). In Washington State 17-year-old Gwen is an Other, a shapeshifter who hides her true nature, until a series of murders of Others forces her into action. (Rev: BL 6/1/10; LMC 10/10; SLJ 7/10)

524 Kitanidis, Phoebe. *Whisper* (8–12). 2010, HarperCollins $16.99 (978-0-06-179925-9). Sisters Joy and Jessica both have the ability to hear others' thoughts, but they use this talent in quite different ways. (Rev: BLO 4/19/10; LMC 10/10; SLJ 6/10; VOYA 8/10)

525 Kizer, Amber. *Meridian* (7–10). 2009, Delacorte $16.99 (978-0-385-73668-8); LB $19.99 (978-0-385-90621-0). After witnessing a traumatizing accident on her 16th birthday, Meridian's parents decide that it's

time to inform their daughter that she is a Fenestra, an angel-like being who helps escort the dying to their final destinations. ℮ Lexile HL590L (Rev: BL 2/17/10; SLJ 12/09; VOYA 2/10)

526 Lackey, Mercedes. *Gwenhwyfar: The White Spirit* (10–12). 2009, DAW $25.95 (978-075640585-4). Although the dutiful Gwenhwyfar puts aside her own desires to become Arthur's queen, she proves herself a force to be reckoned with in the king's court as she battles to keep the throne from falling into conspiring hands. ⌒ ℮ (Rev: BL 10/15/09)

527 Lackey, Mercedes, and James Mallory. *The Phoenix Endangered* (10–12). Series: Enduring Flame. 2008, Tor $27.95 (978-076531594-6). This second installment in the series finds young Tiercel and Harrier on a quest to find the Lake of Fire and defeat darkness; an entertaining fantasy full of humor and adventure. ⌒ (Rev: BL 9/15/08)

528 Lake, Nick. *Blood Ninja* (7–11). 2009, Simon & Schuster $16.99 (978-1-4169-8627-0). In 16th-century Japan teenage Taro is saved from certain death by a bite from a ninja vampire. ℮ Lexile 870L (Rev: BL 12/1/09; SLJ 12/09; VOYA 2/10)

529 Lanagan, Margo. *Tender Morsels* (10–12). 2008, Knopf $16.99 (978-037584811-7); LB $19.99 (978-037594811-4). Fifteen-year-old Liga and her two daughters are magically transported to a realm beyond the horrors they've encountered. ⌒ Lexile 950L (Rev: BL 8/08*; HB 9–10/08; SLJ 11/1/08*)

530 Lang, Michele. *Lady Lazarus* (10–12). 2010, Tor paper $14.99 (978-076532317-0). A 20-year-old witch and the angel she has summoned must save the continent of Europe from Nazi wizards in this urban fantasy that features supernatural characters of all kinds. ℮ (Rev: BL 9/1/10)

531 Larbalestier, Justine. *Liar* (9–12). 2009, Bloomsbury $16.99 (978-1-59990-305-7). Her predisposition for lying calls 17-year-old Micah Wilkins's integrity into question when her boyfriend dies under mysterious circumstances. Lexile HL470L (Rev: BL 9/1/09; HB 11–12/09; LMC 10/09; SLJ 10/09; VOYA 12/09)

532 Link, Kelly. *Pretty Monsters: Stories* (9–12). Illus. by Shaun Tan. 2008, Viking $19.99 (978-0-670-01090-5). A collection of strange stories with elements of horror, science fiction, and fantasy. (Rev: BL 9/15/08*; LMC 1–2/09; SLJ 10/1/08)

533 Livingston, Lesley. *Darklight* (7–10). 2010, HarperCollins $16.99 (978-0-06-157540-2). In this sequel to *Wondrous Strange* (2009), actress Kelley is transported from New York to the Otherworld where she faces many challenges — including resurrecting her relationship with her beloved Sonny. Lexile 880L (Rev: BL 12/15/09; LMC 3–4/10; SLJ 2/10)

534 Livingston, Lesley. *Wondrous Strange* (7–10). Series: Wondrous Strange. 2009, HarperCollins $16.99

(978-006157537-2). Kelley, 17, is acting in a New York City production of "A Midsummer Night's Dream" when she discovers she has a connection to a magic faerie world inhabited by mystical creatures. ℮ Lexile 840L (Rev: BL 1/1–15/09; HB 3–4/09; SLJ 1/1/09; VOYA 4/09)

535 Lo, Malinda. *Ash* (9–12). 2009, Little, Brown $16.99 (978-0-316-04009-9). In this Cinderella-esque tale, Ash falls in love not with the prince but with another female character, the King's huntress. ℮ (Rev: BL 9/15/09; HB 11–12/09; LMC 11–12/09; SLJ 9/09; VOYA 10/09)

536 Lord, Karen. *Redemption in Indigo* (10–12). 2010, Small Beer paper $16 (978-193152066-9). In this modern adaptation of a Senegalese legend, the spirit of Patience has bestowed the Chaos Stick on the likable Paama, a female human, and the spirit of Chance tries every trick in the book to win it back. ∩ ℮ (Rev: BL 5/15/10*)

537 McBride, Regina. *The Fire Opal* (7–10). 2010, Delacorte LB $19.99 (978-0-385-90692-0). In late-16th-century Ireland, 14-year-old Maeve must retrieve a precious fire opal from the corpse goddess Uria in order to save the souls of her mother and sister. Lexile 970L (Rev: BL 5/15/10; LMC 8–9/10; SLJ 8/10)

538 McCaffrey, Todd. *Dragongirl* (10–12). Series: Dragonriders of Pern. 2010, Del Rey $26 (978-034549116-9). Young Fiona and her dragon Talenth are charged with recruiting and leading new dragons and riders as a mysterious plague ravages Pern. ∩ ℮ (Rev: BL 5/15/10)

539 MacCullough, Carolyn. *Once a Witch* (8–11). 2009, Clarion $16 (978-0-547-22399-5). Tamsin is bitter that her family's predisposition toward great talents has forsaken her, until a journey through time sets off a sinister chain of events and allows the edgy heroine to realize her true potential. ℮ Lexile HL790L (Rev: BL 10/1/09; SLJ 10/09; VOYA 10/09)

540 McDonald, Sandra. *Diana Comet and Other Improbable Stories* (11–12). 2010, Lethe paper $15 (978-159021094-9). In this compelling collection of short stories, the lives of three quirky characters intersect as they navigate their fantastical world and its perils; for mature readers. (Rev: BL 6/1–15/10*)

541 Macela, Ann. *Wild Magic* (11–12). 2009, Medallion paper $7.95 (978-193383699-7). Irenee, who finds ancient powerful pieces before they can be misused, and Jim, whose psychic powers help him fight crime, meet and together fight forces of evil; for mature readers. (Rev: BL 9/15/09)

542 McKillip, Patricia A. *The Bell at Sealey Head* (10–12). 2008, Ace $23.95 (978-044101630-3). Two different worlds coexist linked by a beautiful coastal house and an unseen ringing bell, and now the link is about to be revealed. (Rev: BL 9/1/08)

543 McKinley, Robin. *Pegasus* (8–11). 2010, Putnam $18.99 (978-0-399-24677-7). Human Princess Sylvi, 12, discovers she can communicate telepathically with Ebon, her personal pegasus, signaling a potential new era of rapprochement between the two species. (Rev: BL 10/1/10; LMC 3-4/11; SLJ 12/1/10)

544 McKinley, Robin, and Peter Dickinson. *Fire: Tales of Elemental Spirits* (6–10). 2009, Putnam $19.99 (978-0-399-25289-1). Five well-crafted tales illustrate contacts between humans and supernatural beings associated with fire; a companion to *Water: Tales of Elemental Spirits* (2002). ℮ (Rev: BL 9/1/09; HB 11–12/09; LMC 11–12/09; SLJ 9/09; VOYA 12/09)

545 McLaughlin, Lauren. *Cycler* (9–12). 2008, Random $17.99 (978-037585191-9); LB $20.99 (978-037595191-6). For four days each month 17-year-old Jill morphs into her male alter-ego, Jack — who's beginning to insist that he be given his freedom — and, on top of worrying about classes and prom and fitting in, Jill must cope with this bizarre situation. Lexile NC720L (Rev: BL 11/15/08; LMC 11–12/08; SLJ 8/08; VOYA 8/08)

546 McLaughlin, Lauren. *(re)Cycler* (9–12). 2009, Random paper $8.99 (978-0-375-85195-7). In this sequel to *Cycler* (2008), 17-year-old Jill is still turning into Jack for four days each month and with some trepidation heads off to New York to share an apartment with her friend Ramie, who is dating Jack. ℮ (Rev: BLO 7/16/09; SLJ 1/10)

547 McMann, Lisa. *Fade* (8–11). Series: Wake Trilogy. 2009, Simon & Schuster $15.99 (978-141695358-6). This gripping sequel to 2008's *Wake* has the heroine, Janie, exploring more deeply her dream-catching abilities and using them to solve a dangerous case of student abuse. ℮ Lexile 570L (Rev: BL 12/1/08; SLJ 5/1/09)

548 McMann, Lisa. *Gone* (8–11). Series: Wake Trilogy. 2010, Simon & Schuster $16.99 (978-1-4169-7918-0). Janie faces tough decisions about her future as she struggles with her alcoholic mother and her father, also a dream-catcher, surprisingly comes into her life when he is in a coma; the final volume in the trilogy that began with *Wake* (2008) and *Fade* (2009). ℮ (Rev: BL 1/1/10; SLJ 2/10)

549 Madigan, L. K. *The Mermaid's Mirror* (8–10). 2010, Houghton $16 (978-0-547-19491-2). Why does the sea call so strongly to Lena, even though her father, a former surfer, has forbidden her to swim in it? (Rev: BL 9/15/10; SLJ 12/1/10)

550 Mahy, Margaret. *The Magician of Hoad* (9–12). 2009, Simon & Schuster $18.99 (978-1-4169-7807-7). Heriot has nightmares that begin to make sense as he is forced into service as the king's magician. ℮ Lexile 1010L (Rev: BL 10/1/09; HB 11–12/09; LMC 1–2/10; SLJ 11/09)

551 Maizel, Rebecca. *Infinite Days* (8–12). 2010, St. Martin's paper $9.99 (978-0-312-64991-3). Lenah Beaudonte, a vampire whose humanity has been restored thanks to the sacrifice of her lover, Rhode, did not believe she would ever be 16 or fall in love again, but she is having those experiences until her past comes back to haunt her. (Rev: BL 7/19/10; SLJ 12/1/10)

552 Malkin, Nina. *Swoon* (10–12). 2009, Simon & Schuster $17.99 (978-141697434-5). Seventeen-year-old Candice (Dice) moves to a Connecticut town and discovers that her cousin Penelope has been possessed by a man named Sin. As Sin seeks revenge for wrongs done to him in the colonial era, the entire town is affected. ◑ Lexile HL710L (Rev: BL 4/1/09; SLJ 6/1/09)

553 Mantchev, Lisa. *Eyes Like Stars* (8–12). Series: Théâtre Illuminata. 2009, Feiwel & Friends $16.99 (978-031238096-0). The magical Théâtre Illuminata — where characters from Shakespeare's plays materialize from thin air — has been Beatrice's home since infancy, and she is determined to save it by putting on a blockbuster. ◑ Lexile HL740L (Rev: BL 5/15/09; LMC 10/09; SLJ 8/09; VOYA 8/09)

554 Marchetta, Melina. *Finnikin of the Rock* (6–10). 2010, Candlewick $18.99 (978-0-7636-4361-4). In this rich, multilayered fantasy, 19-year-old Finnikin prepares to return from exile and, with the help of a mysterious young woman Evanjalin and other refugees, restore the kingdom of Lumatere to its former glory. ◑ Lexile 820L (Rev: BL 3/1/10*; HB 5–6/10; LMC 5–6/10; SLJ 3/10)

555 Marillier, Juliet. *Cybele's Secret* (7–10). 2008, Knopf $16.99 (978-0-375-83365-6). Scholarly Paula, 17, accompanies her father on a trip to Istanbul to buy a treasured artifact, the remnant of a pagan cult, only to find herself in a dangerous and challenging position; a companion to *Wildwood Dancing* (2007). ◑ (Rev: BL 7/08*; HB 11–12/08; LMC 11–12/08; SLJ 9/1/08; VOYA 12/08)

556 Marillier, Juliet. *Heart's Blood* (11–12). 2009, Roc $24.95 (978-045146293-0). In 12th-century Ireland young scribe Catrin seeks to free the crippled chieftain Anluan from a centuries-old curse; for mature readers. (Rev: BL 11/15/09)

557 Marr, Melissa. *Fragile Eternity* (10–12). 2009, HarperCollins $16.99 (978-006121471-4); LB $17.89 (978-006121472-1). Aislinn is in love with Seth, a mortal, but is also attracted to Keenan, the faerie summer king, in this sequel to *Wicked Lovely* (2007). ℮ Lexile HL650L (Rev: BL 4/1/09; SLJ 6/1/09)

558 Marriott, Zoe. *Daughter of the Flames* (7–11). 2009, Candlewick $17.99 (978-076363749-1). Zira, who is part Ruan and part Sedorne, is caught up in a battle between the two tribes in this sweeping story. (Rev: BL 2/15/09; LMC 8–9/09; SLJ 8/09; VOYA 4/09)

559 Martinez, A. Lee. *Too Many Curses* (10–12). 2008, Tor paper $14.95 (978-076531835-0). A humble housekeeper turns heroine when her employer, a powerful wizard, dies leaving behind many angry cursed beings and a wicked sorceress who wants to take over the castle. ◑ (Rev: BL 9/1/08; SLJ 2/09)

560 Melling, O. R. *The Book of Dreams* (7–12). Series: The Chronicles of Faerie. 2009, Abrams $19.95 (978-0-8109-8346-5). Dana, a 13-year-old who is half faerie, now lives unhappily in Canada but travels to the land of Faerie to find the Book of Dreams. Lexile 670L (Rev: BL 10/1/09; SLJ 8/09; VOYA 6/09)

561 Meyer, Stephenie. *Breaking Dawn* (9–12). Series: Twilight. 2008, Little, Brown $22.99 (978-031606792-8). Bella Swan marries handsome vampire Edward Cullen, but her connection with werewolf Jacob is still strong in this final volume in the popular series. ◑ ℮ Lexile 690L (Rev: BLO 8/08; SLJ 10/1/08; VOYA 8/08)

562 Michaelis, Antonia. *Dragons of Darkness* (9–12). Trans. from German by Anthea Bell. 2010, Abrams $18.95 (978-0-8109-4074-1). Magic and realism are interwoven in this story set in Nepal and featuring 14-year-old Christopher, a German searching for his older brother, and young prince Jumar; the two band together to destroy the dragons that have been disrupting the nation. Lexile 800L (Rev: BL 3/1/10*; SLJ 3/10; VOYA 2/10)

563 Michaelis, Antonia. *Tiger Moon* (9–12). Trans. by Anthea Bell. 2008, Abrams $18.95 (978-081099481-2). In early 20th-century India, young Raka weaves a magical, compelling tale in an effort to escape a miserable arranged marriage. Lexile 820L (Rev: BL 10/15/08*; HB 11–12/08; LMC 5–6/09; SLJ 11/1/08*)

564 Micklem, Sarah. *Wildfire* (11–12). 2009, Scribner $26 (978-074326524-9). When Firethorn defies her master Sir Galan and follows him into war, she is hit by lightning and loses her power of speech, after which she is hailed as a prophet; a sequel to *Firethorn* (2004), ℮ (Rev: BL 7/09)

565 Miller, Kirsten. *The Eternal Ones* (8–11). 2010, Penguin $17.99 (978-1-595-14308-2). This suspenseful tale mixes fantasy, mystery, and romance as 17-year-old Haven faces discrimination because of her visions of previous lives and flees from small-town Tennessee to New York City. ◑ ℮ Lexile HL760L (Rev: BL 6/1/10; LMC 11–12/10; SLJ 8/10)

566 Mitchard, Jacquelyn. *Look Both Ways* (7–10). Series: Midnight Twins. 2009, Penguin $16.99 (978-159514161-3). Twins Merry and Mallory, who can "see" the future and the past, try to sort out their latest cryptic vision with the help of Native American friends. ◑ Lexile 710L (Rev: BL 2/15/09; SLJ 5/1/09)

567 Mlynowski, Sarah. *Gimme a Call* (7–10). 2010, Delacorte $17.99 (978-0-385-73588-9); LB $20.99

(978-0-385-90574-9). When Devi's boyfriend dumps her just before senior prom, she decides to rewrite her own present by summoning her 14-year-old self and attempting to avert her current problems from happening in this light novel with a time travel twist. ꩜ ℮ Lexile HL440L (Rev: BL 3/1/10; SLJ 3/10; VOYA 10/10)

568 Mourlevat, Jean-Claude. *Winter's End* (9–12). Trans. from French by Anthea Bell. 2009, Candlewick $17.99 (978-0-7636-4450-5). Four teenagers escape their repressive boarding schools and, pursued by terrifying dog-men, set out on a dangerous mission to avenge the deaths of their parents. (Rev: BL 12/15/09*; LMC 11–12/09; SLJ 12/09)

569 Mullin, Caryl Cude. *Rough Magic* (7–10). 2009, Second Story paper $9.95 (978-1-897187-63-0). This fantasy based on Shakespeare's *The Tempest* is presented in five acts and tells the story of three generations of Caliban's family. Lexile HL610L (Rev: BL 8/09; LMC 3–4/10)

570 Niffenegger, Audrey. *Her Fearful Symmetry* (11–12). 2009, Scribner $26.99 (978-143916539-3). When an aunt bequeaths 20-year-old twins Valentina and Julia a flat next to London's Highgate Cemetery, they become involved in an intricately woven tale of spirits, family secrets, and love lost and gained; for mature readers. ꩜ (Rev: BL 9/09*)

571 Nix, Garth. *Superior Saturday* (8–11). Series: Keys to the Kingdom. 2008, Scholastic $17.99 (978-043970089-4). In this sixth installment in the series, Arthur is revealed as heir to the kingdom and must obtain the Sixth Key from the powerful Saturday in the face of many challenges. ꩜ ℮ Lexile 930L (Rev: BL 11/15/08; VOYA 8/08)

572 Noël, Alyson. *Blue Moon* (8–11). Series: The Immortals. 2009, St. Martin's paper $9.99 (978-031253276-5). In this sequel to *Evermore* (2008), 600-year-old Damen's powers are weakening and 16-year-old Ever knows she must save him from the evil perpetrated by the newly arrived Roman. ꩜ (Rev: BL 7/09)

573 Noël, Alyson. *Evermore* (8–10). Series: The Immortals. 2009, St. Martin's $8.95 (978-031253275-8). The first book in the Immortals series introduces Ever, who finds she has supernatural powers as a result of the car crash that killed the rest of her family. Lexile 940L (Rev: BL 2/1/09; SLJ 4/1/09)

574 Noël, Alyson. *Shadowland* (8–11). Series: The Immortals. 2009, St. Martin's $17.99 (978-0-312-59044-4). Girlfriend (Ever) and boyfriend (Damen) have achieved immortality but at a cost — they are never allowed to touch each other. Lexile 960L (Rev: BLO 11/17/09; SLJ 2/10)

575 North, Pearl. *Libyrinth* (8–11). 2009, Tor $17.95 (978-076532096-4). In a distant future, Haly, who has the ability to hear books, finds herself between competing forces: the Libyrarians, who protect and preserve

ancient books, and the Eradicants, who seek to destroy the printed word. (Rev: BLO 6/17/09; LMC 11–12/09; SLJ 9/09)

576 Novik, Naomi. *Tongues of Serpents* (10–12). Series: Temeraire. 2010, Del Rey $25 (978-034549689-8). In this sixth installment of Novik's fantastical series, Temeraire and Laurence find themselves embroiled in a mission to safely transport dragon eggs through a land fraught with mutiny, betrayal, and thievery. ꩜ (Rev: BL 6/1–15/10)

577 Nylund, Eric. *All That Lives Must Die* (10–12). 2010, Tor paper $14.99 (978-076532304-0). Twins Eliot and Fiona — part devil, part deity — attend the challenging Paxington Institute and hone their powers as danger and intrigue surround them; a sequel to *Mortal Coils* (2009). (Rev: BL 7/10)

578 Oppel, Kenneth. *Starclimber* (6–10). 2009, HarperTeen $17.99 (978-006085057-9); LB $18.89 (978-006085058-6). Matt and Kate rocket into space aboard a Canadian spaceship in this exciting sequel to *Airborn* (2004) and *Skybreaker* (2005). ℮ (Rev: BLO 6/16/09; SLJ 6/1/09*)

579 Palmer, Robin. *Little Miss Red* (7–11). 2010, Penguin paper $7.99 (978-0-14-241123-0). A frothy romantic fairy tale in which 16-year-old, Jewish Sophie, on her way to visit her grandmother in Florida, meets bad boy Jack, who is charming but somehow scary. Lexile 890L (Rev: BL 2/1/10; SLJ 2/10; VOYA 4/10)

580 Parks, Richard. *The Long Look* (10–12). 2008, Five Star $25.95 (978-159414704-3). The evil magician is not who he seems to be in this entertaining story of one man's attempt to change the future. (Rev: BL 9/1/08)

581 Pauley, Kimberly. *Sucks to Be Me: The All-True Confessions of Mina Hamilton, Teen Vampire (Maybe)* (7–10). 2008, Mirrorstone $14.95 (978-078695028-7). Sixteen-year-old Mina must decide between staying human and becoming a vampire in this light, often funny story. ℮ Lexile HL740L (Rev: BL 11/15/08; VOYA 10/08)

582 Pearce, Jackson. *As You Wish* (8–10). 2009, HarperTeen $16.99 (978-006166152-5). Upset when her boyfriend declares that he is gay, 16-year-old Viola accidentally summons a genie and her wish to be popular comes true. But does she prefer the genie to her new status? (Rev: BLO 5/15/09; SLJ 1/10; VOYA 8/09)

583 Peterfreund, Diana. *Rampant* (9–12). 2009, HarperTeen $17.99 (978-0-06-149000-2). Astrid learns she is destined to be a unicorn hunter, a dangerous and crucial calling that requires she remain a virgin. ℮ Lexile 750L (Rev: BL 10/7/09; SLJ 8/09; VOYA 6/09)

584 Pierce, Tamora. *Melting Stones* (6–10). 2008, Scholastic $17.99 (978-054505264-1). Evvy helps to save the Battle Islands from mysterious environmental ailments by using her magical powers. ꩜ ℮ Lexile 590L

(Rev: BLO 5/27/09; LMC 5–6/09; SLJ 12/08; VOYA 12/08)

585 Pike, Aprilynne. *Spells* (7–10). 2010, HarperTeen $16.99 (978-0-06-166806-7). In this sequel to *Wings* (2009), 16-year-old Laurel is studying at the faerie academy and feeling tensions between her two worlds and her romantic relationships. ∩ (Rev: BL 3/15/10*; SLJ 8/10; VOYA 8/10)

586 Pon, Cindy. *Silver Phoenix: Beyond the Kingdom of Xia* (9–12). 2009, Greenwillow $17.99 (978-006173021-4). Ai Ling faces danger as she searches for her missing father in this otherworldly adventure set in ancient China. Lexile 760L (Rev: BL 4/1/09*; SLJ 12/09)

587 Pratchett, Terry. *Unseen Academicals* (10–12). Series: Discworld. 2009, Harper $25.99 (978-006116170-4). This fantasy is a humorous story of an unlikely group from Unseen University who are forced to learn how to play football. ∩ e (Rev: BL 9/09)

588 Raedeke, Christy. *The Daykeeper's Grimoire* (7–10). Series: Prophecy of Days. 2010, Flux paper $9.95 (978-0-73871-576-6). Caity decodes a message she finds in a room in her parents' Scottish castle and is sent on a crucial mission that takes her around the world. e (Rev: BL 5/15/10; LMC 8–9/10)

589 Rice, Patricia. *Mystic Warrior* (11–12). Series: Mystic Isle. 2009, Signet paper $7.99 (978-045122747-8). A misfit warrior with supernatural powers tries to control his anger, which has dire consequences for his surroundings. (Rev: BLO 7/09)

590 Scott, Michael. *The Sorceress* (7–10). Series: The Secrets of the Immortal Nicholas Flamel. 2009, Delacorte $17.99 (978-038573529-2); LB $20.99 (978-038590515-2). Twins Josh and Sophie, along with Nicolas Flamel, are still on the run in this third book in the series. Shakespeare, Billy the Kid, and Gilgamesh are some of the characters that pop up along the journey. Lexile 840L (Rev: BLO 4/24/09; SLJ 7/1/09)

591 Selfors, Suzanne. *Coffeehouse Angel* (7–10). 2009, Walker $16.99 (978-0-8027-9812-1). Katrina helps a young man who turns out to be an angel, ready to grant her her heart's desire . . . once she figures out what that is. e Lexile HL620L (Rev: BL 9/15/09; SLJ 8/09; VOYA 12/09)

592 Selzer, Adam. *I Kissed a Zombie, and I Liked It* (9–12). 2010, Delacorte LB $12.99 (978-0-385-90497-1); paper $7.99 (978-0-385-73503-2). Ambitious 18-year-old Ally Rhodes resists the peer pressure to "convert" to vampirism but instead falls in love with a zombie musician named Doug in this witty romance. e Lexile 820L (Rev: BL 4/15/10; SLJ 1/10)

593 Shan, Darren. *The Thin Executioner* (9–12). 2010, Little, Brown $17.99 (978-0-316-07865-8). Hoping despite evidence to the contrary to become an executioner like his father, Jebel Rum undertakes a quest for invincibility and must face many violent challenges; he is accompanied by a slave called Tel Hasani whom he intends to sacrifice. e Lexile 850L (Rev: BL 7/10; LMC 10/10; SLJ 7/10; VOYA 12/10)

594 Shaw, Ali. *The Girl with the Glass Feet* (10–12). 2010, Holt $24 (978-080509114-4). Young Ida Maclaird realizes she is slowly turning to glass, and she and lonely Midas Crook become romantically involved as they seek a cure in this novel full of magical realism on remote islands. (Rev: BL 10/15/09)

595 Shinn, Sharon. *Gateway* (9–12). 2009, Viking $17.99 (978-0-670-01178-0). Walking under the Gateway Arch in St. Louis, Chinese American teen Daiyu finds herself whisked away to a parallel world where she is given a dangerous task; this exciting fantasy is sprinkled with romance. (Rev: BL 9/15/09; LMC 11–12/09*; SLJ 12/09)

596 Showalter, Gena. *Intertwined* (7–10). 2009, Harlequin $15.99 (978-0-373-21002-2). Misdiagnosed as a schizophrenic, 16-year-old Aden Stone in fact has four souls with special powers living inside his body; the complex plot involves vampires, werewolves, assorted magical beings, and a touch of romance. (Rev: BL 9/15/09; SLJ 12/09)

597 Shusterman, Neal. *Everwild* (7–10). Series: The Skinjacker Trilogy. 2009, Simon & Schuster $16.99 (978-1-4169-5863-5). Nick, known as the dreaded "chocolate ogre," is trying to find all the children in Everlost and release them from the limbo they are in, while Mikey and Allie have joined a band of skinjackers and are putting themselves in danger by visiting the world of the living. Allie, Nick, and Mikey split up to pursue different and dangerous avenues in their quest to help the children of Everlost. (Rev: BLO 11/5/09; SLJ 12/09)

598 Simner, Janni Lee. *Bones of Faerie* (7–10). 2009, Random $16.99 (978-037584563-5); LB $19.99 (978-037594563-2). In a world devastated by a war between faeries and humans, 15-year-old Liza finds herself in danger when she discovers she's gained faerie powers. e Lexile HL670L (Rev: BL 12/1/08; LMC 5–6/09; SLJ 4/1/09)

599 Simner, Janni Lee. *Thief Eyes* (7–10). 2010, Random $16.99 (978-0-375-86770-8). While in Iceland with her father, 16-year-old Haley discovers that she is related to the Hallgerd of Icelandic mythology and that this relationship is linked with her mother's disappearance. (Rev: BL 4/1/10; LMC 8–9/10; SLJ 5/10)

600 Singleton, Sarah. *Out of the Shadows* (8–10). 2008, Clarion $16.00 (978-061892722-7). A complicated plot makes knowledge of the time period's political and religious scheming necessary to fully understand this tale of friendship between a time-traveling faerie girl and a young Catholic teen in Elizabethan England. Lexile 770L (Rev: BL 12/1/08; LMC 3–4/09; SLJ 6/1/09)

601 Slade, Arthur. *The Hunchback Assignments* (7–10). 2009, Random $15.99 (978-0-385-73784-5); LB $18.99 (978-0-385-90694-4). A complex steampunk adventure set in Victorian London in which 14-year-old Modo, a shape-shifting hunchback, joins the Permanent Association, an organization formed to fight the evil Clockwork Guild. ∩ (Rev: BL 8/09; LMC 11–12/09; SLJ 12/09)

602 Smith, L. J. *The Initiation and the Captive, Part 1* (7–10). Series: The Secret Circle. 2008, HarperTeen paper $8.99 (978-006167085-5). Cassie discovers that she is part witch — and that there are others like her — when she and her mother move to New Salem, Massachusetts. (Rev: BLO 3/5/09)

603 Smith, Linda. *The Broken Thread* (8–11). 2009, Coteau paper $12.95 (978-155050398-2). Alina must care for a young prince who is fated to grow up to be a tyrant unless she intervenes. (Rev: BL 4/1/09)

604 Smith, Sherwood. *Coronets and Steel* (10–12). 2010, DAW $24.95 (978-075640642-4). This urban-fantasy fairy tale set in Eastern Europe follows the journey of 23-year-old Kim who, while exploring her grandmother's past, discovers her own power to see ghosts. ℮ (Rev: BL 9/15/10)

605 Sniegoski, Thomas E. *Legacy* (8–11). 2009, Delacorte $15.99 (978-0-385-73714-2); LB $18.99 (978-0-385-90648-7). When his mother is killed, 18-year-old Lucas changes his mind and agrees to take on his father's role as Seraph City superhero and crime fighter. (Rev: BL 9/1/09; SLJ 12/09)

606 Spinner, Stephanie. *Damosel: In Which the Lady of the Lake Renders a Frank and Often Startling Account of Her Wondrous Life and Times* (6–10). 2008, Knopf $16.99 (978-037583634-3); LB $19.99 (978-037593634-0). Elegantly told, this Arthurian-based tale tells of the Lady of the Lake's magical creation of the sword Excalibur and the loyal support of Twixt, a dwarf jester in Arthur's court. ℮ Lexile 830L (Rev: BL 10/1/08; LMC 3–4/09; SLJ 12/08; VOYA 2/09)

607 Stewart, Sean, and Jordan Weisman. *Cathy's Ring: If Found, Please Call 650-266-8263* (8–11). Illus. by author. Series: Cathy. 2009, Running Press $17.95 (978-076243530-2). The page-turning final volume in the trilogy features the familiar format (doodles and designs on each page) and Cathy is still in love with an immortal and running from assassins. (Rev: BL 4/15/09; SLJ 6/09)

608 Stiefvater, Maggie. *Lament: The Faerie Queen's Deception* (9–12). Illus. by Julia Jeffrey. 2008, Flux paper $9.95 (978-073871370-0). Fantasy, danger, and romance are intertwined in this book about Deirdre, a 16-year-old harpist who meets the boy of her dreams only to discover that she has dangerous telekinetic powers, and that he has been sent by the Queen of Faeries to assassinate her. ℮ (Rev: BL 12/1/08; VOYA 12/08)

609 Stiefvater, Maggie. *Linger* (8–11). 2010, Scholastic $17.99 (978-0-545-12328-0). In this sequel to *Shiver* (2009), Sam is close to leaving his werewolf status and achieving humanity, but his girlfriend Grace is now suffering from illnesses that may be related to a wolf bite; at the same time a new wolf pack member called Cole threatens the group's stability. ∩ ℮ Lexile 800L (Rev: BL 6/1/10; HB 7–8/10; LMC 10/10; SLJ 8/10; VOYA 8/10)

610 Strahan, Jonathan, and Marianne S. J. Jablon, eds. *Wings of Fire* (10–12). 2010, Night Shade paper $15.95 (978-159780187-4). A collection of 26 diverse dragon stories by well-known authors. (Rev: BLO 7/10; SLJ 10/1/10)

611 Stroud, Jonathan. *Heroes of the Valley* (6–10). 2009, Hyperion $17.99 (978-142310966-2). A rollicking fantasy about Halli Sveinsson, the young descendent of a legendary Nordic hero, who finds himself on an epic journey to avenge his uncle's death, in the process spawning his own, brand-new legend. ∩ Lexile 770L (Rev: BL 12/1/08*; HB 1–2/09; LMC 8–9/09; SLJ 1/1/09*)

612 Tanigawa, Nagaru. *The Sigh of Haruhi Suzumiya* (9–12). Illus. by Noizi Ito. 2009, Little, Brown paper $8.99 (978-0-316-03879-9). In this followup to 2009's *The Melancholy of Haruhi Suzumiya*, the omnipotent protagonist decides to film a movie for the school's cultural festival, and her fellow SOS Brigade members have no choice but to follow along. (Rev: BLO 9/11/09; SLJ 3/10; VOYA 4/10)

613 Taylor, Laini. *Silksinger* (7–10). Illus. by Jim Di Bartolo. Series: Dreamdark. 2009, Putnam $18.99 (978-0-399-24631-9). Full of fast-paced adventure, this second volume in the series has Magpie and the other fairies discovering long-lost clans as they try to save the world from destruction. ∩ Lexile 870L (Rev: BLO 8/20/09; SLJ 9/09)

614 Telep, Trisha, ed. *The Eternal Kiss: 13 Vampire Tales of Blood and Desire* (8–12). 2009, Running Press paper $9.95 (978-0-7624-3717-7). Vampires of all kinds populate these diverse stories featuring comedy, romance, violence, mystery, and so forth. (Rev: BL 9/1/09; SLJ 12/09)

615 Tomlinson, Heather. *Aurelie: A Faerie Tale* (7–10). 2008, Holt $16.95 (978-080508276-0). As gifted friends Aurelie, Garin, and Netta come of age in their intricate, fantastical world, they cope with distance, physical struggles, familial obligations, and a complex and ill-fated love story. ℮ Lexile 780L (Rev: BL 9/1/08; HB 9–10/08; SLJ 12/08)

616 Tomlinson, Heather. *Toads and Diamonds* (8–12). 2010, Henry Holt $16.99 (978-0-8050-8968-4). Perrault's classic tale is reimagined in a fictional Indian land, where stepsisters Diribani and Tana have very different experiences as they use the gifts bestowed on them by a goddess. ⌂ **e** Lexile 820L (Rev: BL 2/15/10; LMC 5–6/10; SLJ 7/10)

617 Turtledove, Harry. *Hitler's War* (11–12). 2009, Del Rey $27 (978-034549182-4). An alternate history full of interesting detail, fascinating characters, and exciting action; for mature readers. ⌂ **e** (Rev: BL 7/09)

618 Turtledove, Harry. *Liberating Atlantis* (10–12). 2009, Roc $25.95 (978-045146296-1). Civil War seems certain in the United States of Atlantis in this concluding volume in the series. ⌂ **e** (Rev: BLO 12/15/09*)

619 Turtledove, Harry. *West and East: The War That Came Early* (11–12). 2010, Del Rey $27 (978-034549184-8). Turtledove's alternate World War II history continues with this sequel to *Hitler's War* (2009) that follows Russian pilot Sergei and British Sergeant Alistair, among many others around the world; for mature readers. (Rev: BL 4/15/10*)

620 Van Lowe, E. *Never Slow Dance with a Zombie* (7–10). 2009, Tor paper $8.99 (978-0-7653-2040-7). A satirically humorous zombie story in which 16-year-old Margot, who longs to be popular, gets her chance for stardom when nearly all her classmates are turned into zombies. **e** Lexile 620L (Rev: BL 9/1/09; LMC 3–4/10; SLJ 1/10)

621 Vandervort, Kim. *The Northern Queen* (10–12). 2010, Hadley Rille $28.95 (978-098294671-8). In the sequel to *The Song and the Sorceress* (2009), Ki'leah, newly crowned Queen of Si'vad, must protect her kingdom from both internal and external threats. (Rev: BL 11/1/10)

622 Vaughn, Carrie. *Voices of Dragons* (7–10). 2010, HarperTeen $16.99 (978-0-06-179894-8). When 17-year-old Kay is rescued from a fall by a friendly dragon named Artegal, the two attempt to negotiate a peace agreement between the warring realms of humans and dragons. **e** Lexile HL690L (Rev: BL 1/1/10; SLJ 3/10; VOYA 8/11)

623 Vaught, S. R, and J. B. Redmond. *Assassin's Apprentice* (7–12). Series: Oathbreaker. 2009, Bloomsbury paper $10.99 (978-1-59990-162-6). When young Aron is chosen to join an elite team of assassins — the Stone Brothers — his considerable aptitude for magic becomes apparent; the first volume in a two-part fantasy set in the world of Eyrie. **e** Lexile 1020L (Rev: SLJ 6/1/09; VOYA 8/09)

624 Walton, Jo. *Among Others* (9–12). 2011, Tor $24.99 (978-076532153-4). Fantasy, science fiction, and coming-of-age story, this book, told in diary format, follows a 15-year-old girl with the ability to cast spells as she fights to escape her evil mother and reconnect with her estranged father, all the while drowning her troubles in her love of books. **e** (Rev: BL 1/1/11)

625 Ward, Rachel. *Numbers* (8–12). 2010, Scholastic $17.99 (978-0-545-14299-1). When Jem, 15, realizes

that all the tourists in line for the London Eye Ferris wheel are scheduled to die that day, she and her friend Spider take off, setting in motion a chain of events. ⌂ **e** Lexile HL650L (Rev: BL 12/15/09; SLJ 1/10; VOYA 4/10)

626 Watt-Evans, Lawrence. *A Young Man Without Magic* (10–12). 2009, Tor $27.99 (978-076532279-1). In the Walasian Empire, where sorcery translates into power, young Anrel Murau wants no part of either, but the death of a close friend inspires him to take action and jeopardize his own safety. **e** (Rev: BLO 10/1/09)

627 Werlin, Nancy. *Extraordinary* (8–12). 2010, Dial $17.99 (978-0-8037-3372-5). Privileged Phoebe's best friend Mallory, and her mysterious half-brother Ryland, are both part fairy, and, as it turns out, they have secretive, sinister plans for their friend. ⌂ (Rev: BL 7/10; HB 9–10/10; LMC 1–2/11; SLJ 10/1/10*; VOYA 10/10)

628 Werlin, Nancy. *Impossible* (7–11). 2008, Dial $17.99 (978-0-8037-3002-1). Magic and reality are intertwined in this tale of 17-year-old Lucy, who becomes pregnant after being raped by her date on prom night and decides to keep the baby even though she must rid herself and the unborn child of a curse. ⌂ (Rev: BL 7/08*; SLJ 9/1/08*)

629 White, Amy Brecount. *Forget-Her-Nots* (7–10). 2010, HarperTeen $16.99 (978-0-06-167298-9); LB $17.89 (978-0-06-167299-6). While at boarding school 14-year-old Laurel learns that her affinity with flowers — and her ability to affect the lives of others through them — is something she has inherited. **e** (Rev: BL 1/1/10; SLJ 3/10; VOYA 6/10)

630 Whitfield, Kit. *In Great Waters* (11–12). 2009, Del Rey paper $15 (978-034549165-7). Power struggles amongst the mer-folk who guard coastal, fantastical Europe create drama in this original tale suitable for mature readers. (Rev: BL 11/15/09)

631 Whitley, David. *The Midnight Charter* (7–10). 2009, Roaring Brook $16.99 (978-1-59643-381-6). In a society where lives are treated as a basic commodity, teens Lily and Mark — sold by their parents — take opposing attitudes to the prevailing system. ⌂ **e** Lexile 790L (Rev: BL 8/09; LMC 1–2/10; SLJ 10/09)

632 Whitman, Emily. *Radiant Darkness* (9–12). 2009, Greenwillow $16.99 (978-006172449-7); LB $17.89 (978-006178035-6). In this retelling of the myth, Persephone is in love with Hades and makes her own seasonal arrangement so she can spend part of the year with her mother, Demeter. (Rev: BL 5/15/09; SLJ 8/09; VOYA 8/09)

633 Willingham, Bill. *Peter and Max: A Fables Novel* (10–12). Illus. Series: Fables. 2009, Vertigo $22.99 (978-140121573-6). Peter Piper has discovered that his brother Max is causing problems in the real world, and so Peter travels to Hamelin to end it; a prose addition to the series. ⌂ **e** (Rev: BL 9/15/09; SLJ 11/09)

634 Willingham, Bill, and Mark Buckingham. *The Dark Ages: Fables 12* (11–12). Illus. Series: Fables. 2009, Vertigo $17.99 (978-140122316-8). Fragmentation after the war between the Fables leads to more dangerous instability in this well-crafted volume for mature readers. (Rev: BL 7/09)

635 Wollman, Jessica. *Second Skin: Appearances Can Be Deceiving* (8–11). 2009, Delacorte $8.99 (978-038573601-5); LB $11.99 (978-038590581-7). Sam steals the invisible second skin that bestowed popularity on Kylie and discovers what it's like to be on top of the high school heap. (Rev: BL 5/15/09; SLJ 10/09)

636 Yansky, Brian. *Alien Invasion and Other Inconveniences* (9–12). 2010, Candlewick $15.99 (978-0-7636-4384-3). Most people die when the Sanginians take control of Earth, but high-schooler Jesse survives and develops his telepathic and other abilities until he feels able to save himself and others. ⌒ ℮ Lexile 530L (Rev: BL 11/1/10; LMC 10/10; SLJ 2/1/11)

637 Zink, Michelle. *Prophecy of the Sisters* (7–10). Series: Prophecy of the Sisters. 2009, Little, Brown $17.99 (978-031602742-7). Twins Lia and Alice, 16, are at the center of a battle against the fallen angel Samael in this complex fantasy set in the late 1800s. (Rev: BL 5/15/09; SLJ 1/10; VOYA 10/09)

Graphic Novels

638 Abouet, Marguerite, and Clément Oubrerie. *Aya of Yop City* (10–12). Illus. 2008, Drawn & Quarterly $19.95 (978-189729941-8). This story of Aya and her friends and family continues where *Aya* (2007) ended, and artfully blends the story of uncertain paternity and other social concerns with Ivory Coast culture; for mature readers. (Rev: BL 9/15/08; SLJ 1/09)

639 Andersen, Hans Christian, et al. *Science Fiction Classics* (9–12). Ed. by Tom Pomplun. Illus. by Hunt Emerson. Series: Graphic Classics. 2009, Eureka paper $17.95 (978-0978-791971). Stories by Andersen, Wells, Jules Verne, Arthur Conan Doyle, and E. M. Forster are among those illustrated in this effective collection in graphic novel format. (Rev: BL 6/1–15/09)

640 Aristophane. *The Zabime Sisters* (7–10). 2010, First Second paper $16.99 (978-1-59643-638-1). On the island of Guadeloupe, three teen sisters enjoy a summer day with adventures including smoking, sneaking a drink, stealing mangoes, and watching a fight.. (Rev: BL 10/15/10; LMC 10/10; SLJ 11/10)

641 Baker, Kevin, and Danijel Zezelj. *Luna Park* (11–12). Illus. 2009, Vertigo $24.99 (978-140121584-2). A Russian immigrant with a brutal past and an increasingly grim future seeks to break free from violence, addiction, and poor choices in 1910 Brooklyn; for mature teens. (Rev: BL 11/15/09)

642 Beddor, Frank, and Liz Cavalier. *Hatter M* (8–12). Illus. by Ben Templesmith. Series: Hatter M. 2008, Automatic Pictures paper $14.95 (978-098187370-1). Fans of Beddor's Looking Glass trilogy will enjoy this dark and complex story of Hatter Madigan and his search for Princess Alyss. (Rev: BL 1/1–15/09; VOYA 2/09)

643 Benjamin. *Orange* (11–12). Illus. by author. 2009, Tokyopop paper $14.99 (978-142781463-0). A girl named Orange is brought back from the brink of suicide by a man who later kills himself. (Rev: BL 4/1/09)

644 Breathed, Berkeley. *Bloom County Library, Vol. 1: 1980–1982* (10–12). Illus. 2009, IDW $39.99 (978-160010531-9). The first installment in a series reintroducing the comic strip about the quirky residents of Bloom County, including Milo Bloom, Steve Dallas, Opus the Penguin, and Bill the Cat. (Rev: BLO 12/15/09)

645 Brosgol, Vera. *Anya's Ghost* (7–12). Illus. by author. 2011, First Second paper $15.99 (978-159643552-0). Teenage Anya, embarrassed by her Russian immigrant family and failing to fit in at school, finds herself making friends with a ghost. (Rev: BL 3/15/11*; HB 7–8/11; SLJ 7/11)

646 Byung-Jun, Byun. *Mijeong* (11–12). Trans. by Joe Johnson. Illus. 2009, NBM/ComicsLit paper $19.95 (978-156163554-2). Mostly dark and gloomy, the stories in this graphic novel are still moving and visually arresting; for mature readers. (Rev: BL 7/09)

647 Campbell, Ross. *Shadoweyes* (8–12). Illus. by author. 2010, SLG paper $14.95 (978-159362189-6). In a future dystopia called Dranac, African American Scout Montana morphs into a superhero but may never have the chance to revert to normal. (Rev: BL 9/15/10*; VOYA 10/10)

648 Card, Orson Scott, and Mike Carey. *Ender's Shadow: Battle School* (10–12). Illus. by Sebastian Fiumara. 2009, Marvel $24.99 (978-078513596-8). A graphic novel adaptation of the classic science fiction tale about an orphan named Bean whose street smarts lead to a place at Battle School, where he befriends and competes with Ender Wiggin. (Rev: BLO 11/17/09*)

649 Carey, Mike, and Peter Gross. *Tommy Taylor and the Bogus Identity* (11–12). Illus. Series: The Unwritten. 2010, Vertigo paper $9.99 (978-140122565-0). Tom Taylor has not been thrilled to be regarded the model for the hero of his father's fantasy novels, but when he discovers he's not in fact Wilson Taylor's child he also begins wonders about his own unusual talents; a suspenseful story that skewers much of fantasy fiction and is the first of a series. (Rev: BL 12/15/09)

650 Castellucci, Cecil. *Janes in Love* (9–12). Illus. by Jim Rugg. 2008, DC Comics paper $9.99 (978-140121387-9). In this tender, quirky comic, the Janes' love of art (and boys) spins a rich, believable background as the Janes navigate all the customary dramas of high school:

romance, self-discovery, and family dysfunction; a sequel to 2007's *The Plain Janes*. (Rev: BL 10/1/08; HB 11–12/08; SLJ 11/08)

651 Colbert, C. C., and Tanitoc. *Booth* (11–12). Illus. 2010, First Second paper $19.99 (978-159643125-6). In graphic-novel form Colbert presents a fictionalized but thoroughly researched account of the life of John Wilkes Booth, Lincoln's assassin, from childhood to Confederate activist and actor. (Rev: BL 2/15/10; SLJ 5/10)

652 Conami, Shoko. *Shinobi Life, Vol. 1* (8–11). Illus. by Vicente Rivera. 2008, Tokyopop paper $9.99 (978-142781111-0). Beni finds herself being shadowed by a very cute time-traveling ninja in this first installment in the series. (Rev: BLO 1/13/09)

653 Crisse, Didier. *Luuna, Vol. 1* (9–12). Illus. by Nicolas Keramidas. Series: Luuna. 2009, Tokyopop paper $12.99 (978-142781412-8). Luuna sets off to find her totem and instead learns that her killer instinct will be released once each month — will she use it for good or evil? (Rev: BL 3/15/09)

654 Dasgupta, Amit, and Neelabh. *Indian by Choice* (10–12). Illus. 2009, Wisdom Tree paper $19.95 (978-818328136-2). This graphic novel tells the story of U.S.-born Mandy's first visit to India, his family's homeland, and how he rediscovers his roots. **℮** (Rev: BL 4/15/09)

655 Davis, Jim. *Garfield: 30 Years of Laughs and Lasagna* (5–10). Illus. by author. 2008, Ballantine $35.00 (978-0-345-50379-4). A collection of the popular comic strip that centers on a grumpy, overweight cat. (Rev: BL 10/15/08; SLJ 1/09)

656 Dembicki, Matt, ed. *Trickster: Native American Tales: A Graphic Collection* (8–12). Illus. 2010, Fulcrum Publishing paper $22.95 (978-1-55591-724-1). More than 20 Native American tales are presented in appealing graphic-novel format, illustrated by a variety of artists. (Rev: BL 5/1/10*; LMC 11–12/10; SLJ 5/10) [398.2]

657 Dini, Paul, and Guillem March. *Gotham City Sirens Union* (10–12). Illus. 2010, DC Comics $19.99 (978-140122570-4). The three femmes fatales of Gotham City — Catwoman, Poison Ivy, and Harley Quinn — move in together, hoping for peace and quiet, but with a violent Batman impostor loose in the city, life is anything but. (Rev: BL 5/15/10)

658 Dostoevsky, Fyodor, and David Zane Mairowitz. *Crime and Punishment* (10–12). Illus. by Alain Korkos. 2009, Sterling paper $14.95 (978-141141594-2). A graphic adaptation of the novel, set in present-day Russia and heavy on atmosphere and angst. (Rev: BL 5/1/09)

659 Dunning, John Harris. *Salem Brownstone: All Along the Watchtowers* (9–12). Illus. by Nikhil Singh. 2010, Candlewick $18.99 (978-0-7636-4735-3). This unusual, oversize graphic novel tells a gothic story of Salem Brownstone inheriting a mansion and a continuing struggle against dark forces. (Rev: BL 7/10*; LMC 11–12/10; SLJ 7/10; VOYA 8/10)

660 Dysart, Joshua, and Cliff Chiang. *Neil Young's Greendale* (11–12). Illus. 2010, Vertigo $19.99 (978-140122820-0). Environmentally conscious 18-year-old Sun Green's charmed life unravels in the face of family drama in this vividly illustrated, political graphic novel inspired by Neil Young's rock opera; for mature teens. (Rev: BL 5/15/10; SLJ 7/10)

661 Fies, Brian. *Whatever Happened to the World of Tomorrow?* (10–12). 2009, Abrams $24.95 (978-0-8109-9636-6). This unique graphic novel captures the feel of the 1939 World's Fair, complete with sepia tones, as a boy views "The Fantastic Future City of 2039," and it then follows him — and the development of technology — through 1975 and the final Apollo mission. (Rev: BLO 6/23/09; LMC 1–2/10)

662 Fillbach, Matt, and Shawn Fillbach. *Roadkill* (10–12). Illus. by author. 2008, Dark Horse paper $9.95 (978-159582169-0). A trucker and his talking dog encounter flesh-eating zombies in a world inhabited by supernatural freaks; humor and horror are here in equal doses. (Rev: BLO 1/13/09)

663 Fitzgerald, F. Scott, and Nunzio DeFilippis. *The Curious Case of Benjamin Button* (10–12). Illus. by Kevin Cornell. 2008, Quirk $15.95 (978-159474281-1). A graphic-novel adaptation of a story recently made into a movie starring Brad Pitt; lovely artwork adds to the charm of this tale of a baby born old. **℮** (Rev: BL 1/1–15/09; SLJ 1/09)

664 Fujishima, Kosuke. *Oh My Goddess! Colors* (8–12). Illus. by author. 2009, Dark Horse paper $19.95 (978-1595822550). Four classic manga stories each focus on a goddess — Belldandy, Urd, Skuld, and Peorth — in this oversized volume that includes a thorough encyclopedia of the series. (Rev: BL 6/1–15/09)

665 Fukushima, Haruka. *Orange Planet, Vol. 1* (8–11). Illus. by author. 2009, Del Rey paper $10.99 (978-034551338-0). In this *shojo* manga, Rui finds herself the object of much male interest — from her contemporaries and from a teacher. (Rev: BLO 4/30/09; SLJ 10/09)

666 Gore, Shawna, ed. *Creepy Archives, Vol. 1* (10–12). Illus. 2008, Dark Horse $49.95 (978-159307973-4). Here is a collection of *Creepy* issues known for their attention-getting covers and boundary-pushing content; the first in a series. (Rev: BL 9/1/08)

667 Heuvel, Eric. *A Family Secret* (7–12). Trans. from Dutch by Lorraine T. Miller. Illus. by Eric Heuvel. 2009, Farrar $18.99. (978-0-374-32271-7). A contemporary teen learns from his grandmother about the Nazi occupation of the Netherlands and the difficult decisions that people had to make. (Rev: BL 9/15/09*; SLJ 5/10)

668 Higuri, You. *Angel's Coffin* (10–12). Illus. by author. 2008, Go! Comi paper $10.99 (978-193361768-8). History and the supernatural mix in this artfully rendered manga novel about the death of Austrian Crown Prince Rudolf in 1889. (Rev: BLO 12/8/08)

669 Hinds, Gareth. *The Odyssey* (7–12). 2010, Candlewick $24.99 (978-0-7636-4266-2). Rich illustrations enhance this faithful graphic-novel rendering of the amazing adventures of Odysseus. Lexile GN840L (Rev: BL 9/15/10*; HB 11–12/10; LMC 11–12/10; SLJ 11/10; VOYA 2/11)

670 Hine, David, and Fabrice Sapolsky. *Spider-Man Noir* (10–12). Illus. by Carmine Di Giandomenico. 2009, Marvel paper $14.99 (978-078512923-3). In 1930s New York City a spider's bite transforms young Peter Parker into a crusader against crime and corruption. (Rev: BL 11/15/09*)

671 Hino, Matsuri. *Captive Hearts, Vol. 2* (8–11). Illus. by author. Series: Captive Hearts. 2009, VIZ Media paper $8.99 (978-142151933-3). Megumi continues to do anything for Suzuka and her love in the second book in this manga series. (Rev: BLO 4/30/09)

672 Hughes, Richard E., and Ogden Whitney. *Herbie Archives; Vol. 1* (10–12). Illus. 2008, Dark Horse $49.95 (978-1-59307-987-1). A collection of the 1960s comics about chunky Herbie Popnecker and his supernatural lollipops and abilities to bend time and space and defeat monsters of all kinds. (Rev: BL 8/08) [741.5]

673 Hwa, Kim Dong. *The Color of Earth* (10–12). Illus. by author. 2009, First Second paper $16.95 (978-159643458-5). This lovely coming-of-age manhwa set in rural Korea traces Ehwa's life from age 7 to 16 and her maturing from childhood into an adolescent interested in her own body and those of young men; she shares a close bond with her widowed mother, who runs a tavern and finds her own new love. (Rev: BL 6/1–15/09*; SLJ 9/09; VOYA 4/09)

674 Igarashi, Daisuke. *Children of the Sea, Vol. 1* (7–12). Illus. by author. 2009, VIZ Media paper $14.99 (978-142152914-1). Fish are disappearing from aquariums around the world and strange children are simultaneously discovered living in the sea; young Ruka feels drawn to the aquarium and sets out to investigate. (Rev: BL 11/1/09*; VOYA 4/10)

675 Immonen, Kathryn, and Stuart Immonen. *Moving Pictures* (10–12). Illus. 2010, Top Shelf paper $14.95 (978-160309049-0). Parisian art curators struggle to protect the masterpieces they love during the Nazi occupation. (Rev: BL 5/1/10*)

676 Inoue, Takehiko. *Real, Vol. 2* (10–12). Illus. by author. Series: Real. 2008, VIZ Media paper $12.99 (978-142151990-6). Athletic Kiyoharu, 14, is confined to a wheelchair after an illness and learns to cope with his limitations. (Rev: BL 3/1/09)

677 Jablonski, Carla. *Resistance* (7–10). Illus. by Leland Purvis. Series: Resistance. 2010, First Second paper $16.99 (978-1-59643-291-8). Marie and Paul help Henri, who is Jewish, reunite with his deported parents in this graphic novel set in World War II. Lexile GN190L (Rev: LMC 8–9/10; SLJ 5/10)

678 Jansson, Tove, and Lars Jansson. *Moomin: The Complete Tove Jansson Comic Strip* (10–12). Illus. 2009, Drawn & Quarterly $19.95 (978-189729978-4). These comic strips based on the Moomin character are filled with time machines, funny situations, and down-to-earth life lessons; (Rev: BL 7/09; SLJ 9/09)

679 Johns, Geoff, and Jeff Katz. *Blue and Gold* (6–12). Illus. by Norm Rapmund. 2008, DC Comics $24.99 (978-140121956-7). Booster Gold and Blue Beetle travel through time and encounter fellow superheroes in this engaging adventure. (Rev: BLO 2/9/09)

680 Johns, Geoff, and Richard Donner. *Last Son: Superman* (10–12). Illus. 2008, DC Comics $19.99 (978-1-4012-1343-5). Elements from the films that Christopher Reeve made famous are captured in this tale that will satisfy fans as they see Superman struggle with his conflicted feelings for humanity and reluctantly turn to arch villains for help to save a Kryptonian boy. (Rev: BL 8/08; SLJ 11/08)

681 Johnson, Nathan, and Matt Yamashita. *Ghostbusters: Ghost Busted* (6–10). Illus. by Chrissy Delk. 2008, Tokyopop $12.99 (978-142781459-3). Based on the 1984 movie about ghostbusting, this manga is filled with comedy, ghosts, and adventure. e (Rev: BL 1/1–15/09; LMC 8–9/09)

682 Johnston, Anthony. *Wolverine: Prodigal Son* (9–12). Illus. by Wilson Tortosa. 2009, Del Rey paper $12.95 (978-034550516-3). A manga reimagining of the Wolverine story, with Logan as a contemporary teen who has lost his memory. (Rev: BL 3/1/09; SLJ 5/09)

683 Jones, Frewin. *Lamia's Revenge: The Serpent Awakes* (8–11). Illus. by Alison Acton. Series: The Faerie Path. 2009, Tokyopop paper $7.99 (978-006145694-7). Teen faerie princess Tania sets out to rescue her mortal parents in this manga version. (Rev: BLO 4/30/09)

684 Kanno, Aya. *Otomen, Vol. 1* (8–12). Illus. by author. 2009, VIZ Media paper $8.99 (978-1-4215-2186-2). Readers meet Asuka, a teenage boy who embraces his feminine side, in this first installment in the series. (Rev: BLO 2/9/09)

685 Kelly, Joe. *I Kill Giants* (9–12). Illus. by J. M. Ken Nimura. 2009, Image Comics paper $15.99 (978-160706092-5). This volume collects the first seven stories about a lonely and frightened but courageous girl named Barbara who battles the monsters in her life. (Rev: BLO 1/31/10*; VOYA 4/10)

686 Kindt, Matt. *Revolver* (11–12). Illus. 2010, Vertigo $24.99 (978-140122241-3). Young journalist Sam is caught between two parallel worlds — one a menial desk-job existence and the other just trying to survive in a nation in post-terrorist-attack shock; for mature readers. (Rev: BL 6/1–15/10)

687 Kindt, Matt. *3 Story: The Secret History of the Giant Man* (10–12). Illus. 2009, Dark Horse $19.95 (978-159582356-4). This intriguing graphic novel recounts the bizarre story of Craig Pressgang, a man who has grown so large that he is rendered incapable of interacting with other humans, leaving him completely alienated from those he loves. (Rev: BL 10/15/09)

688 Kiyuouki, Satoko. *Shoulder-A-Coffin Kuro, Vol. 2* (8–11). Illus. by author. Series: Shoulder-A-Coffin Kuro. 2008, Yen paper $10.99 (978-075952901-4). Little Kuro seeks to rid herself of her coffin as she travels through an eerie land and encounters creepy and dangerous characters; an unusual manga full of humor. (Rev: BLO 1/13/09; SLJ 5/09)

689 Knauf, Charles, and Daniel Knauf. *The Eternals: To Slay a God* (9–12). Illus. by Daniel Acuna. 2009, Marvel paper $19.99 (978-078512978-3). There is trouble among the Eternals, superhumans created millions of years before, in this collection of the first six issues of the comic book. (Rev: BL 6/1–15/09)

690 Kubert, Joe. *Dong Xoai: Vietnam 1965* (9–12). 2010, DC Comics $24.99 (978-1-4012-2142-3). The 1965 battle over the village of Dong Xoia is the focus of this graphic-novel account that is fictional but conveys an accurate picture of the U.S. Special Forces that took part and of their adversaries. (Rev: BL 5/15/10; LMC 11–12/10)

691 Kusakabe, Rei. *Nephylym, Vol. 2* (8–12). Illus. by author. Series: Nephylym. 2008, DrMaster paper $9.99 (978-159796182-0). Sexy yet cute creatures team with humans to battle Noir, the personification of negativity. (Rev: BLO 2/9/09)

692 Kwitney, Alisa. *Token* (8–10). Illus. by Joelle Jones. 2008, DC Comics paper $9.99 (978-140121538-5). Jewish 15-year-old Shira and her widowed father struggle to cope with their changing lives — which include Shira's father's relationship with his secretary and her own romance with a young Spaniard — in 1980s Miami Beach. (Rev: BL 11/15/08; LMC 5–6/09)

693 Larson, Hope. *Mercury* (9–12). 2010, Simon & Schuster $19.99 (978-1-4169-3585-8). With touch of magic realism, this graphic novel interweaves the stories of contemporary Tara and her ancestor Josey, and rumors of buried gold. (Rev: BL 11/1/09*; HB 3–4/10; LMC 11–12/10; SLJ 3/10; VOYA 12/09)

694 Lasko-Gross, Miss. *A Mess of Everything* (11–12). Illus. 2009, Fantagraphics paper $19.99 (978-156097956-2). A sequel to the semi-autobiographic *Escape from "Special"* (2007), this story deals with Melissa's experiences in high school — her friends, and her mistakes along the way to finding herself; for mature readers. (Rev: BL 5/1/09*; SLJ SLJ 7/09)

695 Lee, Stan. *The Fantastic Four, Vol. 1* (5–10). Illus. by Jack Kirby. 2009, Marvel paper $24.99 (978-0-7851-3710-8). This volume collects the first 10 stories about the four who returned to Earth with superhuman abilities after being exposed to cosmic rays. (Rev: BLO 4/30/09)

696 Lemire, Jeff. *The Nobody* (10–12). Illus. 2009, Vertigo $19.99 (978-140122080-8). Inspired by H. G. Wells's *The Invisible Man*, this graphic novel's bandaged stranger comes to a small town and causes tension that leads to violence; for mature readers. (Rev: BL 5/1/09; SLJ 11/09)

697 Lemire, Jeff. *Out of the Deep Woods: Sweet Tooth 1* (10–12). Illus. 2010, Vertigo paper $9.99 (978-1-4012-2696-1). A deer-like young boy is rescued from bounty hunters by a man who endeavors to build his trust. (Rev: BL 4/1/10)

698 Lia, Simone. *Fluffy* (11–12). Illus. 2008, Dark Horse $19.95 (978-1-59307-972-7). *Fluffy*, a graphic novel, details the emotional ups and downs of bachelor Michael and his bunny son as they figure out life and relationships; for mature readers. (Rev: BL 8/08)

699 Loeb, Jeph. *Hulk, Vol. 1: Red Hulk* (6–12). Illus. by Ed McGuinness. Series: Hulk. 2009, Marvel paper $19.99 (978-078512882-3). Good old-fashioned superhero action for Marvel comics fans. (Rev: BL 4/15/09)

700 Love, Jeremy. *Bayou, Vol. 1* (9–12). Illus. by author. 2009, DC Comics paper $14.99 (978-140122382-3). In this historical fantasy set in the South during the Depression, Lily, a white girl, is abducted, and her black friend Lee must brave a frightening parallel universe to rescue her. (Rev: BL 7/09)

701 McCann, Jim. *Return of the Dapper Men* (7–10). Illus. by Janet Lee. 2010, Archaia $24.95 (978-193238690-5). In a world where children live underground and robots inhabit houses overhead, time has stopped and is only restarted with the arrival of 314 Dapper Men. (Rev: BL 2/15/11*)

702 McCloud, Scott. *Zot! 1987–1991* (10–12). Illus. 2008, Harper paper $24.95 (978-006153727-1). *Zot!* tells the story of two worlds through the interaction of Zot, a superhero teen from an alternate futuristic Earth, and Jenny, an ordinary, discontented girl from ours. (Rev: BL 9/1/08)

703 Madison, Ivory. *Huntress: Year One* (10–12). Illus. by Cliff Richards. Series: Huntress. 2009, DC Comics paper $17.99 (978-140122126-3). Superhero Helena seeks revenge after her family is killed by the Mafia; an engaging and sometimes violent thriller. (Rev: BLO 3/24/09)

704 Maeda, Mahiro. *Gankutsuou: The Count of Monte Cristo, Vol. 1* (10–12). Illus. by author. 2008, Del Rey paper $10.95 (978-034550520-0). This graphic-novel retelling of Dumas's classic story with a science fiction twist begins with a trip to another planet, where two young men meet a gothic version of the count of Monte Cristo and are drawn into a dangerous intrigue. (Rev: BL 12/1/08; SLJ 1/09)

705 Marder, Larry. *Beanworld: Wahoolazuma* (8–12). Illus. by author. Series: Beanworld. 2009, Dark Horse $19.95 (978-159582240-6). A collection of comics first published in the 1980s, *Wahoolazuma* features a world populated by beans who learn they are dependent on one another and on the environment. (Rev: BL 4/15/09)

706 Marr, Melissa. *Sanctuary: Desert Tales, Vol. 1* (8–11). Illus. by Xian Nu Studio. Series: Wicked Lovely: Desert Tales. 2009, Tokyopop paper $9.99 (978-006149354-6). This first volume in a new manga trilogy is set in a world familiar to Marr's readers and features Rika, a faery living in the Mojave Desert who becomes involved with a mortal young man. **e** (Rev: BLO 6/16/09; SLJ 7/09)

707 Matsumoto, Taiyo. *Gogo Monster* (10–12). Illus. 2009, VIZ Media $27.99 (978-142153209-7). In this manga tale, a young boy struggles to live in two worlds: a fantasy realm and one full of the reality of cruel classmates. (Rev: BL 12/1/09)

708 Mechner, Jordan. *Solomon's Thieves* (6–10). Illus. by Pham LeUyen and Alex Puvilland. 2010, First Second paper $12.99 (978-1-59643-391-5). The very existence of the Knights Templar is threatened and they must fight for their lives and their treasure in early 14th-century France. (Rev: BL 4/15/10; LMC 8–9/10; SLJ 7/10)

709 Mechner, Jordan, and A. B. Sina. *Prince of Persia: The Graphic Novel* (9–12). Illus. by LeUyen Pham. 2008, First Second paper $16.95 (978-159643207-9). Loosely based on the popular Prince of Persia video game, this tale weaves together the stories of the prince's origins and destiny through visual clues and a richly imagined color palette. (Rev: BL 9/1/08*; VOYA 8/08)

710 Mignola, Mike, et al. *The Black Goddess* (9–12). Illus. Series: B.P.R.D. 2009, Dark Horse paper $17.95 (978-159582411-0). With Liz gone and their most powerful enemies banding together for a final, catastrophic attack, Abe, Kate, and Johann must determine the price of their souls as they decide where their loyalties lie - and whether the life of a friend is more valuable than the fate of the world. B.P.R.D.: The Black Goddess collects the second arc of the Scorched Earth trilogy, pulling together threads from the beginning of the series, with a twist that will shake the worlds of B.P.R.D. agents and readers alike. (Rev: BLO 10/1/09)

711 Millionaire, Tony. *Billy Hazelnuts and the Crazy Bird* (10–12). Illus. by author. 2010, Fantagraphics $19.99 (978-156097917-3). In this funny sequel to 2006's *Billy Hazelnuts,* our garbage-constructed hero embarks on a crazy quest to reunite a young owl with its mother, even as his charge chomps away at him. (Rev: BL 7/10)

712 Modan, Rutu. *Jamilti and Other Stories* (11–12). Trans. by Noah Stollman. Illus. 2008, Drawn & Quarterly $19.95 (978-189729954-8). This book contains seven short stories that vary in plot but are united by Modan's artistic style and sharp characterization; for mature readers. (Rev: BL 9/15/08; SLJ 3/09)

713 Mori, Kaoru. *Shirley, Vol. 1* (7–10). Illus. by author. 2008, DC Comics paper $9.99 (978-1-4012-1777-8). Set in Edwardian England, this manga novel follows the life of an endearing 13-year-old orphan who gets a job as a maid for a cafe owner. (Rev: BLO 12/30/08)

714 Natsume, Yoshinori. *Batman: Death Mask* (9–12). Illus. by author. 2008, DC Comics paper $9.99 (978-140121924-6). This dark manga version of the Batman story will attract fans of Japanese comics. (Rev: BL 2/1/09)

715 Nelson, Arvid, and Juan Ferreyra. *Gate of God: Rex Mundi 6* (10–12). Illus. 2010, Dark Horse paper $17.99 (978-159582403-5). This sixth installment is the conclusion to the alternate history graphic novel series set in the 1930s, and provides lots of action, adventure, and a high body count as the hero, Julien Sauniere, searches for the Holy Grail in the mountains of France. (Rev: BL 2/15/10)

716 Nicolle, Malachai. *Axe Cop, Vol. 1* (9–12). Illus. by Ethan Nicolle. 2011, Dark Horse paper $14.99 (978-159582681-7). The wacky imaginings of 5-year-old Malachai (involving an axe-wielding policeman and a motley crew of superheroes, aliens, dinosaurs, werewolves, and so forth) are illustrated by his older brother in this stirring collection. (Rev: BL 3/15/11*)

717 Okazaki, Takashi. *Afro Samurai* (10–12). Trans. by Greg Moore. Illus. by author. 2008, Tor paper $10.99 (978-076532123-7). Best for older teens because of violence and brief nudity, this is a complex manga story about a futuristic samurai's quest to best the warrior who murdered his father. (Rev: BL 12/1/08; LMC 5–6/09; SLJ 1/09)

718 Oliver, Simon. *Gen13: 15 Minutes (Volume 3)* (9–12). Illus. by Carlo Barberi. 2008, DC Comics $14.99 (978-140122002-0). The members of Gen13 find themselves in New York City in this installment, but they are again in grave danger. (Rev: BLO 1/7/09)

719 O'Malley, Bryan Lee. *Scott Pilgrim vs. the Universe, Vol. 5* (11–12). Illus. by author. Series: Scott Pilgrim. 2009, Oni paper $11.95 (978-193496410-1). (Rev: BL 4/1/09)

720 Panagariya, Ananth. *Applegeeks, Vol. 1: Freshman Year* (10–12). Illus. by Mohammad F. Haque. 2009, Dark Horse paper $14.95 (978-159582174-4). A collection of the first two years of the Webcomic starring college students Hawk and Jayce and their usual and unusual adventures. (Rev: BLO 6/17/09)

721 Patterson, James. *Maximum Ride, Vol. 1* (7–10). Illus. by NaRae Lee. Series: Maximum Ride. 2009, Yen paper $10.99 (978-075952951-9). A manga adaptation of the series by the same name, this story introduces readers to a group of mutant teenagers living in a dangerous world. ℮ (Rev: BL 3/1/09; SLJ 5/09)

722 Powell, Nate. *Swallow Me Whole* (10–12). Illus. 2008, Top Shelf $20.95 (978-160309033-9). *Swallow Me Whole* is a graphic novel that skillfully portrays two teen step-siblings as they struggle with their mental illnesses. (Rev: BL 9/1/08; LMC 3–4/09; SLJ 1/09)

723 Raicht, Mike, and Brian Smith. *The Stuff of Legend, Vol. 1: The Dark* (10–12). Illus. by Charles Paul Wilson. 2010, Villard paper $13 (978-034552100-2). A troupe of toys sets off to do battle with the Boogeyman when their keeper — a young boy — is kidnapped in this creepy thriller set during World War II. (Rev: BL 7/10)

724 Robinson, Alex. *Too Cool to Be Forgotten* (10–12). Illus. 2008, Top Shelf paper $12.95 (978-189183098-3). Andy visits a hypnotherapist to cure his tobacco addiction and ends up traveling back in time to high school, when he has the chance to date his crush, say goodbye to his dying father, and decline that first offer of a cigarette. ℮ (Rev: BL 6/1–15/08; LMC 1–2/09; SLJ 1/09)

725 Robinson, James, and Tony Harris. *The Starman Omnibus 1* (10–12). Illus. 2008, DC Comics $49.99 (978-140121699-3). A collection of the comics featuring Jack Knight, son of a superhero, who suddenly and reluctantly finds himself inheriting his father's role; first in a series. (Rev: BL 9/1/08)

726 Ryukishi07. *Higurashi When They Cry: Abducted by Demons Arc, Vol. 1* (10–12). Illus. by Karin Suzuragi. 2008, Yen paper $10.99 (978-075952983-0). Keiichi tries to solve the mystery behind a string of gory murders in this manga adaptation of a computer game. (Rev: BLO 2/9/09; LMC 8–9/09; SLJ 3/09)

727 Sala, Richard. *Cat Burglar Black* (7–10). Illus. by author. 2009, First Second paper $16.99 (978-159643144-7). K (Katherine), already quite skilled as a burglar, finds herself investigating the motives of an art theft group she has been working with. (Rev: BL 7/09; LMC 11–12/09; SLJ 11/09)

728 Schweizer, Chris. *Crogan's March* (7–12). 2009, Oni $14.95 (978-1-934964-24-8). Peter Crogan is a legionnaire fighting for France in North Africa in 1912 in this action-packed addition to the legends of this unusual family. (Rev: BL 3/15/10*; SLJ 5/10)

729 Schweizer, Chris. *Crogan's Vengeance* (7–12). Illus. by author. 2008, Oni $14.95 (978-193496406-4). Catfish Crogan and his crewmates fight off pirates on the high seas in this adventure tale set in 1701. (Rev: BL 1/1–15/09; SLJ 5/09)

730 Serling, Rod, and Mark Kneece. *Death's-Head Revisited* (7–10). Illus. by Chris Lie. Series: Twilight Zone. 2009, Walker $16.99 (978-080279722-3); paper $9.99 (978-080279723-0). A faithful adaptation of an episode of the *Twilight Zone* television show in which a former concentration camp guard is judged by the souls of the people he murdered. (Rev: BL 3/1/09; SLJ 5/09)

731 Shakespeare, William. *Julius Caesar* (8–12). Adapted by Richard Appignanesi. Illus. by Mustashrik. Series: Manga Shakespeare. 2008, Abrams paper $9.95 (978-081097072-4). Abridged text and expressive illustrations tell the story of the play with a manga twist. (Rev: BL 10/1/08*; SLJ 1/09) [741.5]

732 Shakespeare, William, and John McDonald. *Macbeth: The Graphic Novel* (6–10). Illus. by Jon Haward. 2008, Classical Comics paper $16.95 (978-190633205-1). This dramatically illustrated, condensed version of the play is accompanied by background information to help students understand its plot, setting, characters and significance. (Rev: BL 1/1–15/09)

733 Shakespeare, William, and Richard Appignanesi. *As You Like It* (8–10). Illus. by Chie Kutsuwada. 2009, Abrams paper $10.95 (978-081098351-9). A manga retelling of the play set in the forest of Arden. (Rev: BL 3/1/09; SLJ 3/09) [823]

734 Shakespeare, William, and Steven Grant. *Hamlet* (8–10). Illus. by Tom Mandrake. Series: Classics Illustrated. 2009, Papercutz $9.95 (978-159707149-9). This graphic-novel adaptation gives an effective rendering of the key events and characters, and will be useful to supplement the play itself. (Rev: BL 6/1–15/09; LMC 10/09) [822]

735 Siddell, Thomas. *Orientation* (6–12). Illus. by author. Series: Gunnerkrigg Court. 2009, Archaia Studios $26.95 (978-193238634-9). Antimony arrives at a creepy boarding school where things get odder every day in this webcomic collection, the first in a series. (Rev: BL 3/15/09*)

736 Simmonds, Posy. *Tamara Drewe* (11–12). Illus. 2008, Houghton paper $16.95 (978-054715412-1). Using both written word and art in this graphic novel loosely based on Hardy's *Far from the Madding Crowd,* Simmonds skillfully portrays a middle-class English country society shaken up by the arrival of a glamorous newspaper columnist; for mature readers. (Rev: BL 9/1/08*)

737 Sizer, Paul. *B. P. M* (10–12). Illus. by author. 2008, Cafe Digital paper $15.99 (978-097685656-6). Roxy dreams of becoming a DJ in a top gay nightclub in this manga that's all about music and the club scene (the title stands for "beats per minute"). (Rev: BLO 4/30/09)

738 Smart, Jamie. *Ubu Bubu: Filth* (11–12). Illus. 2009, SLG paper $12.95 (978-159362198-8). Full of anime-influenced artwork and dry British wit, this is the story of a destructive demon that inhabits the body of a kitten and attempts to bring about an apocalypse. (Rev: BL 11/15/09)

739 Smith, Jeff, and Tom Sniegoski. *Bone: Tall Tales* (6–12). 2010, Graphix $22.99 (978-0-545-14095-9). A collection of stories featuring the founder of Boneville, Big Johnson Bone, and his intrepid adventures. Lexile GN560L (Rev: BL 3/15/10; LMC 10/10; SLJ 7/10)

740 Stanley, John. *Melvin Monster: The John Stanley Library* (6–12). Illus. 2009, Drawn & Quarterly $19.95 (978-189729963-0). Stanley's monster kid, Melvin, is funny and sympathetic in this reprinted comic book series. (Rev: BL 7/09; SLJ 11/09)

741 Stanley, John, and Irving Tripp. *Miss Feeny's Folly and Other Stories: Little Lulu 21* (6–12). Illus. 2009, Dark Horse paper $14.95 (978-159582365-6). This 21st volume continues the meticulous reprinting of the delightful Little Lulu series. (Rev: BL 12/1/09)

742 Sumerak, Marc, and Fred Van Lente. *Wolverine: Tales of Weapon X* (8–12). Illus. by Mark Robinson. 2009, Marvel $14.99 (978-078513936-2). Six lively comics combine humor and adventure with details of Wolverine's past. (Rev: BLO 6/16/09)

743 Suzuki, Yasushi. *Goths Cage* (9–12). Illus. by author. 2008, DrMaster $12.95 (978-159796157-8). The focus is on the artwork in these three dark fantasies loosely based on folk and fairy tales. (Rev: BLO 1/13/09)

744 Takada, Rie. *Gaba Kawa, Vol. 1* (8–12). Illus. by author. 2008, VIZ Media paper $8.99 (978-142152259-3). Rara is a high-school demon who falls in love with a human classmate in this funny yet sometimes disturbing story. (Rev: BLO 2/9/09)

745 Takaya, Natsuki. *Phantom Dream, Vol. 1* (10–12). Trans. by Beni Axia Conrad. Illus. by author. 2009, Tokyopop paper $9.99 (978-142781089-2). Tamaki and Asahi learn that they come from warring families in this manga that combines romance and the supernatural. (Rev: BL 3/1/09)

746 Takeuchi, Mick. *Bound Beauty* (8–11). Illus. by author. 2008, Go! Comi $10.99 (978-1-60510-008-1). This manga novel about a teenage matchmaker contains lots of great information about Japanese folklore, history, and traditions. (Rev: BLO 12/30/08)

747 Tamaki, Mariko. *Emiko Superstar* (8–12). Illus. by Steve Rolston. 2008, DC Comics paper $9.99 (978-140121536-1). Asian Canadian Emiko discovers she can use performance art to be someone completely different from the geeky teen she believes she is. (Rev: BL 12/1/08; LMC 5–6/09; SLJ 11/08)

748 Tan, Shaun. *The Arrival* (6–12). Illus. by author. 2007, Scholastic $19.99 (978-043989529-3). This wordless graphic novel tells the moving story of a man who migrates to a new country hoping to build a new life. (Rev: BL 9/1/07*)

749 Tan, Shaun. *Tales from Outer Suburbia* (7–12). Illus. by author. 2009, Scholastic $19.99 (978-054505587-1). These fifteen diverse short tales are beautifully illustrated with Tan's evocative artwork. Lexile 1100L (Rev: BL 12/1/08*; HB 3–4/09; LMC 5–6/09; SLJ 3/1/09*; VOYA 6/09)

750 TenNapel, Doug. *Bad Island* (6–10). Illus. by author. 2011, Graphix $24.99 (978-054531479-4); paper $12.99 (978-054531480-0). On a boat trip with his family, Reese finds himself washed up on an island inhabited by weird beings from a distant galaxy. (Rev: BL 3/15/11*)

751 Tobe, Keiko. *With the Light: Raising an Autistic Child 2* (10–12). Trans. by Satsuki Yamashita. Illus. 2008, Yen paper $14.99 (978-075952359-3). In this second volume about an autistic child and the impact on the family, Hikaru is now in 4th grade and striving to cope with special-ed classes and social interactions. (Rev: BL 6/1–15/08*)

752 Truman, Timothy, and Mark Schultz. *Star Wars Omnibus: Emissaries and Assassins* (6–12). Illus. by Tim Bradstreet. 2009, Dark Horse paper $24.95 (978-159582229-1). A collection of comics based on movies *Episode I* and *II,* with different styles of artwork and featuring favorite characters. (Rev: BLO 5/27/09)

753 Tsuda, Masami. *Castle of Dreams: Stories from the Kare Kano Creator* (8–12). Illus. Series: Sorcerer. 2009, Tokyopop paper $12.99 (978-142781227-8). Teenage romance, fantasy, and modern life mix in this collection of sweet stories. (Rev: BLO 2/9/09)

754 Type-Moon. *Fate/Stay Night* (8–11). Illus. by Dat Nishiwaki. Series: Fate/Stay Night. 2008, Tokyopop $9.99 (978-142781037-3). Emiya faces danger and evil forces in his ongoing fight for the powerful Holy Grail; an action-packed manga with mythological references. (Rev: BLO 1/21/09)

755 Ueda, Miwa. *Papillon, Vol. 1* (8–11). Illus. by author. 2008, Del Rey paper $10.95 (978-0-345-50519-4). High school student Ageha is always upstaged by her twin sister Hana in this manga novel until her sister steals the boy Ageha likes and she decides, with the encouragement of a friend and her school guidance counselor, that it's time to make a change. (Rev: BLO 12/8/08; SLJ 11/08)

756 Urasawa, Naoki, et al. *Pluto, Vol. 1* (10–12). Illus. by author. 2009, VIZ Media paper $12.99 (978-142151918-0). Gesicht, a humanoid robot detective for Europol, investigates a serial murderer. (Rev: BLO 10/27/09*)

757 Urrea, Luis Alberto. *Mr. Mendoza's Paintbrush* (9–12). Illus. by Christopher Carinale. 2010, Cinco Puntos paper $17.95 (978-1-933693-23-1). Mr. Mendoza's graffiti adorn the Mexican village of Rosario, portraying various social problems. (Rev: BL 5/1–15/10; HB 7–8/10; LMC 11–12/10; SLJ 7/10)

758 Venditti, Robert, and Brett Weldele. *Flesh and Bone* (10–12). Illus. Series: The Surrogates. 2009, Top Shelf paper $14.95 (978-160309018-6). It is the year 2039 and wealthy people have avatars, or "surrogates," who go about their daily lives in their place, while revolution brews among those who can't afford this technology; a prequel to *The Surrogates* (2006). (Rev: BL 7/09; SLJ 11/09)

759 Wada, Shinji. *Crown* (9–12). Illus. by You Higuri. Series: Crown. 2008, Go! Comi paper $10.99 (978-160510005-0). This first volume in a series introduces Mahiro, whose long-lost brother and his friend show up to protect her from evil forces after her parents die in a car crash. (Rev: BL 3/1/09)

760 Weing, Drew. *Set to Sea* (8–12). Illus. by Drew Weing. 2010, Fantagraphics $16.99 (978-160699368-2). After years of glorifying the sea in his mind, the unnamed main character of this simple fable suddenly finds himself aboard a clipper bound for Hong Kong. (Rev: BL 10/15/10*)

761 Whedon, Joss, et al. *MySpace Dark Horse Presents, Vol. 2* (11–12). Ed. by Zack Whedon. Illus. by Eric Canete. 2009, Dark Horse paper $19.95 (978-159582248-2). The second volume in this series features a collection of mysterious, romantic, and supernatural comic adventures by many different artists. (Rev: BLO 2/9/09)

762 White, James L., and Dalibor Talajic. *Hunter's Moon* (10–12). Illus. 2008, Boom! Studios paper $14.99 (978-193450622-6). African American Lincoln Greer takes his son Wendell on a hunting trip to the mountains, only to find himself framed for murder and ensnared in racial prejudice. (Rev: BL 6/1–15/08)

763 Yang, Gene Luen. *The Eternal Smile* (9–12). Illus. by Derek Kirk Kim. 2009, First Second paper $16.95 (978-159643156-0). Three complex and engaging stories about imagination, fantasy, and reality; beautiful artwork enhances the text. (Rev: BL 3/1/09; LMC 8–9/09; SLJ 5/09)

764 Yang, Gene Luen. *Prime Baby* (10–12). Illus. 2010, First Second paper $6.99 (978-159643612-1). Brilliant though jealous 8-year-old Thaddeus Fong fights his social insecurities with the help of patient space aliens in this richly imagined, spirited graphic novel with political undertones. (Rev: BL 3/15/10)

765 Yang, Song. *Wild Animals, Vol. 1* (10–12). Illus. by author. 2008, Yen paper $10.99 (978-075952938-0). Expressive artwork punctuates this graphic novel that examines the life and growing awareness of a school boy during China's Cultural Revolution. (Rev: BL 12/1/08)

766 Yolen, Jane. *Foiled* (6–10). Illus. by Mike Cavallaro. 2010, First Second paper $15.99 (978-1-59643-279-6). Reality morphs into fantasy (and black and white into color) when Aliera dons her fencing mask and wields her new ruby-handled foil; the first installment in a series. Lexile GN460L (Rev: HB 7–8/10; LMC 8–9/10; SLJ 3/10)

767 Yuzuki, Jun. *Gakuen Prince, Vol. 1* (10–12). Trans. by Harumi Ueno. Illus. by author. 2009, Del Rey paper $10.99 (978-034550895-9). A new boy at a previously all-girls school, Azusa is pursued by packs of rapacious female students in this raunchy manga. (Rev: BLO 2/9/0; SLJ 5/09)

Historical Fiction and Foreign Lands

Ancient and Medieval History

GENERAL AND MISCELLANEOUS

768 Gormley, Beatrice. *Poisoned Honey* (8–12). 2010, Knopf $16.99 (978-0-375-85207-7). Gormley reimagines the life of Mary Magdalene before she became a follower of Jesus Christ, with anecdotes about the evolution of Matthew the tax collector plus an author's note about various versions of Mary's story. ℮ Lexile HL780L (Rev: BL 5/15/10; LMC 5–6/10; SLJ 2/10)

769 Moran, Katy. *Bloodline* (9–12). 2009, Candlewick $16.99 (978-076364083-5). Essa, who is of uncertain ancestry, must choose which king to serve and whom to fight for in this story set in Britain in the 7th century. Lexile 830L (Rev: BL 2/15/09; LMC 8–9/09; SLJ 5/1/09*)

GREECE AND ROME

770 Saylor, Steven. *Empire: The Novel of Imperial Rome* (10–12). 2010, St. Martin's $25.99 (978-0-312-38101-1). Saylor portrays the rise and fall of the Roman Empire through the life of one aristocratic family — the Pinarii — in this sequel to 2007's *Roma* that includes the Great Fire, military campaigns, and the insane whims of emperors. (Rev: BL 8/10)

MIDDLE AGES

771 Bell, Hilari. *Player's Ruse* (7–10). Series: Knight and Rogue. 2010, HarperTeen $17.99 (978-0-06-082509-6). Sir Michael and his squire Fisk visit a port town, Huckerston, in an effort to solve a maritime mystery and perhaps woo the fair Rosamund. Lexile 910L (Rev: BL 12/1/09; HB 1–2/10; SLJ 1/10; VOYA 2/10)

772 Coventry, Susan. *The Queen's Daughter* (9–12). 2010, Henry Holt $16.99 (978-0-8050-8992-9). Set in 12th-century Europe, this novel focuses on the life of Joan, daughter of Henry II of England and Eleanor Aquitaine, and provides lots of details of court life and the expectations of a princess of the time. Lexile 690L (Rev: LMC 8–9/10; SLJ 7/10)

773 Grant, K. M. *Blue Flame* (7–10). Series: Perfect Fire. 2008, Walker $16.99 (978-080279694-3). Young lovers Raimon and Yolanda's religious differences suddenly become cause for conflict when a powerful beacon of Christ reappears in 13th-century France. Lexile 890L (Rev: BL 10/15/08*; HB 11–12/08; LMC 1–2/09; SLJ 12/08; VOYA 2/09)

774 Hatcher, John. *The Black Death: A Personal History* (10–12). 2008, Da Capo $27.50 (9780306815713). In this fictional story rooted in fact, the Black Death is ravaging feudal Walsham, England, and its residents speculate about God and eternity as they struggle to bury their dead and carry on with life. **e** (Rev: BL 6/1–15/08)

775 Jinks, Catherine. *Babylonne* (8–12). 2008, Candlewick $18.99 (978-076363650-0). Sixteen-year-old Babylonne, daughter of Pagan Kidrouk, escapes her arranged marriage to an old man by teaming up with a priest in a daring journey through the 13th-century French countryside. (Rev: BL 10/15/08; HB 1–2/09; LMC 3–4/09; SLJ 12/08; VOYA 2/09)

776 McKenzie, Nancy. *Guinevere's Gamble* (6–10). Series: Chrysalis Queen Quartet. 2009, Knopf/Borzoi $16.99 (978-0-375-84346-4); LB $19.99 (978-0-375-94346-1). In the second installment in the series, Guinevere, 13, uses her wit to battle Morgan le Fey's conniving, sinister nature as she progresses toward maturity and eventual queendom. **e** Lexile 780L (Rev: SLJ 10/09; VOYA 10/09)

777 Reeve, Philip. *Here Lies Arthur* (7–10). 2008, Scholastic $17.99 (978-0-545-09334-7). The story of King Arthur is told from the viewpoint of young Gwyna, a peasant girl given shelter by Myrddin, the Merlin figure. (Rev: BL 8/08*; LMC 3–4/09*)

Africa

778 Badoe, Adwoa. *Between Sisters* (8–12). 2010, Groundwood $18.95 (978-0-88899-996-2); paper $12.95 (978-0-88899-997-9). Sixteen-year-old Ghanaian Gloria dreams of escaping a life of illiteracy, poverty, and AIDS in this poignant story, eventually befriending a young doctor who teaches her to read. (Rev: BL 10/1/10; HB 11–12/10; SLJ 10/1/10; VOYA 12/10)

779 Combres, Élisabeth. *Broken Memory: A Novel of Rwanda* (9–12). Trans. by Shelley Tanaka. 2009, Groundwood $17.95 (978-0-88899-892-7). Inspired by interviews with survivors and narrated by 14-year-old Emma, who was just 5 when she witnessed the murder of her mother by Hutu soldiers, this fictionalized account of the 1994 Rwanda genocide and its aftermath recounts the young woman's struggle to come to terms with her traumatic past and move forward with her life. Lexile 890L (Rev: BL 9/1/09; LMC 11–12/09; SLJ 12/09)

780 Mankell, Henning. *Shadow of the Leopard* (10–12). Trans. from Swedish by Anna Paterson. 2009, Annick $19.95 (978-1-55451-200-3); paper $10.95 (978-1-55451-199-0). Sofia, last seen in *Secrets in the Fire* (2003) when she had lost her legs in a landmine ac-

cident, is now married with three children and living in a Mozambique village; her discovery that her husband Armando is having an affair sets off a chain of events. (Rev: BL 12/1/09*; SLJ 12/09)

781 Naidoo, Beverley. *Burn My Heart* (7–12). 2009, Amistad $15.99 (978-006143297-2); LB $16.89 (978-006143298-9). In the turbulent Kenya of the 1950s, the tenuous friendship of a privileged white boy and a disenfranchised black boy — whose family has been accused of arson — unravels against a dramatic backdrop of prejudice and racial inequality. Lexile 740L (Rev: BL 10/1/08*; LMC 8–9/09; SLJ 2/1/09*; VOYA 4/09)

782 Oron, Judie. *Cry of the Giraffe* (9–12). 2010, Annick $21.95 (978-1-55451-272-0); paper $12.95 (978-1-55451-271-3). Thirteen-year-old Wuditu and her Ethiopian Jewish family travel to Sudan in hopes of finding a way to get to Israel but Wuditu is separated from her family and must return to Ethiopia alone, where she becomes a slave; a grim story that mirrors the experiences of many in the 1980s. (Rev: BLO 10/21/10; SLJ 12/1/10)

783 Sabatini, Irene. *The Boy Next Door* (11–12). 2009, Little, Brown $23.99 (978-031604993-1). Sabatini tells a story set in Zimbabwe of a black girl and white boy who become attached despite their differences and separate only to reunite several years later; for mature readers. ∩ **e** (Rev: BL 9/15/09)

Asia and the Pacific

784 Bobis, Merlinda. *The Solemn Lantern Maker* (10–12). 2009, Delta paper $14 (978-0-385-34113-4). Life is cheap in the slums of Manila, and when 6-year-old Noland brings home an American woman who has been shot, he soon finds himself suffering at the hands of his own government. **e** (Rev: SLJ 12/09)

785 Busfield, Andrea. *Born Under a Million Shadows* (11–12). 2010, Holt paper $14 (978-080509061-1). In Kabul after the fall of the Taliban, 11-year-old Fawad's life changes after his mother gets a job working for three Americans; for mature readers. (Rev: BL 2/1–15/10; SLJ 2/10)

786 Doshi, Tishani. *The Pleasure Seekers* (11–12). 2010, Bloomsbury paper $15 (978-160819277-9). This saga follows three generations of the Patel family, who live in Madras, India, as they deal with challenges including cross-cultural marriage and leaving home to study in England; for mature readers. **e** (Rev: BL 9/1/10)

787 Feiyu, Bi. *Three Sisters* (11–12). 2010, Houghton $24 (978-015101364-7). In Communist China in the 1970s and 1980s three sisters from a small village use different strategies to escape from their confining boundaries; for mature, advanced readers. (Rev: BL 7/10)

788 Finn, Mary. *Anila's Journey* (9–12). 2008, Candlewick $16.99 (978-076363916-7). Talented 14-year-old orphan Anila — half Indian, half Irish — lands a job aboard a naturalist's river expedition and forges a sense of identity and belonging as she faces down sexist taunting in this tale set in 18th-century India. (Rev: BL 10/1/08; LMC 3–4/09; SLJ 1/1/09; VOYA 2/09)

789 Foxlee, Karen. *The Anatomy of Wings* (9–12). 2009, Knopf $16.99 (978-037585643-3); LB $19.99 (978-037595643-0). Jennifer searches for answers about her older sister's death and her own losses in this lyrical story set in Australia in the 1980s; for sophisticated readers. ℮ Lexile 710L (Rev: BL 1/1–15/09*; HB 3–4/09; LMC 5–6/09; SLJ 7/1/09; VOYA 4/09)

790 Frazier, Angie. *Everlasting* (8–10). 2010, Scholastic $17.99 (978-0-545-11473-8). In 1885 independent-minded 17-year-old Camille sets off across Australia in search of her long-lost mother, whose existence her father revealed before the shipwreck that killed him. ℮ Lexile 790L (Rev: LMC 10/10; SLJ 9/1/10; VOYA 6/10)

791 Guo, Xiaolu. *Twenty Fragments of a Ravenous Youth* (11–12). Illus. 2008, Doubleday $22.95 (978-038552592-3). Fenfang trades the isolation of her small village for Beijing, where she encounters violence, resentment, and poverty as she struggles to make a living; for mature readers. ℮ (Rev: BL 7/08)

792 Herrick, Steven. *Cold Skin* (8–12). 2009, Front Street $18.95 (978-159078572-0). The murder of a pretty girl sets an Australian town on edge in this story set just after World War II. (Rev: BL 4/15/09; SLJ 5/1/09)

793 Howell, Simmone. *Everything Beautiful* (10–12). 2008, Bloomsbury $16.99 (978-159990042-1). Rebellious 16-year-old Riley escapes from her despised Christian summer camp — along with paraplegic Dylan — for a vision quest in the Australian desert in this tough-talking first-person narrative. ℮ (Rev: BL 10/1/08; LMC 3–4/09; SLJ 1/1/09)

794 Kadohata, Cynthia. *A Million Shades of Gray* (7–12). 2010, Simon & Schuster $16.99 (978-1-4169-1883-7). In 1975 Vietnam, Y'Tin, 13, survives a massacre and is able to find his favorite elephant, Lady, and take her deep into the jungle, but the stress of this flight lingers with him for years. ℮ Lexile 700L (Rev: BL 12/1/09; SLJ 3/10; VOYA 2/10)

795 Kim, Eugenia. *The Calligrapher's Daughter* (11–12). Illus. 2009, Holt $26 (978-0-8050-8912-7). In the early part of the 20th century, during the brutal Japanese occupation of Korea, a young woman's life reflects the tumultuous political and social atmosphere of her homeland after she flees an arranged marriage; for mature readers. (Rev: BL 7-09; SLJ 12/09)

796 Kirino, Natsuo. *Real World* (11–12). Trans. by Philip Gabriel. 2008, Knopf $22.95 (978-030726757-3). Four teenage girls struggling through summer cramming classes in suburban Tokyo are inexplicably sympathetic toward a matricidal boy named Toshi in this dark coming-of-age story. ℮ (Rev: BL 7/08*; SLJ 12/08)

797 Knight, Dominic. *Disco Boy* (10–12). 2010, IPG/Bantam $22.95 (978-174166626-7). Paul is a self-conscious, 25-year-old Australian DJ and law school grad, still living with his parents and looking for love in this funny, touching novel about finding one's place in the world. (Rev: BL 2/1/10)

798 McKay, Sharon E. *Thunder over Kandahar* (7–12). Photos by Rafal Gerszak. 2010, Annick LB $21.95 (978-1-55451-267-6); paper $12.95 (978-1-55451-266-9). Two Afghan teens, Yasmine and Tamanna, are from very different backgrounds but become friends as they flee the Taliban. ∩ (Rev: BL 12/1/10; SLJ 12/1/10)

799 Manivong, Laura. *Escaping the Tiger* (9–12). 2010, HarperCollins $15.99 (978-0-06-166177-8). Twelve-year-old Vonlai Sirivong and his family escape from Communist Laos in 1982 only to find new miseries in a UN refugee camp in Thailand; based on experiences of the author's husband. Lexile 750L (Rev: BL 1/1/10; LMC 5–6/10; SLJ 3/10)

800 Marchetta, Melina. *Jellicoe Road* (9–12). 2008, HarperTeen $17.99 (978-006143183-8); LB $18.89 (978-006143184-5). Seventeen-year-old Taylor leads the Underground Community — a student faction that battles the Cadets (led by the attractive Jonah) and the Townies — and hopes to unlock her mother's secret identity in this melodramatic tale that combines mystery and romance and is infused with its Australian environment. ∩ ℮ Lexile 820L (Rev: BL 11/1/08; HB 11–12/08; SLJ 12/08; VOYA 12/08)

801 Millard, Glenda. *A Small Free Kiss in the Dark* (7–10). 2010, Holiday House $16.95 (978-0-8234-2264-7). When war strikes unexpectedly, four unlikely allies — 12-year-old runaway Skip, homeless man Billy, 6-year-old Max, and teen mother Tia — flee their Australian city. Lexile 840L (Rev: BL 3/1/10; LMC 10/10; SLJ 3/10)

802 Mohan, Suruchi. *Divine Music* (11–12). 2009, Bayeux paper $19.95 (978-189741106-3). In 1970s India a young music student becomes aware of the double-standard imposed on women in her culture when she finds herself romantically involved with her married music teacher; for mature readers. (Rev: BLO 10/1/09)

803 Rippin, Sally. *Chenxi and the Foreigner* (10–12). 2009, Annick $21.95 (978-155451173-0); paper $10.95 (978-155451172-3). Anna visits China in 1989 and has an affair that opens her eyes to the Chinese government's reach and power over its citizens. (Rev: BL 4/15/09; SLJ 7/1/09)

Europe and the Middle East

804 Abi-Ezzi, Nathalie. *A Girl Made of Dust* (10–12). 2009, Grove $24 (978-080211895-0). Set in Lebanon during the Israeli invasion, this story of war is told from the perspective of 9-year-old Christian Maronite Ruba, who has trouble understanding the reasons for the upheaval. ℮ (Rev: BL 5/1/09)

805 Almond, David. *Raven Summer* (7–12). 2009, Delacorte $16.99 (978-0-385-73806-4); LB $19.99 (978-0-385-90715-6). War and violence are at the heart of this novel set in northern England during the Iraq War, in which teenage Liam copes with an abandoned child, a Liberian refugee, and a prejudiced bully. ℮ Lexile HL480L (Rev: BL 9/15/09*; HB 11–12/09; LMC 11–12/09; SLJ 12/09; VOYA 12/09)

806 Banks, Iain. *The Crow Road* (11–12). 2008, MacAdam/Cage $25.00 (978-1-59692-306-5). Young, self-involved Prentice McHoan of Glasgow searches for answers to his life questions about love, family, and religion in this often humorous novel suitable for mature readers. ∩ (Rev: BL 8/08)

807 Baratz-Logsted, Lauren. *The Education of Bet* (8–11). 2010, Houghton $16 (978-0-547-22308-7). In 19th-century England 16-year-old Elizabeth poses as her brother Will, who has joined the army, and takes his place at boarding school, hoping to gain an education but also facing quite a few challenges. (Rev: BL 5/1/10; SLJ 12/1/10)

808 Baratz-Logsted, Lauren. *The Twin's Daughter* (7–11). 2010, Bloomsbury $16.99 (978-1-59990-513-6). Thirteen-year-old Lucy Sexton's peaceful, privileged life in Victorian London is upset when her mother's identical twin sister turns up, starting a series of events that ends in murder. ℮ Lexile 910L (Rev: BL 9/1/10; LMC 10/10; SLJ 12/1/10; VOYA 12/10)

809 Barratt, Mark. *Joe Rat* (7–10). 2009, Eerdmans paper $9 (978-0-8028-5356-1). In 19th-century London orphan Joe escapes his bleak future in the sewers by choosing to trust his new friend Bess Farleigh and a madman who gives the two sanctuary. (Rev: HB 1–2/10; SLJ 10/09)

810 Baugh, Carolyn. *The View from Garden City* (11–12). 2008, Forge $24.95 (978-076531657-8). In this stereotype-busting novel, the often heartbreaking story of arranged marriage and female circumcision in the Islamic world is told through the stories of six Egyptian women; for mature readers. ℮ (Rev: BL 7/08)

811 Benjamin, Melanie. *Alice I Have Been* (11–12). 2010, Delacorte $25 (978-0-385-34413-5). This fictionalized account of the life of Alice Liddell Hargreaves, the young girl who served as the inspiration for Lewis Carroll's Alice, recounts her childhood experiences with the author and the impact that relationship had on the rest of her life; for mature readers. (Rev: SLJ 2/10)

812 Bronsky, Alina. *Broken Glass Park* (11–12). Trans. by Tim Mohr. 2010, Europa paper $15 (978-193337296-9). In this fast-paced novel translated from German, Russian-born 17-year-old Sacha, who is now living in the projects in Berlin, cares for her siblings and plots revenge after her stepfather murders her mother; for mature readers. (Rev: BLO 2/4/10)

813 Burgis, Stephanie. *A Most Improper Magick* (6–10). Series: Unladylike Adventures of Kat Stephenson. 2010, Simon & Schuster $16.99 (978-1-4169-9447-3). Romance, historical fiction, literary allusions, and humor are interwoven in this story, set in England in the early 19th century, about 12-year-old Kat who seeks to use her magic powers to help her siblings. ℮ Lexile 740L (Rev: BL 2/15/10; LMC 11–12/10; SLJ 12/10)

814 Cadnum, Michael. *Peril on the Sea* (7–10). 2009, Farrar $16.95 (978-037435823-5). Sherwin, an 18-year-old crew member on Captain Fletcher's *Vixen,* is charged with recording the captain's memoirs as they fight the Spanish Armada in 1588. (Rev: BL 4/15/09; VOYA 10/09)

815 Carter, Anne Laurel. *The Shepherd's Granddaughter* (7–12). 2008, Groundwood $17.95 (978-0-88899-902-3). Palestinian Amani, 15, witnesses the heartbreak and destruction of displacement firsthand in this story of the volatile Israeli-Palestinian conflict. ℮ (Rev: BLO 10/7/08; LMC 5–6/09; SLJ 12/08)

816 Collins, Pat Lowery. *Hidden Voices: The Orphan Musicians of Venice* (8–10). 2009, Candlewick $17.99 (978-076363917-4). Set in an orphanage where composer Antonio Vivaldi teaches, this story is about three of his young students — Anetta, Rosalba, and Luisa — and their differing aspirations. Lexile 1040L (Rev: BL 4/15/09; HB 7–8/09; LMC 8–9/09; SLJ 5/09; VOYA 6/09)

817 Cooper, Michelle. *A Brief History of Montmaray* (7–10). 2009, Knopf/Borzoi $16.99 (978-0-375-85864-2); LB $19.99 (978-0-375-95864-9). On the invented island nation of Montmaray in 1936, Sophie FitzOsborne, niece to the rather nutty king, lives in a castle with her family and starts a diary in which she records the struggle to escape Nazi domination; romance, conspiracy, ghosts, murder — they're all here. ∩ ℮ Lexile 1000L (Rev: BL 9/15/09*; HB 11–12/09; LMC 10/09; SLJ 12/09; VOYA 4/10)

818 Crowley, Suzanne. *The Stolen One* (8–12). 2009, Greenwillow $17.99 (978-006123200-8); LB $18.89 (978-006123201-5). Could Kat, an orphan, really be Mary Seymour, the daughter of Katherine Parr and Thomas Seymour? This tale of romance and court intrigue, set in Elizabethan England, is full of historical detail. Lexile HL740L (Rev: BL 5/1/09; HB 7–8/09; SLJ 8/09; VOYA 4/09)

819 Cummins, Jeanine. *The Outside Boy* (10–12). 2010, NAL paper $15 (978-045122948-9). Family secrets begin to spill out after young Christy's Grandda dies,

51

leaving Christy to ponder his identity in this evocative, detailed Irish story about the Pavee, a nomadic group of gypsies. **e** (Rev: BL 5/15/10*)

820 Dent, Grace. *Diary of a Chav* (8–11). 2008, Little, Brown $16.99 (978-031603483-8). Fifteen-year-old Shiraz is already a bit of a trouble-maker when things go awry both at home and with her friends. **e** Lexile 1090L (Rev: BLO 3/16/09; SLJ 12/08; VOYA 12/08)

821 Dent, Grace. *Posh and Prejudice* (10–12). 2009, Little, Brown paper $7.99 (978-0-31603-484-5). In this humorous sequel to *Diary of a Chav* (2008), British teen Shiraz is now in the 6th form at school and finds herself caught between the limited opportunities afforded by her working-class upbringing and the equally unappealing prospect of attending college. **e** Lexile 1160L (Rev: BLO 10/27/09; SLJ 12/09; VOYA 2/10)

822 Donovan, Anne. *Being Emily* (11–12). 2010, Canongate $12.95 (978-184767125-7). With Emily Brontë as a role model, teenage artist Fiona navigates the prickly drama of grief, ungrateful siblings, and a gorgeous crush in working-class Glasgow; for mature readers. (Rev: BL 7/10)

823 Dunlap, Susanne. *Anastasia's Secret* (8–11). 2010, Bloomsbury $16.99 (978-1-59990-420-7). The Russian Revolution is on the horizon as young Anastasia falls in love with one of the royal guards; historical details add to this story of doomed romance. (Rev: BL 2/1/10; LMC 3–4/10; SLJ 3/10)

824 Dunlap, Susanne. *The Musician's Daughter* (8–11). 2009, Bloomsbury $16.99 (978-159990332-3). Fifteen-year-old viola virtuoso Theresa Maria gets a boost from her godfather — who conveniently turns out to be composer Franz Joseph Haydn — as she struggles to support her family after her father's murder. **e** Lexile 950L (Rev: BL 11/1/08*; LMC 5–6/09; SLJ 5/1/09; VOYA 2/09)

825 Eberstadt, Fernanda. *Rat* (11–12). 2010, Knopf $25.95 (978-030727183-9). In this gritty novel appropriate for older teens, bold-spirited 15-year-old Celia, who calls herself "Rat," lives in the south of France with her mother and an orphaned 9-year-old Algerian boy named Morgan; when her mother's new boyfriend sexually abuses the boy, Rat escapes with Morgan to London to search for the father she never knew. **e** (Rev: BL 2/1/10)

826 Elliott, Patricia. *The Pale Assassin* (7–10). 2009, Holiday House $17.95 (978-0-8234-2250-0). Pampered aristocrat Eugénie, 15, must leave behind her posh lifestyle to flee an arranged marriage and the turmoil of the French Revolution in this historical adventure full of political intrigue. Lexile 840L (Rev: BL 10/1/09*; SLJ 12/09)

827 Gill, Elizabeth. *Paradise Lane* (11–12). 2010, Severn $28.95 (978-072786832-9). When a deathbed confession by wealthy Annabel's father throws her privileged

life — and impending propitious marriage — into chaos, Annabel sets out to uncover the truth about her history; this novel set in turn-of-the-20th-century Britain is suitable for mature readers. (Rev: BL 3/15/10)

828 Gray, Keith. *Ostrich Boys* (8–12). 2010, Random LB $20.99 (978-0-375-95843-4). When Ross, 15, dies in an accident, his three best friends decide to take his ashes from England to the village of Ross in Scotland for the burial he would have wanted, encountering many challenges along the way. ∩ Lexile HL630L (Rev: BL 2/1/10; LMC 5–6/10; SLJ 2/10)

829 Gregson, Julia. *Band of Angels* (10–12). 2010, Touchstone $16 (978-143910113-1). In this adventure-filled novel, young Catherine disobeys her family to join up with Florence Nightingale's "band of angels," and encounters danger, harsh truths, and romance during the Crimean War. **e** (Rev: BL 4/15/10)

830 Hinton, Nigel. *The Road from Home* (6–10). 2009, Sourcebooks paper $13.99 (978-1-4022-2461-4). Eleven-year-old Leo leaves his native Poland in 1870 and sets out for America, encountering many adventures on the way. (Rev: BLO 12/8/09; LMC 1–2/10; SLJ 11/09)

831 Jebreal, Rula. *Miral* (11–12). Trans. by John Cullen. 2010, Penguin paper $15 (978-014311619-6). This complex and thoughtful novel follows the life of Miral, a young woman growing up in a West Bank orphanage after the 1948 war, and provides a human perspective on the Arab-Israeli conflict; for mature readers. (Rev: BLO 7/10)

832 Jiji, Jessica. *Sweet Dates in Basra* (10–12). 2010, Avon paper $14.99 (978-006168930-7). Iraqi Jew Sharif acquires an ill-fated fascination with Kathmiya, a traditional Muslim girl seeking the safety of an arranged marriage in WWII-era Iraq, where the shadow of Hitler adds to the suspense. ∩ **e** (Rev: BL 5/1/10)

833 Jocelyn, Marthe. *Folly* (8–12). 2010, Random $15.99 (978-0-385-73846-0). In alternating sequences set in late-19th-century London, this book tells the stories of homeless, unmarried Mary Finn and of the son she must send to the Foundling Hospital so that he will have a chance for a decent future. Lexile 850L (Rev: BL 4/15/10; HB 5–6/10; LMC 8–9/10; SLJ 7/10)

834 Kirkwood, Gwen. *Heart of the Home* (11–12). 2011, Severn $28.95 (978-072786963-0). A Scottish dairy farm provides the setting for this story about young Avril, who must give up her dreams of university education to return to the farm, and her love for Dean, whose mother is intent on breaking up their relationship; for mature readers. (Rev: BLO 1/26/11)

835 Klein, Lisa. *Lady Macbeth's Daughter* (7–12). 2009, Bloomsbury $16.99 (978-1-59990-347-7). This re-imagining of Shakespeare's *Macbeth* is delivered in alternating chapters by Lady Macbeth and Albia, Macbeth's banished daughter. **e** Lexile 730L (Rev: BL 8/09; LMC 11–12/09; SLJ 12/09; VOYA 2/10)

836 Kolosov, Jacqueline. *A Sweet Disorder* (7–12). 2009, Hyperion $16.99 (978-1-4231-1245-7). Sixteen-year-old seamstress Miranda hopes to avoid an unfavorable arranged marriage by winning the favor of Queen Elizabeth I. Lexile 1080L (Rev: SLJ 12/09; VOYA 12/09)

837 Lasky, Kathryn. *Ashes* (6–12). 2010, Viking $16.99 (978-0-670-01157-5). In 1932 Berlin, Gabriella, 13, watches as Hitler's rise affects society, she is pressured to join the Hitler Youth, her sister dates a Nazi, and her astrophysicist father helps his friend Einstein. ℮ Lexile 770L (Rev: BL 1/1/10*; HB 3–4/10; SLJ 2/10; VOYA 4/10)

838 Levine, Anna. *Freefall* (7–12). 2008, Greenwillow $16.99 (978-006157654-6); LB $17.89 (978-006157656-0). Eighteen-year-old Aggie is determined to do her compulsory service in the Israeli army as a soldier, not stuck in an office job, in this apolitical story with a touch of romance. ℮ Lexile HL600L (Rev: BL 10/15/08; HB 1–2/09; SLJ 1/1/09)

839 Libby, Alisa M. *The King's Rose* (8–11). 2009, Dutton $17.99 (978-052547970-3). A well-written account of the tragic life of Catherine Howard, the doomed fifth wife of King Henry VIII, full of court intrigue. ℮ Lexile HL810L (Rev: BL 3/1/09; LMC 5–6/09; SLJ 5/1/09; VOYA 6/09)

840 Maccoll, Michaela. *Prisoners in the Palace: How Victoria Became Queen with the Help of Her Maid, a Reporter, and a Scoundrel* (7–12). 2010, Chronicle $16.99 (978-0-8118-7300-0). Liza Hastings, a 17-year-old orphan, finds work as a lady's maid to 16-year-old Princess Victoria in 1835, the year before Victoria becomes queen, and helps her employer navigate the ins and outs of court life. (Rev: LMC 1/2/11; SLJ 12/1/10*)

841 McGowan, Anthony. *The Knife that Killed Me* (10–12). 2010, Delacorte LB $19.99 (978-0-385-90716-3). In a depressed area of Leeds, England, Paul Vardeman is struggling to find his place in his school's social structure and finds himself seduced by the power of a knife handed to him by a gang leader. ℮ Lexile HL720L (Rev: BL 3/15/10*; LMC 8–9/10; SLJ 6/10)

842 Madoc, Gwen. *Keeping Secrets* (11–12). 2008, Severn $27.95 (978-072786667-7). In the 1930s in Wales two young women, first cousins, fall in love with the same forbidden man and the repercussions reveal many hidden family secrets; for mature readers. ♫ (Rev: BL 9/1/08)

843 Masson, Sophie. *The Madman of Venice* (7–10). 2010, Delacorte $17.99 (978-0-385-73843-9). In the early 17th century young Ned travels to Venice with his employer and his daughter Celia; there they investigate piracy and a disappearance as the two young people fall for each other. Lexile 740L (Rev: BLO 7/19; LMC 11–12/10; SLJ 8/10; VOYA 12/10)

844 Meyer, Carolyn. *The True Adventures of Charley Darwin* (9–12). 2009, Houghton $17.00 (978-015206194-4). This fictionalized, first-person account of the early years of Charles Darwin offers romance, humor, and adventure as well as details of his scientific interests. Lexile 1060L (Rev: BL 1/1–15/09; SLJ 1/1/09; VOYA 4/09)

845 Mosse, Kate. *The Winter Ghosts* (10–12). 2011, Putnam $24.95 (978-039915715-8). Freddie Watson is touring the French Pyrenees while recovering from the death of his brother in World War I when he comes across a quaint village with a ghostly history, and a mysterious woman who helps him heal and promptly disappears. ♫ ℮ (Rev: BL 1/1/11)

846 Nicholson, Christopher. *The Elephant Keeper* (11–12). 2009, Morrow $24.99 (978-006165160-1). In 18th-century England young Tom Page is so devoted to an elephant named Jenny that his relationship with his sweetheart suffers; for mature readers. (Rev: BL 7/09)

847 O'Brien, Anne. *The Virgin Widow* (10–12). 2010, NAL paper $15 (978-045123129-1). Set in England in the late 15th century, this historical romance is a fictionalized account of the life of Anne Neville and her romance with the man who would become Richard III, king of England. (Rev: BL 11/1/10)

848 Oldfield, Pamela. *The Birthday Present* (11–12). 2010, Severn $27.95 (978-072786839-8). In this coming-of-age novel best suited to older teens and set in 1890s London, young music-hall singer Rose Paton finds herself entangled in the dramas of the wealthy Bennley siblings, including the fatally ill Marie; for mature readers. (Rev: BLO 2/4/10)

849 Pignat, Caroline. *Greener Grass* (7–10). 2009, Red Deer paper $12.95 (978-088995402-1). In 1847, 14-year-od Kit's family is threatened by the Irish potato famine. When she loses her job as a kitchen maid, escaping to Canada may be her only hope. Lexile 650L (Rev: BL 4/15/09; LMC 5–6/09; VOYA 6/09)

850 Pitkeathley, Jill. *Cassandra and Jane: A Jane Austen Novel* (10–12). Illus. 2008, HarperCollins paper $13.95 (978-006144639-9). Cassandra Austen's voice is heard in this novel depicting her strong relationship with her sister Jane and how dreams, disappointments, and family expectations shaped their lives. ℮ (Rev: BL 9/15/08)

851 Quick, Barbara. *A Golden Web* (7–10). 2010, HarperCollins $16.99 (978-0-06-144887-4). In 14th-century Italy, 15-year-old Alessandra rebels against the arranged marriage that awaits her and, disguised as a boy, studies anatomy at the university. ℮ (Rev: BL 4/15/10; LMC 5–6/10; SLJ 5/10)

852 Rees, Celia. *The Fool's Girl* (8–11). 2010, Bloomsbury $16.99 (978-1-59990-486-3). Violetta and Feste go to London to retrieve from Malvolio a stolen holy relic; they meet William Shakespeare, who joins the quest and includes elements of *Twelfth Night*. **e** Lexile HL780L (Rev: BL 4/15/10; LMC 10/10; SLJ 8/10; VOYA 10/10)

853 Rees, Celia. *Sovay* (7–10). 2008, Bloomsbury $16.99 (978-159990203-6). In this fictional tale rooted in history, beautiful 17-year-old Sovay abandons her pastime as a highwayman and becomes caught up in the danger and intrigue surrounding the French Revolution as she endeavors to clear her father's name. ⌒ **e** Lexile 810L (Rev: BLO 11/6/08; LMC 1–2/09; SLJ 10/1/08; VOYA 8/08)

854 Reynolds, Abigail. *Mr. Darcy's Obsession* (11–12). 2010, Sourcebooks paper $14.99 (978-1-4022-4092-8). This "alternate-history" Austen story explores what might have happened to Elizabeth Bennett and Darcy had Elizabeth's father died; for mature readers. **e** (Rev: BL 9/1/10)

855 Robert, Na'ima B. *From Somalia, with Love* (7–10). 2009, Frances Lincoln $15.95 (978-184507831-7); paper $7.95 (978-184507832-4). Safia, a 14-year-old Muslim girl, has grown up in East London and finds her whole life changing when her father arrives from Somalia after a 12-year absence with different expectations. (Rev: BL 7/09; SLJ 7/1/09)

856 Rosoff, Meg. *The Bride's Farewell* (11–12). 2009, Viking $24.95 (978-0-670-02099-7). Faced with the stifling prospect of life as a housewife in mid-19th-century England, Pell's adventures begin when she runs off on her wedding day to attend the Salisbury Horse Fair; for mature readers. (Rev: BL 8/09; SLJ 12/09)

857 Seraji, Mahbod. *Rooftops of Tehran* (11–12). 2009, NAL paper $15 (978-045122681-5). Set in Iran during the Shah's regime, this is the story of young love, joy, accidental betrayal to the secret police, and heartbreak experienced by Pasha, a 17-year-old boy; for mature readers. ⌒ **e** (Rev: BL 4/15/09)

858 Sturtevant, Katherine. *The Brothers Story* (9–12). 2009, Farrar $16.99 (978-0-374-30992-3). In the 17th century, during a "Great Frost," 15-year-old Kit heads for London in hopes of finding the wherewithal to support his "simple" twin brother Christy. **e** Lexile 920L (Rev: BL 11/1/09*; HB 11–12/09; LMC 5–6/10; SLJ 1/10)

859 Thompson, Kate. *Creature of the Night* (9–12). 2009, Roaring Brook $17.95 (978-159643511-7). Bobby and his mother move from the slums of Dublin to a haunted house in the Irish countryside. Lexile HL670L (Rev: BL 4/1/09*; HB 5–6/09; SLJ 8/09; VOYA 2/10)

860 Thompson, Ricki. *City of Cannibals* (9–12). 2010, Front Street $18.95 (978-1-59078-623-9). Dell travels to London, where she falls in love with a young monk and learns to be a puppeteer in this story set in 1536. Lexile HL660L (Rev: BL 1/1/10; HB 5–6/10; LMC 8–9/10; SLJ 3/10)

861 Weyn, Suzanne. *Distant Waves: A Novel of the Titanic* (8–11). 2009, Scholastic $17.99 (978-054508572-4). Spiritualism and science intersect in this novel featuring Jane, 16-year-old daughter of a spirit medium, and inventor Nikola Tesla, who are traveling aboard the *Titanic*. Lexile 790L (Rev: BL 4/15/09*; LMC 10/09; SLJ 9/09)

862 Wiseman, Eva. *Puppet* (7–12). 2009, Tundra $17.95 (978-088776828-6). A Jewish boy is forced into giving false witness in this story based on an actual case of anti-Semitic violence in Hungary in 1883. **e** Lexile HL660L (Rev: BL 2/15/09; SLJ 3/1/09)

Latin America and Canada

863 Hearn, Julie. *Hazel* (9–12). 2009, Simon & Schuster $17.99 (978-1-4169-2504-0). Having disgraced her upper-class family by participating in a suffragist protest in 1913 London, Hazel Mull-Dare, 13, is sent into exile on a Caribbean sugar plantation where she is forced to confront the racial inequities that have allowed her family to enjoy generations of privilege. **e** (Rev: BL 9/1/09; HB 11–12/09; SLJ 12/09; VOYA 2/10)

864 Hiatt, Shelby. *Panama* (10–12). 2009, Houghton $16.00 (978-054719600-8). This novel combines material on the building of the Panama Canal with an affair between a 15-year-old American girl, daughter of an engineer, and an older Spaniard named Federico who introduces her to new socioeconomic ideas and to sex. (Rev: BL 7/09; LMC 1–2/10; SLJ 12/09; VOYA 12/09)

865 Jefferson, Joanne K. *Lightning and Blackberries* (7–10). 2008, Nimbus paper $10.95 (978-155109654-4). In 1774 Nova Scotia 17-year-old Elizabeth longs for independence but knows she must settle for marriage and domesticity until she meets an Acadian woman who widens her horizons. **e** (Rev: BLO 11/11/08; VOYA 10/08)

866 Landman, Tanya. *The Goldsmith's Daughter* (9–12). 2009, Candlewick $16.99 (978-076364219-8). Itacate, an Aztec girl, faces many challenges even before the arrival of the Spanish. (Rev: BL 7/09*; LMC 11–12/09)

867 Montoya, Maceo. *The Scoundrel and the Optimist* (11–12). 2009, Bilingual $28 (978-193101065-8); paper $18 (978-193101067-2). When abusive Filastro is nearly killed in a skirmish with police and gangsters — and undergoes a personal transformation, his son Edmund nurses him back to physical and emotional health; the humor balances the violence in this coming-of-age tale suitable for mature readers. (Rev: BL 12/1/09)

868 Resau, Laura, and Maria Virginia Farinango. *The Queen of Water* (8–12). 2011, Delacorte $16.99 (978-038573897-2); LB $19.99 (978-038590761-3). Virginia, 7, is sent by her poor Quechua Indian family to be an indentured servant to a mestizo family; there she learns some skills and puts up with a certain amount of abuse, but can she ever go back home? (Rev: BL 2/15/11*; HB 7–8/11; SLJ 6/11)

869 Weber, Lori. *If You Live Like Me* (7–10). 2009, Lobster $14.95 (978-189755012-0). After a series of moves, Cheryl learns to love Newfoundland and her new neighbor, Jim, only to learn that she can finally return to Montreal. (Rev: BL 4/15/09; SLJ 6/1/09)

Polar Regions

870 Farr, Richard. *Emperors of the Ice: A True Story of Disaster and Survival in the Antarctic, 1910–13* (10–12). Illus. 2008, Farrar $19.95 (978-037431975-5). In this journal-style fiction rooted in history, Apsley Cherry-Garrard, one of the men in Robert Scott's ill-fated Antarctic expedition, provides a glimpse into their struggle for survival. ⌒ Lexile 1050L (Rev: BL 9/1/08; HB 11–12/08; SLJ 12/08; VOYA 8/08)

United States

NATIVE AMERICANS

871 Landman, Tanya. *I Am Apache* (8–12). 2008, Candlewick $17.99 (978-076363664-7). When 14-year-old Apache Siki witnesses her brother's death at the hands of brutal Mexican raiders in the late 19th century, she vows to avenge him by earning her stripes as a daring, if unlikely, warrior. Lexile 860L (Rev: BL 10/1/08; LMC 3–4/09; SLJ 8/08; VOYA 12/08)

COLONIAL PERIOD AND FRENCH AND INDIAN WARS

872 Hemphill, Stephanie. *Wicked Girls: A Novel of the Salem Witch Trials* (7–12). 2010, HarperCollins LB $16.99 (978-0-06-185328-9). Three of the Salem accusers relate the story of the false testimony and resulting deaths in alternate verse voices. e Lexile 700L (Rev: BL 6/1/10*; HB 7–8/10; LMC 10/10; SLJ 8/10; VOYA 10/10)

873 Steinmetz, Karen. *The Mourning Wars* (7–10). 2010, Roaring Brook $18.99 (978-1-59643-290-1). In 1704 young Eunice Williams is seized by Mohawk Indians and adopted by Atironta and Kenniontie, whose daughter has died; she soon adjusts to her new life and must make a difficult choice when her father finally comes looking for her. Based on a true story. e Lexile 910L (Rev: BL 6/1/10; LMC 11–12/10; SLJ 11/1/10; VOYA 10/10)

REVOLUTIONARY PERIOD AND THE YOUNG NATION (1775–1809)

874 Anderson, Laurie Halse. *Chains* (7–10). 2008, Simon & Schuster $16.99 (978-141690585-1). Hoping to gain her freedom — and learn the whereabouts of her missing sister — slave Isabel decides to spy for the

rebels in American Revolution-era New York City. ⌒ e Lexile 780L (Rev: BL 11/1/08*; HB 11–12/09; LMC 1–2/09; SLJ 10/1/08; VOYA 10/08)

NINETEENTH CENTURY TO THE CIVIL WAR (1809–1861)

875 Noble, Diane. *The Sister Wife* (11–12). 2010, Avon paper $12.99 (978-006196222-6). In this evenhanded look at the beginnings of polygamy set in the mid-19th century, Noble tells the story of Mary Rose, a recent covert to Mormonism, who is dismayed when her husband is advised to take a second wife; for mature readers. (Rev: BL 6/1–15/10)

876 Preus, Margi. *Heart of a Samurai: Based on the True Story of Nakahama Manjiro* (7–11). Illus. 2010, Abrams $15.95 (978-0-8109-8981-8). This is a fictionalized version of the true story of Manjiro, the 14-year-old Japanese boy rescued from the sea by an American whaling ship in 1841; he becomes known as the first Japanese to set foot in the United States and must make many adjustments. (Rev: BL 7/10*; HB 9–10/10; LMC 1–2/11; SLJ 9/1/10*)

877 Salerni, Dianne K. *We Hear the Dead* (8–11). 2010, Sourcebooks paper $12.99 (978-1-4022-3092-9). Explorer Elisha Kane falls in love with beautiful "spiritualist" Maggie Fox in this story based on actual events in the mid-19th century. e Lexile 1070L (Rev: BL 4/15/10; LMC 8–9/10; SLJ 6/10)

878 Tinti, Hannah. *The Good Thief* (11–12). 2008, Dial $25.00 (978-038533745-8). Despairing orphan Ren's purported long-lost younger brother turns out to be a con-man in this darkly comedic book set in 19th-century New England; for mature readers. ⌒ e (Rev: BL 6/1–15/08*)

THE CIVIL WAR (1861–1865)

879 Brown, Linda Beatrice. *Black Angels* (9–12). 2009, Putnam $16.99 (978-0-399-25030-9). Toward the end of the Civil War, three children — two black and one white — become unlikely companions and bond over the violence they've witnessed. e Lexile 840L (Rev: BL 9/1/09; LMC 11–12/09; SLJ 1/10)

880 Gourley, Catherine. *The Horrors of Andersonville: Life and Death Inside a Civil War Prison* (9–12). 2010, Lerner LB $38.60 (978-0-7613-4212-0). Gourley draws on primary sources including soldiers' memoirs to tell the story of the Confederate prisoner-of-war camp and the dreadful conditions there. Lexile 990L (Rev: BL 3/1/10; LMC 8–9/10; SLJ 4/10)

881 Klein, Lisa. *Two Girls of Gettysburg* (7–10). 2008, Bloomsbury $16.99 (978-159990105-3). The voices of two young women — quiet, dutiful Lizzie and frivolous Rosanna — are woven together to tell the story of the Battle of Gettysburg. Lexile 830L (Rev: BL 9/1/08; SLJ 11/1/08; VOYA 12/08)

882 Myers, Walter Dean. *Riot* (7–12). 2009, Egmont USA $16.99 (978-1-60684-000-9); LB $19.99 (978-1-60684-042-9). Set in New York City in the summer of 1863, this story presented in screenplay format follows Claire, a biracial teen who lives amidst the chaos, ethnic tension, and anxiety of the Civil War and the riots that took place when Irish immigrants protested the draft. ∩ ℮ (Rev: BL 8/09*; LMC 11–12/09; SLJ 9/09; VOYA 12/09)

883 Wilson, John. *Death on the River* (8–10). 2009, Orca paper $12.95 (978-1-55469-111-1). Jake, a young Union soldier, survives the horrors of Andersonville prison but then worries about the support he gets from a fellow prisoner. ℮ Lexile 890 (Rev: BL 10/15/09; LMC 1–2/10; SLJ 11/09)

WESTWARD EXPANSION AND PIONEER LIFE

884 Hemphill, Helen. *The Adventurous Deeds of Deadwood Jones* (7–12). 2008, Front Street $16.95 (978-159078637-6). Inspired by the true story of an African American cowboy, this book tells the story of Prometheus Jones, who rides a raffle-won horse away from racist-riddled Tennessee to adventure in the Wild West. ℮ Lexile 720L (Rev: BL 10/1/08; HB 1–2/09; LMC 1–2/09; SLJ 12/08)

885 Holt, Kimberly Willis. *The Water Seeker* (7–12). 2010, Henry Holt $16.99 (978-0-8050-8020-9). Young Amos travels the Oregon Trail with his father and takes on adult responsibilities out of necessity. Lexile 730L (Rev: BL 8/15/10; LMC 8–9/10; SLJ 7/10)

886 McKernan, Victoria. *The Devil's Paintbox* (8–12). 2009, Knopf $16.99 (978-037583750-0). Orphans Aiden, 15, and his younger sister Maddy face disease, death, and disasters as they travel with a wagon train from Kansas to Oregon in 1866. ℮ Lexile 740L (Rev: BL 1/1–15/09; LMC 5–6/09; SLJ 2/1/09*; VOYA 4/09)

887 Nowak, Pamela. *Choices* (11–12). 2009, Five Star $25.95 (978-159414810-1). In 1876 Miriam reluctantly leaves boarding school and returns to her military family in the Dakota Territory, where she must endure the harsh treatment of her drug-addicted mother and prejudices that stifle her independence. (Rev: BL 10/1/09*)

888 Whitson, Stephanie Grace. *Sixteen Brides* (10–12). 2010, Bethany paper $14.99 (978-076420513-2). Aghast to find they'd been promised as frontier brides, a group of women arrive on the Nebraska prairie and decide to overcome their troubled pasts by pooling their resources and building a house together. ∩ ℮ (Rev: BL 4/1/10*)

RECONSTRUCTION TO WORLD WAR I (1865–1914)

889 Davies, Jacqueline. *Lost* (7–10). 2009, Marshall Cavendish $16.99 (978-076145535-6). Sixteen-year-old Essie, who works in the Triangle Shirtwaist Factory in the early 1900s, must come to terms with losses in her life in this multilayered story. Lexile 680L (Rev: BL 3/15/09; LMC 8–9/09; SLJ 4/1/09; VOYA 8/09)

890 Hale, Marian. *The Goodbye Season* (7–10). 2009, Holt $16.99 (978-080508855-7). Sixteen-year-old Mercy Kaplan, daughter of a Texas sharecropper, struggles to make her way after her family dies in the 1918 flu epidemic. (Rev: BL 7/09; SLJ 10/09)

891 Hatcher, Robin Lee. *A Matter of Character* (11–12). Series: Sisters of Bethlehem Springs. 2010, Zondervan paper $14.99 (978-031025807-0). Daphne decides to reveal the truth — that she's been writing dime novels under a pseudonym — when she encounters a man determined to clear the reputation of one of her characters in this faith-based romance set in 1918. (Rev: BL 6/1–15/10)

892 Kephart, Beth. *Dangerous Neighbors* (8–12). 2010, Egmont USA $16.99 (978-1-60684-080-1); LB $19.99 (978-1-60684-106-8). In 1876 during the Philadelphia Centennial Exhibition 17-year-old Katherine is contemplating suicide in her grief over her twin sister's death, but the celebration itself serves to bring her out of her despondency. ℮ Lexile 930L (Rev: BL 9/1/10; LMC 1-2/11; SLJ 10/1/10)

893 LaFaye, A. *The Keening* (7–10). 2010, Milkweed $17 (978-1-57131-692-9). When 14-year-old Lyza's mother dies in the flu epidemic of 1918, her father begins acting strangely and Lyza learns that both she and her father can communicate with the dead. (Rev: BL 4/15/10; LMC 8–9/10; SLJ 6/10)

894 Napoli, Donna Jo. *Alligator Bayou* (7–10). 2009, Random $16.99 (978-038574654-0). Based on a true event — a lynching of Sicilian immigrants in Louisiana in 1899 — this novel follows young Calogero, who is shut out of both black and white society. Lexile HL430L (Rev: BL 2/15/09; LMC 8–9/09; SLJ 5/1/09; VOYA 4/09)

895 Richards, Jame. *Three Rivers Rising* (7–11). 2010, Knopf $16.99 (978-0-375-85885-7). Three characters caught up in the disaster tell their stories of survival following the 1889 Johnstown Flood. ∩ Lexile HL780L (Rev: BL 4/15/10; LMC 8–9/10; SLJ 4/10)

896 Sawyer, Kim Vogel. *In Every Heartbeat* (10–12). 2010, Bethany $19.99 (978-076420510-1); paper $14.99 (978-076420510-1). Three friends get scholarships to college in 1914, and cope with the competition, strife, and differing ambitions that opportunity brings in this novel with a Christian message. ∩ (Rev: BL 8/10)

897 Tall, Eve. *Cursing Columbus* (7–10). 2009, Cinco Puntos $16.95 (978-1-933693-59-0). In this sequel to *Double Crossing* (2005), 14-year-old Raizel and her younger brother Lemmel react in opposite ways to the challenges of being Ukrainian Jewish immigrants on the Lower East Side of Manhattan in 1908. ℮ Lexile 500L (Rev: BL 10/15/09; LMC 5–6/10; SLJ 1/10)

BETWEEN THE WARS AND THE GREAT DEPRESSION (1919–1941)

898 Bryant, Jen. *Ringside, 1925: Views from the Scopes Trial* (6–10). 2008, Knopf $15.99 (978-037584047-0); LB $18.99 (978-037594047-7). A series of first-person free-verse poems brings to life the events of the Scopes Monkey Trial and the divisive, circus-like atmosphere it brought to town as citizens debated the teaching of evolution. (Rev: BLO 10/30/08; HB 5–6/08; LMC 4–5/08; SLJ 3/08; VOYA 6/08)

899 Gabhart, Ann H. *Angel Sister* (10–12). 2011, Revell paper $14.99 (978-080073381-0). In this Christian novel set in the 1930s, young Kate, the middle child in a troubled family, rescues an abandoned 5-year-old-girl on the steps of a church. ℮ (Rev: BLO 1/26/11)

900 Luper, Eric. *Bug Boy* (8–12). 2009, Farrar $16.99 (978-0-374-31000-4). Set at the Saratoga Race Track during the Depression, this is the story of 15-year-old Jack, an apprentice jockey whose dreams of racing are almost sidetracked by shady characters and his own father's betrayal. ℮ (Rev: BL 9/1/09; SLJ 9/09)

901 Prasad, Chandra. *Breathe the Sky* (10–12). 2009, Wyatt-MacKenzie $14.99 (978-193227939-9). This novelized account of the life of famed aviator Amelia Earhart focuses on her adult years and explores her fascination with flying and the accompanying celebrity, as well as her romance with the PR man who would further her career. (Rev: BL 10/1/09)

902 Stuber, Barbara. *Crossing the Tracks* (7–12). 2010, Simon & Schuster $16.99 (978-1-4169-9703-0). In 1930s Missouri, 15-year-old Iris is sent to be a caregiver to an elderly woman and despite initial trepidation finds herself making a happy new home. ℮ Lexile 680L (Rev: BL 7/10; LMC 10/10; SLJ 8/10; VOYA 10/10)

POST WORLD WAR II UNITED STATES (1945–)

903 Beard, Jo Ann. *In Zanesville* (11–12). 2011, Little, Brown $23.99 (978-031608447-5). A witty and charming coming-of-age novel about an everyday girl struggling with friendship, family, and fitting in, set in the 1970s in small-town Illinois. ∩ (Rev: BL 3/15/11)

904 Blundell, Judy. *What I Saw and How I Lied* (8–12). 2008, Scholastic $16.99 (978-043990346-2). Fifteen-year-old Evie uncovers unsettling truths about her family while on vacation in Palm Beach in 1947. ∩ ℮ Lexile HL620L (Rev: BL 11/1/08*; SLJ 12/08; VOYA 2/09)

905 Brown, Chris Carlton. *Hoppergrass* (7–10). 2009, Holt $17.95 (978-080508879-3). This dark novel about 15-year-old Bowser's experiences in an institution for

delinquent teens is set in 1969 Virginia. Lexile 850L (Rev: BL 4/15/09; SLJ 7/1/09)

906 Cady, Jack. *Rules of '48* (11–12). 2010, Night Shade paper $14.95 (978-159780085-3). Cady portrays Louisville, Kentucky, as it was in 1948, when the town found itself in the midst of business and race-related clashes in this fictionalized memoir; for mature readers. (Rev: BL 1/1/10)

907 Gwin, Minrose. *The Queen of Palmyra* (11–12). 2010, Harper paper $14.99 (978-006184032-6). In 1960s Mississippi, neglected 11-year-old Florence is torn between her family's racist attitudes and her feelings for the black woman who raised her; for mature readers. (Rev: BL 3/15/10)

908 Hegedus, Bethany. *Between Us Baxters* (7–10). 2009, WestSide $17.95 (978-193481302-7). In late 1950s Georgia, 12-year-old Polly, from a struggling white family, and black 14-year-old Timbre Ann find their friendship threatened by the turmoil around them. Lexile 610L (Rev: BL 3/15/09; SLJ 5/1/09; VOYA 10/09)

909 Hostetter, Joyce Moyer. *Comfort* (6–10). 2009, Boyds Mills $17.95 (978-159078606-2). Ann Fay, although reluctant to leave her troubled family, goes to Warm Springs in Georgia to receive therapy for her polio. Lexile 680L (Rev: BLO 3/24/09; LMC 10/09; SLJ 5/1/09)

910 Lester, Julius. *Guardian* (9–12). 2008, Amistad $16.99 (978-006155890-0); LB $17.89 (978-006155891-7). In the South in 1946 a white man and his 14-year-old son fail to act to stop the lynching of a black man falsely accused of raping and killing a white teenager. (Rev: BL 9/15/08; HB 11–12/08; SLJ 11/1/08; VOYA 2/09)

911 Levchuk, Lisa. *Everything Beautiful in the World* (9–12). 2008, Farrar $16.95 (978-037432238-0). Emotionally numb, 17-year-old Edna escapes her mother's cancer and her father's icy neglect in the arms of her handsome though devious art teacher in this story set in 1980s New Jersey. Lexile 960L (Rev: BL 11/15/08*; SLJ 1/1/09; VOYA 8/08)

912 MacEnulty, Pat. *Picara* (10–12). 2009, Livingston LB $27 (978-160489037-2); paper $16.95 (978-160489038-9). As the turbulent 1960s draw to a close, the death of the grandmother who has raised her prompts 14-year-old Eli to flee to St. Louis where she finds herself suddenly immersed in the counterculture in which her activist father is deeply engaged. (Rev: BL 10/15/09)

913 McGuigan, Mary Ann. *Morning in a Different Place* (8–11). 2009, Front Street $17.95 (978-159078551-5). Friendship between white Fiona and black Yolanda causes problems in 1963 New York. Lexile HL710L (Rev: BL 2/1/09; LMC 8–9/09; SLJ 3/1/09; VOYA 8/09)

914 Magoon, Kekla. *The Rock and the River* (6–10). 2009, Aladdin $15.99 (978-141697582-3). Fourteen-year-old Sam considers turning to violence and the Black Panthers when peaceful attempts to gain civil rights seem to fail in this novel set in 1968 Chicago. ♫ Lexile HL550L (Rev: BL 2/1/09; LMC 8–9/09; SLJ 2/1/09)

915 Neri, G. *Yummy: The Last Days of a Southside Shorty* (8–12). Illus. by Randy DuBurke. 2010, Lee Low paper $16.95 (978-158430267-4). Yummy, an 11-year-old African American with a sweet tooth, was a gang member in Chicago in the 1990s; this graphic novel based on documented sources describes his life on the streets, his shooting of a young girl, and his death at the hands of his own gang. (Rev: BL 8/10*; HB 11–12/10; SLJ 9/10; VOYA 10/10)

916 Tucker, Todd. *Over and Under* (9–12). 2008, St. Martin's $23.95 (978-0-312-37990-2). The tight friendship between two boys growing up in 1979 Indiana is strained by a strike at their fathers' workplace in this nostalgic coming-of-age story. ♥ (Rev: BL 6/1–15/08*)

Twentieth-Century Wars

WORLD WAR I

917 Frost, Helen. *Crossing Stones* (7–12). 2009, Farrar $16.99 (978-0-374-31653-2). Siblings Muriel and Ollie and their friends Emma and Frank describe in heartfelt, evocative verse their experiences as the young men leave for World War I and Muriel and Emma take separate paths toward womanhood. ♫ (Rev: BL 10/1/09*; HB 11–12/09; LMC 11–12/09; SLJ 10/09; VOYA 10/09)

918 Lottridge, Celia Barker. *Home Is Beyond the Mountains* (7–10). 2010, Groundwood $16.95 (978-0-88899-932-0). A moving story, based on the experiences of the author's aunt, about Assyrian children who become orphaned refugees during World War I. Lexile 680L (Rev: BL 4/15/10; LMC 8–9/10; SLJ 4/10)

WORLD WAR II AND THE HOLOCAUST

919 Chapman, Fern Schumer. *Is It Night or Day?* (6–10). 2010, Farrar $17.99 (978-0-374-17744-7). In 1938, 12-year-old Edith's German Jewish parents send her to Chicago where she leads a miserable, anxious life apart from her fondness for baseball; this story is based on the life of the author's mother. ♥ (Rev: BL 2/1/10*; LMC 5–6/10; SLJ 5/10)

920 Engle, Margarita. *Tropical Secrets: Holocaust Refugees in Cuba* (7–11). 2009, Holt $16.95 (978-080508936-3). Paloma, a Cuban girl, and Daniel, a German Jew who fled to Cuba to escape the Nazis, become friends in this story told in verse. ♫ ♥ Lexile 1170L (Rev: BL 1/1–15/09; LMC 10/09; SLJ 6/1/09*; VOYA 4/09)

921 Gleitzman, Morris. *Once* (7–10). 2010, Holt $16.99 (978-0-8050-9026-0). After living in a Catholic orphanage for four years, young Felix, a Polish Jew, runs away to find his parents and experiences directly the horrors of the Holocaust. ♫ ♥ (Rev: BL 2/15/10; HB 3–4/10; SLJ 4/10)

922 Gower, Iris. *Bomber's Moon* (10–12). 2009, Severn $28.95 (978-072786765-0). Set in Britain and Germany during World War II, this novel follows teens who experience fear, romance, death, and destruction. (Rev: BLO 7/09)

923 Goyer, Tricia, and Mike Yorkey. *The Swiss Courier* (11–12). 2009, Revell paper $13.99 (978-080073336-0). Gabi Mueller, who is working for the United States as a spy, is assigned to rescue a German scientist in this fast-paced novel set in Hitler's Germany; for mature readers. (Rev: BL 10/15/09)

924 McMorris, Kristina. *Letters from Home* (11–12). 2011, Kensington paper $15 (978-075824684-4). A sweeping saga told through letters about three young women whose lives take many unexpected twists and turns as they live, love, and work during World War II; for mature readers. ♥ (Rev: BLO 1/26/11)

925 Polak, Monique. *What World Is Left* (7–12). 2008, Orca $12.95 (978-155143847-4). When 14-year-old Anneke and her Jewish family are taken from Holland to Theresienstadt, she suffers filthy, overcrowded conditions and the terror of the gas chambers while her artist father is charged with painting scenery that will make the town look hospitable to Red Cross inspectors, in this powerful book written in memoir format. (Rev: BL 12/15/08*; LMC 5–6/09; SLJ 4/09)

926 Riordan, James. *The Sniper* (9–12). 2009, Frances Lincoln paper $8.95 (978-1-84507-884-3). Teen sniper Tania Belova courageously defends Stalingrad against the invading Germans in this World War II novel based on a true story. (Rev: SLJ 1/10)

927 Smith, Sherri L. *Flygirl* (7–10). 2009, Putnam $16.99 (978-039924709-5). Even though she is black, Ida Mae manages to become a pilot in the WASP (Women Airforce Service Program) during World War II. ♥ Lexile 680L (Rev: BL 1/1–15/09*; HB 5–6/09; LMC 5–6/09; SLJ 2/1/09; VOYA 2/09)

928 Vincenzi, Penny. *Forbidden Places* (11–12). 2010, Overlook $26.95 (978-159020356-9). Set in World War II England, this saga focuses on three women and their relationships with men and their families; for mature readers. (Rev: BL 9/15/10)

929 Whitney, Kim Ablon. *The Other Half of Life* (7–10). 2009, Knopf $16.99 (978-037585219-0); LB $19.99 (978-037595219-7). This moving story of Jewish refugees in 1939 is based on the true-life experiences of those aboard the MS *St. Louis,* which was denied entry to Cuba and the United States. Lexile HL730L (Rev: BL 4/15/09; LMC 10/09; SLJ 7/1/09; VOYA 6/09)

KOREAN, VIETNAM, AND OTHER WARS

930 Burg, Ann. *All the Broken Pieces* (6–10). 2009, Scholastic $16.99 (978-054508092-7). Told in free verse, this is the story of a boy adopted from Vietnam in the 1970s and his conflicting emotions. ∩ Lexile HL680L (Rev: BL 2/15/09; HB 5–6/09; LMC 5–6/09; SLJ 5/1/09)

931 Crocker, Gareth. *Finding Jack* (10–12). 2011, St. Martin's $23.99 (978-031262172-8). This is the moving story of a U.S. army sniper who stays behind after the Vietnam War, endangering his own life to rescue an injured scouting dog. e (Rev: BL 1/1/11)

932 House, Silas. *Eli the Good* (9–12). 2009, Candlewick $16.99 (978-0-7636-4341-6). Perceptive 10-year-old Eli copes with the changing family dynamics when his war-protesting aunt clashes with his Vietnam veteran father and his mother and sister disagree in this novel set in 1976. ∩ e (Rev: BL 10/1/09; SLJ 1/10)

933 Smith, Andrew. *In the Path of Falling Objects* (10–12). 2009, Feiwel & Friends $17.99 (978-0-312-37558-4). Jonah, 16, and his younger brother Simon miss their older brother who is experiencing a miserable war in Vietnam; they take to the road and unfortunately hitch a ride with a violent killer. ∩ e Lexile 840L (Rev: BL 11/1/09; SLJ 11/09)

934 Soli, Tatjana. *The Lotus Eaters* (11–12). 2010, St. Martin's $24.99 (978-031261157-6). This novel follows the lives of two war photographers — Sam and Helen — who become involved while working in Vietnam and their separate relationships with the Vietnamese assistant Linh; for mature readers. ∩ e (Rev: BL 3/15/10)

Horror Stories and the Supernatural

935 Adams, John Joseph, ed. *By Blood We Live* (10–12). 2009, Night Shade paper $15.95 (978-1-59780-156-0). This provocative collection presents 30 vampire tales written over the past 30 years by a diverse group of authors including Anne Rice, Neil Gaiman, and Stephen King. (Rev: BL 10/15/09; SLJ 12/09)

936 Alender, Katie. *Bad Girls Don't Die* (7–10). 2009, Hyperion $15.99 (978-142310876-4). Alexis must determine why her little sister is possessed by the spirit of a child who died long ago. Lexile HL670L (Rev: BL 4/1/09; SLJ 8/09)

937 Atwater-Rhodes, Amelia. *Persistence of Memory* (7–10). 2008, Delacorte $15.99 (978-038573437-0); LB $18.99 (978-038590443-8). Sixteen-year-old Erin has been treated for schizophrenia for most of her life, but after a two-year hiatus from her alter-ego Shevaun, she discovers she isn't mentally ill at all, but entwined with the soul of a 500-year-old vampire. e Lexile 860L (Rev: BL 12/1/08; LMC 5–6/09; SLJ 2/1/09)

938 Atwater-Rhodes, Amelia. *Token of Darkness* (6–10). 2010, Delacorte $16.99 (978-0-385-73750-0). A strange spectral girl named Samantha has remained at Cooper's side since his car accident, but who is she and how can he help her in her quest for a physical presence? e Lexile 900L (Rev: BLO 11/19/10; LMC 5–6/10; SLJ 1/10)

939 Becker, Robin. *Brains: A Zombie Memoir* (11–12). 2010, Eos paper $13.99 (978-006197405-2). A troupe of zombies sets off to find the virus that caused their condition —and to end the war between the living and the undead — in this violent yet funny novel for mature readers. e (Rev: BL 6/1–15/10)

940 Block, Francesca Lia. *The Frenzy* (9–12). 2010, HarperTeen $16.99 (978-0-06-192666-2). Something happened to Liv when she was 13, and now that she is 17 she finally comes to understand that she is a werewolf and that both she and her family must learn to cope with this fact. (Rev: BL 9/1/10; SLJ 12/1/10)

941 Block, Francesca Lia. *Pretty Dead* (9–12). 2009, HarperTeen $16.99 (978-006154785-0); LB $17.89 (978-006154786-7). Vampire Charlotte is just getting close to human Jared when William, the vampire who transformed her in 1925, comes back into her life. (Rev: BL 5/15/09*; HB 1–2/10; SLJ 10/09; VOYA 10/09)

942 Bray, Libba, et al. *Vacations from Hell* (8–11). 2009, HarperTeen $16.99 (978-0-06-168873-7); paper $9.99 (978-0-06-168872-0). A collection of stories by well-known authors about teens whose vacations take scary turns. (Rev: BL 8/09; SLJ 8/09; VOYA 10/09)

943 Brewer, Heather. *Tenth Grade Bleeds* (6–10). Series: The Chronicles of Vladimir Tod. 2009, Dutton $16.99 (978-0-525-42135-1). Half-vampire Vlad, now in 10th grade in the third volume in the series, is grappling with teen angst while at the same time fighting the supernatural forces seeking to destroy him. ∩ e Lexile 820L (Rev: SLJ 9/09; VOYA 6/09)

944 Caine, Rachel. *Ghost Town* (10–12). Series: Morganville Vampires. 2010, NAL $17.99 (978-045123161-1). This installment in the vampire series finds Claire fighting to save her community after widespread memory loss creates havoc. (Rev: BL 11/1/10)

945 Chadda, Sarwat. *Devil's Kiss* (7–10). 2009, Hyperion $17.99 (978-1-4231-1999-9). Fifteen-year-old Billi SanGreal is secretly a Templar Knight in training in this complex and compelling novel that features the Angel of Death on a rampage. ∩ Lexile HL620L (Rev: BL 10/15/09; LMC 1–2/10; SLJ 11/09)

946 Connolly, John. *The Gates* (10–12). 2009, Atria $24 (978-143917263-6). Weirdness abounds this in this comedic horror-fantasy as the neighborhood's adult population is inhabited by demons who are preparing for the Great Malevolence; fortunately for 11-year-old Samuel, the hapless demon who shows up in his bedroom takes a shine to him. ∩ ℮ (Rev: BL 10/15/09)

947 Davis, Heather. *Never Cry Werewolf* (7–10). 2009, HarperTeen $16.99 (978-006134923-2). At a "brat camp," willful 16-year-old Shelby meets an attractive young werewolf named Austin Bridges III. (Rev: BL 7/09; SLJ 12/09)

948 Dunkle, Clare B. *The House of Dead Maids* (7–10). 2010, Henry Holt $15.99 (978-0-8050-9116-8). In this prequel to *Wuthering Heights,* 11-year-old Tabby arrives at the spooky Seldon House to be a nursemaid to the young Heathcliff (here called Himself) and learns about many previous housemaids who did not survive. ∩ ℮ (Rev: BL 8/10; HB 11–12/10; LMC 11–12/10; SLJ 11/1/10; VOYA 12/10)

949 Fahy, Thomas. *Sleepless* (8–11). 2009, Simon & Schuster $15.99 (978-141695901-4). Emma and her friends are sleepwalking and having horrible nightmares. Could they be responsible for the deaths of some of their classmates? Lexile 710L (Rev: BLO 5/27/09; SLJ 12/09)

950 Gibson, Marley. *The Awakening* (7–10). Series: Ghost Huntress. 2009, Harcourt paper $8.99 (978-054715093-2). Newly moved from Chicago to a tiny town in Georgia, 16-year-old Kendall finds herself part of a ghost-hunting team that seeks to free Kendall's father of a troublesome spirit. (Rev: BL 5/15/09; LMC 10/09; SLJ 6/1/09)

951 Gill, David Macinnis. *Soul Enchilada* (7–10). 2009, Greenwillow $16.99 (978-006167301-6); LB $17.89 (978-006167302-3). A quirky story in which 18-year-old Bug Smoot, whose prize possession is a 1958 Cadillac Biarritz, discovers that the car — and her soul — are part of a deal with the Devil made years before by her grandfather. (Rev: BL 11/15/08; SLJ 4/1/09)

952 Golden, Christopher. *Poison Ink* (9–12). 2008, Delacorte LB $12.99 (978-0-385-90481-0); paper $8.99 (978-0-385-73483-7). Teenage angst and isolation are amplified as Sammi's friends abandon her after getting tattoos that seem to wield a negative, otherworldly influence. ℮ (Rev: SLJ 10/1/08; VOYA 10/08)

953 Grahame-Smith, Seth. *Abraham Lincoln: Vampire Hunter* (10–12). 2010, Grand Central $21.99 (978-044656308-6). Grahame-Smith tells the "true story" of Abraham Lincoln, revealed by a passage in Honest Abe's secret journal that outlines his lifelong campaign against vampires. ∩ Lexile 960L (Rev: BL 1/1/10)

954 Grahame-Smith, Seth. *Pride and Prejudice and Zombies* (10–12). 2009, Quirk paper $12.95 (978-159474334-4). An entertaining mingling of disparate genres that has the ultra-mannered characters of *Pride and Prejudice* (much of Austen's text is kept) training for combat and happily killing zombies. ∩ ℮ (Rev: BL 5/1/09)

955 Gray, Claudia. *Stargazer* (9–12). 2009, HarperTeen $16.99 (978-006128440-3); LB $17.89 (978-006128445-8). At Evernight, a boarding school for vampires, Bianca is torn between Balthazar and Lucas—and between the human realm and the world of the undead; a sequel to *Evernight* (2008). Lexile HL750L (Rev: BL 2/15/09; SLJ 5/1/09)

956 Harris, Charlaine. *Dead and Gone* (11–12). 2009, Ace $25.95 (978-044101715-7). In the latest installment of the series on which HBO's *True Blood* is based, barmaid Sookie Stackhouse investigates as werewolves follow vampires' lead in going public; for mature readers. ∩ (Rev: BL 4/15/09)

957 Harrison, Kim. *Once Dead, Twice Shy* (8–11). Series: Madison Avery. 2009, HarperTeen $16.99 (978-006171816-8). Madison joins angels, "timekeepers," and other supernatural beings when her soul hovers between life and death following a car crash. ℮ (Rev: BL 2/1/09; SLJ 7/1/09; VOYA 8/09)

958 Harvey, Alyxandra. *Hearts at Stake* (8–10). Series: Drake Chronicles. 2010, Walker $16.99 (978-0-8027-9840-4). This funny, coming-of-age vampire story — involving 15-year-old Solange (vampire queen to be), her seven protective older brothers, and her feisty mortal friend Lucy — is the first in a series. ℮ Lexile HL660L (Rev: BL 12/1/09; LMC 3–4/10; SLJ 3/10)

959 Henry, Mark. *Battle of the Network Zombies* (11–12). 2010, Kensington paper $15 (978-075822526-9). In fashion-conscious zombie Amanda Feral's third adventure, a snarky sendup of reality TV, the undead owner of an ad company finds herself investigating the fame-seeking contestants she's living with in Minions Mansion — including a yeti stripper and a cross-dressing werewolf — in the murder of a promiscuous male wood-nymph named Johnny Birch. For mature readers. (Rev: BLO 2/4/10)

960 Hightman, J. P. *Spirit* (6–10). 2008, HarperTeen $16.99 (978-006085063-0); LB $17.89 (978-006085064-7). Depraved, ghostly Old Widow Malgore haunts 1892 Blackthorne, Massachusetts, and newlyweds Tess and Tobias have their share of gruesome, eerie encounters as they explore the abandoned town and try to wrest Blackthorn's secret from its keeper. ℮ Lexile NC800L (Rev: BL 8/08; SLJ 9/1/08; VOYA 12/08)

961 Hockensmith, Steve. *Dawn of the Dreadfuls* (10–12). 2010, Quirk paper $12.95 (978-159474454-9). Providing backstory to 2009's *Pride and Prejudice and Zombies,* Hockensmith explores the origin of the Bennett sisters' gifts as zombie killers. (Rev: BL 3/1/10)

962 Holder, Nancy, and Debbie Viguié. *Crusade* (7–11). 2010, Simon & Schuster $16.99 (978-1-4169-9802-0). Jenn has trained at Spain's Salamanca Academy for vampire hunters and is now part of a teenage team battling power-hungry vampires. ℮ (Rev: BL 9/15/10; SLJ 12/1/10)

963 Holmes, Jeannie. *Blood Law* (11–12). 2010, Dell paper $7.99 (978-055359267-2). In small-town Mississippi, Alexandra Sabian, a vampire herself, is charged with keeping the peace between humans and vampires at a time when vampires start showing up murdered; a complex, violent novel for mature readers. ℮ (Rev: BL 5/1/10)

964 Holt, Simon. *Soulstice* (8–12). 2009, Little, Brown $16.99 (978-0-316-03571-2). In this sequel to 2008's *The Devouring,* the evil Vours return, and Reggie — who can access the "fearscape" and retrieve human spirits — faces more demons in order to protect those she holds dear. ℮ Lexile HL750L (Rev: SLJ 1/10; VOYA 2/10)

965 Horowitz, Anthony. *Bloody Horowitz* (9–12). 2010, Philomel $12.99 (978-0-399-25451-2). A collection of gruesome stories, many with a technological twist. (Rev: BL 9/1/10; SLJ 12/1/10)

966 Hubbard, Susan. *The Season of Risks* (10–12). Series: Ethical Vampire. 2010, Simon & Schuster paper $14 (978-143918342-7). Half-vampire Ari yearns for adulthood — and the chance to travel in elite political circles with fellow vampire presidential candidate Neil Cameron. (Rev: BL 7/10)

967 Kadrey, Richard. *Sandman Slim* (11–12). 2009, Eos $24.99 (978-006171430-6). After a long stint in hell, a tough-guy magician seeks revenge on the "Circle" responsible for putting him there; for mature readers. ∩ (Rev: BL 7/09)

968 Kate, Lauren. *Fallen* (9–12). 2010, Delacorte $17.99 (978-0-385-73893-4). This tale of fallen angels involves 17-year-old Luce, who is sent to a boarding school after the mysterious death of her boyfriend, and the gorgeous Daniel, who also attends the same school and is strangely familiar. ∩ ℮ Lexile 830L (Rev: BL 12/1/09; LMC 3–4/10; SLJ 1/10)

969 Kelly, Ronald. *Hell Hollow* (11–12). 2009, Cemetery Dance $40 (978-158767186-9). In this coming-of-age horror story, 12-year old Keith Bishop encounters a fugitive murderer while visiting his grandfather's Tennessee farm. (Rev: BL 11/15/09)

970 Kenyon, Nate. *Sparrow Rock* (11–12). 2010, Leisure paper $7.99 (978-084396377-9). A group of teenagers find themselves trapped in a bomb shelter as a nuclear holocaust takes place outside, and they face both external and internal challenges; for mature readers. ℮ (Rev: BLO 5/3/10)

971 King, Stephen. *Just After Sunset* (10–12). 2008, Scribner $28.00 (978-141658408-7). A typical anthology of short stories from the master of horror. ∩ ℮ (Rev: BL 9/15/08)

972 Krinard, Susan. *Come the Night* (10–12). 2008, HQN paper $6.99 (978-037377315-2). A werewolf story and a tale of searching for one's identity combine in this romantic tale of forbidden love. ℮ (Rev: BL 9/15/08*)

973 Lumley, Brian. *Harry and the Pirates: Necroscope* (10–12). Series: Necroscope. 2009, Tor $23.95 (978-076532338-5). Harry's encounters with strange souls continue in this cleverly written story. (Rev: BL 7/09)

974 MacHale, D. H. *The Light* (6–10). Series: Morpheus Road. 2010, Aladdin $17.99 (978-1-4169-6516-9). A fast-paced fantasy thriller in which Marshall has frightening visions and is pursued by a figure called Gravedigger while he searches for his missing friend Coop. ∩ ℮ (Rev: BLO 4/23/10; LMC 8–9/10; SLJ 5/10)

975 McMahon, Jennifer. *Don't Breathe a Word* (10–12). 2011, Harper $14.99 (978-006168937-6). Lisa walked away from her dysfunctional family at the age of 12, saying she was going to become queen of the fairy world, but 15 years later, her brother Sam, who was convinced she had been abducted, faces a series of mysterious occurrences that make him wonder if Lisa is still alive in this supernatural thriller. (Rev: BL 3/1–15/11)

976 Marr, Melissa, et al. *Love Is Hell* (9–12). 2008, HarperTeen $16.99 (978-0-06-144305-3). Supernatural romance is the theme of these five short stories by writers including Justine Larbalestier and Scott Westerfeld. (Rev: SLJ 2/1/09)

977 Masterton, Graham. *Blind Panic* (10–12). 2009, Severn $28.95 (978-072786820-6). Chaos ensues when the entire U.S. population is simultaneously stricken blind in this gripping thriller that features familiar characters Misquamacus (the ancient shaman) and charlatan-psychic Harry Erskine. (Rev: BL 10/15/09)

978 Moore, Christopher. *Bite Me: A Love Story* (11–12). 2010, Morrow $23.99 (978-006177972-5). In this funny sequel to 2008's *You Suck,* vampire couple Tommy and Jody escape from the Rodin statue in which they were imprisoned and join up with a legion of vampire cats, much to the concern of Abby Normal and her boyfriend; for mature readers. ℮ (Rev: BL 2/1/10)

979 Mullany, Janet. *Jane and the Damned* (11–12). 2010, Avon paper $13.99 (978-006195830-4). Jane Austen, now a vampire, must help defeat the French militia when they invade Bath, England. ℮ (Rev: BL 9/1/10)

980 Myracle, Lauren. *Bliss* (9–12). 2008, Abrams $16.95 (978-081097071-7). Bliss, new girl at a fancy Atlanta school, uncovers some violent history in this scary tale with a backdrop of late-1960s culture. Lexile HL640L (Rev: BL 11/1/08*; LMC 3–4/09; SLJ 10/1/08; VOYA 12/08)

981 Nayeri, Daniel, and Dina Nayeri. *Another Faust* (8–10). 2009, Candlewick $16.99 (978-0-7636-3707-1). In this well-written, Faustian tale, a wicked governess leads five siblings to exchange their souls for supernatural gifts. ∩ ℮ Lexile 740L (Rev: BL 9/15/09; LMC 10/09; SLJ 9/09; VOYA 8/09)

982 Nelson, Marilyn, and Tonya C. Hegamin. *Pemba's Song: A Ghost Story* (7–10). 2008, Scholastic $16.99 (978-054502076-3). African American 14-year-old

Pemba is aghast when her family relocates from Brooklyn to rural Connecticut, and unsettled when she starts having dreams about an 18th-century slave girl. Lexile 730L (Rev: BL 11/1/08; LMC 3–4/09; SLJ 12/08)

983 Pearce, Jackson. *Sisters Red* (8–12). 2010, Little, Brown $16.99 (978-0-316-06868-0). Sisters Scarlett and Rosie set out for revenge when a werewolf kills their grandmother and injures Scarlett; a retelling of the Little Red Riding Hood story with a twist that will appeal to fans of werewolves and vampires. (Rev: BL 4/15/10; HB 9–10/10; LMC 8–9/10; SLJ 5/10)

984 Perez, Marlene. *Dead Is a State of Mind* (7–10). 2009, Graphia paper $7.99 (978-015206210-1). In this sequel to *Dead Is the New Black* (2008), 17-year-old Daisy and other residents of Nightshade, California — some of them with supernatural abilities — are shaken when a teacher at the high school is murdered. An entertaining combination of romance, mystery, and the paranormal. e Lexile HL620L (Rev: BLO 1/7/09; SLJ 2/1/09)

985 Poblocki, Dan. *The Nightmarys* (6–10). 2010, Random $16.99 (978-0-375-84256-6). In this scary mystery story 7th-grader Timothy and his new classmate Abigail try to undo the curse on Abigail's family that is having an impact on them all. e Lexile 680L (Rev: BL 8/10; LMC 11–12/10; SLJ 12/1/10)

986 Priest, Cherie. *Boneshaker* (10–12). 2009, Tor paper $15.99 (978-076531841-1). Zeke is aware that his father is responsible for the zombies that roam the streets of lawless mid-19th-century Seattle; however, there are more bizarre discoveries to come about his parents' past in this atmospheric steampunk novel. (Rev: BL 10/15/09)

987 Radford, Michelle. *Totally Fabulous* (7–10). 2009, HarperTeen paper $8.99 (978-006128531-8). British 14-year-old Fiona travels to New Jersey to spend time with her long-lost father and attend an ESP boot camp to hone her psychic powers. (Rev: BL 7/09)

988 Ruby, Lois. *The Secret of Laurel Oaks* (7–10). 2008, Tor $16.95 (978-076531366-9). Siblings Lila and Gabe set out to solve the puzzle of who really poisoned the owner of Laurel Oaks Plantation in 1839; the narration alternates between Lila and Gabe and Daphne, the slave girl wrongly blamed for the murder. e Lexile 850L (Rev: BLO 10/30/08; LMC 5–6/09; SLJ 11/1/08; VOYA 12/08)

989 Ryan, Carrie. *The Forest of Hands and Teeth* (9–12). 2009, Delacorte $17.99 (978-038573681-7); LB $20.99 (978-038590631-9). In this gory story, Mary faces terrifying flesh-eating zombies and the prospect of marriage to a man she does not love. ∩ e Lexile 900L (Rev: BL 1/1–15/09; LMC 8–9/09; SLJ 5/1/09*)

990 Saul, John. *House of Reckoning* (10–12). 2009, Ballantine $26 (978-034551424-0). When teenaged Sarah finds herself in an oppressive foster home in the town where her drunken father is imprisoned, a troubled peer and mysterious teacher help her to overcome increasingly dire straits. ∩ e (Rev: BL 9/09)

991 Shusterman, Neal. *Bruiser* (8–12). 2010, HarperCollins $16.99 (978-0-06-113408-1). When Bronte, 16, starts dating the seemingly inappropriate Bruiser and her twin brother Tennyson comes to accept this, they are amazed to find that Bruiser absorbs all their physical and emotional pains; told from four perspectives. ∩ e Lexile 820L (Rev: BL 5/1/10; LMC 10/10; SLJ 8/10; VOYA 8/10)

992 Sigler, Scott. *Ancestor* (11–12). 2010, Crown $24.99 (978-030740633-0). On a small island in Lake Superior, two researchers endeavoring to engineer and clone an ancient human ancestor step into a genetic minefield in this action-packed thriller suitable for mature teens. ∩ e (Rev: BL 5/1/10)

993 Smith, Cynthia Leitich. *Eternal* (9–12). 2009, Candlewick $17.99 (978-076363573-2). Miranda, a vampire princess, and Zachary, her guardian angel, find love in the tenuous and frightening world of the dead; a companion novel to *Tantalize* (2007). ∩ e Lexile HL690L (Rev: BLO 2/9/09; HB 3–4/09; LMC 8–9/09; SLJ 7/1/09)

994 St. Crow, Lili. *Strange Angels* (8–11). Series: Strange Angels. 2009, Penguin paper $9.99 (978-159514251-1). Dru's mother is dead and she was forced to kill her father, who was turned into a zombie, in this first book in the series populated by vampires, werewolves, and demons. e Lexile HL810L (Rev: BL 5/15/09; SLJ 7/1/09)

995 Staub, Wendy Corsi. *Lily Dale: Connecting* (7–10). 2008, Walker $16.99 (978-0-8027-9785-8). Still in the spiritualist community of Lily Dale, Calla is preoccupied with romance and friendship even as she investigates her mother's death with the aid of the Internet and spirit guides; the third book in the series. e Lexile 1230 (Rev: BL 2/1/09; SLJ 2/1/09)

996 Stiefvater, Maggie. *Shiver* (9–12). 2009, Scholastic $17.99 (978-0-545-12326-6). A refreshing take on the supernatural/human romance fad, this well-written novel features a werewolf and the teenage girl who loves him. ∩ Lexile 740L (Rev: BL 8/09; HB 3–4/10; LMC 1–2/10; SLJ 10/09)

997 Straub, Peter. *A Dark Matter* (11–12). 2010, Doubleday $26.95 (978-038551638-9). Forty years after a small group of Wisconsin students fell under the sway of a mystic, novelist Lee Harwell attempts to unravel the strange occurrences of 1966 when an occult ritual resulted in the death of one student and the disappearance of another; for mature readers. (Rev: BL 10/1/09)

998 Straub, Peter. *A Special Place: The Heart of a Dark Matter* (11–12). 2010, Pegasus paper $12.95 (978-160598102-4). This disturbing novella relays the backstory of serial murderer Keith Hayward — the focus of

A Dark Matter (2010) — and describes Keith's education in the art of killing by his Uncle Till; for mature readers. (Rev: BL 7/10)

999 Taylor, Laini. *Lips Touch Three Times* (8–12). Illus. by Jim Di Bartolo. 2009, Scholastic $16.99 (978-0-545-05585-7). Three supernatural short stories feature kisses that change lives. ∩ ℮ Lexile 990L (Rev: BL 10/1/09*; SLJ 11/09)

1000 Turner, Joan Frances. *Dust* (10–12). 2010, Ace $24.95 (978-044101928-1). Chicago teenager Jessica Ann Porter is a thinking, feeling, and relatively contented zombie when a new virus appears and threatens both the living and the undead. ∩ (Rev: BL 9/1/10*)

1001 Warrington, Freda. *Dracula the Undead* (9–12). 2009, Severn $28.95 (978-072786817-6). Told through letters and journal entries, this sequel to Bram Stoker's *Dracula* finds several of the characters returning to Transylvania seven years after the vampire's apparent death only to find that their bloodthirsty adversary is back. (Rev: BL 10/15/09)

1002 Weldon, Phaedra. *Spectre* (11–12). 2008, Ace paper $14.00 (978-044101593-1). In this followup to *Wraith* (2007), Zoe, an investigator with paranormal abilities, copes with the sudden loss of her voice, her budding romance with Daniel, and a mysterious mission that turns out to be far more dangerous than she bargained for; for mature readers. ℮ (Rev: BL 6/1–15/08)

1003 Whitcomb, Laura. *The Fetch* (9–12). 2009, Houghton $17.00 (978-061889131-3). When Calder, a ghost who escorts souls from Earth to Heaven, interferes with a soul on Earth, he enters the body of Rasputin on the eve of the Russian Revolution and finds himself in league with the souls of Anastasia and Alexi Romanov in this complex and sophisticated novel that will raise questions about history and spirituality. ∩ Lexile 890L (Rev: BL 12/1/08*; LMC 8–9/09; SLJ 3/1/09)

1004 Winters, Ben H. *Sense and Sensibility and Sea Monsters* (10–12). Illus. 2009, Quirk paper $12.95 (978-159474442-6). The Dashwood women fight sea creatures and find true love in this mingling of horror and proper English manners. ∩ ℮ (Rev: BL 9/15/09)

1005 Yancey, Rick. *The Monstrumologist* (9–12). Series: The Monstrumologist. 2009, Simon & Schuster $17.99 (978-1-4169-8448-1). In 1888, 12-year-old Will Henry is an apprentice to Pellinore Warthrop, a scientist who hunts and studies real-life monsters. ∩ ℮ Lexile 990L (Rev: BL 9/1/09*; LMC 11–12/09; SLJ 11/09)

1006 Yovanoff, Brenna. *The Replacement* (9–12). 2010, Penguin $17.99 (978-159514337-2). Sixteen-year-old Mackie, who lives in a small town called Gentry that tries to ignore the supernatural beings that live underground, decides to challenge the status quo. (Rev: BL 9/1/10*; LMC 1–2/11; SLJ 12/1/10)

Humor

1007 Crawford, Brent. *Carter Finally Gets It* (7–10). 2009, Hyperion $15.99 (978-142311246-4). Clumsy, ADD-suffering freshman Will Carter attempts to talk to girls, cope with humiliation, and survive sports in this funny, believable account of high school from a hormone-crazed boy's perspective. ∩ ℮ Lexile HL760L (Rev: BL 11/15/08; SLJ 3/1/09; VOYA 4/09)

1008 Geerling, Marjetta. *Fancy White Trash* (9–12). 2008, Viking $15.99 (978-0-670-01082-0). A humorous story about 15-year-old Abby, her out-of-control family — her mother and one of her sisters may be simultaneously pregnant by the same man — and her steadying friendship with gay neighbor Cody. (Rev: SLJ 10/1/08)

1009 Hiaasen, Carl. *Star Island* (11–12). 2010, Knopf $26.95 (978-030727258-4). Things get complicated when out-of-control pop star Cherry Pye's body double is kidnapped, and the star's managers have to figure out a way to get the double back without Cherry finding out that she exists; for mature readers. ∩ ℮ (Rev: BL 7/10)

1010 Ives, David. *Voss: How I Come to America and Am Hero, Mostly* (7–10). 2008, Putnam $17.99 (978-039924722-4). The hilarious misadventures of Voss, a 15-year-old immigrant, are populated with larger-than-life characters including gangsters, socialites, and crazy relatives, and are told in broken English through letters to a friend back home in Slobovia. (Rev: BL 12/1/08; LMC 1–2/09; SLJ 12/08)

1011 Kinsella, Sophie. *Mini Shopaholic* (10–12). 2010, Dial $25 (978-038534204-9). In this followup to 2007's *Shopaholic and Baby,* the Brandons' toddler daughter, Minnie, begins exhibiting worrisome fashionista tendencies that create strife between Becky and Luke. ∩ (Rev: BL 8/10)

1012 McGowan, Anthony. *Jack Tumor* (7–10). 2009, Farrar $17.95 (978-037432955-6). Funny and vulgar, this British novel features a teen boy named Hector and his brain tumor, Jack; Jack and Hector face an uncertain future and an interesting present as Jack tries to improve Hector's social life. (Rev: BL 6/1–15/09; SLJ 6/1/09)

1013 McLaughlin, Emma, and Nicola Kraus. *Nanny Returns* (11–12). 2009, Atria $25 (978-141658567-1). This sequel to *The Nanny Diaries* (2002) finds Nan settling into married life and a new job when an unexpected visitor from her past draws her back into the lives of the X family; for mature readers. (Rev: BL 10/1/09)

1014 Snow, Carol. *Just Like Me, Only Better* (11–12). 2010, Berkley paper $14 (978-042523248-4). Struggling young mom Veronica gets a big break when she's picked as star Haley Rush's celebrity double — but finds that balancing reality with stardom is far from easy street; for mature students. ℮ (Rev: BL 4/1/10)

Mysteries, Thrillers, and Spy Stories

1015 Abrahams, Peter. *Reality Check* (8–11). 2009, HarperTeen $16.99 (978-006122766-0); LB $17.89 (978-006122767-7). Cody Laredo is already facing difficulties — a knee injury keeps him off the football team and ruins his chances of a college scholarship — when his rich girlfriend Clea disappears from her boarding school in Vermont and he sets off from Colorado to find her. ∩ **e** (Rev: BL 7/09; SLJ 5/1/09; VOYA 4/09*)

1016 Atkins, Charles. *Mother's Milk* (11–12). 2009, Severn $28.95 (978-072786795-7). The discovery of two dead teenagers and the disappearance of one of her patients, now the prime suspect, send forensic psychiatrist Barratt Conyers on a twisting search for the truth. (Rev: BL 10/1/09)

1017 Barclay, Linwood. *Never Look Away* (11–12). 2010, Delacorte $25 (978-055380717-2). When average joe David becomes a suspect in his troubled wife's disappearance, he sets out to discover the truth — and clear his own name — in this engrossing family thriller suitable for mature readers. (Rev: BL 3/1/10)

1018 Beaufrand, Mary Jane. *The River* (8–12). 2010, Little, Brown $16.99 (978-0-316-04168-3). Ronnie, unhappy following her family's move from Portland to rural Oregon, is overwhelmed when the 10-year-old girl she has been babysitting drowns; suspicious about the circumstances, she sets out to discover what happened. Lexile HL730L (Rev: BL 12/15/09; HB 5–6/10; SLJ 2/10; VOYA 4/10)

1019 Bebris, Carrie. *The Intrigue at Highbury; or, Emma's Match* (10–12). Series: Mr. and Mrs. Darcy Mysteries. 2010, Tor $22.99 (978-076531848-0). In this Austen-flavored whodunit, Mr. Knightley agrees to help the Darcys to find the highwayman who robbed them, in return for help investigating the unexpected death of Frank Churchill's guardian, Edgar. (Rev: BL 3/15/10)

1020 Bebris, Carrie. *The Matters at Mansfield; or, The Crawford Affair* (10–12). Series: Mr. and Mrs. Darcy Mysteries. 2008, Forge $22.95 (978-0-7653-1847-3). Darcy and Elizabeth visit Mansfield Park in this murder mystery written in Austen's style. **e** (Rev: BL 8/08)

1021 Bond, Stephanie. *5 Bodies to Die For* (11–12). Series: Body Movers. 2009, Harlequin paper $7.99 (978-077832705-9). In this fifth volume in the series Carlotta is dodging a serial killer and romantic entanglements; for mature readers ∩ **e** (Rev: BL 5/1/09*)

1022 Bond, Stephanie. *6 Killer Bodies* (11–12). Series: Body Movers. 2009, MIRA paper $7.99 (978-077832707-3). Carlotta tracks a killer who leaves bracelet charms in the mouths of his victims; for mature readers. ∩ **e** (Rev: BL 7/09)

1023 Bradley, Alan. *The Weed That Strings the Hangman's Bag* (9–12). 2010, Delacorte $24 (978-038534231-5). When a puppeteer is electrocuted in the middle of a performance at the local church, 11-year-old Flavia DeLuce is on the case; set in 1950s England. ∩ **e** (Rev: BL 2/15/10)

1024 Cantor, Jillian. *The September Sisters* (7–12). 2009, HarperCollins $16.99 (978-006168648-1); LB $17.89 (978-006168649-8). Abigail's sister, missing for two years, is found dead in this story about grief, anger, suspicion, and loneliness. Lexile 850L (Rev: BL 2/1/09; SLJ 6/1/09; VOYA 6/09)

1025 Carey, Benedict. *The Unknowns* (6–10). 2009, Abrams $16.95 (978-081097991-8). A group of preteens sets out to solve a mystery on their island, home to a nuclear power plant. Their math teacher has left behind clues in the form of equations and geometry puzzles. Lexile 760L (Rev: BL 5/1/09; LMC 10/09; SLJ 10/09)

1026 Carman, Patrick. *Thirteen Days to Midnight* (7–10). 2010, Little, Brown $16.99 (978-0-316-00403-9). When his foster father dies in an accident, Jacob discovers that he has a unique power to ward off death but that this power is not without pitfalls; a suspenseful read. ∩ Lexile 1010L (Rev: BL 5/1/10; LMC 8–9/10; SLJ 5/10)

1027 Causey, Toni McGee. *Bobbie Faye's (Kinda, Sorta, Not-exactly) Family Jewels* (11–12). 2008, St. Martin's paper $13.95 (978-031235450-3). In this second book about Bobbie Faye, the witty, feisty heroine must evade the FBI, Homeland Security, the Irish mob, and unsavory members of her own family as she tries to convince everyone she that doesn't know where the diamonds are hidden; for mature readers. **e** (Rev: BL 6/1–15/08*)

1028 Clare, Alys. *Mist over the Water* (11–12). Series: Aelf Fen. 2010, Severn $28.95 (978-072786848-0). This Aelf Fen mystery set in Norman England follows the healer Lassair, 16, as she becomes embroiled in a mystery involving a monastery on Ely Island; for mature readers. **e** (Rev: BL 12/1/09*)

1029 Clare, Alys. *Out of the Dawn Light* (10–12). Series: Aelf Fen. 2009, Severn $27.95 (978-072786763-6). This blend of mystery and romance set in medieval England features 14-year-old Lassair, who finds herself embroiled in a dangerous quest for a magic crown. (Rev: BL 7/09)

1030 Collins, Brandilyn, and Amberly Collins. *Final Touch* (8–12). 2010, Zondervan paper $9.99 (978-0-310-71933-5). On the very day her mother, rock star Rayne O'Connor, is to get remarried, teenage Shaley is abducted by a stalker. (Rev: BL 9/1/10; SLJ 12/1/10)

1031 Cooney, Caroline B. *If the Witness Lied* (7–10). 2009, Delacorte $16.99 (978-0-385-73448-6); LB $19.99 (978-0-385-90451-3). After their mother's death from cancer and their father's demise in an accident, siblings Smithy, Madison, and Jack must act to keep their toddler brother safe from their evil aunt and the threat of a reality TV show about their grief. ℮ Lexile HL670L (Rev: BL 5/1/09; HB 5–6/09; LMC 8–9/09; SLJ 5/1/09; VOYA 6/09)

1032 Cotterill, Colin. *The Merry Misogynist* (10–12). Series: Dr. Siri. 2009, Soho Crime $24 (978-1-56947-556-0). Set in Laos in the 1970s, this sixth installment in the mystery series finds quirky coroner Dr. Siri Paiboun on the trail of a serial killer who is victimizing young women from rural villages. (Rev: SLJ 8/09)

1033 Coulter, Catherine. *KnockOut* (11–12). 2009, Putnam $26.95 (978-039915584-0). Married FBI agents Savich and Sherlock deal with psychic powers in this tense page-turner suitable for mature readers. ∩ ℮ (Rev: BL 5/1/09)

1034 Davis, Lindsey. *Alexandria* (10–12). 2009, Minotaur $24.95 (978-0-312-37901-8). The 17th installment in the Marcus Didius Falco stories finds Roman private detective Falco in 1st-century Alexandria charged with solving the mystery of the dead librarian. (Rev: SLJ 12/09)

1035 Derting, Kimberly. *The Body Finder* (7–12). 2010, HarperCollins $16.99 (978-0-06-177981-7). Violet's ability to sense the bodies of murdered people brings her anxious moments even as she is absorbed in her growing fascination with her best friend Jay; this suspenseful thriller, with a dollop of romance, contains language and sexual content that may limit the grade range. ℮ Lexile 940L (Rev: BL 10/15/09; LMC 3–4/10; SLJ 5/10)

1036 Ebisch, Glen. *Ghosts from the Past* (11–12). 2009, Avalon $23.95 (978-080349978-2). Young ghost hunter Marcie Ducasse finds herself with an additional death on her hands as she sets out to investigate the apparitions of three men who were hanged decades ago; for mature readers. (Rev: BL 10/15/09)

1037 Ehrenhaft, Daniel. *Dirty Laundry* (8–11). 2009, HarperTeen $16.99 (978-006113103-5). A playful mystery about a teen actress who goes undercover at a New England boarding school in order to research a part, but becomes embroiled in the mystery of a missing student. ℮ Lexile HL630L (Rev: BL 12/15/08; SLJ 3/1/09)

1038 Ferraris, Zoe. *City of Veils* (10–12). 2010, Little, Brown $24.99 (978-031607427-8). Detective Osama Ibrahim investigates the death of a young filmmaker with the help of forensic expert Katya in this suspenseful novel that exposes the strictures of Saudi life. ∩ (Rev: BL 7/10)

1039 Fleischman, A. S. *Danger in Paradise / Malay Woman* (10–12). 2010, Stark House paper $19.95 (978-193358628-1). Originally published in the 1950s, these two mysteries by children's author Sid Fleischman offer exotic glimpses into a world of espionage, seduction, and betrayal. (Rev: BL 8/10)

1040 Ford, John C. *The Morgue and Me* (9–12). 2009, Viking $17.99 (978-067001096-7). Christopher has a summer job at a morgue and stumbles across a mystery involving the medical examiner and a suspicious dead body. ℮ Lexile HL720L (Rev: BL 5/1/09; LMC 11–12/09; SLJ 8/09; VOYA 8/09)

1041 Fuerst, James W. *Huge* (10–12). 2009, Crown $23.95 (978-030745249-8). Eugene "Huge" Smalls is indeed small for his 12 years and compensates with his tough guy attitude and detective skills as he tries to solve a mystery at his grandma's nursing home. ∩ ℮ (Rev: BL 5/1/09*; SLJ 9/09)

1042 Gavin, Jamila. *See No Evil* (7–10). 2009, Farrar $16.95 (978-037436333-8). Nettie, 12, searches her family's London mansion for the secrets to her father's vast wealth after her tutor mysteriously disappears. (Rev: BL 5/1/09; SLJ 7/1/09; VOYA 2/09)

1043 Gerber, Linda. *Death by Denim* (7–10). Series: Death By. 2009, Penguin paper $7.99 (978-014241119-3). Sixteen-year-old Aphra and her mother, a CIA agent, race through Europe to escape the Mole and save Aphra's boyfriend, Seth. The third book after *Death by Bikini* and *Death by Latte* (both 2008). Lexile HL740L (Rev: BL 5/1/09; SLJ 6/1/09)

1044 Gist, Deeanne, and J. Mark Bertrand. *Beguiled* (11–12). 2010, Bethany paper $14.99 (978-076420628-3). Charleston provides the setting for this blend of romance and suspense about a female dog-walker and a male newspaper journalist who together try to discover the true identity of a modern-day Robin Hood; for mature readers. ∩ ℮ (Rev: BL 2/15/10)

1045 Gonzales, Laurence. *Lucy* (11–12). 2010, Knopf $24.95 (978-030727260-7). Forced to flee the Congolese jungle, scientist Jenny and orphaned 14-year-old Lucy arrive in Chicago, where the truth about Lucy's heritage (she is half human and half bonobo) makes her the center of attention; for mature readers. ∩ ℮ (Rev: BL 6/1–15/10)

1046 Goodman, Carol. *The Night Villa* (11–12). 2008, Ballantine paper $14.00 (978-034547960-0). Classics professor Sophie Chase travels to the island of Capri to solve two murder mysteries, one past and one present, in this exciting, clever, and romantic novel; for mature teens. ∩ (Rev: BL 8/08)

1047 Gordon-Smith, Dolores. *A Hundred Thousand Dragons* (10–12). 2010, Severn $28.95 (978-072786910-4). Home in England after World War II, Jack Haldean has a chance meeting with an Arabian explorer that draws him into a web of mystery and adventure. ℮ (Rev: BL 7/10)

1048 Grant, Helen. *The Vanishing of Katharina Linden* (11–12). 2010, Delacorte $24 (978-038534417-3). In this suspenseful coming-of-age story, two adventure-seeking 10-year-olds set out to apprehend a real-live boogeyman, who's been kidnapping young girls from their German village; for mature readers. ᙁ ℮ (Rev: BL 6/1–15/10)

1049 Green, John. *Paper Towns* (9–12). 2008, Dutton $17.99 (978-0-525-47818-8). High school senior Quentin "Q" has been crazy about his neighbor Margo for years, and when she disappears he and his friends set out to investigate. ᙁ (Rev: BL 12/1/08*; LMC 1–2/09*; SLJ 10/1/08)

1050 Harrison, Cora. *Writ in Stone* (10–12). 2009, Severn $27.95 (978-072786812-1). In 16th-century Ireland Mara seeks justice — and the motive of the killer — when a man is murdered in the village, perhaps in the place of her fiancé, the King? The fourth installment in the series. ℮ (Rev: BL 11/15/09)

1051 Harrod-Eagles, Cynthia. *Fell Purpose* (11–12). Series: Detective Inspector Bill Slider Mysteries. 2010, Severn $28.95 (978-072786842-8). This entry in the series finds Slider investigating the murder of a well-heeled young woman whose secret life informs the violent circumstances of her death; for mature readers. ℮ (Rev: BL 12/1/09)

1052 Hart, Carolyn. *Merry, Merry Ghost* (10–12). 2009, Morrow $24.99 (978-006087437-7). Second in a series, *Merry, Merry Ghost* marks the return of Bailey Ruth, a lovable yet often misguided spirit who helps a young orphan and solves the murder of his wealthy grandmother. (Rev: BL 9/15/09)

1053 Healy, Erin. *Never Let You Go* (11–12). 2010, Thomas Nelson $21.99 (978-159554750-7). In this faith-based thriller, single mother Lexi is backed into a dangerous situation by one mishap after another —and it's only through hope, and one well-timed miracle, that she manages to persevere; for mature readers. ᙁ ℮ (Rev: BLO 4/30/10)

1054 Henderson, Lauren. *Kisses and Lies* (9–12). 2009, Random $16.99 (978-038573489-9); LB $19.99 (978-038590486-5). British socialite Scarlett, whose crush, Dan, died mysteriously in *Kiss Me Kill Me* (2008), travels to Scotland to find his killer. (Rev: BL 5/1/09; SLJ 5/1/09)

1055 Henry, April. *Girl, Stolen!* (7–10). 2010, Henry Holt $16.99 (978-0-8050-9005-5). Things go from bad to worse when a young carjacker steals Cheyenne's mother's car — not realizing the blind, pneumonia-stricken teen is in the back seat. ℮ Lexile HL700L (Rev: BL 9/15/10; SLJ 10/1/10)

1056 Hoag, Tami. *Deeper Than the Dead* (11–12). 2009, Dutton $26.95 (978-052595130-8). Set in 1985 in the sleepy town of Oak Knoll, California, this scary thriller thrusts four fifth-graders into the center of a hunt for a psychotic serial killer; for mature readers. ᙁ ℮ (Rev: BL 10/15/09)

1057 Huston, Charlie. *Sleepless* (10–12). 2010, Ballantine $25 (978-034550113-4). When a plague of termi-

nal insomnia strikes, a police officer assigned to bust a gang trafficking in the cure is further motivated by his stricken wife. ᙁ ℮ (Rev: BLO 12/1/09)

1058 Jaffarian, Sue Ann. *Ghost a la Mode* (10–12). 2009, Midnight Ink paper $14.95 (978-073871380-9). *Ghost a la Mode* introduces divorcee Emma Whitecastle and her relative, the long-dead Granny Apples, who solve mysteries together beginning with clearing Granny of her husband's murder. (Rev: BL 9/09)

1059 Jarzab, Anna. *All Unquiet Things* (9–12). 2010, Delacorte $17.99 (978-0-385-73835-4); LB $20.99 (978-0-385-90723-1). Neily and Audrey, students at a classy high school, join together to investigate the death of Carly, who was Neily's ex-girlfriend and whose murderer has been identified as Audrey's father. ᙁ ℮ Lexile HL780L (Rev: BL 10/15/09; LMC 11–12/09; SLJ 2/10; VOYA 2/10)

1060 Johansen, Iris. *Eight Days to Live* (11–12). 2010, St. Martin's $27.99 (978-031236815-9). Jane MacGuire, adoptive daughter of Eve Duncan and an artist mysteriously targeted by a religious cult, seeks help as she receives death threats; for mature readers. (Rev: BL 1/1–15/10)

1061 Kenner, Julie. *Demon Ex Machina: Tales of a Demon-Hunting Soccer Mom* (11–12). 2009, Berkley paper $14 (978-042522964-4). Soccer-mom-turned-demon-hunter Kate enlists the help of her current and ex-husbands, as well as her surprisingly capable teenage daughter, to rid the sleepy hamlet of San Diablo, California of a growing number of demons; for mature readers. ℮ (Rev: BL 10/15/09)

1062 Kephart, Beth. *Nothing but Ghosts* (8–11). 2009, HarperCollins $17.95 (978-006166796-1); LB $18.89 (978-006166797-8). Katie, 16, in an effort to recover from her mother's death, works on the construction of a gazebo at a nearby estate and stumbles on a mystery that she investigates with some help from her art restorer father and fellow worker Danny. (Rev: BL 4/1/09; LMC 1–2/10; SLJ 7/09; VOYA 8/09)

1063 Lee, Y. S. *A Spy in the House* (8–12). Series: Mary Quinn Mysteries. 2010, Candlewick $16.99 (978-0-7636-4067-5); paper $11.20 (978-1-4063-1516-5). Saved from hanging in 1850s London five years earlier, Mary Quinn, now 17, is part of an all-female detective agency and charged with tracing some missing cargo ships; this first installment in a series is full of Victorian details. ᙁ ℮ (Rev: BL 1/1/10; LMC 5–6/10; SLJ 4/10)

1064 Lelic, Simon. *A Thousand Cuts* (10–12). 2010, Viking $24.95 (978-067002150-5). Detective Lucia May investigates a brutal shooting at a school in which a newly hired teacher kills three students, another teacher, and himself in this thought-provoking novel about bullying and retribution. (Rev: BL 2/1/10)

1065 Lippman, Laura. *I'd Know You Anywhere* (11–12). 2010, Morrow $25.99 (978-006170655-4). Housewife

Eliza looks back at her dreadful experiences when she was kidnapped at age 15 by a manipulative serial rapist; for mature readers. ∩ e (Rev: BL 5/1/10*)

1066 Littlewood, Ann. *Night Kill* (10–12). 2008, Poisoned Pen $24.95 (978-1-59058-504-7). *Night Kill* combines the thrill and danger of solving a murder mystery with a glimpse into the internal workings of a zoo. e (Rev: BL 8/08)

1067 Lourey, Jess. *September Fair* (10–12). 2009, Midnight Ink paper $14.95 (978-073871872-9). When the newly elected Queen of the Dairy is killed at the fair, it is up to reporter Mira James to solve the crime in this amusing tale of jealousy and dairy business. e (Rev: BL 9/09*)

1068 McClintock, Norah. *Homicide Related* (9–12). 2009, Fitzhenry & Whiteside paper $12.95 (978-0-88995-431-1). Now living with his strict uncle, Ryan Dooley is recovering from his abuse of drugs and alcohol when his mother is found dead, supposedly from an overdose; Dooley decides to investigate. (Rev: BL 10/15/09; LMC 1–2/10; SLJ 12/09)

1069 McDonnell, Margot. *Torn to Pieces* (8–11). 2008, Delacorte $15.99 (978-038573559-9); LB $18.99 (978-038590542-8). Anne, 17, discovers the horrifying truth about her mother's past in this occasionally violent teen thriller. e Lexile NC510L (Rev: BL 11/1/08; SLJ 1/1/09)

1070 McNab, Andy, and Robert Rigby. *Meltdown* (8–11). 2008, Putnam $16.99 (978-0-399-24686-9). Danny and his secret agent grandfather Fergus investigate a new — and fatal — designer drug called Meltdown in this action-packed British story. (Rev: BL 7/08; SLJ 1/1/09)

1071 McNamara, Mary. *The Starlet* (11–12). 2010, Simon & Schuster paper $15 (978-143914984-3). In this followup to 2008's *Oscar Season,* Juliette hopes to recover from Hollywood stress in Italy, and finds herself rescuing Mercy, a young, drugged-out actress, from a Florence fountain; suspicious deaths add to the drama in this mystery suitable for mature readers. (Rev: BL 6/1–15/10)

1072 McNamee, Graham. *Bonechiller* (7–10). 2008, Random $15.99 (978-038574658-8); LB $18.99 (978-038590895-5). High schoolers Danny and Howie grapple with a merciless, bloodthirsty beast in this supernatural thriller set in the Canadian tundra. Lexile 580L (Rev: BL 11/1/08*; LMC 11–12/08; SLJ 1/1/09)

1073 Marrone, Amanda. *Devoured* (8–12). 2009, Simon & Schuster paper $9.99 (978-1-4169-7890-9). In this fast-paced murder mystery, 17-year-old Megan grapples with volatile politics at her summer job, her distant mother, and her dead twin sister's increasingly foreboding ghost. e (Rev: BLO 8/20/09; SLJ 10/09)

1074 Mitchard, Jacquelyn. *The Midnight Twins* (6–12). 2008, Penguin $16.99 (978-159514160-6). Identical

twins Meredith and Mallory's eerie ability to communicate with each other forms the heart of this thrilling series starter. e (Rev: BL 7/08; LMC 11–12/08; SLJ 10/1/08)

1075 Mitchell, Saundra. *Shadowed Summer* (8–12). 2009, Delacorte $15.99 (978-038573571-1); LB $18.99 (978-038590560-2). Iris, 14, accidentally contacts a ghost who pressures her to solve the mystery of his long-ago murder; her investigation uncovers unpleasant secrets about her Louisiana town. e Lexile 760L (Rev: BL 2/15/09; SLJ 4/1/09)

1076 Nikitas, Derek. *The Long Division* (11–12). 2009, Minotaur $24.99 (978-031236398-7). A 15-year-old boy, the mother who gave him up, a policeman, and other characters' story lines intertwine in this fast-paced novel about bad choices and inevitable outcomes; suitable for mature readers. (Rev: BL 9/15/09; SLJ 2/10)

1077 Norman, Hilary. *Ralph's Children* (11–12). 2008, Severn $27.95 (978-072786673-8). Four abused orphans bond as they secretly read *Lord of the Flies*, and as adults, decide to play their *Lord of the Flies* game to retaliate against perceived wrongdoing; for mature teens. (Rev: BL 9/1/08)

1078 Northrop, Michael. *Gentlemen* (10–12). 2009, Scholastic $16.99 (978-054509749-9). Mike, Mixer, and Bones suspect that their English teacher may be responsible for the disappearance of their friend Tommy. Lexile HL860L (Rev: BL 5/1/09; LMC 10/09; SLJ 8/09; VOYA 6/09)

1079 Nugent, Andrew. *Soul Murder* (10–12). 2009, Minotaur $24.95 (978-031253656-5). Irish police Superintendent Denis Lennon and Sergeant Molly Power investigate a murder at a boys' boarding school in this compelling and suspenseful novel. e (Rev: BL 7/09*)

1080 Oldham, Nick. *Screen of Deceit* (11–12). 2008, Severn $27.95 (978-0-7278-6646-2). In this story for mature readers, 14-year-old Mark sets out to solve the puzzle of his drug-addicted sister's death and quickly finds himself between a rock and hard place: wear a wire for DCI Henry Christie, or let the bad guy go free. (Rev: BL 6/1–15/08)

1081 Parker, Robert B. *Chasing the Bear: A Young Spenser Novel* (7–10). 2009, Philomel $17.99 (978-039924776-7). An adult Spenser tells his girlfriend the story of being brought up by his rough-and-tumble father and uncles. ∩ e Lexile HL500L (Rev: BL 5/1/09; SLJ 8/09; VOYA 8/09)

1082 Patterson, James, and Maxine Paetro. *10th Anniversary* (10–12). Series: Women's Murder Club. 2011, Little, Brown $27.99 (978-031603626-9). This tense thriller finds Sergeant Lindsay Boxer, Assistant DA Yuki Castellano, and reporter Cindy Thomas embroiled in mysterious cases involving young women, drugs ,and crime in the San Francisco area. (Rev: BL 3/15/11)

1083 Peacock, Shane. *Vanishing Girl* (7–10). Series: The Boy Sherlock Holmes. 2009, Tundra $19.95 (978-0-88776-852-1). The young daughter of a government official disappears, a ransom note arrives, and young Sherlock investigates in this fast-paced mystery full of Victorian atmosphere. ℮ Lexile 810L (Rev: BLO 11/20/09; SLJ 2/10)

1084 Quinn, Spencer. *Thereby Hangs a Tail* (10–12). Series: Chet and Bernie Mysteries. 2010, Atria $25 (978-141658585-5). In this entertaining followup to *Dog on It* (2009), Bernie and Chet (Bernie's canine partner, who tells the story) investigate a missing show dog. ⌒ ℮ (Rev: BL 12/1/09)

1085 Reger, Rob, and Jessica Gruner. *The Lost Days* (7–10). Illus. by author. Series: Emily the Strange. 2009, HarperCollins $16.99 (978-006145229-1); LB $17.89 (978-006145230-7). Emily (first featured in graphic-novel form) has amnesia and uses her diary to sort out who she is. Lexile 870L (Rev: BL 5/1/09; SLJ 6/1/09)

1086 Reger, Rob, and Jessica Gruner. *Stranger and Stranger* (7–10). Illus. by author and Buzz Parker. Series: Emily the Strange. 2010, HarperTeen $16.99 (978-0-06-145232-1); LB $17.89 (978-0-06-145233-8). In a series of diary entries with manga-style cartoons, this quirky story follows Emily through a confusing cloning experience full of dark humor; a sequel to 2009's *The Lost Days*. Lexile 900L (Rev: BL 1/1/10; SLJ 1/10; VOYA 8/10)

1087 Reiken, Frederick. *Day for Night* (11–12). 2010, Little, Brown $24.99 (978-031607756-9). Historically and emotionally diverse characters propel this complex, ambitious psychological suspense novel that explores the underlying, often surprising connections between strangers; for mature readers. (Rev: BL 3/15/10*)

1088 Rice, Luanne. *Last Kiss* (11–12). 2008, Bantam $25.00 (978-0-553-80512-3). When Nell's first love, Charlie, is mysteriously murdered, she hires a private investigator to solve the puzzle in this engrossing, multifaceted story for mature readers. ⌒ ℮ (Rev: BL 6/1–15/08)

1089 Richmond, Michelle. *No One You Know* (10–12). 2008, Delacorte $23.00 (978-0-385-34013-7). Ellie is determined to regain control of the story of her sister's murder — which became a best-selling crime novel — in this incisive, travel-rich literary thriller. ⌒ ℮ (Rev: BL 6/1–15/08*)

1090 Ritari, Jacob. *Taroko Gorge* (10–12). 2010, Unbridled paper $15.95 (978-193607165-4). In this suspenseful novel set in a Taiwanese national park, two American journalists and a group of Japanese teens find themselves trapped as a cyclone bears down on the area. ℮ (Rev: BL 5/1/10)

1091 Schrefer, Eliot. *The Deadly Sister* (9–12). 2010, Scholastic $17.99 (978-0-545-16574-7). When Abby finds the body of her sister Maya's former boyfriend

and her sister Maya's cell phone nearby, she is determined to find her missing sister and prove her innocent. ℮ Lexile HL720L (Rev: LMC 10/10; SLJ 8/10)

1092 Sedgwick, Marcus. *Revolver* (7–10). 2010, Roaring Brook $16.99 (978-1-59643-592-6). In the early 20th century above the Arctic Circle, young Sig's father has been found frozen to death; Sig's sister and stepmother go for help and Sig is alone when a stranger bearing a Colt revolver arrives demanding gold he is owed. ⌒ ℮ Lexile 890L (Rev: BL 5/1/10; HB 3–4/10; LMC 5–6/10; SLJ 4/10)

1093 Sorrells, Walter. *Whiteout* (7–12). Series: Hunted. 2009, Dutton $15.99 (978-0-525-42141-2). Sixteen-year-old Chass is determined to work out who's stalking herself and her mother rather than relocate yet again in this third installment in the series. ℮ Lexile HL530L (Rev: BLO 8/20/09; SLJ 1/10; VOYA 10/09)

1094 Steinbeck, Thomas. *In the Shadow of the Cypress* (10–12). 2010, Gallery $25 (978-143916825-7). When marine biologist Luke finds a 1906 diary mentioning ancient Chinese treasure lost along the California coast, he sets out to look for it and finds more than he anticipated. ⌒ ℮ (Rev: BL 4/1/10*)

1095 Strachan, Mari. *The Earth Hums in B Flat* (10–12). 2009, Canongate $24 (978-184767192-9). As she dreams, 12-year-old Gwenni happily glides above her Welsh village watching the people below until she spies something strange that causes her to seek answers and unravel lives. ℮ (Rev: BL 5/1/09)

1096 Strasser, Todd. *Wish You Were Dead* (8–12). 2009, Egmont USA $16.99 (978-1-60684-007-8); LB $19.99 (978-1-60684-049-8). In this technology-filled thriller, Madison seeks the identity of a local killer — and her own cyberstalker — by unraveling clues in blog posts and Facebook conversations. ⌒ ℮ Lexile HL650L (Rev: BL 10/1/09; LMC 11–12/09; SLJ 10/09; VOYA 12/09)

1097 Sturman, Jennifer. *And Then Everything Unraveled* (7–10). 2009, Scholastic $16.99 (978-054508722-3). Delia Truesdale investigates her mother's disappearance at the same time as she tries to adapt to her new life in Manhattan with two very different aunts. ℮ (Rev: BL 7/09; SLJ 8/09)

1098 Unger, Lisa. *Fragile* (11–12). 2010, Crown $24 (978-030739399-9). When a teen girl goes missing in a quiet suburban town, the adults must sort out the web of secrets and hidden relationships of their own lives as they continue to search; for mature readers. ⌒ ℮ (Rev: BL 7/10)

1099 Webb, Betty. *The Koala of Death* (10–12). Series: Gunn Zoo. 2010, Poisoned Pen $24.95 (978-159058756-0). When zookeeper Teddy Bentley's coworker Kate is found murdered, Teddy finds herself struggling to fill Kate's shoes — and solve the crime — before the killer strikes again. ⌒ ℮ (Rev: BL 6/1–15/10)

1100 Wiesel, Elie. *The Sonderberg Case* (10–12). 2010, Knopf $25 (978-030727220-1). In this tense, mature courtroom drama, an ex-Nazi falls to his death in the Adirondack mountains. **e** (Rev: BL 4/1/10)

1101 Williams, Carol Lynch. *The Chosen One* (7–10). 2009, St. Martin's $16.95 (978-031255511-5). In this compelling novel, 13-year-old Kyra is commanded to marry her uncle and plans a daring escape from the polygamous sect in which she has been raised. ∩ Lexile HL480L (Rev: BL 2/15/09; HB 5–6/09; LMC 10/09; SLJ 7/1/09)

1102 Williams, Katie. *The Space Between Trees* (8–12). 2010, Chronicle $16.99 (978-0-8118-7175-4). Sixteen-year-old Evie, a loner given to making up stories, must grow up when the body of a classmate is found and she is drawn into the investigation. **e** Lexile 850L (Rev: BLO 4/12/10; LMC 8–9/10; SLJ 5/10)

1103 Windle, J. M. *Veiled Freedom* (11–12). 2009, Tyndale paper $13.99 (978-141431475-4). Two Americans — a female Christian relief worker and a Special Forces veteran — and an Afghani interpreter find themselves embroiled in political intrigue and unrest in Afghanistan; for mature readers. **e** (Rev: BL 5/1/09)

1104 Winslow, Emily. *The Whole World* (11–12). 2010, Delacorte $25 (978-038534288-9). American college students Polly and Liv meet while studying abroad at Cambridge University and become fast friends, but dark secrets are revealed when they both develop a crush on a male student who ends up dead; for mature readers. (Rev: BLO 2/17/10)

1105 Wynne-Jones, Tim. *The Uninvited* (9–12). 2009, Candlewick $16.99 (978-076363984-6). NYU student Mimi Shapiro, recovering from an affair with a professor, retreats to her father's remote house in Canada and there discovers a hitherto-unknown half-brother and an unsettling intruder. Lexile HL630L (Rev: BL 5/1/09; HB 5–6/09*; LMC 8–9/09; SLJ 7/1/09; VOYA 6/09)

Romances

1106 Arnold, Judith. *Meet Me in Manhattan* (11–12). 2010, Health Communications paper $13.95 (978-075731533-6). High school sweethearts Erika and Ted reconnect years later when they are both successful and working in Manhattan, but Ted wonders whether to give his heart again; for mature readers. **e** (Rev: BLO 9/9/10)

1107 Baratz-Logsted, Lauren. *Crazy Beautiful* (7–10). 2009, Houghton $16 (978-0-547-22307-0). This high school romance chronicles the unlikely attraction between the beautiful and popular Aurora and Lucius, the alienated loner who sports steel hooks after accidentally blowing his hands off in a mysterious accident.

e Lexile 910L (Rev: BLO 8/20/09; SLJ 12/09; VOYA 12/09)

1108 Blackwell, Lawana. *The Jewel of Gresham Green* (11–12). 2008, Bethany paper $13.99 (978-076420511-8). Fourth in the *Gresham Cronicles*, this novel set in 1880s England tells the story of Jewel and her young daughter, who leave the dangers of the city for the safety of Gresham Green and wind up making a difference in the vicar's family. (Rev: BL 8/08)

1109 Boschee, Rebecca L. *Mulligan Girl* (10–12). 2010, Avalon $23.95 (978-080349992-8). Ren Edwards has every single girl's dream job, shopping at upscale stores to rate the service, but her personal life is lacking until she meets golf pro Adan Bennett. (Rev: BL 2/1/10)

1110 Brabant, Loretta. *Kiss and Tell* (11–12). 2009, Avalon $23.95 (978-080349974-4). Irresponsible Alexis is suddenly the guardian of her two nieces and is desperate to break into celebrity journalism when she becomes entangled with Max, a hugely popular jazz singer; for mature readers. (Rev: BL 9/15/09)

1111 Brown, Carolyn. *Come High Water* (10–12). 2010, Avalon $23.95 (978-080347766-7). Left to run her family's inn by herself, troubled 19-year-old Bridget O'Shea seeks help from wealthy, heartbroken Wyatt Ferguson in this novel set in 1920 Huttig, Arkansas. (Rev: BL 6/1–15/10)

1112 Brown, Carolyn. *From Wine to Water* (10–12). Series: Angels and Outlaws. 2011, Avalon $23.95 (978-080347706-3). Three cousins charged with escorting three women from Texas to Louisiana in 1836 get more than they bargained for with the high-spirited, sassy sisters; the first book in a new series. (Rev: BLO 1/26/11)

1113 Caletti, Deb. *The Six Rules of Maybe* (8–12). 2010, Simon & Schuster $16.99 (978-1-4169-7969-2). When Scarlet's beautiful older sister returns home with doting new husband Hayden in tow and a baby on the way, Scarlet finds herself increasingly drawn to Hayden. ∩ **e** Lexile 820L (Rev: BL 2/15/10; HB 5–6/10; SLJ 3/10)

1114 Calvert, Candace. *Disaster Status* (11–12). 2010, Tyndale paper $12.99 (978-141432544-6). In this suspenseful, faith-based story, fire chief Scott McKenna must cope with his hospitalized nephew Cody — and Cody's new orphan status — as well as romantic advances from Cody's nurse, as he reconciles his guilt over the accident; for mature readers. **e** (Rev: BL 4/1/10)

1115 Coble, Colleen. *Lonestar Homecoming* (10–12). 2010, Thomas Nelson paper $14.99 (978-159554734-7). Two adults with troubled pasts agree to a mutually beneficial marriage of convenience — but issues from their past lives keep getting in the way in this action-packed Christian romance. ∩ **e** (Rev: BL 4/1/10)

1116 Colasanti, Susane. *Waiting for You* (7–10). 2009, Viking $17.99 (978-067001130-8). Marisa learns about heartbreak when her handsome boyfriend's eye begins to wander and her parents' marriage falls apart. Lexile HL570L (Rev: BLO 3/24/09; SLJ 8/09; VOYA 8/09)

1117 Delsol, Wendy. *Stork* (7–11). 2010, Candlewick $15.99 (978-0-7636-4844-2). Romance and Norse mythology blend in this story of 16-year-old Kat, who returns to a Minnesota town and discovers some startling facts about herself while falling for the young man, Jack, who rescued her from a long-ago accident. e Lexile 680L (Rev: BL 10/15/10; LMC 11–12/10; SLJ 1/1/11; VOYA 12/10)

1118 Eulberg, Elizabeth. *The Lonely Hearts Club* (7–10). 2010, Scholastic $17.99 (978-0-545-14031-7). Disillusioned with high school boys, Penny Lane Bloom starts a no-dating Lonely Hearts Club that proves very successful until a nice guy enters Penny's life and club rules are amended. Lexile HL640L (Rev: BL 1/1/10; SLJ 2/10)

1119 Fortier, Anne. *Juliet* (11–12). 2010, Ballantine $25 (978-034551610-7). Julie Jacobs, 25, inherits a key to a safe-deposit box in Siena, Italy, and travels there only to discover a centuries-old feud and a handsome young man called Alessandro; a lively and suspenseful story for mature readers. ∩ e (Rev: BL 7/10)

1120 Gist, Deeanne. *Maid to Match* (11–12). 2010, Bethany $19.99 (978-076420806-5); paper $14.99 (978-076420408-1). In this star-crossed love story, Mack and Tillie must fight their forbidden attraction for each other — for they're both servants in Vanderbilt's Biltmore Estate — and cope with sometimes demeaning, physically demanding work in an opulent environment; set in the late 19th century, this romance is suitable for mature readers. ∩ e (Rev: BL 6/1–15/10*)

1121 Goldblatt, Stacey. *Girl to the Core* (7–10). 2009, Delacorte $16.99 (978-0-385-73609-1); LB $19.99 (978-0-385-90587-9). Molly grows more self-confident over the course of this book as the motherless 15-year-old learns valuable lessons about friendship and dating, partly through her exposure to the younger girls in the Girl Corps. (Rev: BL 9/15/09; SLJ 9/09)

1122 Gordon, Victoria. *Wolf in Tiger's Stripes* (11–12). 2010, Five Star $25.95 (978-159414844-6). Journalist Judith finds herself hoodwinked into following an expedition searching for the fabled Tasmanian tiger in this suspenseful romance suitable for mature readers. (Rev: BL 1/1/10*)

1123 Greenfield, Jacquie. *Colorado Pride* (11–12). 2010, Five Star $25.95 (978-159414919-1). Wealthy womanizer Seth has taken custody of his orphaned 12-year-old niece Nicole when he falls for Nicole's counselor at an outreach camp for troubled kids in this Rocky Mountain romance; for mature teens. (Rev: BL 9/15/10)

1124 Griggs, Vanessa Davis. *Practicing What You Preach* (10–12). 2009, Kensington paper $15 (978-075823222-9). Complications arise when Melissa Anderson finds

out that the seemingly perfect man she is dating is divorced; for readers who enjoy Christian romance. ∩ e (Rev: BL 5/1/09)

1125 Han, Jenny. *The Summer I Turned Pretty* (7–10). 2009, Simon & Schuster $16.99 (978-141696823-8). The summer she is 15, Belly is finally noticed by two boys she's known all her life and finds that other boys are starting to appreciate her too. ∩ Lexile HL600L (Rev: BLO 5/28/09; SLJ 4/1/09*; VOYA 8/09)

1126 Harper, Karen. *Down River* (11–12). 2010, MIRA paper $7.99 (978-077832747-9). Set in the Alaskan wilderness, this suspenseful romance suitable for older teens features lots of fast-paced adventure as Lisa and her ex-boyfriend Mitch fight to survive after Lisa is pushed into the white-rapids river. (Rev: BL 2/1/10)

1127 Harris, Lisa. *Blood Ransom* (11–12). Series: Mission Hope. 2010, Zondervan paper $14.99 (978-031031905-4). Surgeon Chad and medical consultant Natalie bond over helping young Joseph heal — physically and emotionally — from the wounds wrought by the slave traders in this romantic and suspenseful novel set in Africa. ∩ e (Rev: BL 4/1/10*)

1128 Harrison, C. C. *Running from Strangers* (11–12). 2008, Five Star $25.95 (978-1-59414-709-8). Child advocate Allie Hudson tries to protect a little boy from being returned to his abusive parents and finds herself on the run and seeking help from an old boyfriend; a suspenseful romance featuring wild mustangs in high Colorado and suitable for mature readers. (Rev: BL 8/08)

1129 Hauck, Rachel. *Dining with Joy* (11–12). 2010, Thomas Nelson paper $14.99 (978-159554339-4). Charming and witty, and in way over her head, Joy Ballard finds herself hosting a television cooking show; now all she needs to do is learn how to cook — and there's handsome chef Luke who may save the day; for mature readers. (Rev: BL 11/1/10)

1130 Herbsman, Cheryl Renee. *Breathing* (7–10). 2009, Viking $16.99 (978-067001123-0). Fifteen-year-old Savannah's asthma begins to ease when she meets gorgeous Jackson Channing in this romance set on the Carolina coast and using local dialect. (Rev: BL 4/1/09; SLJ 6/1/09; VOYA 8/09)

1131 Hogan, Mary. *Pretty Face* (10–12). 2008, HarperTeen $16.99 (978-006084111-9); LB $17.89 (978-006084112-6). Overweight 16-year-old Haley travels to Italy on summer break, finding romance and self-acceptance in this girl-empowerment story. e Lexile 620L (Rev: BL 8/08; SLJ 4/08; VOYA 8/08)

1132 Jackson, Jane. *Heart of Stone* (11–12). 2010, Severn $27.95 (978-072786825-1). Young unwed mother Sarah reaches out to battle-scarred James for help in saving her father's granite quarry in this historical romance set in 1840s Cornwall; for mature readers. (Rev: BL 1/1/10)

1133 Jacobs, Anna. *Saving Willowbrook* (11–12). 2009, Severn $28.95 (978-072786738-4). Ella Turner's life is already challenging when she discovers that her devious ex-husband plans to sell her lovely property to a cutthroat company, and she seeks to protect her sick daughter from him; a romance for mature readers. (Rev: BL 5/1/09)

1134 Jacobs, Jenny. *Cold Hands, Warm Hearts* (11–12). 2010, Avalon $23.95 (978-080347775-9). Troubled single mom Char falls for charming Max as she copes with her ailing daughter Abby in this suspenseful yet tender romance; for mature readers. (Rev: BL 7/10)

1135 Judd, Wynonna, and LuAnn McLane. *Restless Heart* (11–12). 2011, NAL $25.95 (978-045122926-7). Judd's knowledge of the country music business sets apart this story of an aspiring country singer in Nashville who reconnects with her high school love just as her career takes off; for mature teens. ℮ (Rev: BLO 1/26/11)

1136 Kennedy, Joanne. *One Fine Cowboy* (11–12). 2010, Sourcebooks paper $6.99 (978-140223670-9). This humorous romance features city girl Charlie and a Wyoming cowboy who are forced together when she is sent to his ranch to research horse-whisperers. ℮ (Rev: BL 9/15/10)

1137 Klein, Lisa. *Cate of the Lost Colony* (7–10). 2010, Bloomsbury $16.99 (978-1-59990-507-5). Lady Catherine (Cate), 14, is banished to Roanoke, Virginia, when she and Sir Walter Ralegh form an attachment; there, however, she meets a handsome Croatoan Indian named Manteo. (Rev: BL 9/15/10; LMC 10/10; SLJ 1/1/11; VOYA 12/10)

1138 Lessman, Julie. *A Hope Undaunted* (11–12). Series: Winds of Change. 2010, Revell paper $14.99 (978-080073415-2). In 1929 Boston privileged Katie O'Connor finds herself working with poor but ambitious Luke McGee to help deprived children; for mature readers. (Rev: BLO 7/10)

1139 Lon, Kiki. *Enter the Parrot* (8–12). Series: Got Kung Fu? 2009, Wild Rose paper $12.99 (978-160154459-9). Romance and mystery feature in this novel about 16-year-old Jade who is learning Cantonese and martial arts while hunting for her grandfather's missing parrot. (Rev: BL 7/09)

1140 MacAlister, Katie. *Steamed* (11–12). 2010, Signet paper $7.99 (978-045122931-1). Dr. Jack Fletcher awakens in an airship captained by a woman in Victorian garb, and soon realizes that an experiment gone awry has landed him smack in the middle of his steampunk fantasies; for mature readers. ☊ ℮ (Rev: BL 2/15/10)

1141 MacLean, Sarah. *The Season* (7–10). 2009, Orchard $16.99 (978-054504886-6). Lady Alexandra Stafford falls in love while solving a murder mystery in this traditional romance set in 1815 but featuring a feisty and independent heroine. Lexile 900L (Rev: BL 2/15/09; LMC 5–6/09; SLJ 6/1/09)

1142 Mallery, Susan. *Sweet Spot* (10–12). Series: Bakery Sisters. 2008, HQN paper $6.99 (978-037377314-5). While running the family bakery and trying to forget the pain of the past, Nicole Keyes finds herself helping a foster boy and guarding her heart from his well-meaning, attractive coach; the second volume in a trilogy. ℮ (Rev: BL 8/08)

1143 Mills, Tricia. *Heartbreak River* (8–12). 2009, Penguin paper $8.99 (978-159514256-6). After her father's death in a whitewater rafting accident, 16-year-old Alex works through her grief and her fear of the water during a difficult summer in which she also struggles with her love for Sean. ℮ (Rev: BL 3/1/09; SLJ 4/1/09)

1144 Napoli, Donna Jo. *The Smile* (8–11). 2008, Dutton $17.99 (978-052547999-4). In this story about the mysterious woman behind daVinci's Mona Lisa, we follow Monna Elisabetta through her tumultuous Italian youth and young womanhood, and her propitious meeting with the artist. Lexile 580L (Rev: BL 10/1/08; HB 11–12/08; LMC 1–2/09; SLJ 11/1/08; VOYA 12/08)

1145 Nicholson, William. *Rich and Mad* (8–12). 2010, Egmont USA $17.99 (978-1-60684-120-4). Seventeen-year-olds Maddy Fisher and Rich Ross yearn for love, and after their first attempts at relationships go awry, they find one another and form a deep bond that can only be expressed one way. (Rev: BLO 8/30/10; SLJ 12/1/10)

1146 Ockler, Sarah. *20 Boy Summer* (9–11). 2009, Little, Brown $16.99 (978-031605159-0). Anna's secret boyfriend, Matt, dies before she can tell her best friend (who is also Matt's sister) about their love. Lexile 940L (Rev: BL 5/1/09; SLJ 6/1/09; VOYA 10/09)

1147 Odiwe, Jane. *Lydia Bennet's Story: A Sequel to Pride and Prejudice* (10–12). 2008, Sourcebooks paper $12.95 (978-140221475-2). Jane Odiwe fills in the tale of the flirtatious Bennet sister Lydia and her life with Mr. Wickham. (Rev: BL 9/15/08)

1148 Odiwe, Jane. *Willoughby's Return* (10–12). 2009, Sourcebooks paper $14.99 (978-140222267-2). In this followup to *Sense and Sensibility,* now-married Marianne is sent into a spiral of self-doubt by the attractive Willoughby, who is now determined to get back in her good graces. (Rev: BL 11/15/09)

1149 Perkins, Stephanie. *Anna and the French Kiss* (9–12). 2010, Dutton $16.99 (978-0-525-42327-0). When Anna's romance-novelist father sends her to an elite American boarding school in Paris for her senior year of high school, she reluctantly goes, and meets an amazing boy who becomes her best friend, in spite of the fact that they both want something more. (Rev: BL 11/15/10; SLJ 12/1/10)

1150 Perl, Erica S. *Vintage Veronica* (9–12). 2010, Knopf/Borzoi $16.99 (978-0-375-85923-6); LB $19.99

(978-0-375-95923-3). Fifteen-year-old Veronica may be overweight but she also has good fashion sense and finds a job in a used-clothing store; there she finds unexpected romance. Lexile 710L (Rev: BL 2/15/10; SLJ 2/10)

1151 Peterson, Tracie. *Embers of Love* (10–12). 2010, Bethany $19.99 (978-076420819-5); paper $14.99 (978-076420612-2). After calling off her marriage to Stuart, young Lizzie escapes to a logging town in Texas where she and her friend Deborah find love and intellectual challenge; this Christian romance is set in 1885. ⌒ ℮ (Rev: BL 9/15/10)

1152 Peterson, Tracie. *A Promise to Believe In* (11–12). Series: Brides of Gallatin County. 2008, Bethany $19.99 (978-076420586-6); paper $13.99 (978-076420148-6). This first volume in a romance trilogy set in Montana Territory begins with several tragedies that leave the three Gallatin sisters alone to run the family hotel and fend off the opposition; for mature readers. ⌒ (Rev: BL 9/15/08*)

1153 Poppen, Nikki. *The Madcap* (11–12). 2010, Avalon $23.95 (978-080349987-4). Audacious (and very wealthy) Marianne, a 19-year-old from San Francisco, sets out to woo a noble but impoverished Brit away from his stiff, proper bride-to-be; for mature readers. (Rev: BLO 1/8/10)

1154 Rallison, Janette. *Just One Wish* (7–11). 2009, Putnam $15.99 (978-039924618-0). Annika, 17, gets more than she bargained for (including romance) when she tries to get Steve Raleigh, a teen TV star, to visit her sick little brother. Lexile HL730L (Rev: BL 2/1/09; SLJ 5/1/09)

1155 Raybourn, Deanna. *The Dead Travel Fast* (11–12). 2010, MIRA paper $13.95 (978-077832765-3). Visiting her friend Cosmina in Transylvania, author Theodora meets a disturbingly attractive count and learns more about the region when a servant girl is found dead with bite marks in her neck; a gothic romance for mature readers. ℮ (Rev: BL 2/15/10)

1156 Resau, Laura. *The Ruby Notebook* (7–11). 2010, Delacorte $16.99 (978-0-385-90615-9); LB $19.99 (978-0-385-73653-4). Recently arrived in France, 16-year-old Zeeta's relationship with her American boyfriend gets complicated when she's enchanted by gorgeous, mysterious Jean-Claude in this sequel to *The Indigo Notebook* (2009). ℮ Lexile HL750L (Rev: BLO 8/30/10; SLJ 10/1/10; VOYA 12/10)

1157 Rice, Patricia. *The Wicked Wyckerly* (11–12). Series: Rebellious Sons. 2010, Signet paper $7.99 (978-045123071-3). Fitz Wyckerly lives a life of excess and irresponsibility — until his father and brother die suddenly, making him an earl overnight and leaving him with a pile of debt and the need to find a rich wife; this humorous romance is suitable for mature readers. ℮ (Rev: BL 7/10)

1158 Roberts, Nora. *The Search* (11–12). 2010, Putnam $26.95 (978-039915657-1). Romance and suspense combine in this novel about independent Fiona, a dog trainer; for mature readers. ℮ (Rev: BL 4/1/10)

1159 Rose, Elisabeth. *Outback Hero* (11–12). 2009, Avalon $23.95 (978-080349982-9). Deceptions threaten to derail romance in this story of singer Stella Starr, traveling incognito in the Australian Outback, and Koologong resident Jonathan who hopes she will model clothing from his factory; for mature readers. (Rev: BL 12/15/09)

1160 Saint James, Joycelyn. *One, Two, Three . . . Together* (11–12). 2010, Avalon $23.95 (978-080347762-9). When Liz's prima ballerina mother breaks her leg, Liz assumes responsibility for running her mom's dance studio — and discovers a pile of financial trouble, and one shining but unlikely way out — in this light romance for mature readers. (Rev: BLO 7/10)

1161 Sawyer, Kim Vogel. *A Hopeful Heart* (11–12). 2010, Bethany paper $14.99 (978-076420509-5). Socially awkward Tressa gains self-confidence, faith, and romance on the American frontier when her aunt sends her west to learn how to be a wife. ⌒ ℮ (Rev: BL 6/1–15/10)

1162 Schroeder, Lisa. *Chasing Brooklyn* (8–12). 2010, Simon & Schuster $15.99 (978-1-4169-9168-7). A year after Lucca died, his girlfriend — Brooklyn — and his brother Nico are still grappling with grief; when Gabe, who was driving that night, dies of an overdose, Brooklyn and Nico experience strange dreams and draw closer together; a moving novel told in verse. ℮ Lexile HL510L (Rev: BLO 11/17/09; SLJ 2/10; VOYA 4/10)

1163 Seilstad, Lorna. *Making Waves* (10–12). 2010, Revell paper $14.99 (978-080073445-9). It's 1895 and Marguerite Westing's independence and interests in astronomy and sailing have attracted only one, wealthy suitor; when she meets the attractive Trip Andrews she must choose between him and the riches that will save her whole family — a light, Christian romance. ℮ (Rev: BL 8/10)

1164 Sheinmel, Alyssa B. *The Beautiful Between* (9–11). 2010, Knopf $16.99 (978-0-375-86182-6). Shy Rapunzel-like Connelly 16, and cool prince-like Jeremy form a deep friendship as Jeremy shares his fears about his sister's leukemia and Connelly reveals her need to find out how her father died. ℮ (Rev: LMC 8–9/10; SLJ 5/10)

1165 Simonsen, Mary Lydon. *The Perfect Bride for Mr. Darcy* (11–12). 2011, Sourcebooks paper $14.99 (978-140224025-6). This retelling of *Pride and Prejudice* allows several minor characters to play larger roles in the future of Darcy and Elizabeth; for mature readers. ℮ (Rev: BL 1/1/11)

1166 Snelling, Lauraine. *A Measure of Mercy* (10–12). Series: Home to Blessing. 2009, Bethany paper $13.99

(978-076420609-2). Astrid is a modern early 1900s young woman who plans to go to Chicago to become a doctor, but economic and romantic factors make this decision difficult in this faith-based novel, the first in a series. ∩ ℮ (Rev: BLO 9/15/09)

1167 Springer, Kristina. *The Espressologist* (7–10). 2009, Farrar $16.99 (978-0-374-32228-1). High school senior Jane's amazing ability to make matches among her coffeehouse customers doesn't extend to herself, but in the end . . . . ℮ Lexile HL640L (Rev: BL 10/15/09; SLJ 9/09)

1168 Stepakoff, Jeffrey. *Fireworks over Toccoa* (11–12). 2010, St. Martin's $22.99 (978-031258158-9). On the eve of her husband's return from combat in World War II Lily meets Jake, a pyrotechnics expert in town to produce a show for the soldiers' homecoming, and falls in love for the first time; suitable for mature readers. ∩ (Rev: BL 2/15/10)

1169 Sundin, Sarah. *A Distant Melody* (10–12). 2010, Revell paper $14.99 (978-080073421-3). Allie Miller is torn between her parents' wishes for her to marry her father's icy employee, and her own attraction to a less-than-perfect Air Force officer in this Christian romance set during World War II. (Rev: BL 2/15/10)

1170 Tahmaseb, Charity, and Darcy Vance. *The Geek Girl's Guide to Cheerleading* (9–12). 2009, Simon & Schuster paper $8.99 (978-141697834-3). Geeky Bethany decides to try cheerleading as a way to the heart of the attractive, sporty Jack. (Rev: BLO 6/19/09)

1171 Tanner, Janet. *Seagull Bay* (10–12). 2010, Severn $28.95 (978-072786822-0). Taken in by her English Aunt Fran, Canadian orphan Dawn Stephens, 17, retreats into fantasies of future stardom until she meets Sandy, a man who absorbs her entirely; set in the 1960s. ∩ (Rev: BL 12/1/09)

1172 Tayleur, Karen. *Chasing Boys* (8–11). 2009, Walker $16.99 (978-080279830-5). El starts at a new school and finds that the boy of her dreams is already taken — by a "perfect" girl named Angelique. ℮ Lexile 690L (Rev: BL 2/15/09; SLJ 6/1/09)

1173 Thomas, Jodi. *Texas Blue* (10–12). Series: Whispering Mountain. 2011, Berkley paper $7.99 (978-042524047-2). High-spirited Emily McMurray poses as a lowly ranch hand when her cousin sends along three men of marrying age, one of whom came to marry a rancher's daughter, but falls in love with the "ranch hand" instead. (Rev: BL 3/1–15/11)

1174 Thompson, Alicia. *Psych Major Syndrome* (8–10). 2009, Hyperion $16.99 (978-1-4231-1457-4). Leigh, a serious-minded college freshman in California, wrestles with her relationships with friends and the opposite sex. (Rev: BL 10/15/09; SLJ 9/09)

1175 Thompson, Renee. *The Bridge at Valentine* (11–12). 2010, Tres Picos paper $14.95 (978-097453092-5). Farmer's daughter July falls for dreamy, introspective

Rory in this 1890s Plains take on the Montagues and Capulets; for mature readers. (Rev: BL 8/10)

1176 Triana, Gaby. *Riding the Universe* (10–12). 2009, HarperTeen $16.99 (978-0-06-088570-0). Seventeen-year-old Chloé suddenly finds herself having to choose between Gordon, her chemistry tutor, and Rock, who has loved her since elementary school. ℮ (Rev: BL 8/09; SLJ 8/09)

1177 Vogts, Deborah. *Seeds of Summer* (11–12). Series: Season of Tallgrass. 2010, Zondervan paper $12.99 (978-031029276-0). Rodeo queen Natalie must choose between faith and anger when she meets a handsome minister who wants to help her cope with bringing up her half siblings; set in rural Kansas this is suitable for mature readers. ℮ (Rev: BL 7/10)

1178 Warner, Ann. *Dreams for Stones* (11–12). 2008, Samhain paper $14.00 (978-159998974-7). Vivid Alaskan scenery and strong emotions color this tale of broken and mended hearts and the struggle to become whole after loss. (Rev: BL 9/15/08)

1179 Wilkins, Kim. *Unclaimed Heart* (9–12). 2009, Penguin paper $8.99 (978-159514258-0). Constance is an adventurous 17-year-old British girl searching for her long-lost mother in this exciting romance set in the 18th century and featuring a sea voyage, stowaways, and Ceylon (now Sri Lanka). (Rev: BL 6/1–15/09)

1180 Willig, Lauren. *The Betrayal of the Blood Lily* (10–12). Series: Pink Carnation. 2010, Dutton $25.95 (978-052595150-6). In her continuing research into 18th-century British spies, contemporary scholar Eloise Kelly investigates the life of rebellious Penelope Deveraux, who moves to India with her aloof, aristocratic husband and finds herself intrigued by their escort, Captain Alex Reid. ∩ ℮ (Rev: BL 12/1/09)

1181 Willig, Lauren. *The Mischief of the Mistletoe* (10–12). Series: Pink Carnation. 2010, Dutton $24.95 (978-052595187-2). A note on the wrapping of a Christmas pudding sets a young teacher and her new beau off on a spying adventure in this Regency romp. ℮ (Rev: BL 9/15/10)

1182 Woods, Janet. *Salting the Wound* (11–12). 2010, Severn $28.95 (978-072786829-9). When Marianne tries to console her sister's spurned beau, she stumbles into the hold of his ship and is not discovered for days — setting in motion a series of misunderstandings and recriminations; this novel, set in 1850, is suitable for mature readers. ∩ (Rev: BL 12/1/09)

1183 Zeises, Lara M. *The Sweet Life of Stella Madison* (8–11). 2009, Delacorte $16.99 (978-0-385-73146-1); LB $19.99 (978-0-385-90178-9). Stella, 17, becomes an intern for Baltimore's *Daily Journal* and, perhaps because of her foodie parents, is assigned to restaurant reviews; she is grateful for the help of the gorgeous Jeremy while fretting about her feelings toward her boyfriend Max. (Rev: BL 9/1/09; SLJ 7/1/09; VOYA 10/09)

Science Fiction

1184 Adams, John Joseph, ed. *Seeds of Change* (10–12). 2008, Prime $19.95 (978-0-8095-7310-3). *Seeds of Change* is an interesting compilation of science fiction stories, mostly by new authors, that center on a small change that affects the world in a big way. (Rev: BL 8/08; SLJ 11/1/08)

1185 Anderson, Taylor. *Crusade* (11–12). Series: Destroyermen. 2008, Roc $26.50 (978-045146230-5). A sequel to *Into the Storm* (2008), this novel set in an alternate world pits Lt. Commander Reddy and the Lemurian allies against the Grik, who are threatening a neighboring society; for mature teens who enjoy science fiction with a military flavor. (Rev: BL 9/1/08*)

1186 Atwood, Margaret. *The Year of the Flood* (11–12). 2009, Doubleday $26 (978-038552877-1). After a pandemic decimates a city, survivors band together in a fragile environment ruled by a sinister government; this novel intersects with the world of *Oryx and Crake* (2003) and is suitable for mature readers. ☊ ℮ (Rev: BL 7/09*)

1187 Bacigalupi, Paolo. *Ship Breaker* (8–12). 2010, Little, Brown $17.99 (978-0-316-05621-2). In a future, chaotic Accelerated Age Nailer and his friend Pima come across a wealthy girl as they scavenge among wrecks on the beach; can they help her and keep her safe from her enemies? ☊ Lexile HL690L (Rev: BL 5/15/10*; HB 7–8/10; LMC 8–9/10; SLJ 6/10)

1188 Bacigalupi, Paolo. *The Windup Girl* (10–12). 2009, Night Shade $24.95 (978-1-59780-157-7). This intricate science fiction novel is set in a grim Thailand of the future, where food is the most valuable asset, and the avaricious search for a new source of nutrition could jeopardize the future of the entire country. (Rev: SLJ 12/09)

1189 Beaudoin, Sean. *Fade to Blue* (8–11). Illus. by author. 2009, Little, Brown $16.99 (978-031601417-5). Goth girl Sophie Blue's father disappears on her 17th birthday and she and her hunk friend Kenny Fade share a feeling they may be losing their minds in this quirky, dark yet funny novel that incorporates a comic book and involves a lab that may be infecting young people with software code. (Rev: BL 6/1–15/09; SLJ 10/09)

1190 Beck, Ian. *Pastworld: A Mystery of the Near Future* (7–10). 2009, Bloomsbury $16.99 (978-1-59990-040-7). The year is 2050 and London has been turned into a Victorian theme park complete with a series of gruesome murders. ℮ Lexile 880L (Rev: BL 11/15/09; LMC 11–12/09; SLJ 12/09)

1191 Bradbury, Ray. *The Martian Chronicles: The Fortieth Anniversary Edition* (10–12). 1950, Doubleday $15.95 (978-0-385-05060-9). Earth's efforts to colonize Mars are recounted in this collection of famous short stories. (Rev: BLO 8/18/08)

1192 Brindley, John. *The Rule of Claw* (7–10). 2009, Carolrhoda $18.95 (978-158013608-2). In a land and time where mutants run wild, 15-year-old Ash is kidnapped by the Raptors and caught up in a war between two genetically altered races. Lexile HL740L (Rev: BLO 2/9/09; SLJ 5/1/09)

1193 Bynum, Laura. *Veracity* (10–12). 2010, Pocket $25 (978-143912334-8). After her daughter is taken away, a mother must fight the dystopian society she had diligently served. ℮ (Rev: BL 12/1/09)

1194 Card, Orson Scott. *Hidden Empire* (10–12). 2009, Tor $24.99 (978-076532004-9). In this thrilling sequel to 2006's *Empire*, a cast of politicians, soldiers, and military advisers copes with conspiracy and imperialist politics in a plague-stricken futuristic Africa. ℮ (Rev: BL 11/15/09)

1195 Card, Orson Scott. *Pathfinder* (8–12). 2010, Simon & Schuster $18.99 (978-1-4169-9176-2). Thirteen-year-old Rigg can see the paths of others' pasts, and revelations after his father's death set him on a dangerous quest accompanied by friends who can bend time. ℮ (Rev: BL 11/1/10; SLJ 12/1/10)

1196 Cheva, Cherry. *DupliKate* (7–10). 2009, HarperTeen $16.99 (978-0-06-128854-8). When 17-year-old Kate's online gaming avatar comes to life, the overbooked teen welcomes the extra set of hands — until her duplicate's wild nature and separate agenda begin to come through. ℮ (Rev: BL 12/1/09; SLJ 10/09)

1197 Collins, Suzanne. *Catching Fire* (9–12). Series: The Hunger Games. 2009, Scholastic $17.99 (978-043902349-8). Katniss and Peeta find unexpected challenges as they travel through Panem in this exciting sequel to *The Hunger Games* (2008). (Rev: BL 7/09; LMC 1–2/10; SLJ 9/09)

1198 Collins, Suzanne. *The Hunger Games* (7–12). 2008, Scholastic $17.99 (978-0-439-02348-1). A tense survival story set in a future dystopian North America, in which 16-year-old Kat is thrust into a fight to the death on live TV. ☊ (Rev: BL 9/1/08*; HB 7–8/08; LMC 11–12/08*; SLJ 9/1/08*; VOYA 4/08)

1199 Dashner, James. *The Scorch Trials. Bk. 2* (9–12). Series: Maze Runner Trilogy. 2010, Delacorte $17.99 (978-0-385-73875-0); LB $20.99 (978-0-385-90745-3). In this sequel to *The Maze Runner* (2009), Thomas and a group of other boys have escaped the horrors of the Maze and now seek an antidote to the insanity disease with which they are told they have been infected. ℮ (Rev: BL 1/1–15/11; SLJ 12/1/10)

1200 DeNiro, Alan. *Total Oblivion, More or Less* (11–12). 2009, Spectra paper $15 (978-055359254-2). Rampant plagues, slave traders, and marauders from the past are laying waste to America; but for 16-year-old Macy, the biggest danger of all may be posed by her conniving younger brother. For mature readers. ❤ (Rev: BL 10/15/09*)

1201 Denning, Troy. *Abyss* (10–12). Series: Star Wars: Fate of the Jedi. 2009, Del Rey $27 (978-034550918-5). The order of the Jedi is in danger of crumbling in this fast-paced Star Wars book (third in a series). (Rev: BL 7/09)

1202 Denning, Troy. *Vortex* (10–12). Series: Star Wars: Fate of the Jedi. 2010, Del Rey $27 (978-034550920-8). Converging plotlines are advanced in this sixth installment of the nine-part Star Wars series. (Rev: BL 11/1/10)

1203 Dick, Philip K. *Nick and the Glimmung* (7–10). 2008, Subterranean $35.00 (978-159606168-2). Die-hard science fiction fans will enjoy this complex story in which Dick travels from Earth to a more animal-friendly planet. (Rev: BL 3/1/09)

1204 Doyle, Larry. *Go, Mutants!* (10–12). 2010, Ecco $23.99 (978-006168655-9). J!m, a 17-year-old alien with blue skin, atomic ape Johnny, and their gooey sidekick Jelly band together to try to outwit bullies and win girls. (Rev: BL 6/1–15/10)

1205 Duane, Diane. *Omnitopia Dawn* (11–12). 2010, DAW $24.95 (978-075640623-3). Video game creator Dev Logan worries about hackers on the eve of a huge new expansion of his intricate, addictive online game, Omnitopia. ❤ (Rev: BL 8/10)

1206 Falkner, Brian. *Brain Jack* (9–12). 2010, Random $17.99 (978-0-375-84366-2); LB $20.99 (978-0-375-93924-2). In a near-future New York City, 14-year-old computer geek Sam Wilson manages to hack into the AT&T network and attracts attention from a government department. ❤ (Rev: BL 10/1/10; SLJ 12/1/10)

1207 Gill, David Macinnis. *Black Hole Sun* (8–11). 2010, Greenwillow $16.99 (978-0-06-167304-7). In this action-packed novel set on a dystopian Mars, 16-year-old Durango and other mercenaries fight to protect mines at the South Pole. (Rev: BL 6/1/10*; SLJ 11/1/10)

1208 Golden, Christie. *Allies* (10–12). Series: Star Wars: Fate of the Jedi. 2010, Del Rey $27 (978-034550914-7). Luke and Ben decide to challenge Abeloth, the evil force that is threatening the young Jedi. ∩ ❤ (Rev: BL 5/1/10)

1209 Golden, Christie. *Omen* (9–12). Series: Star Wars: Fate of the Jedi. 2009, Del Rey $27 (978-034550912-3). Second in a series, *Omen* opens with many Jedi mysteriously insane, and Luke and Ben trying to discover why, following Jacen, and getting closer to an unknown planet full of Sith. ❤ (Rev: BL 5/1/09)

1210 Haldeman, Joe. *Marsbound* (10–12). 2008, Ace $24.95 (978-0-441-01595-5). Carmen Dula has just graduated from high school when her family wins a chance to live on Mars, and while she knows it will be an adventure, Carmen has no idea what she is in for. ❤ (Rev: BL 8/08)

1211 Hauge, Lesley. *Nomansland* (8–11). 2010, Henry Holt $16.99 (978-0-8050-9064-2). In a future dystopian world, members of a society of women discover a trove of fashion magazines , with unsettling results. ∩ (Rev: BL 5/15/10; HB 7–8/10; LMC 8–9/10; SLJ 8/10)

1212 Helfers, John, and Martin H. Greenberg, eds. *Future Americas* (10–12). 2008, DAW paper $7.99 (978-075640508-3). Themes ranging from ecology to criminal investigation to designer fetuses are examined in these thought-provoking stories from a variety of authors. ❤ (Rev: BL 6/1–15/08)

1213 Herbert, Brian, and Kevin J. Anderson. *Paul of Dune* (10–12). 2008, Tor $27.95 (978-0-7653-1294-5). Good on its own or as a link between *Dune* (1965) and *Dune: Messiah* (1970), this novel tells of Paul Muad-dib as the emperor and explains how he became the messiah. ∩ ❤ (Rev: BL 8/08)

1214 Jinks, Catherine. *Living Hell* (7–10). 2010, Houghton $17 (978-0-15-206193-7). On a spaceship on a long journey to find a habitable planet, 17-year-old Cheney finds the peaceful routine turned on its head when they pass through a radiation field. ❤ Lexile 600L (Rev: BL 2/15/10; HB 3–4/10; SLJ 4/10; VOYA 6/10)

1215 Kellerman, Faye, and Aliza Kellerman. *Prism* (9–12). 2009, Harper $16.99 (978-006168721-1); LB $17.89 (978-006168722-8). A bus crash propels three high school students into a parallel universe in which illness and medicine are not recognized. ❤ (Rev: BL 7/09; SLJ 8/09)

1216 Kelly, James Patrick. *The Wreck of the Godspeed and Other Stories* (10–12). 2008, Golden Gryphon $24.95 (978-1-930846-51-7). This volume contains previously published science fiction short stories that evoke a surreal atmosphere through the strangeness of the settings while dealing with basic human emotions. (Rev: BL 8/08)

1217 Koontz, Dean. *Breathless* (10–12). 2009, Bantam $28 (978-055380715-8). In this trademark Koontz alien-encounter tale, two furry, pint-size beings arrive on Earth and set about applying their superhuman intelligence to the turmoil they encounter. (Rev: BL 11/15/09)

1218 Landon, Kristen. *The Limit* (8–11). 2010, Simon & Schuster $15.99 (978-1-4424-0271-3). When his family goes over its spending limit, 13-year-old Matt is sent to the Federal Debt Rehabilitation Agency, where his own living conditions are tolerable, but he recognizes that others are suffering and must be rescued. ❤ (Rev: BL 10/1/10; SLJ 12/1/10)

1219 Lerner, Edward M. *Fools' Experiments* (11–12). 2008, Tor $25.95 (978-076531901-2). *Fools' Experi-*

ments is a clever, suspenseful science fiction novel that uses the possibilities of computer technology's evolution to chill and thrill; for mature readers. ☊ (Rev: BL 9/15/08)

1220 Lloyd, Saci. *The Carbon Diaries 2015* (9–12). 2009, Holiday $17.95 (978-082342190-9). Teenager Laura documents daily life in London after climate change has led to carbon rationing and drastic changes in energy use. Lexile HL690L (Rev: BL 2/15/09; HB 5–6/09; SLJ 5/1/09*)

1221 Lloyd, Saci. *The Carbon Diaries 2017* (9–12). 2010, Holiday House $17.95 (978-0-8234-2260-9). In the aftermath of the global disaster seen in *The Carbon Diaries 2015,* new carbon rationing has been introduced in Great Britain, the population is abandoning London, and new right-wing political groups are in ascendance; these upheavals disrupt Laura Brown's studies and her punk group's tour of Europe. Lexile 690L (Rev: BL 2/15/10; HB 3–4/10; SLJ 4/10)

1222 Locke, M. J. *Up Against It* (10–12). 2011, Tor $25.99 (978-076531515-1). On the asteroid colony of Phoecaea rocket-bike-riding teens expose a scheme by the Martian mob to gain control of the colony through the water supply, and cameras everywhere film the colonists for a reality TV show running back on Earth. (Rev: BL 3/1–15/11)

1223 McDevitt, Jack. *Time Travelers Never Die* (10–12). 2009, Ace $24.95 (978-044101763-8). Plucky protagonist Shel learns of his impending demise when he stumbles upon his father's time travel devices, and desperately searches for a way to change his future. (Rev: BL 11/15/09)

1224 Malley, Gemma. *The Resistance* (9–12). 2008, Bloomsbury $16.99 (978-159990302-6). Teens Peter and Anna are working for the resistance, determined to restore the world's natural order and deliver it from the grips of Longevity — the drug that offers eternal life but renders unapproved reproduction a criminal act. ℮ Lexile 750L (Rev: BL 11/1/08; SLJ 12/08; VOYA 10/08)

1225 Mancusi, Marianne. *Razor Girl* (11–12). 2008, Love Spell paper $6.99 (978-050552780-6). An apocalyptic thriller combines with a tense romance in this story of survival in a world devastated by a Super Flu; for mature readers. (Rev: BL 9/15/08)

1226 Mariz, Rae. *The Unidentified* (7–11). 2010, HarperCollins $16.99 (978-0-06-180208-9). Kid rejects the corporate, technology-based education system in which students learn by playing games in malls, and is drawn toward the underground activists called the Unidentified. ℮ Lexile HL740L (Rev: BL 9/15/10; SLJ 10/1/10; VOYA 12/10)

1227 Ness, Patrick. *The Ask and the Answer* (9–12). Series: Chaos Walking. 2009, Candlewick $18.99 (978-0-7636-4490-1). Alternating chapters follow teens Todd

and Viola as they are separated by the brutal regime in New Prentisstown, a space colony inhabited by men who can hear others' thoughts; a sequel to *The Knife of Never Letting Go* (2008). ☊ ℮ Lexile 770L (Rev: BL 8/09*; HB 9–10/09; SLJ 1/10)

1228 Ness, Patrick. *The Knife of Never Letting Go* (8–12). Series: Chaos Walking. 2008, Candlewick $18.99 (978-076363931-0). Young Todd Hewitt realizes that there is a hole in the Noise — which makes the thoughts of men and animals audible — and sets off with his talking dog Viola to seek answers; the opening volume in a trilogy. ☊ ℮ Lexile 860L (Rev: BL 9/1/08*; HB 11–12/08; SLJ 11/1/08; VOYA 10/08)

1229 Ness, Patrick. *Monsters of Men* (9–12). Series: Chaos Walking. 2010, Candlewick $18.99 (978-0-7636-4751-3). War is at the center of this conclusion to the trilogy involving Todd and Viola, who must make difficult decisions. ☊ ℮ (Rev: BL 7/10*; HB 11–12/10; SLJ 9/1/10)

1230 Nye, Jody Lynne. *View from the Imperium* (10–12). 2011, Baen paper $7.99 (978-143913430-6). This fast-paced, often humorous space opera follows the adventures of Ensign Thomas Innes Loche, who is enlisted to travel to the far reaches of the empire to inspect a military installation and runs into a band of dangerous space pirates. (Rev: BLO 3/1–15/11)

1231 O'Brien, Caragh M. *Birthmarked* (9–12). 2010, Roaring Brook $16.99 (978-1-59643-569-8). As a midwife in her village outside the ramparts, 16-year-old Gaia must each month deliver the first three babies to the walled Enclave; she does not doubt the status quo until her parents are arrested, and she then sets out to rescue them and question the system. ℮ Lexile HL800L (Rev: BL 2/15/10; LMC 5–6/10; SLJ 5/10)

1232 Osterlund, Anne. *Academy 7* (8–12). 2009, Penguin paper $8.99 (978-014241437-8). Aerin and Dane both attend the elite Academy 7 but come from very different worlds. They find themselves attracted to each other as they navigate the demands of school and political intrigue. Lexile 760L (Rev: BL 5/15/09; SLJ 9/09; VOYA 4/10)

1233 Patneaude, David. *Epitaph Road* (9–12). 2010, Egmont USA $16.99 (978-1-60684-055-9). In 2097 young Kellen, a 14-year-old boy in a population where males are restricted to a mere 5 percent, seeks to protect his rebellious father. ℮ Lexile HL720L (Rev: BL 1/1/10; LMC 10/10; SLJ 4/10)

1234 Polansky, Steven. *The Bradbury Report* (10–12). 2010, Weinstein $24.95 (978-160286122-0). In this complex thriller set in 2071, Anna recognizes an escaped clone as her old boyfriend, and sets out to reunite the clone with his original. ℮ (Rev: BL 4/1/10*)

1235 Priest, Cherie. *Clementine* (11–12). Series: Clockwork Century. 2010, Subterranean $25 (978-159606308-2). In this steampunk take on the Civil War,

76

Confederate spy Belle Boyd has taken a job with the Pinkerton detective agency and must investigate who's threatening the *Clementine,* a blimp carrying needed supplies over the Rocky Mountains. ∩ ℮ (Rev: BLO 5/3/10)

1236 Ringo, John. *Live Free or Die* (11–12). 2010, Baen $26 (978-143913332-3). An unfriendly breed of extra-terrestrials is at war with Earth, and an unlikely protagonist — Vermont native Tyler Vernon — saves the day; for mature readers. (Rev: BLO 1/8/10)

1237 Sawyer, Robert J. *WWW: Wake* (10–12). 2009, Ace $24.95 (978-044101679-2). Hoping to break out of the darkness, 10th-grader Caitlin opts for experimental eye surgery and realizes afterward that she is seeing the World Wide Web instead of real life. ℮ (Rev: BL 4/15/09)

1238 Scalzi, John. *Zoe's Tale* (10–12). Series: Old Man's War. 2008, Tor $24.95 (978-0-7653-1698-1). This addition to the trilogy is told from 15-year-old Zoe Perry's point of view as she helps defend the colony against an alien alliance. (Rev: BL 8/08)

1239 Scarrow, Alex. *Time Riders* (9–12). 2010, Walker $16.99 (978-0-8027-2172-3). Three teens join forces to travel through time and correct changes in history made by other time travelers. (Rev: LMC 11–12/10; SLJ 6/11)

1240 Schubert, Edmund R., and Orson Scott Card, eds. *Orson Scott Card's InterGalatic Medicine Show* (10–12). 2008, Tor paper $15.95 (978-076532000-1). Likening fantasy stories to an old-time medicine show, Schubert and Card present 17 new stories — 5 from the Ender series — that have appeared in Card's e-zine. ℮ (Rev: BL 6/1–15/08)

1241 Testa, Dom. *The Comet's Curse* (7–10). Series: Galahad. 2009, Tor $16.95 (978-076532107-7). The first book in a six-part series, this sci-fi drama starts when a comet spews deadly dust, killing the adults on Earth and forcing 250 teens into space to colonize a safer planet. ℮ Lexile 840L (Rev: BL 12/15/08; LMC 8–9/09; SLJ 3/1/09; VOYA 4/09)

1242 Turtledove, Harry. *The Valley-Westside War* (10–12). 2008, Tor $24.95 (978-0-7653-1487-1). In post-nuclear Los Angeles, two teens struggle to overcome the prejudices of their warring principalities as they learn that even leaders make mistakes. (Rev: BL 6/1–15/08; SLJ 9/08)

1243 Waldrop, Howard. *Other Worlds, Better Lives: A Howard Waldrop Reader: Selected Long Fiction, 1989–2003* (10–12). 2008, Old Earth paper $15.00 (978-188296838-1). The seven novellas found in this book are fine examples of the author's skill and artistry as a writer of science fiction. (Rev: BL 9/15/08)

1244 Wasserman, Robin. *Crashed* (9–12). 2009, Simon & Schuster $16.99 (978-1-4169-7453-6). "Mech" — or

synthetic human — Lia fights a conspiracy to destroy her and her kind in this sequel to 2008's *Skinned.* ∩ ℮ Lexile HL770L (Rev: BLO 10/21/09; SLJ 1/10; VOYA 8/09)

1245 Wasserman, Robin. *Skinned* (9–12). 2008, Simon & Schuster $15.99 (978-141693634-3). Although 17-year-old Lia's body was destroyed in a car accident, her mind lives on in her new persona as a "mech"— a mechanical replica — and the previously popular and glamorous girl must cope with being ostracized and isolated. ℮ Lexile HL630L (Rev: BL 10/15/08; LMC 5–6/09; SLJ 1/1/09)

1246 Weber, David. *Worlds of Weber: Ms. Midshipwoman Harrington and Other Stories* (10–12). 2008, Subterranean $45.00 (978-159606177-4). An interesting and lengthy compilation of Weber's short stories full of fascinating characters and science fiction adventure. (Rev: BL 9/1/08)

1247 Willis, Connie. *Blackout* (11–12). 2010, Spectra $26 (978-055380319-8). Three researchers from the future (2060) travel back in time to 1940 London, where they face the perils of the Blitz, including evacuations, blackouts, and bombings. ℮ (Rev: BL 2/1/10)

1248 Winters, Ben H. *Android Karenina* (10–12). 2010, Quirk paper $12.95 (978-159474460-0). Winters implants numerous robots, cyborgs, and other sci-fi elements into Tolstoy's classic tale of ill-fated love. (Rev: BL 6/1–15/10)

1249 Yu, Charles. *How to Live Safely in a Science Fictional Universe* (11–12). 2010, Pantheon $24 (978-030737920-7). Charles, a bumbling time-machine repair man in a futuristic universe, seeks answers about his inventor father's disappearance; for mature readers. (Rev: BL 8/10)

1250 Zahn, Timothy. *Odd Girl Out* (10–12). Series: Quadrail. 2008, Tor $24.95 (978-076531733-9). The third in the Quadrail series, this book delivers action and adventure in an interstellar setting. ∩ ℮ (Rev: BL 9/15/08)

Sports

1251 Cohen, Joshua C. *Leverage* (10–12). 2011, Dutton $16.99 (978-052542306-5). Diminutive gymnastics star Danny finds unlikely support against bullying in Kurt, the new football fullback who stutters. ∩ ℮ (Rev: BL 12/15/10*; LMC 5–6/11; SLJ 4/11; VOYA 2/11)

1252 Deuker, Carl. *Payback Time* (7–10). 2010, Houghton $16 (978-0-547-27981-7). Student reporter Mitch finds himself in a tough situation as he investigates a potential football cheating scandal. ℮ (Rev: BL 9/1/10*; HB 11–12/10; SLJ 9/1/10; VOYA 12/10)

1253 Flynn, Pat. *Out of His League* (9–12). 2008, Walker $16.95 (978-080279776-6). Australian exchange student Ozzie uses his rugby skills to lead the football team to victory for his Texas high school. Lexile 750L (Rev: BLO 8/08; SLJ 9/1/08)

1254 Halpin, Brendan. *Shutout* (8–10). 2010, Farrar $16.99 (978-0-374-36899-9). Amanda and Lena's long-standing friendship begins to fray when they enter high school and Lena makes the varsity soccer team while Amanda's sore heel disqualifies her. (Rev: BL 9/1/10*; SLJ 8/10)

1255 McKissack, Fredrick, Jr. *Shooting Star* (9–12). 2009, Simon & Schuster $16.99 (978-1-4169-4745-5). Steroids initially help Jomo build up his body, but the African American football player soon experiences mood swings that lead him to regret this drug use. ℮ Lexile HL720L (Rev: BL 9/1/09; SLJ 9/09)

1256 MacLeod, J. E. *Waiting to Score* (9–12). 2009, WestSide $16.95 (978-193481301-0). Zack is a sensitive hockey player interested in Jane, a Goth girl who comes to see that he's not a sexist jock. (Rev: BL 5/15/09; SLJ 5/1/09; VOYA 10/09)

1257 Martino, Alfred C. *Over the End Line* (7–10). 2009, Harcourt $17 (978-0-15-206121-0). Jonny Fehey enjoys his celebrity when he scores a winning soccer goal during his senior year at high school, but the pleasure is brief when he realizes that the exchange student he has been seeing has been raped. ℮ Lexile HL660L (Rev: BL 9/15/09; SLJ 9/09; VOYA 10/09)

1258 Peet, Mal. *Exposure* (9–12). 2009, Candlewick $18.99 (978-0-7636-3941-9). Soccer journalist Paul Faustino recounts the sorry story of star Otello's fall from grace in this novel loosely based on Shakespeare's *Othello*. (Rev: BL 8/09; SLJ 12/09)

1259 Weaver, Will. *Super Stock Rookie* (8–11). Series: Motor Novels. 2009, Farrar $14.95 (978-037435061-1). High-schooler Trace wins a corporate sponsorship, giving him the chance to compete on the stock-car circuit, but is suspicious about the motives of Team Blu. Lexile HL720L (Rev: BL 2/15/09; SLJ 3/1/09; VOYA 6/09)

1260 Zadoff, Allen. *Food, Girls, and Other Things I Can't Have* (8–10). 2009, Egmont USA $16.99 (978-1-60684-004-7); LB $19.99 (978-1-60684-051-1). Overweight high school sophomore Andy Zansky finds his popularity soaring when he joins the football team but soon discovers that many pitfalls await him.. ℮ Lexile HL520L (Rev: BL 10/15/09; HB 11–12/09; LMC 11–12/09; SLJ 9/09; VOYA 10/09)

Short Stories and General Anthologies

1261 Allen, Jeffery Renard. *Holding Pattern* (11–12). 2008, Graywolf paper $16.00 (978-155597509-8). Strong characters and vivid settings burst to life in this collection of short stories suitable for mature readers. (Rev: BL 9/15/08*)

1262 Amnesty International. *Free? Stories About Human Rights* (9–12). 2010, Candlewick $17.99 (978-0-7636-4703-2). Short stories written by 14 popular YA authors (Eoin Colfer, Roddy Doyle, David Almond, and Rita Williams-Garcia, for example) are linked to articles from the United Nations Declaration of Human Rights. Lexile 750L (Rev: LMC 5–6/10; SLJ 6/10)

1263 Atta, Sefi. *News from Home* (11–12). 2010, Interlink paper $15 (978-156656803-6). Eleven moving stories portray the anxieties and challenges facing Nigerians both at home and as they move away seeking better opportunities; for mature readers. (Rev: BL 9/1/10)

1264 Beattie, Ann. *The New Yorker Stories* (11–12). 2010, Scribner $30 (978-143916874-5). Forty-eight of Beattie's masterful stories — which deal with such universal themes as loneliness, family strife, and the consequences of violence — are presented in this collection for mature readers. (Rev: BL 8/10)

1265 Black, Holly, and Cecil Castellucci, eds. *Geektastic: Stories from the Nerd Herd* (8–12). 2009, Little, Brown $16.99 (978-0-316-00809-9). A collection of short stories that will please fans of everything from Star Trek to Dungeon Maters, underlining some of the difficult sides of geekiness. ℮ (Rev: BL 9/09; HB 9–10/09; LMC 1–2/10; SLJ 8/09)

1266 Ellis, Deborah. *Lunch with Lenin and Other Stories* (7–12). 2008, Fitzhenry & Whiteside $14.95 (978-155455105-7). This collection of uneven but nonetheless worthy short stories centers around the theme of drugs and drug addiction in different countries around the world. (Rev: BL 12/1/08; SLJ 2/1/09; VOYA 2/09)

1267 Evans, Danielle. *Before You Suffocate Your Own Fool Self* (11–12). 2010, Riverhead $25.95 (978-159448769-9). This compelling collection of short stories covers such universal themes as race, class, and coming-of-age; for mature readers. (Rev: BL 8/10)

1268 Frosch, Mary, ed. *Coming of Age in the 21st Century: Growing Up in America Today* (10–12). Series: Coming of Age. 2008, New Press paper $17.95 (978-159558055-9). Well-written short stories and selections taken from acclaimed novels and memoirs examine themes that deal with the interpersonal and societal issues of today's teens and young adults; the accompanying critical material may be less appealing to teen readers. (Rev: BL 8/08)

1269 Hopkins, Ellen, et al. *Does This Book Make Me Look Fat? Stories About Loving — and Loathing — Your Body* (7–12). Ed. by Marissa Walsh. 2008, Clarion $16.00 (978-054701496-8). A primarily fiction-based collection of essays and short stories by multiple YA authors that focus on various aspects of body image. (Rev: BL 12/15/08; LMC 3–4/09; SLJ 1/1/09; VOYA 2/09)

1270 Kyle, Aryn. *Boys and Girls Like You and Me* (11–12). 2010, Scribner $24 (978-141659480-2). A bleak, darkly rendered collection of stories for older teens, featuring mostly girls and young women protagonists who make universally bad choices while searching for meaning and identity in their lives; for mature readers. (Rev: BL 2/15/10)

1271 Loughead, Deb, and Jocelyn Shipley, eds. *Cleavage: Breakaway Fiction for Real Girls* (8–12). 2009, Sumach, dist. by Orca paper $12.95 (978-1-894549-76-9). Fifteen diverse stories by Canadian writers explore the relationship between teen girls and their mothers, many with a focus on different perspectives of body image. (Rev: SLJ 2/1/09; VOYA 2/09)

1272 MacLeod, Alexander. *Light Lifting* (11–12). 2011, Biblioasis paper $16.95 (978-189723194-4). This gritty collection of short stories, often violent and uncompromising, features protagonists who test the limits of the human body, spirit, and psyche; for mature readers (Rev: BLO 3/1–15/11)

1273 Na, An, and M. T. Anderson. *No Such Thing as the Real World: Stories About Growing Up and Getting a Life* (9–12). 2009, HarperTeen $16.99 (978-006147058-5); LB $17.89 (978-006147059-2). Short stories about young people facing the "real world" are written by An Na, M. T. Anderson, K. L. Going, Beth Kephart, Chris Lynch, and Jacqueline Woodson. (Rev: BL 7/09; SLJ 4/1/09)

1274 November, Sharyn, ed. *Firebirds Soaring: An Anthology of Original Speculative Fiction* (7–12). Illus. by Mike Dringenberg. Series: Firebirds. 2008, Penguin $19.99 (978-014240552-9). Nancy Springer, Nancy Farmer, Jane Yolen, Carol Emshwiller, and Kara Dalkey are among the authors of the 19 short stories included in this volume, diverse tales that reflect a number of genres. Lexile 820L (Rev: BL 1/1–15/09; LMC 5–6/09; SLJ 12/08)

1275 Noyes, Deborah, ed. *Sideshow: Ten Original Tales of Freaks, Illusionists, and Other Matters Odd and Magical* (9–12). Illus. 2009, Candlewick $16.99 (978-076363752-1). A creepy collection of short stories about the grotesque, the strange, and the spooky. Lexile 790L (Rev: BL 4/15/09; LMC 11–12/09; SLJ 7/09)

1276 Penzler, Otto, ed. *The Vampire Archives: The Most Complete Volume of Vampire Tales Ever Published* (9–12). 2009, Vintage paper $25 (978-0-307-47389-9). Edgar Allan Poe, Stephen King, and Ray Bradbury are among the writers represented in this collection of more than 80 tales and poems. (Rev: SLJ 12/09)

1277 Vonnegut, Kurt. *While Mortals Sleep: Unpublished Short Fiction* (11–12). 2011, Delacorte $27 (978-038534373-2). These sixteen unpublished short stories from the author of *Slaughterhouse-Five* are culled from Vonnegut's early career and show some of the cynicism of his later work. (Rev: BL 11/1/10)

1278 Waters, Sarah, ed. *Dancing with Mr. Darcy: Stories Inspired by Jane Austen and Chawton House Library* (11–12). 2010, Harper paper $13.99 (978-006199906-2). A collection of short stories from the Chawton House Library competition, featuring an eclectic mix of tales based on Jane Austen's characters, her stories, and her life; for mature readers. **e** (Rev: BL 9/1/10)

1279 Wilson, Kevin. *Tunneling to the Center of the Earth* (11–12). 2009, HarperPerennial paper $13.95 (978-006157902-8). A well-written collection of humorous and sometimes disturbing short stories suitable for mature readers. (Rev: BL 4/15/09)

Plays

General and Miscellaneous Collections

1280 Allen, Laurie. *Comedy Scenes for Student Actors: Short Sketches for Young Performers* (9–12). 2009, Meriwether paper $17.95 (978-1-56608-159-7). This well-written collection of 31 comic two-person sketch-es includes a good mix of male and female parts. (Rev: SLJ 10/09; VOYA 12/10) [792.9]

1281 Slaight, Craig, and Jack Sharrar, eds. *Great Monologues for Young Actors* (9–12). Series: Young Actors. 2009, Smith and Kraus paper $14.95 (978-1-57525-408-1). Presenting a wide range of monologues, this volume also gives advice on presentation and contact information for those wishing to produce public performances. (Rev: SLJ 5/1/09) [808.82]

Poetry

General and Miscellaneous Collections

1282 Mora, Pat. *Dizzy in Your Eyes: Poems About Love* (7–10). 2010, Knopf $15.99 (978-0-375-84375-4). Typical teen experiences with young love are covered in a collection of poems written in a wide variety of formats. ☺ (Rev: BL 11/15/09; LMC 1–2/10; SLJ 1/10) [811]

1283 Nye, Naomi Shihab, sel. *Time You Let Me In: 25 Poets Under 25* (7–12). 2010, Greenwillow $16.99 (978-0-06-189637-8); LB $17.89 (978-0-06-189638-5). Diverse poems by young writers deal with contemporary themes both personal and political. (Rev: BL 1/1/10; SLJ 2/10) [811]

Geographical Regions

Europe

GREAT BRITAIN AND IRELAND

1284 Duffy, Carol Ann. *Mrs. Scrooge: A Christmas Poem* (9–12). Illus. 2009, Simon & Schuster $12.99 (978-143917633-7). Ebenezer Scrooge's widow is swept away from her dogged anti-materialism protest by the ghosts of Christmas past, present, and future, who reveal the true meaning of the gifts we receive. (Rev: BL 11/15/09) [811]

United States

1285 Dungy, Camille T., ed. *Black Nature: Four Centuries of African American Nature Poetry* (10–12). 2009, Univ. of Georgia paper $24.95 (978-082033431-8). Perceptive essays introduce each section in this collection of poems about nature written by nearly 100 African Americans. (Rev: BL 2/1/10) [808.81]

1286 Giovanni, Nikki, ed. *The 100 Best African American Poems* (10–12). 2010, Sourcebooks $22.99 (978-140222111-8). Noted poet Nikki Giovanni brings together more than 100 of the best poems by African American writers. (Rev: BL 11/1/10) [811]

1287 Reynolds, Jason, and Jason Griffin. *My Name Is Jason. Mine Too: Our Story. Our Way* (9–12). Illus. by authors. 2009, HarperCollins paper $12.99 (978-0-06-154788-1). Written in hip, gritty poetic prose, this book chronicles the trials of two young men named Jason — one a painter and one a writer, one white and one black — as they learn the value of taking risks and cultivating friendships while finding their way in New York City. (Rev: SLJ 10/09; VOYA 8/09) [811]

1288 Spires, Elizabeth. *I Heard God Talking to Me: William Edmondson and His Stone Carvings* (6–12). Illus. 2009, Farrar $17.95 (978-037433528-1). Poems celebrate the art of African American sculptor William Edmondson, who started carving tombstones in 1931 when he was in his 50s; with photographs of the artist and his works. (Rev: BL 2/1/09; SLJ 3/1/09*) [811]

1289 *Tell the World: Teen Poems from Writerscorps* (7–12). 2008, HarperTeen $16.99 (978-0-06-134505-0). Brief poems by teen participants in WritersCorps workshops are organized in chapters titled "Who We Are," "Where We're From," "What We Love," "What We Think," "How It Feels," and "Why We Hope." (Rev: SLJ 1/1/09) [811]

1290 Young, Kevin. *Dear Darkness* (11–12). 2008, Knopf $26.00 (978-030726434-3). This unique collection of poetry captures the Southern way of life, the sadness of death, and the sweet bizarreness of family; for mature teens. (Rev: BL 9/1/08) [811]

1291 Zucker, Rachel, and Arielle Greenberg, eds. *Starting Today: 100 Poems for Obama's First 100 Days* (11–12). 2010, Univ. of Iowa paper $20 (978-158729871-4). One hundred poems by a wide range of poets record Obama's first 100 days and reflect an initial blaze of hope and slowly mounting disappointment in the face of the continuing poor economy, two wars, and political gridlock. (Rev: BL 4/1/10) [811]

Other Regions

1292 Engle, Margarita. *The Firefly Letters: A Suffragette's Journey to Cuba* (6–12). 2010, Holt $16.99 (978-0-8050-9082-6). In alternating free-verse narratives Swedish suffragist Frederika Bremer, her teenage slave Cecilia, and a privileged 12-year-old daughter of a planter describe their lives and quite different experiences. ℮ Lexile NC1230L (Rev: BL 12/15/09; HB 3–4/10; LMC 11–12/09; SLJ 2/10) [813]

1293 Engle, Margarita. *The Surrender Tree: Poems of Cuba's Struggle for Freedom* (6–12). 2008, Henry Holt $16.95 (978-0-8050-8674-4). In free verse Engle describes the lives of residents of Cuba in the mid- to late-19th century who fought for freedom. (Rev: BL 3/15/08*; LMC 11–12/08) [811]

Folklore and Fairy Tales

General and Miscellaneous

1294 Schwartz, Howard, ed. *Leaves from the Garden of Eden: One Hundred Classic Jewish Tales* (10–12). Illus. by Kirstina Swarner. 2008, Oxford $34.95 (978-0-19-533565-1). This large volume of diverse tales spans countries and traditions while explaining the common thread that makes them all Jewish. ℮ (Rev: BL 9/15/08) [398]

1295 Vande Velde, Vivian. *Cloaked in Red* (7–10). 2010, Marshall Cavendish $15.99 (978-0-7614-5793-0). A collection of eight diverse stories that give new twists to the well-known tale. Lexile 920L (Rev: BL 9/15/10; LMC 11–12/10; SLJ 12/1/10; VOYA 10/10)

Geographical Regions

North America

GENERAL AND MISCELLANEOUS

1296 Currie, Stephen. *African American Folklore* (7–12). Series: Lucent Library of Black History. 2008, Gale/Lucent $32.45 (978-1-4205-0082-0). In chapters on folk stories, folk songs, jokes and rhymes, and roots and influences, Currie explores the genre. (Rev: SLJ 2/1/09) [398.08996]

Mythology

General and Miscellaneous

1297 Lavers, Chris. *The Natural History of Unicorns* (10–12). Illus. 2009, Morrow $26.99 (978-006087414-8). This volume explores how different cultures throughout history have viewed this mythical animal. (Rev: BL 7/09) [398.24]

Humor and Satire

1298 Martin, Demetri. *This Is a Book* (10–12). Illus. 2011, Grand Central $24.99 (978-044653970-8). Fans of Martin from "The Daily Show" will appreciate his cutting, intelligent sense of humor in this collection of musings on history, pop culture, family and more. (Rev: BL 3/15/11) [818]

Speeches, Essays, and General Literary Works

1299 Burford, Brendan, ed. *Syncopated: An Anthology of Nonfiction Picto-Essays* (10–12). Illus. 2009, Villard paper $16 (978-034550529-3). Covering topics ranging from the mundane baling of hay to the 1921 Tulsa race riot, this volume collects 16 essays rendered by different artists in a selection of engaging comic formats. (Rev: BL 5/1/09*; SLJ 7/09) [741.5]

1300 Remini, Robert V., and Terry Golway, eds. *Fellow Citizens: The Penguin Book of U.S. Presidential Addresses* (10–12). 2008, Penguin paper $16.00 (978-014311453-6). Well-respected historians Remini and Golway examine every presidential inaugural speech and comment on each one's eloquence and historical impact. (Rev: BL 8/08) [352.23]

1301 Roosevelt, Theodore. *Theodore Roosevelt's History of the United States: His Own Words, Selected and Arranged by Daniel Ruddy* (10–12). Ed. by Daniel Ruddy. 2010, HarperCollins $27.99 (978-006183432-5). The outspoken former president offers his frequently blunt opinions on everything from discrimination to history to Jefferson Davis in this collection of writings and speeches. ℮ (Rev: BLO 5/3/10) [973.91]

1302 Stavans, Ilan, ed. *The Norton Anthology of Latino Literature* (10–12). 2010, Norton $59.95 (978-039308007-0). This engaging collection of Latino literature spanning four centuries is an excellent resource for those who want to explore Latino poetry, letters, stories, and more. (Rev: BL 9/15/10) [810.8]

Literary History and Criticism

Fiction

Europe

Great Britain and Ireland

1303 Johnson, Claudia Durst, ed. *Issues of Class in Jane Austen's Pride and Prejudice* (10–12). Illus. Series: Social Issues in Literature. 2008, Gale/Greenhaven $36.20 (978-073774258-9); paper $24.95 (978-073774259-6). High schoolers studying *Pride and Prejudice* will find this collection of essays useful for reports and class discussions; also included are a chronology of Austen's life, discussion questions, and a bibliography. (Rev: BL 1/1–15/09) [823]

Other Countries

1304 Prose, Francine. *Anne Frank: The Book, the Life, the Afterlife* (10–12). 2009, Harper $24.99 (978-006143079-4). Francine Prose makes the case that Anne Frank was a skilled young writer, well aware of the darker aspects of the Holocaust, and that her diary has not been served well by later editing and portrayals on stage and film that portray her as a somewhat naive idealist. (Rev: BL 9/09*) [940.53]

United States

1305 Bloom, Harold, ed. *Asian-American Writers* (10–12). Series: Bloom's Modern Critical Views. 2009, Bloom's Literary Criticism $45 (978-1-60413-401-8). Intended for students in advanced courses, this volume contains scholarly essays that examine Asian American fiction writers and how cultural identity is manifested in their writing. (Rev: SLJ 9/09)

1306 Jones, Sharon S. *Critical Companion to Zora Neale Hurston: A Literary Reference to Her Life and Work* (10–12). Illus. 2009, Facts on File $75 (978-081606885-2). This is a comprehensive book detailing the life and work of Zora Neale Hurston including

critical essays, influences, and photographs. (Rev: BL 5/1/09) [813]

1307 Ladd, Andrew, and Karen Meyers. *Romanticism and Transcendentalism, 1800–1860* (9–12). Series: Backgrounds to American Literature. 2010, Chelsea House $40 (978-1-60413-486-5). An appealing, well-illustrated guide to the romantic and transcendentalist era in American literature with discussion of the foundations of the movement and some of the key writers involved, including Hawthorne and Melville. ℮ (Rev: LMC 11–12/10) [810.9]

1308 Lathbury, Roger, and Karen Meyers. *Realism and Regionalism, 1860–1910* (9–12). Series: Backgrounds to American Literature. 2010, Chelsea House $40 (978-1-60413-487-2). An appealing, well-illustrated guide to realism and regionalism in American literature with discussion of the foundations of the movements, slave narratives, and some of the key writers involved, including Twain, James, Wharton, Crane, Sinclair, and Dreiser. ℮ (Rev: LMC 11–12/10) [810.9]

1309 Meyers, Karen. *Colonialism and the Revolutionary Period, Beginnings to 1800* (9–12). Series: Backgrounds to American Literature. 2010, Chelsea House $40 (978-1-60413-485-8). An appealing, well-illustrated guide to American literature in the early years of the nation with discussion of the historical context. ℮ (Rev: LMC 11–12/10) [810.9]

1310 Rangno, Erik V. R., and Karen Meyers. *Contemporary American Literature, 1945 to Present* (9–12). Series: Backgrounds to American Literature. 2010, Chelsea House $40 (978-1-60413-489-6). With chapters on the 1950s, 1960s, contemporary poetry, new voices, the "postmodern moment," and millenial voices, this volume places the literature of this period in historical and social context. ℮ (Rev: LMC 11–12/10) [810.0]

1311 Showalter, Elaine, ed. *The Vintage Book of American Women Writers* (10–12). 2011, Vintage paper $17.95 (978-140003445-1). A rich anthology featuring the works of 79 American women writers who shaped the country's literary history, from Puritan poet to modern literary novelist. ℮ (Rev: BL 1/1/11) [810.8]

Plays and Poetry

Europe

Great Britain

1312 Johanson, Paula. *Early British Poetry: "Words That Burn"* (9–12). Series: Poetry Rocks! 2009, Enslow LB $34.60 (978-0-7660-3276-7). Chaucer, Spenser, Shakespeare, Donne, Milton, Blake, Wordsworth, and Keats are among the poets introduced in this volume that provides brief biographical information, two or more poems or excerpts, and discussion of themes and techniques. (Rev: BL 10/1/09; LMC 3–4/10) [821.009]

Language and Communication

Words and Languages

1313 Gorrell, Gena K. *Say What? The Weird and Mysterious Journey of the English Language* (7–12). 2009, Tundra paper $10.95 (978-0-88776-878-1). A clever and often amusing history of the English language that emphasizes external influences and language's ability to change with the times, with word exercises and guessing games. (Rev: SLJ 1/10; VOYA 2/10) [420.9]

1314 Harrison, K. David. *The Last Speakers: The Quest to Save the World's Most Endangered Languages* (10–12). 2010, National Geographic $27 (978-142620461-6). A fascinating exploration of the world's disappearing languages and some of their last speakers. **e** (Rev: BLO 9/21/10) [408.9]

Writing and the Media

General and Miscellaneous

1315 Friedman, Lauri S., ed. *The Iraq War* (9–12). Series: Writing the Critical Essay, An Opposing Viewpoints Guide. 2008, Gale/Greenhaven $29.95 (978-0-7377-4037-0). Articles presenting opposing views about the war in Iraq are juxtaposed with chapters explaining how to write your own analytical essay — creating an outline, presenting theories and conclusions, using quotations, finding and citing information, and so forth. (Rev: SLJ 1/1/09) [956]

Books and Publishing

1316 Barry, Lynda. *What It Is* (9–12). Illus. 2008, Drawn & Quarterly $24.95 (978-189729935-7). Comics illustrator Barry presents an array of scrapbook-style collages and text as she explores the creative process and encourages teens with imaginative activities. (Rev: BL 6/1–15/08; SLJ 9/08) [741.5]

1317 Collins, Paul. *The Book of William: How Shakespeare's First Folio Conquered the World* (10–12). 2009, Bloomsbury $25 (978-159691195-6). A fascinating glimpse at the history of the surviving copies of Shakespeare's first collected edition of plays. (Rev: BL 7/09*) [016.8223]

1318 Pennac, Daniel. *The Rights of the Reader* (9–12). Trans. by Sarah Adams. Illus. by Quentin Blake. 2008, Candlewick $17.99 (978-076363801-6). This new translation of the 1992 French celebration of reading features playful illustration as it emphasizes the joys of literature. (Rev: BL 10/15/08; HB 5–6/09*) [028]

Print and Other Media

1319 Connolly, Sean. *Advertisements* (10–12). Series: Getting the Message. 2010, Smart Apple Media LB $34.25 (978-1-59920-345-4). Each volume in this series explores an area of mass communication and how it has changed over time. (Rev: LMC 1–2/10)

1320 Ellis, Sherry, and Laurie Lamson, eds. *Now Write! Screenwriting: Screenwriting Exercises from Today's Best Writers and Teachers* (10–12). 2011, Tarcher paper $14.95 (978-158542851-9). With essays by some of Hollywood's most successful screenwriters, this volume offers helpful tips on how to craft a screenplay, writing exercises, and advice on what to do with the script when it's finished. ℮ (Rev: BL 1/1/11) [808.2]

1321 Wallace, Mike, and Beth Knobel. *Heat and Light: Advice for the Next Generation of Journalists* (10–12). 2010, Three Rivers paper $14 (978-030746465-1). Two seasoned TV journalists offer valuable advice on the changing world of journalism, the importance of objectivity, and the traditional skills that remain applicable in the new environment. (Rev: BL 7/10) [070.92]

Biography, Memoirs, Etc.

Adventurers and Explorers

Collective

1322 MacPhee, Ross D. E. *Race to the End: Amundsen, Scott, and the Attainment of the South Pole* (10–12). Illus. 2010, Sterling $27.95 (978-140277029-6). Numerous photographs and Arctic artifacts enhance this account of Scott's and Amundsen's heroic treks to the South Pole. (Rev: BL 4/15/10) [920]

Individual

EARHART, AMELIA

1323 Wels, Susan. *Amelia Earhart: The Thrill of It* (9–12). Illus. 2009, Running Press $35 (978-0-7624-3763-4). This photo-biography recounts Earhart's life and pres-

ents recent attempts to unravel the circumstances around her disappearance in 1937. (Rev: BL 10/1/09) [921]

HILLARY, SIR EDMUND

1324 Crompton, Samuel Willard. *Sir Edmund Hillary* (6–12). Series: Great Explorers. 2009, Chelsea House $30 (978-1-60413-420-9). With photographs and journal excerpts, this biography gives an overview of the life of the mountaineer, his celebrated expeditions, his relationship with the Sherpa people, and other exploration taking place at that time. (Rev: LMC 3–4/10) [921]

LEWIS AND CLARK

1325 Crompton, Samuel Willard. *Lewis and Clark* (6–12). Series: Great Explorers. 2009, Chelsea House $30 (978-1-60413-418-6). With photographs and journal excerpts, this biography gives an overview of the lives of these two explorers, their celebrated expedition, their treatment of the native peoples, and other exploration taking place at that time. ℮ (Rev: LMC 3–4/10) [920]

Artists, Authors, Composers, and Entertainers

Collective

1326 Amend, Allison. *Hispanic-American Writers* (8–12). Series: Multicultural Voices. 2010, Chelsea House $35 (978-1-60413-312-7). Rudolfo Anaya, Julia Alvarez, and Sandra Cisneros are among the eight writers introduced in this volume that places them in historical and cultural context and examines major themes in their work. ℮ (Rev: LMC 10/10; SLJ 9/1/10) [920]

1327 Austerlitz, Saul. *Another Fine Mess: A History of American Film Comedy* (10–12). Illus. 2010, Chicago Review paper $24.95 (978-155652951-1). More than 100 movie comics are included here in admiring profiles. ℮ (Rev: BL 9/15/10) [920]

1328 Leiber, Jerry, et al. *Hound Dog: The Leiber and Stoller Autobiography* (10–12). Illus. 2009, Simon & Schuster $25 (978-141655938-2). Here is the story of songwriters Jerry Leiber and Mike Stoller, who wrote famous hits during the 1950s for the Coasters, Elvis, and many more. ℮ (Rev: BLO 4/30/09) [920]

1329 Otfinoski, Steven. *Native American Writers* (10–12). Series: Multicultural Voices. 2010, Chelsea House $35 (978-1-60413-314-1). Louise Erdrich and Sherman Alexie are among the ten writers introduced in this volume that places them in historical and cultural context and examines major themes in their work. ℮ (Rev: LMC 10/10; SLJ 8/10) [920]

Artists and Architects

DITKO, STEVE

1330 Bell, Blake. *Strange and Stranger: The World of Steve Ditko* (10–12). Illus. 2008, Fantagraphics $39.95

(978-1-56097-921-0). With Ditko's forceful artwork and Bell's perceptive comments, this book provides comic fans with a wealth of information about the very private artist. (Rev: BL 8/08) [921]

1331 Ditko, Steve. *Strange Suspense: The Steve Ditko Archives* (9–12). Illus. 2009, Fantagraphics $39.99 (978-160699289-0). Idiosyncratic and sometimes blunt, this book features three dozen of Spider Man co-creator Steve Ditko's earliest works. (Rev: BL 11/15/09)

KAMBALU, SAMSON

1332 Kambalu, Samson. *The Jive Talker* (11–12). 2008, Free Press $24.00 (978-1-4165-5931-3). Internationally known artist Kambalu tells the story of growing up poor in Malawi, of his father who was an educated man who loved words, and of his own struggle to find himself; for mature teens. ℮ (Rev: BL 8/08) [921]

KIRBY, JACK

1333 Kirby, Jack. *Kirby Five-Oh! Celebrating 50 Years of the "King" of Comics* (10–12). Ed. by John Morrow. Illus. 2008, TwoMorrows paper $19.95 (978-189390589-4). This admiring volume is filled with large layouts of the creator of *Iron Man*'s drawings including pencil originals, previously unpublished artwork, and accolades from many artists and authors. (Rev: BL 8/08) [921]

MONET, CLAUDE

1334 Kallen, Stuart A. *Claude Monet* (7–10). Series: Eye on Art. 2008, Gale/Lucent $32.45 (978-1-4205-0074-5). This attractive Monet biography offers a compelling glimpse at the man behind the famed artwork, including his personal struggles, flaws, and volatile genius. (Rev: SLJ 6/1/09) [921]

RIVERA, DIEGO

1335 Bernier-Grand, Carmen T. *Diego: Bigger Than Life* (7–10). Illus. by David Diaz. 2009, Marshall Cavendish $18.99 (978-076145383-3). The story of artist Diego Rivera's life is told using first-person free-verse poems; fact and fiction are defined in the informative back matter. (Rev: BL 2/15/09; HB 5–6/09; LMC 8–9/09; SLJ 4/1/09) [921]

VAN GOGH, VINCENT

1336 Crispino, Enrica. *Van Gogh* (6–10). Illus. Series: Art Masters. 2008, Oliver LB $27.95 (978-193454505-8). This insightful look at Van Gogh's work focuses more on the painter in the context of his times rather than providing a chronology of personal events. (Rev: BL 12/15/08; LMC 11–12/08) [921]

Authors

ALCOTT, LOUISA MAY

1337 Reisen, Harriet. *Louisa May Alcott: The Woman Behind Little Women* (9–12). 2009, Holt $26 (978-080508299-9). This lively biography describes the tumultuous childhood, varied careers, and struggles of the well-known author. ◯ (Rev: BL 10/1/09*) [921]

ANGELOU, MAYA

1338 Angelou, Maya. *Letter to My Daughter* (11–12). 2008, Random $25.00 (978-140006612-4). Angelou writes short stories, poems, and anecdotes of her life that serve as helpful advice and often warnings to the daughter she never had; for mature readers. ◯ ℮ (Rev: BL 9/15/08) [921]

BROWN, RITA MAE

1339 Brown, Rita Mae. *Animal Magnetism: My Life with Creatures Great and Small* (10–12). Illus. 2009, Ballantine $25 (978-034551179-9). Brown fondly recounts memories of her family, friends, and their animals and focuses on the life-lessons they have taught her. ◯ (Rev: BL 10/15/09) [921]

DAHL, ROALD

1340 Dahl, Roald. *More About Boy: Roald Dahl's Tales from Childhood* (6–12). Illus. by Quentin Blake. 2009, Farrar $24.99 (978-0-374-35055-0). This updated and expanded scrapbook-style version of Dahl's original autobiography *Boy* (1984) includes personal artifacts (report cards, photographs, letters, and so forth) as well as new anecdotes and a quiz. (Rev: HB 11–12/09; LMC 3–4/10; SLJ 1/10) [921]

1341 Sturrock, Donald. *Storyteller: The Authorized Biography of Roald Dahl* (10–12). 2010, Simon & Schus-

ter $30 (978-141655082-2). A highly readable profile that brings the author's oversized personality to life. ℮ (Rev: BL 9/15/10) [921]

DIAKITE, BABA WAGUE

1342 Diakité, Baba Wagué. *A Gift from Childhood: Memories of an African Boyhood* (6–10). 2010, Groundwood $18.95 (978-0-88899-931-3). The author relates his childhood living with his grandparents in a village in Mali and recalls the wisdom and folklore he learned there along with many practical lessons. (Rev: HB 7–8/10; LMC 8–9/10; SLJ 5/10) [921]

GEISEL, THEODOR SEUSS

1343 Pease, Donald E. *Theodor Seuss Geisel* (10–12). Illus. Series: Lives and Legacies. 2010, Oxford $19.95 (978-019532302-3). A concise, engaging look at one of children's literature's greats, covering his childhood as well as his work and his adult experiences. ℮ (Rev: BL 4/15/10) [921]

GROGAN, JOHN

1344 Grogan, John. *The Longest Trip Home* (11–12). 2008, Morrow $25.95 (978-006171324-8). This memoir explains the author of *Marley and Me*'s rejection and final acceptance of his Catholic faith; for mature readers. ◯ ℮ (Rev: BL 9/15/08) [921]

HEMINGWAY, ERNEST

1345 Reef, Catherine. *Ernest Hemingway: A Writer's Life* (8–12). Illus. 2009, Clarion $20.00 (978-061898705-4). With many quotations from Hemingway's contemporaries, Reef creates a vivid and balanced portrait of the author's complex life. ◯ (Rev: BL 6/1–15/09*; SLJ 8/09) [921]

KIRN, WALTER

1346 Kirn, Walter. *Lost in the Meritocracy: The Undereducation of an Overachiever* (11–12). 2009, Doubleday $24.95 (978-038552128-4). This is Kirn's account of how he learned to coast through prestigious schools by playing the system rather than pursuing knowledge. ℮ (Rev: BL 4/15/09) [921]

LEE, HARPER

1347 Madden, Kerry. *Harper Lee* (7–12). Illus. Series: Up Close. 2009, Viking $16.99 (978-067001095-0). An introduction to the life and work of the reclusive author of *To Kill a Mockingbird*. Lexile 1210 (Rev: BL 4/15/09; HB 3–4/09; SLJ 6/09) [921]

MEYER, STEPHENIE

1348 Krohn, Katherine. *Stephenie Meyer: Dreaming of Twilight* (6–12). Illus. Series: Lifeline Biographies. 2010, Lerner LB $33.26 (978-076135220-4). This attractive biography draws on the archives of *USA Today* to describe the author's life and publishing career. (Rev: BL 9/1/10*) [921]

RICE, ANNE

1349 Rice, Anne. *Called Out of Darkness: A Spiritual Confession* (10–12). 2008, Knopf $23.95 (978-030726827-3). Author Anne Rice examines her loss of faith and her eventual path back to Catholicism; fans of her witch and vampire books will be interested in this memoir. ∩ e (Rev: BL 8/08) [921]

SANDELL, LAURIE

1350 Sandell, Laurie. *The Impostor's Daughter: A True Memoir* (10–12). Illus. 2009, Little, Brown $24.99 (978-031603305-3). Sandell recounts her experiences growing up as the daughter of a highly deceptive father; the graphic-novel format conveys her own maturing. (Rev: BL 7/09) [921]

TWAIN, MARK

1351 Caravantes, Peggy. *A Great and Sublime Fool: The Story of Mark Twain* (7–10). Illus. Series: World Writers. 2009, Morgan Reynolds LB $28.95 (978-159935088-2). Well-chosen illustrations add to this informative survey of Twain's life and work. (Rev: BL 6/1–15/09; SLJ 7/1/09) [921]

WHARTON, EDITH

1352 Wooldridge, Connie Nordhielm. *The Brave Escape of Edith Wharton: A Biography* (7–10). 2010, Clarion $20 (978-0-547-23630-8). Explaining the social structure of the Gilded Age, this biography reveals Wharton's own rebellion against conventions and shows how her experiences are reflected in those of her literary characters. (Rev: BL 10/1/10*; LMC 3–4/11; SLJ 9/1/10; VOYA 12/10) [921]

Performers and Media Personalities

BERNSTEIN, LEONARD

1353 Bernstein, Burton. *Leonard Bernstein: American Original* (10–12). Ed. by Barbara B. Haws. Illus. 2008, Collins $29.95 (978-0-06-153786-8). Revisiting a New York Philharmonic on the verge of bankruptcy and the unexpected young conductor who saved it, this portrait features an array of warm first-person stories about Leonard Bernstein from a variety of different authors. e (Rev: BL 6/1–15/08*) [921]

CHAPLIN, CHARLIE

1354 Fleischman, Sid. *Sir Charlie: Chaplin, The Funniest Man in the World* (6–10). 2010, Greenwillow $19.99

(978-0-06-189640-8). This engaging profile covers Chaplin's life from his start in the slums of London through a Vaudeville career, success in Hollywood, and eventual move to Switzerland and relative obscurity. (Rev: BL 6/1/10*; LMC 11–12/10; SLJ 6/10; VOYA 6/10) [921]

DEGENERES, ELLEN

1355 Paprocki, Sherry Beck. *Ellen DeGeneres: Entertainer* (6–10). Series: Women of Achievement. 2009, Chelsea House $30 (978-1-60413-082-9). This is a balanced profile of the popular TV host and her impact on pop culture. (Rev: SLJ 5/1/09) [921]

HERSH, KRISTIN

1356 Hersh, Kristin. *Rat Girl* (11–12). 2010, Penguin paper $15 (978-014311739-1). Throwing Muses founder Hersh chronicles her teenage experiences as her band found success, she was diagnosed with bipolar disorder, and she discovered she was pregnant; for mature readers. e (Rev: BL 8/10) [921]

JACKSON, MICHAEL

1357 George, Nelson. *Thriller: The Musical Life of Michael Jackson* (10–12). Illus. 2010, Da Capo $25 (978-030681878-3). Focusing more on Jackson's contributions to the music industry than on the scandals that plagued his later years, this book offers a well-researched look into the hardworking, barrier-busting King of Pop. (Rev: BL 6/1–15/10) [921]

JOPLIN, JANIS

1358 Angel, Ann. *Janis Joplin: Rise Up Singing* (9–12). 2010, Abrams $19.95 (978-0-8109-8349-6). This well-researched account of the short life of passionate, enigmatic Janis Joplin contains many photographs and quotations from friends and family. (Rev: BL 11/1/10*; LMC 1–2/11; SLJ 10/1/10*) [921]

LANG, LANG

1359 Lang, Lang, and David Ritz. *Journey of a Thousand Miles: My Story* (10–12). Illus. 2008, Spiegel & Grau $24.95 (978-0-385-52456-8). Pianist Lang chronicles his youth in China and the supportive, though often tense relationship with his parents who sacrificed much for the son they had determined would become a star. ∩ e (Rev: BL 6/1–15/08; SLJ 1/09) [921]

LENNON, JOHN

1360 Blaney, John. *John Lennon: In His Life* (10–12). Ed. by Valeria Manferto de Fabianis. Illus. 2010, Sterling paper $39.95 (978-885440449-6). The life and career of seminal rock musician John Lennon is revealed through many photographs and a narrative that covers his private and public life from a young age. (Rev: BL 11/1/10) [921]

MARLEY, BOB

1361 Salewicz, Chris. *Bob Marley: The Untold Story* (10–12). Illus. 2010, Farrar $27 (978-086547999-9). Drawing on interviews with band mates, friends, and Marley himself, this biography tells of the culture, influence, and controversial legacy of the reggae star. (Rev: BL 4/1/10) [921]

SHAKUR, TUPAC

1362 Golus, Carrie. *Tupac Shakur: Hip-Hop Idol* (6–12). Illus. Series: Lifeline Biographies. 2010, Lerner LB $33.26 (978-076135473-4). This attractive biography draws on the archives of *USA Today* to give an unvarnished account of the rap star's life. (Rev: BL 9/1/10*) [921]

SMITH, PATTI

1363 Smith, Patti. *Just Kids* (11–12). Illus. 2010, Ecco $27 (978-006621131-2). A cast of notable characters from the 1960s and 1970s creative scene in New York City populates this memoir by punk rocker/poet Patti Smith that chronicles both her own life and her relationship with photographer Robert Mapplethorpe; for mature readers. (Rev: BLO 2/15/10) [921]

Contemporary and Historical Americans

Collective

1364 Adams, Katherine H., and Michael L. Keene. *After the Vote Was Won: The Later Achievements of Fifteen Suffragists* (11–12). 2010, McFarland paper $45 (978-078644938-5). Adams and Keene profile 15 suffragists and describe the challenges they faced after the 19th Amendment was ratified and the achievements of their later lives. (Rev: BLO 9/23/10) [920]

1365 Fleming, Thomas. *The Intimate Lives of the Founding Fathers* (10–12). 2009, Smithsonian $27.99 (978-0-06113-912-3). Fleming explores the home lives of George Washington, Ben Franklin, John Adams, Thomas Jefferson, Alexander Hamilton, and James Madison and the roles their wives played. e (Rev: BL 10/15/09; LMC 5–6/10) [920]

1366 Morgan, Edmund S. *American Heroes: Profiles of Men and Women Who Shaped Early America* (10–12). 2009, Norton $27.95 (978-039307010-1). Morgan sheds new light on some old truths in his essays about early America and its prominent individuals. e (Rev: BL 4/15/09) [920]

1367 Raphael, Ray. *Founders: The People Who Brought You a Nation* (10–12). Illus. 2009, New Press $35 (978-159558327-7). Raphael chooses seven notable people, three upper class and four middle class, whose significant contributions shaped the American Revolution. (Rev: BL 4/15/09) [920]

1368 Sanders, Nancy I. *America's Black Founders: Revolutionary Heroes and Early Leaders with 21 Activities* (6–10). 2010, Chicago Review paper $16.95 (978-1-55652-811-8). With archival prints and extracts from primary sources as well as activities, this volume tells the stories of African Americans who made significant contributions during the colonial period. (Rev: BL 2/1/10; LMC 3–4/10; SLJ 1/10) [920]

1369 Wong, Andrea, and Rosario Dawson. *Secrets of Powerful Women: Leading Change for a New Generation* (10–12). 2010, Hyperion/Voice paper $14.99 (978-140134111-4). Participants at 2008's Future Frontrunners Summit such as Congresswoman Jan Schakowsky and actress Fran Drescher recount for a teen audience their stories of succeeding as leaders. e (Rev: BLO 12/1/09) [920]

Civil and Human Rights Leaders

ANTHONY, SUSAN B.

1370 Todd, Anne M. *Susan B. Anthony: Activist* (6–10). Series: Women of Achievement. 2009, Chelsea House $30 (978-1-60413-087-4). This concise and balanced profile is a good starting place for anyone researching the famous suffragette and her legacy. (Rev: SLJ 5/1/09) [921]

DOUGLASS, FREDERICK

1371 Adler, David A. *Frederick Douglass: A Noble Life* (6–10). 2010, Holiday House $18.95 (978-0-8234-2056-8). With many quotations from Douglass's own writings, this generally admiring profile tells the story of his life and considerable achievements. (Rev: BL 6/1/10*; LMC 1–2/11; SLJ 9/1/10*) [921]

DU BOIS, W. E. B.

1372 Bolden, Tonya. *W. E. B. Du Bois: A Twentieth-Century Life* (7–10). Illus. Series: Up Close. 2008, Viking $16.99 (978-067006302-4). A look at the life of the complex African American leader, this will be helpful to report writers and others interested in important civil rights figures. (Rev: BL 2/1/09; HB 3–4/09; SLJ 1/1/09) [921]

Presidents and Their Families

JACKSON, ANDREW

1373 Remini, Robert V. *Andrew Jackson* (10–12). Illus. Series: Great Generals. 2008, Palgrave $21.95 (978-023060015-7). This biography of Andrew Jackson focuses on his military skill and reasons for his actions, especially when fighting against the Creek and Seminole tribes. ∩ (Rev: BL 9/15/08) [921]

LINCOLN, ABRAHAM AND MARY TODD

1374 Fleming, Candace. *The Lincolns: A Scrapbook Look at Abraham and Mary* (7–12). 2008, Random LB $28.99 (978-0-375-93618-0). With a pleasing mix of narrative, documents, paintings and etchings, and political cartoons, this attractive volume provides a detailed life of both Abraham and Mary. (Rev: BL 9/15/08; LMC 1–2/09; SLJ 10/1/08*) [921]

PIERCE, FRANKLIN

1375 Holt, Michael F. *Franklin Pierce* (10–12). Series: American Presidents. 2010, Times $23 (978-080508719-2). Holt examines the life and contributions of dark-horse president Franklin Pierce, who failed to achieve a second term in office thanks mostly to the divisive Kansas-Nebraska Act. (Rev: BL 3/1/10) [921]

ROOSEVELT, ELEANOR

1376 Hubbard-Brown, Janet. *Eleanor Roosevelt: First Lady* (6–10). Series: Women of Achievement. 2009, Chelsea House $30 (978-1-60413-076-8). This volume is a good source of basic information on former First Lady Eleanor Roosevelt and her influence on American culture. (Rev: SLJ 5/1/09) [921]

ROOSEVELT, FRANKLIN D.

1377 Brinkley, Alan. *Franklin Delano Roosevelt* (9–12). 2010, Oxford paper $12.95 (978-019973202-9). Personal and professional roles are both covered in this even-handed introduction to Roosevelt's life from childhood. (Rev: BL 12/15/09) [921]

TRUMAN, HARRY S

1378 Dallek, Robert. *Harry S. Truman* (10–12). Series: American Presidents. 2008, Times $22.00 (978-0-8050-6938-9). This biography of Harry Truman focuses on the struggles he faced during his presidency. ∩ ℮ (Rev: BL 8/08) [921]

Other Government and Public Figures

CLINTON, HILLARY RODHAM

1379 Abrams, Dennis. *Hillary Rodham Clinton: Politician* (6–10). Series: Women of Achievement. 2009, Chelsea House $30 (978-1-60413-077-5). Covering her youth, her university career, her marriage and political life with Bill Clinton, and her election to the Senate and run for the White House, this volume provides a balanced account. (Rev: LMC 10/09; SLJ 5/1/09) [921]

FRANKLIN, BENJAMIN

1380 Miller, Brandon Marie. *Benjamin Franklin, American Genius: His Life and Ideas with 21 Activities* (7–12). Illus. 2009, Chicago Review paper $16.95 (978-1-55652-757-9). The life and times of Benjamin Franklin — inventor, publisher, scientist, founding father — are presented clearly and engagingly in this illustrated, large-format biography. (Rev: BL 12/15/09; SLJ 10/09) [921]

GREENE, NATHANAEL

1381 Carbone, Gerald M. *Nathanael Greene: A Biography of the American Revolution* (10–12). 2008, Palgrave $27.95 (978-0-230-60271-7). A fast-paced tour through the 44-year-long life of Nathanael Greene, one of Washington's top generals during the Revolutionary War. ℮ (Rev: BL 6/1–15/08) [921]

MCCARTHY, JOSEPH

1382 Giblin, James Cross. *The Rise and Fall of Senator Joe McCarthy* (8–12). 2010, Clarion $22 (978-0-618-61058-7). This well-researched biography of McCarthy includes photographs, quotes, and little-known facts to provide a complete portrait of the man and his life. Lexile 1400 (Rev: BL 10/15/09; HB 11–12/09; LMC 1–2/10; SLJ 12/09) [921]

PATTON, GEORGE S.

1383 Gitlin, Martin. *George S. Patton: World War II General and Military Innovator* (7–10). Series: Military Heroes. 2010, ABDO LB $32.79 (978-1-60453-964-6). A well-written and richly illustrated account of the life of the World War II commander, covering his childhood, education, military career, and his strengths and weaknesses. (Rev: BL 4/1/10; LMC 10/10; SLJ 4/10) [921]

PELOSI, NANCY

1384 Pelosi, Nancy. *Know Your Power: A Message to America's Daughters* (9–12). 2008, Doubleday $23.95 (978-0-385-52586-2). Pelosi combines information about her youth and rise to power with (fairly standard) advice on achieving one's dreams. **e** (Rev: BL 6/1–15/08) [921]

Miscellaneous Persons

BOOTH, JOHN WILKES

1385 Swanson, James L. *Chasing Lincoln's Killer: The Search for John Wilkes Booth* (7–12). Illus. 2009, Scholastic $16.99 (978-043990354-7). This engaging account of the hunt for John Wilkes Booth in the 12 days following Lincoln's assassination is adapted from the author's 2006 adult book, "Manhunt," but lacks source notes and bibliography. ∩ Lexile 980L (Rev: BL 12/1/08; LMC 5–6/09; SLJ 1/1/09*; VOYA 12/08) [921]

COLVIN, CLAUDETTE

1386 Hoose, Phillip. *Claudette Colvin: Twice Toward Justice* (7–12). Illus. 2009, Farrar $19.95 (978-037431322-7). Readers will be inspired by the story of teenager Claudette Colvin, who was arrested when she refused to give up her seat on a bus months before Rosa Parks made her famous stand; with photographs and background information about the civil rights movement. Lexile 1000L (Rev: BL 2/1/09; LMC 8–9/09; SLJ 2/1/09*) [921]

JACOBS, JANE

1387 Lang, Glenna, and Marjory Wunsch. *Genius of Common Sense: Jane Jacobs and the Story of the Death and Life of Great American Cities* (7–12). 2009, Godine $17.95 (978-1-56792-384-1). Jane Jacobs fought against urban renewal projects she feared would do more harm to New York City than good, changing the way Americans view cities and city life. (Rev: BL 9/1/09; HB 7–8/09; SLJ 4/1/09) [921]

MARTIN, LUTHER

1388 Kauffman, Bill. *Forgotten Founder, Drunken Prophet: The Life of Luther Martin* (10–12). Series: Lives of the Founders. 2008, ISI $25.00 (978-193385973-6). Kauffman brings to life Luther Martin who, as the Constitution was being written, argued against a centralized government, was harshly criticized, and went on as Maryland's attorney general to defend Samuel Chase and Aaron Burr. (Rev: BL 9/1/08) [921]

MORRIS, GOUVERNEUR

1389 Miller, Melanie. *An Incautious Man: The Life of Gouverneur Morris* (10–12). Series: Lives of the

Founders. 2008, ISI $25.00 (978-193385972-9). Miller presents not only the role Morris played in the Constitutional Convention but also his work as a diplomat in France during the tumultuous times before and during the French Revolution. (Rev: BL 9/1/08) [921]

ROSS, BETSY

1390 Miller, Marla R. *Betsy Ross and the Making of America* (10–12). 2010, Holt $30 (978-080508297-5). This accessible portrait paints a vivid picture of Ross's life and times, showing the contributions of working men and women to the formation of a new nation. ∩ **e** (Rev: BL 4/15/10) [921]

SABERI, ROXANA

1391 Saberi, Roxana. *Between Two Worlds: My Life and Captivity in Iran* (11–12). 2010, Harper $25.99 (978-006196528-9). Journalist Roxana Saberi recounts the 100 days spent in an Iranian prison after her arrest in 2009, and the lessons she learned from her experience; for mature readers. (Rev: BL 4/1/10*) [921]

SITIKI

1392 Sitiki . *The Odyssey of an African Slave* (10–12). Ed. by Patricia C. Griffin. Illus. 2009, Univ. Press of Florida $24.95 (978-081303391-4). Griffin adds explanatory notes to the autobiography of an African slave named Sitki, who was captured in Africa at a young age and transported to America in the early 1800s. (Rev: BL 9/15/09) [306.3]

SMITH, VENTURE

1393 Nelson, Marilyn. *The Freedom Business: Including a Narrative of the Life and Adventures of Venture, a Native of Africa* (9–12). Illus. by Deborah Dancy. 2008, Boyds Mills $18.95 (978-193242557-4). The story of Venture Smith, an 18th-century slave, is told through evocative poetry and illustrations set alongside Venture's original account published in 1798. Lexile 1200L (Rev: BL 10/1/08*; HB 11–12/08; LMC 1–2/09; SLJ 10/1/08) [921]

TILL, EMMETT

1394 Wright, Simeon, and Herb Boyd. *Simeon's Story: An Eyewitness Account of the Kidnapping of Emmett Till* (6–10). 2010, Chicago Review $19.95 (978-1-55652-783-8). Author Wright was just 12 years old when his cousin Till came from the North to visit relatives in Mississippi, and he gives real insight into the murder of the 14-year-old African American and the events that followed. (Rev: BL 2/1/10; SLJ 2/10; VOYA 12/09) [921]

Science, Medicine, Industry, and Business Figures

Collective

1395 Hall, Derek, ed. *Philosophy, Invention, and Engineering* (8–11). Illus. Series: Facts at Your Fingertips: Great Scientists. 2009, Brown Bear LB $24.95 (978-193383448-1). Aristotle, Thomas Edison, Alan Turing, and Jonas Salk are among the scientists profiled in this attractive and informative volume. (Rev: BL 10/1/09*; LMC 5–6/10) [920]

1396 Rohmer, Harriet. *Heroes of the Environment: True Stories of People Who Are Helping to Protect Our Planet* (6–10). Illus. by Julie McLaughlin. 2009, Chronicle $16.99 (978-0-8118-6779-5). This book highlights 12 environmental crusaders — many of them teens or young adults — and their work to end pollution and industrial development from Appalachia to Alaska. (Rev: BLO 11/5/09; SLJ 1/10; VOYA 12/09) [920]

Science and Medicine

ATANASOFF, JOHN V.

1397 Smiley, Jane. *The Man Who Invented the Computer: The Biography of John Atanasoff, Digital Pioneer* (10–12). Series: Great Innovators. 2010, Doubleday $25.95 (978-038552713-2). A look into the earliest years of computer science, this fascinating biography examines the life and inventions of physicist John Atanasoff, who many believe invented the first computer. e (Rev: BL 9/15/10) [921]

CURIE, MARIE

1398 Koestler-Grack, Rachel A. *Marie Curie: Scientist* (6–10). Series: Women of Achievement. 2009, Chelsea House $30 (978-1-60413-086-7). This is a balanced profile that provides good basic information on Curie and her impact on the world of science. (Rev: SLJ 5/1/09) [921]

DARWIN, CHARLES

1399 Eldredge, Niles, and Susan Pearson. *Charles Darwin and the Mystery of Mysteries* (7–10). 2010, Flash Point (Roaring Brook Press LB $19.99 (978-1-59643-374-8). This engaging biography gives lots of information on Darwin's youth and private life as well as his research and the voyages of the *Beagle*. (Rev: BL 7/10; LMC 5–6/10; SLJ 6/10) [921]

DARWIN, CHARLES AND EMMA

1400 Heiligman, Deborah. *Charles and Emma: The Darwins' Leap of Faith* (8–12). 2009, Holt $18.95 (978-080508721-5). The story of Charles Darwin and his relationship with his wife (and cousin) Emma; family letters and other primary sources document a loving marriage between two very different people. ⌒ e Lexile 1020L (Rev: BL 1/1–15/09*; HB 1–2/09; LMC 8–9/09; SLJ 1/1/09*; VOYA 12/08) [920]

LEVI-MONTALCINI, RITA

1401 Yount, Lisa. *Rita Levi-Montalcini: Discoverer of Nerve Growth Factor* (9–12). Series: Makers of Modern Science. 2009, Chelsea House LB $35.00 (978-081606171-6). A clear and thorough account of the long and eventful life of the Nobel-winning scientist who was born in Italy in 1909. (Rev: BLO 6/17/09) [921]

SLOWINSKI, JOSEPH

1402 James, Jamie. *The Snake Charmer: A Life and Death in Pursuit of Knowledge* (10–12). Illus. 2008, Hyperion $24.95 (978-140130213-9). James explores the passion, personality, and tragic death of Joe Slowinski, a wildlife adventurer and herpetologist who died after being bitten by a deadly snake in the Burmese jungle. **e** (Rev: BL 7/08) [921]

Industry and Business

BUFFETT, WARREN

1403 Johnson, Anne Janette. *Warren Buffett* (7–12). Series: Business Leaders. 2008, Morgan Reynolds LB $27.95 (978-1-59935-080-6). This biography of Buffett covers both the personal and professional milestones of his life in clear, accessible prose. (Rev: SLJ 10/1/08) [921]

GATES, BILL

1404 Aronson, Marc. *Bill Gates* (6–10). Illus. Series: Up Close. 2008, Viking $16.99 (978-067006348-2). This book provides an insightful and evenhanded glimpse into Bill Gates's world, from his ultra-competitive childhood to his business practices and philanthropic works. (Rev: BL 12/1/08) [921]

GATES, BILL AND MELINDA

1405 Isaacs, Sally. *Bill and Melinda Gates* (6–10). Series: Front-Page Lives. 2010, Heinemann-Raintree $38.93 (978-1-4329-3220-6). Using a headlines format that highlights events, Isaacs covers the Gates's lives from childhood and includes a timeline, glossary, and other useful back matter. (Rev: LMC 3–4/10) [921]

JOBS, STEVE

1406 Imbimbo, Anthony. *Steve Jobs: The Brilliant Mind Behind Apple* (7–10). Illus. Series: Life Portraits. 2009, Gareth Stevens LB $34.00 (978-143390060-0). Photographs and anecdotes add interest to this profile of the inventive computer engineer. Lexile 980L (Rev: BL 4/1/09; LMC 8–9/09) [921]

LAUREN, RALPH

1407 Weatherly, Myra. *Business Leaders: Ralph Lauren* (7–12). 2008, Morgan Reynolds LB $27.95 (978-1-59935-084-4). This volume covers Lauren's successful career in the fashion industry. (Rev: SLJ 10/1/08) [921]

RAY, RACHAEL

1408 Abrams, Dennis. *Rachael Ray: Food Entrepreneur* (6–10). Illus. Series: Women of Achievement. 2009, Chelsea House LB $30.00 (978-160413078-2). The popular TV personality and cookbook author is profiled here in appealing text with many interesting quotations. (Rev: BL 4/1/09; SLJ 5/09) [921]

STEWART, MARTHA

1409 Paprocki, Sherry Beck. *Martha Stewart: Lifestyle Entrepreneur* (6–10). Series: Women of Achievement. 2009, Chelsea House $30 (978-1-60413-083-6). Paprocki does not shy away from controversy in this evenhanded profile of the business and lifestyle maven and her impact on American culture. (Rev: SLJ 5/1/09) [921]

SUI, ANNA

1410 Darraj, Susan Muaddi. *Anna Sui* (7–10). Series: Asian Americans of Achievement. 2009, Chelsea House $30 (978-1-60413-570-1). Sui's devotion to fashion — and her success at creating an international company with interests in fragrance, cosmetics, and even cell phones — are documented here, with interesting sidebars on culture and business. (Rev: BL 5/26/10; SLJ 2/10) [921]

WALKER, MADAM C. J.

1411 Bundles, A'Lelia. *Madam C. J. Walker: Entrepreneur* (7–12). Illus. Series: Black Americans of Achievement. 2008, Chelsea House $30.00 (978-160413072-0). The story of the successful African American businesswoman, complete with photographs and background information. (Rev: BLO 1/13/09) [921]

Sports Figures

Collective

1412 Grange, Michael. *Basketball's Greatest Stars* (9–12). Illus. 2010, Firefly $35 (978-155407637-6). An eye-catching, photo-filled survey of the 50 greatest players, with biographical information and analysis of their strengths. (Rev: BL 9/1/10) [920]

Automobile Racing

SCOTT, WENDELL

1413 Donovan, Brian. *Hard Driving: The Wendell Scott Story; The American Odyssey of NASCAR's First Black Driver* (10–12). Illus. 2008, Steerforth $25.95 (978-158642144-1). Scott, the first black man to compete in 1950s NASCAR racing, faced hate, verbal and physical abuse, and a lack of sponsors, yet he persevered, gaining respect and popularity. (Rev: BL 9/1/08*) [921]

Baseball

AARON, HENRY

1414 Bryant, Howard. *The Last Hero: A Life of Henry Aaron* (10–12). Illus. 2010, Pantheon $29.95 (978-037542485-4). Aaron goes from rural, poor Alabama to breaking Babe Ruth's home run record in this athletic rags-to-riches biography that includes photos and statistics. ⌒ **e** (Rev: BL 4/15/10*) [921]

Basketball

JAMES, LEBRON

1415 James, LeBron, and Buzz Bissinger. *Shooting Stars* (10–12). Illus. 2009, Penguin $26.95 (978-159420232-2). LeBron James describes his early life in Akron, Ohio, including the hardships that came with poverty and all the people who helped him succeed. ⌒ (Rev: BL 9/09) [921]

Football

BURRESS, PLAXICO

1416 Burress, Plaxico, and Jason Cole. *Giant: The Road to the Super Bowl* (10–12). Illus. 2008, HarperEntertainment $24.95 (978-0-06-169574-2). A likable account of Burress's road to success, with insight into football in general and the New York Giants in particular. (Rev: BLO 8/28/08) [921]

FAVRE, BRETT

1417 Funk, Joe, ed. *Favre: The Man, The Legend* (9–12). Illus. 2008, Triumph $27.95 (978-157243920-7). Here is a chronological account of Brett Favre's career including quotes from those who played with him and against him, statistics, and plenty of terrific photographs. (Rev: BL 9/1/08) [921]

MANNING, PEYTON

1418 Crompton, Samuel Willard. *Peyton Manning* (7–10). Illus. Series: Football Superstars. 2008, Chelsea House LB $30 (978-079109605-5). Star quarterback Peyton Manning's childhood, school years, and early career are documented in this well-organized book with a chronology, statistics, and play-by-plays. (Rev: BLO 8/08) [921]

Ice Skating and Hockey

OHNO, APOLO ANTON

1419 Aldridge, Rebecca. *Apolo Anton Ohno* (7–10). Series: Asian Americans of Achievement. 2009, Chelsea House $30 (978-1-60413-565-7). Son of a Japanese father, Ohno has won medals as a speed skater at the Olympics. (Rev: SLJ 2/10) [921]

Tennis

MCENROE, PATRICK

1420 McEnroe, Patrick, and Peter Bodo. *Hardcourt Confidential: Tales from Twenty Years in the Pro Tennis Trenches* (10–12). 2010, Hyperion $25.99 (978-140132381-3). Tennis pro McEnroe serves up a collection of wry anecdotes from his career playing, observing, administrating, and commenting on professional tennis. (Rev: BL 6/1–15/10) [921]

Track and Field

JONES, MARION

1421 Jones, Marion. *On the Right Track: From Olympic Downfall to Finding Forgiveness and the Strength to Overcome and Succeed* (10–12). Illus. 2010, Simon & Schuster $25 (978-145161082-6). Olympic Gold Medalist Marion Jones recounts her rise to the pinnacle of her sport and the scandal and subsequent incarceration resulting from her use of performance-enhancing drugs. (Rev: BL 11/1/10) [921]

THORPE, JIM

1422 Buford, Kate. *Native American Son: The Life and Sporting Legend of Jim Thorpe* (10–12). Illus. 2010, Knopf $35 (978-037541324-7). An in-depth look at the life of the great athlete, placing his importance in historical context and examining his personal struggles. e (Rev: BL 9/1/10) [921]

Miscellaneous Sports

ARMSTRONG, LANCE

1423 Strickland, Bill. *Tour de Lance: The Extraordinary Story of Lance Armstrong's Fight to Reclaim the Tour de France* (10–12). Illus. 2010, Harmony $25.99 (978-0-307-58984-2). Strickland tells the story of Armstrong's 2009 effort to make a comeback. e (Rev: BL 5/15/10*) [921]

EDERLE, GERTRUDE

1424 Dahlberg, Tim, et al, and Brenda Greene. *America's Girl: The Incredible Story of How Swimmer Gertrude Ederle Changed the Nation* (9–12). 2009, St. Martin's $25.99 (978-0-312-38265-0). The story of 20-year-old Gertrude Ederle's historic 1926 swim across the English Channel, not only the first woman to do so but beating the men's record by nearly two hours. (Rev: SLJ 12/09) [921]

LOPEZ, NANCY

1425 Sharp, Anne Wallace. *Nancy Lopez: Golf Hall of Famer* (6–10). Illus. Series: 20th Century's Most Influential Hispanics. 2008, Gale/Lucent LB $32.45 (978-1-4205-0060-8). Sharp highlights the various obstacles Lopez faced as she rose to prominence in a male-dominated sport in this appealing profile. (Rev: BL 9/1/08) [921]

MAY-TREANOR, MISTY

1426 May-Treanor, Misty, and Jill Lieber Steeg. *Misty: Digging Deep in Volleyball and Life* (10–12). Illus. 2010, Scribner $25 (978-143914854-9). Volleyball star May-Treanor details her wins, losses, injuries, and coach changes — as well as her mother's death from cancer — in this approachable sports autobiography. (Rev: BL 6/1–15/10) [921]

PARKIN, JOE

1427 Parkin, Joe. *A Dog in a Hat: An American Bike Racer's Story of Mud, Drugs, Blood, Betrayal, and Beauty in Belguim* (10–12). 2008, Velo paper $21.95 (978-193403026-4). Parkin tells the story of his life as a young American bike racer in Belgium who strove to fit in amid the stress of racing, the illegal drugs, and the fierce competition. (Rev: BL 9/1/08) [921]

SPITZ, MARK

1428 Foster, Richard J. *Mark Spitz: The Extraordinary Life of an Olympic Champion* (10–12). Illus. 2008, Santa Monica $24.95 (978-159580039-8). Mark Spitz's life, from his humble beginnings to Olympic glory, is detailed in this inspiring biography. (Rev: BL 9/1/08) [921]

WHITFIELD, SIMON

1429 Whitfield, Simon, and Cleve Dheensaw. *Simon Says Gold: Simon Whitfield's Pursuit of Athletic Excellence* (7–12). 2009, Orca paper $14 (978-1-55469-141-8). In this illustrated biography, Whitfield chronicles his successes, failures, and eventual rise to Olympic stardom. (Rev: BLO 11/20/09; SLJ 1/10; VOYA 6/10) [921]

World Figures

Collective

1430 Pouy, Jean-Bernard. *The Big Book of Dummies, Rebels and Other Geniuses* (7–10). Illus. by Serge Bloch. 2008, Enchanted Lion $19.95 (978-159270103-2). This often funny, irreverently illustrated book showcases the unlikely, often chaotic beginnings of 26 prominent figures in art, science, literature, and history, from Charlemagne and Dumas to Pablo Picasso and Agatha Christie. (Rev: BLO 10/7/08; SLJ 9/1/08; VOYA 8/08) [920]

Africa

BASHIR, HALIMA

1431 Bashir, Halima, and Damien Lewis. *Tears of the Desert: A Memoir of Survival in Darfur* (11–12). 2008, Ballantine $25.00 (978-0-345-50625-2). Bashir recounts her work as a doctor in Darfur during the civil war, the atrocities that took place, and her efforts to gain global recognition of this genocide; for mature readers. ⌒ e (Rev: BL 8/08) [921]

HANNIBAL

1432 Mills, Clifford W. *Hannibal* (6–10). Series: Ancient World Leaders. 2008, Chelsea House LB $30 (978-0-7910-9580-5). Mills covers the founding of Carthage and Hannibal's famous journey through the Alps and campaign against Rome. (Rev: SLJ 1/1/09) [921]

MANDELA, NELSON

1433 Cohen, David Elliot. *Nelson Mandela: A Life in Photographs* (10–12). Illus. 2010, Sterling $24.95 (978-140277707-3). Featuring more than 100 color photographs, a brief history of apartheid, and six of Mandela's historic speeches dating from the 1960s to the 1990s, this oversize volume rewards browsers and researchers. (Rev: BL 2/1/10) [921]

NEFERTITI

1434 Lange, Brenda. *Nefertiti* (6–12). Series: Ancient World Leaders. 2008, Chelsea House $30 (978-0-7910-9581-2). Full of illustrations that complement the text, this volume describes everyday life in ancient Egypt and the importance of religion and royalty as well as documenting what we know about the queen's life. (Rev: SLJ 3/1/09) [921]

Asia and the Middle East

DALAI LAMA

1435 Talty, Stephan. *Escape from the Land of Snows: The Young Dalai Lama's Harrowing Flight to Freedom and the Making of a Spiritual Hero* (11–12). Illus. 2011, Crown $26 (978-030746095-0). A gripping account of the life of the current Dalai Lama, from young monk to courageous leader in Tibet's uprising against invading China and during his long exile. ⌒ e (Rev: BL 1/1/11) [921]

JUNDI, SAMI AL

1436 Al Jundi, Sami, and Jen Marlowe. *The Hour of Sunlight: One Palestinian's Journey from Prisoner to Peacemaker* (10–12). 2011, Nation paper $16.95 (978-156858448-5). The Palestinian founder of the Seeds of Peace program, which brings together Israeli and Palestinian teens in the Middle East, describes his stay in an

109

Israeli prison and how it led him to change his politics and the course of his life. ℮ (Rev: BL 1/1/11) [921]

SHEBA, QUEEN OF

1437 Lucks, Naomi. *Queen of Sheba* (6–12). Series: Ancient World Leaders. 2008, Chelsea House $30 (978-0-7910-9579-9). Lucks provides a glimpse into the past with this well-illustrated volume that documents what we know about the Queen of Sheba. (Rev: SLJ 3/1/09) [921]

Europe

FRANK, ANNE

1438 Metselaar, Menno, and Ruud van der Rol. *Anne Frank: Her Life in Words and Pictures* (6–12). Trans. by Arnold J. Pomerans. 2009, Flash Point $19.99 (978-1-59643-546-9); paper $12.99 (978-1-59643-547-6). Short excerpts from Anne Frank's diary are interspersed with news photos, scrapbook pages, and family history to paint a rich and harrowing picture of Nazism, World War II, and the Frank family's place in history. (Rev: BL 11/1/09*; HB 1–2/11; LMC 11/09; SLJ 10/09) [921]

SARKOZY, NICOLAS

1439 Abrams, Dennis. *Nicolas Sarkozy* (7–10). Illus. Series: Modern World Leaders. 2009, Chelsea House $30.00 (978-160413081-2). With many quotations from Sarkozy and others, Abrams covers the French president's private life and public achievements. (Rev: BL 6/1–15/09) [921]

South and Central America, Canada, and Mexico

CALCINES, EDUARDO F.

1440 Calcines, Eduardo F. *Leaving Glorytown: One Boy's Struggle Under Castro* (7–10). 2009, Farrar $16.95 (978-037434394-1). The author writes of his childhood in Communist Cuba in the 1960s, the hardships that Castro's regime brought to Cuba, and how they affected one close family. ∩ Lexile 800L (Rev: BL 4/1/09; SLJ 6/1/09*; VOYA 4/09) [921]

ROMERO, OSCAR

1441 Wright, Scott. *Oscar Romero and the Communion of Saints* (10–12). Illus. 2010, Orbis paper $20 (978-157075839-3). Wright tells the life story of Oscar Romero, the Catholic archbishop of El Salvador who was assassinated in 1980. (Rev: BLO 12/1/09) [921]

Miscellaneous Interesting Lives

Collective

1442 Baggett, Jennifer, et al. *The Lost Girls: Three Friends, Four Continents, One Unconventional Detour Around the World* (10–12). 2010, Harper $24.99 (978-006168906-2). Three young women in their 20s encounter plenty of adventure — as well as questions about leadership, teamwork, careers, and self-preservation — as they travel the world during a year off work. ℮ (Rev: BL 4/15/10) [920]

1443 Deng, Ayuel Leek, et al. *Courageous Journey: Walking the Lost Boys' Path from the Sudan to America* (11–12). Illus. 2008, New Horizon $24.95 (978-088282334-8). Deng and Ngor, refugees from Sudan's brutal civil war, tell the story of their harrowing survival and long journey to the United States; for mature teens. (Rev: BL 8/08) [920]

1444 Murphy, Bill. *In a Time of War: The Proud and Perilous Journey of West Point's Class of 2002* (10–12). Illus. 2008, Holt $27.50 (978-0-8050-8679-9). Murphy follows the lives of several West Point graduates as they choose their specialties, form personal relationships, and are posted to combat zones. ℮ (Rev: BL 8/08) [920]

1445 Silverwood, John, and Jean Silverwood. *Black Wave: A Family's Adventure at Sea and the Disaster That Saved Them* (10–12). 2008, Random $25.00 (978-1-4000-6655-1). A dramatic account of a how the family's devastating wreck at sea turned into an event that pulled the family closer together. ⌒ ℮ (Rev: BLO 8/28/08; SLJ 9/08) [920]

1446 Welch, Liz, et al. *The Kids Are All Right* (10–12). 2009, Harmony $24.99 (978-030739604-4). Four chil-

dren, who are suddenly orphaned and split up, strive to keep in touch with each other and make sense of the tragedy that has befallen them; for mature readers. (Rev: BL 9/15/09) [306.88]

Individual

AFZAL-KHAN, FAWZIA

1447 Afzal-Khan, Fawzia. *Lahore with Love: Growing Up with Girlfriends, Pakistani-Style* (11–12). 2010, Syracuse Univ. paper $19.95 (978-081560924-7). Describing her life in Pakistan (and telling the story of her arrival and work in the United States), Afzal-Khan emphasizes the importance of female friendship in a country where women face so many challenges; for mature readers. (Rev: BL 4/15/10) [921]

ALI, NUJOOD

1448 Ali, Nujood, and Delphine Minoui. *I Am Nujood, Age 10 and Divorced* (11–12). 2010, Three Rivers paper $12 (978-030758967-5). This is the extraordinary first-person story of a brave 10-year-old Yemeni girl, named *Glamour* magazine's Woman of the Year in 2008, who fled the husband three times her age who repeatedly raped and beat her — and headed straight for the courthouse; for mature readers. (Rev: BL 2/1/10) [921]

BARKER, ADELE

1449 Barker, Adele. *Not Quite Paradise: An American Sojourn in Sri Lanka* (11–12). Illus. 2010, Beacon $24.95 (978-080700061-8). Barker details her time spent teaching in Sri Lanka, from her life as a university professor to mundane aspects of everyday life to the civil unrest gripping the country; for mature readers. (Rev: BL 1/1/10) [921]

BELLIL, SAMIRA

1450 Bellil, Samira. *To Hell and Back: The Life of Samira Bellil* (11–12). Trans. by Lucy R. McNair. 2008, Univ. of Nebraska $19.95 (978-080321356-2). After years of life on the streets in a rough suburb of Paris, including degradation and rape, author Samira Bellil chose to be heard, not only for herself but for all abused women; for mature readers. (Rev: BL 9/15/08) [921]

BOYLE, BRIAN

1451 Boyle, Brian, and Bill Katovsky. *Iron Heart: The True Story of How I Came Back from the Dead* (10–12). Illus. 2009, Skyhorse $24.95 (978-160239771-2). Brian Boyle survives a horrific car crash, a nearly fatal coma, and goes on to compete in an Iron Man triathlon. (Rev: BL 9/09) [921]

BRILL, LEIGH

1452 Brill, Leigh. *A Dog Named Slugger* (10–12). 2010, BelleBooks paper $14.95 (978-098432565-8). In this inspiring memoir subtitled *The True Story of the Friend Who Changed My World,* Brill chronicles her struggle with cerebral palsy and celebrates the big-hearted dog — Slugger — who helped her cope with and accept her condition. **e** (Rev: BL 4/15/10) [921]

BUCKLEY, BRYAN AND UMBRELL, COLBY

1453 Sielski, Mike. *Fading Echoes: A True Story of Rivalry and Brotherhood from the Football Field to the Fields of Honor* (10–12). Illus. 2009, Berkley $24.95 (978-042522974-3). Sielski tells the story of two football stars, from opposing high school teams in Pennsylvania, who both join the military after 9/11 and fight in Iraq; their lives reflect much of the turmoil of the early 21st century. (Rev: BL 9/09) [921]

BUSBY, CYLIN AND JOHN

1454 Busby, Cylin, and John Busby. *The Year We Disappeared: A Father-Daughter Memoir* (9–12). 2008, Bloomsbury $16.99 (978-159990141-1). The sometimes violent true story of a Cape Cod policeman and his attacker is told here through the alternating voices of the policeman himself and his daughter, Cylin, who was 9 years old when the family was forced to go into hiding. **e** Lexile 940L (Rev: BL 9/1/08; HB 11–12/08; SLJ 10/1/08; VOYA 10/08) [921]

CAPOTORTO, CARL

1455 Capotorto, Carl. *Twisted Head: An Italian American Memoir* (10–12). 2008, Broadway $23.95 (978-076792861-8). Vivid descriptions and skillful writing evoke Capotorto's experience growing up gay in the Bronx in the 1970s. (Rev: BL 9/1/08) [921]

CHIN, STACEYANN

1456 Chin, Staceyann. *The Other Side of Paradise* (11–12). 2009, Scribner $24 (978-074329290-0). Jamaican-born Staceyann Chin is a well-known New York City political activist and performance artist whose poignant memoir depicts her horrible childhood and how she overcame her many setbacks and came out as a lesbian; for mature readers. (Rev: BLO 9/09) [921]

COOK, PAUL

1457 Cook, Paul. *Cooked in LA: I Shot for the Stars and Hit Bottom* (11–12). Illus. 2009, Kunati $24.95 (978-160164193-9). Drug and alcohol problems, combined with the pressures of trying to succeed in the entertainment business, cause Paul Cook to spiral out of control; for mature readers. (Rev: BL 4/15/09) [921]

DAVIS, MATTHEW

1458 Davis, Matthew. *When Things Get Dark: A Mongolian Winter's Tale* (11–12). 2010, St. Martin's $25.99 (978-031260773-9). Mongolian history, culture, and its changing identity are interwoven in this memoir of a Peace Corps teacher sent to live in a yurt in a small village for two years; there he finds himself struggling with the same issues of drinking and violence to which many Mongolian men fall prey; for mature readers. (Rev: BL 2/1/10) [921]

DEN HARTOG FAMILY

1459 den Hartog, Kristen, and Tracy Kasaboski. *The Occupied Garden: A Family Memoir of War-Torn Holland* (10–12). Illus. 2009, St. Martin's $24.95 (978-031256157-4). Using the photos, diaries, and letters of their grandparents, the authors recreate the daily effort it took to survive in Holland during World War II. **e** (Rev: BL 4/15/09) [921]

EIRE, CARLOS

1460 Eire, Carlos. *Learning to Die in Miami: Confessions of a Refugee Boy* (10–12). 2010, Free Press $26 (978-143918190-4). Picking up where his award-winning *Waiting for Snow in Havana* (2002) left off, Eire describes his arrival in America in 1962, his journey through foster homes, and living with an uncle in Chicago as he tries to assimilate to his new surroundings. **e** (Rev: BL 9/15/10) [921]

FRIEDMAN, HANNAH

1461 Friedman, Hannah. *Everything Sucks: Losing My Mind and Finding Myself in a High School Quest for Cool* (9–12). 2009, Health Communications paper $12.95 (978-0-7573-0775-1). In this sassy, wry memoir, Hannah Friedman recounts her no-holds-barred campaign to gain popularity and her self-destructive behaviors (drugs, eating disorders, and superficiality). (Rev: SLJ 10/09; VOYA 10/09) [921]

GOLDSWORTHY, ANNA

1462 Goldsworthy, Anna. *Piano Lessons* (10–12). 2010, St. Martin's $24.99 (978-031264628-8). This touching memoir documents how the author's childhood piano teacher helped shape her future. ℮ (Rev: BL 9/1/10) [921]

GUIDRY, JEFF

1463 Guidry, Jeff. *An Eagle Named Freedom: My True Story of a Remarkable Friendship* (10–12). 2010, Morrow $21.99 (978-006199435-7). The true story of a man's deep kinship with a rehabilitated bald eagle he met while volunteering at a wildlife rescue center. ℮ (Rev: BLO 1/18/11) [921]

JENKINS, MISSY

1464 Jenkins, Missy, and William Croyle. *I Choose to Be Happy: A School Shooting Survivor's Triumph Over Tragedy* (6–12). 2008, LangMarc paper $16.95 (978-1-880292-31-0). School shooting survivor Missy Jenkins documents the horrific events of December 1, 1997, in West Paducah, Kentucky, and the long road to hope and forgiveness. (Rev: SLJ 3/1/09; VOYA 6/09) [921]

JUNGER, SEBASTIAN

1465 Junger, Sebastian. *War* (11–12). 2010, Twelve $26.99 (978-044655624-8). Junger recounts his thrilling, dangerous experiences embedded with the Second Platoon, Battle Company, in eastern Afghanistan in this inside look at life in combat; for mature teens. ℮ (Rev: BL 3/15/10) [921]

KAMARA, MARIATU

1466 Kamara, Mariatu, and Susan McClelland. *The Bite of the Mango* (9–12). Illus. 2008, Annick paper $12.95 (978-155451158-7). A disturbing but hopeful memoir of a young woman who was maimed and raped during the civil war in Sierra Leone. ℮ (Rev: BL 1/1–15/09; SLJ 11/1/08*; VOYA 2/09) [921]

KANTNER, SETH

1467 Kantner, Seth. *Shopping for Porcupine: A Life in Arctic Alaska* (10–12). Illus. 2008, Milkweed $28.00 (978-157131301-0). In this photo-filled volume Kantner shares poignant first-person stories from the Alaskan tundra that touch on environmental calamity, the displacement of Inuit elders, and the slow attrition of an ancient culture. (Rev: BL 6/1–15/08*) [921]

KEAT, NAWUTH

1468 Keat, Nawuth, and Martha Kendall. *Alive in the Killing Fields: The True Story of Nawuth Keat, a Khmer Rouge Survivor* (7–12). 2009, National Geographic $15.95 (978-1-4263-0515-3); LB $23.90 (978-1-4263-0516-0). In this stirring memoir, Cambodian Nawuth Keat provides a graphic, wrenching picture of the life of

a young refugee and his struggle toward freedom. (Rev: BL 8/09; LMC 11–12/09; SLJ 10/09) [921]

KERMAN, PIPER

1469 Kerman, Piper. *Orange Is the New Black: My Year in a Women's Prison* (11–12). 2010, Spiegel & Grau $25 (978-038552338-7). Indicted ten years after her nonviolent crime, Kerman spends a year absorbing the engrossing — and often unexpectedly kind — culture of a federal women's prison; for mature readers. (Rev: BL 3/15/10) [921]

KLEIN, STEPHANIE

1470 Klein, Stephanie. *Moose: A Memoir of a Fat Camp* (10–12). 2008, Morrow $24.95 (978-006084329-8). With humor and pain, Klein describes her summer fat camp experience and speaks of how it had lasting effects on her adult life; for mature teens. ℮ (Rev: BLO 9/2/08; SLJ 11/08) [921]

KOHLER, DEAN ELLIS

1471 Kohler, Dean Ellis. *Rock 'n' Roll Soldier* (9–12). 2009, HarperTeen $16.99 (978-006124255-7). A memoir of the Vietnam War and the author's band, the Electrical Banana. ℮ (Rev: BL 7/09; SLJ 9/09) [921]

KOPELMAN, JAY

1472 Kopelman, Jay. *From Baghdad to America: Life Lessons from a Dog Named Lava* (9–12). 2008, Skyhorse $23.95 (978-160239264-9). In this followup to 2006's *From Baghdad, with Love*, Kopelman and his inspiring canine dog struggle with the transition to civilian life after the war. ⌒ (Rev: BL 7/08) [921]

KOR, EVA MOZES

1473 Kor, Eva Mozes, and Lisa Rojany Buccieri. *Surviving the Angel of Death: The Story of a Mengele Twin in Auschwitz* (6–10). 2009, Tanglewood Press $14.95 (978-1-933718-28-6). Kor tells the horrifying story of her treatment — with her twin sister — at the hands of Mengele in Auschwitz. (Rev: LMC 5–6/10; SLJ 5/10) [921]

LAUREN, JILLIAN

1474 Lauren, Jillian. *Some Girls: My Life in a Harem* (11–12). 2010, Plume paper $15 (978-045229631-2). Lauren chronicles her time spent in the harem of Prince Jefri of Borneo: first exotic and exciting, the atmosphere grows increasingly paranoid and catty as Lauren vies for the prince's affections; for mature readers. (Rev: BL 3/15/10) [921]

LUCAS, FRANK

1475 Lucas, Frank, and Aliya S. King. *Original Gangster: The Real Life Story of One of America's Most Notorious Drug Lords* (11–12). Illus. 2010, St. Martin's

$25.99 (978-031254489-8). Lucas's view of the world was changed forever when at the age of 6 he watched his cousin murdered by a couple of hate-filled white men; in this confessional memoir suitable for mature readers, he owns up to his drug lord career with honesty and bluntness. ∩ ℮ (Rev: BL 5/1/10) [921]

LUKAS, CHRISTOPHER

1476 Lukas, Christopher. *Blue Genes: A Memoir of Loss and Survival* (11–12). 2008, Doubleday $24.95 (978-0-385-52520-6). Lukas writes of his family's struggle with depression and suicide and how it has affected them all; for mature readers. (Rev: BL 8/08) [616.85]

MARIC, VESNA

1477 Maric, Vesna. *Bluebird* (10–12). 2009, Soft Skull paper $14.95 (978-159376258-2). Sprinkling wit among the sorrow, Maric, a Bosnian teen living in England, describes life as a refugee and includes letters from her father describing the horrors at home. (Rev: BLO 9/15/09) [325.]

MASTERS, JARVIS JAY

1478 Masters, Jarvis Jay. *That Bird Has My Wings: The Autobiography of an Innocent Man on Death Row* (11–12). 2009, HarperOne $24.99 (978-006173045-0). Death-row inmate Masters's memoir eloquently recounts the unfortunate lead-up to his incarceration; suitable for mature readers. ℮ (Rev: BL 9/09) [921]

MAYOR, MIREYA

1479 Mayor, Mireya. *Pink Boots and a Machete: My Journey from NFL Cheerleader to National Geographic Explorer* (10–12). Illus. 2011, National Geographic $26 (978-142620786-0). Former Miami Dolphins cheerleader and current co-host of "National Geographic Wild," Mireya Mayor writes about her experiences in the wild and how we can protect our endangered lands and animals. (Rev: BL 3/15/11) [921]

MONAQUE, MATHILDE

1480 Monaque, Mathilde. *Trouble in My Head: A Young Girl's Fight with Depression* (7–12). Trans. by Lorenza Garcia. 2009, Trafalgar paper $15.95 (978-009191723-4). A memoir of a French teen's struggle to overcome depression. (Rev: BL 4/1/09; SLJ 9/09) [921]

MONTANA-LEBLANC, PHYLLIS

1481 Leblanc, Phyllis Montana. *Not Just the Levees Broke: My Story During and After Hurricane Katrina* (10–12). 2008, Atria $20.00 (978-1-4165-6346-4). In this personal account of New Orleans during and after Katrina, Montana-Leblanc tells of her fears, anger, and bewilderment at the politics involved. ∩ ℮ (Rev: BL 8/08) [921]

MURRAY, LIZ

1482 Murray, Liz. *Breaking Night* (11–12). 2010, Hyperion $24.99 (978-078686891-9). Murray unflinchingly relates the story of her own childhood — cocaine-addicted parents, domestic instability, and life on the streets — in this straightforward, surprisingly unsentimental memoir for mature readers subtitled *A Memoir of Forgiveness, Survival, and My Journey from Homeless to Harvard.* ∩ ℮ (Rev: BL 8/10) [921]

NIVEN, JENNIFER

1483 Niven, Jennifer. *The Aqua Net Diaries: Big Hair, Big Dreams, Small Town* (10–12). Illus. 2010, Simon & Schuster $24 (978-141695429-3). Niven describes her high school years in rural Indiana in the 1980s, complete with irreverent fashion commentary and frank tales of less successful moments. (Rev: BLO 3/2/10) [921]

NORRIS, MICHELE

1484 Norris, Michele. *The Grace of Silence* (11–12). 2010, Pantheon $24.95 (978-030737876-7). NPR journalist Norris explores her African American family's history in this account of an investigation that took her to surprising places. (Rev: BL 9/1/10) [921]

OPPENHEIMER, MARK

1485 Oppenheimer, Mark. *Wisenheimer: A Childhood Subject to Debate* (10–12). 2010, Free Press $25 (978-143912864-0). Oppenheimer manages to achieve success — despite being his teacher's worst nightmare — by joining the debate club in middle school and discovering his aptitude for language and logic; an exuberant and compelling memoir. (Rev: BL 3/1/10) [921]

PETERSON, BRENDA

1486 Peterson, Brenda. *I Want to Be Left Behind: Finding Rapture Here on Earth* (11–12). 2010, Da Capo $25 (978-030681804-2). Peterson's memoir about being raised a Southern Baptist explains her struggles to find common ground between radical evangelists and environmentalists. ℮ (Rev: BL 12/1/09*) [921]

POOLE, ERIC

1487 Poole, Eric. *Where's My Wand? One Boy's Magical Triumph over Alienation and Shag Carpeting* (10–12). 2010, Putnam $24.95 (978-039915655-7). Poole navigates a minefield of family dysfunction, romantic obsession, and anxiety about his homosexuality in this amusing memoir of 1970s St. Louis. ℮ (Rev: BL 4/15/10) [921]

RICHARDS, SUSAN

1488 Richards, Susan. *Saddled: How a Spirited Horse Reined Me In and Set Me Free* (10–12). 2010, Harcourt $24 (978-054724172-2). Richards's powerful connection to her horse helps her recover from a troubled past and present filled with depression and alcoholism. ⌒ ℮ (Rev: BLO 1/24/11) [921]

ROBINSON, HOLLY

1489 Robinson, Holly. *The Gerbil Farmer's Daughter* (10–12). Illus. 2009, Harmony $23 (978-030733745-0). Holly Robinson's memoir is unusual as it turns from growing up as a military daughter to her father's secret, intense study of gerbils. (Rev: BL 5/1/09) [921]

SANCHEZ, IVAN

1490 Sanchez, Ivan. *Next Stop: Growing Up Wild-Style in the Bronx* (11–12). Illus. 2008, Touchstone paper $14.00 (978-141656267-2). A violent memoir about the daily danger, crime, and sadness that Sanchez experienced while growing up in the Bronx; for mature teens. (Rev: BL 9/1/08) [921]

SELLERS, HEATHER

1491 Sellers, Heather. *You Don't Look Like Anyone I Know: A True Story of Family, Face Blindness, and Forgiveness* (11–12). 2010, Riverhead $25.95 (978-159448773-6). A diagnosis of prosopagnosia — the inability to recognize faces — rescues Sellers from fear that she has inherited her parents' mental illnesses; for mature readers. ⌒ ℮ (Rev: BL 9/1/10) [921]

SHEFF, NIC

1492 Sheff, Nic. *We All Fall Down: Living with Addiction* (10–12). 2011, Little, Brown $17.99 (978-031608082-8). This soul-baring sequel to *Tweak* (2008) documents Sheff's continuing difficulties with addictions and generally bad decision-making. (Rev: BL 2/15/11*; SLJ 4/11; VOYA 6/11) [362]

SMALL, DAVID

1493 Small, David. *Stitches* (10–12). Illus. 2009, Norton $24.95 (978-039306857-3). In graphic novel format, Small tells the sad tale of his youth in a joyless home and the surgery that rendered him mute for many years. (Rev: BL 7/09*; SLJ 9/09) [921]

SMITHSON, RYAN

1494 Smithson, Ryan. *Ghosts of War: The True Story of a 19-Year-Old GI* (9–12). 2009, Collins $16.99 (978-006166468-7); LB $17.89 (978-006166470-0). Smithson describes his decision after 9/11 to join the Army, basic training, his experiences in Iraq including worthwhile interactions with poverty-stricken Iraqi children and the night terrors he suffered afterward. (Rev: BL 7/09; SLJ 3/09*; VOYA 8/09) [921]

SUKRUNGRUANG, IRA

1495 Sukrungruang, Ira. *Talk Thai: The Adventures of Buddhist Boy* (11–12). 2010, Univ. of Missouri $24.95

(978-082621889-6). Growing up in the Chicago suburbs in the 1980s, Thai American Ira Sukrungruang tries hard to reconcile his family's resistance to assimilation and his own need to fit in with his white suburban neighbors; this sometimes hilarious, sometimes painful memoir is suitable for mature readers. (Rev: BLO 2/17/10) [921]

SUNDQUIST, JOSH

1496 Sundquist, Josh. *Just Don't Fall: How I Grew Up, Conquered Illness, and Made It Down the Mountain* (10–12). 2010, Viking $25.95 (978-067002146-8). Sundquist lost a leg to cancer as an adolescent and describes with wry humor his struggles at home and at school, and his eventual success on the ski slopes, competing in the 2006 Paralympics in Italy. ⌒ ℮ (Rev: BLO 12/15/09) [921]

SUPERNAW, SUSAN

1497 Supernaw, Susan. *Muscogee Daughter: My Sojourn to the Miss America Pageant* (10–12). Series: American Indian Lives. 2010, Univ. of Nebraska $24.95 (978-080322971-6). The first Native American to win the title of Miss Oklahoma tells the story of her difficult youth and road to academic success, emphasizing the importance of the Native traditions inculcated by her grandmother and other mentors. (Rev: BL 9/1/10) [921]

SWAN, ROBERT

1498 Swan, Robert, and Gil Reavill. *Antarctica 2041: My Quest to Save the Earth's Last Wilderness* (10–12). 2009, Broadway $24.99 (978-076793175-5). This book has two purposes: to give an account of the explorer's journey to the poles and to call attention to Antarctica's environmental needs. (Rev: BL 9/15/09) [577.5]

TAMM, JAYANTI

1499 Tamm, Jayanti. *Cartwheels in a Sari: A Memoir of Growing Up Cult* (10–12). 2009, Harmony $22.95 (978-030739392-0). With humor and frankness, the author writes of her life in a controlling popular cult from childhood to young adulthood when she broke free. (Rev: BL 4/15/09) [921]

UMRIGAR, THRITY N

1500 Umrigar, Thrity. *First Darling of the Morning: Selected Memories of an Indian Childhood* (10–12). 2008, HarperCollins paper $14.95 (978-006145161-4). In this compelling coming-of-age memoir, Umrigar describes her middle-class childhood in India, a life-changing meeting and subsequent rebellion against her family, and her move to America where she is an author and university teacher. ℮ (Rev: BL 9/1/08*) [921]

UNFERTH, DEB OLIN

1501 Unferth, Deb Olin. *Revolution: The Year I Fell in Love and Went to Join the War* (11–12). 2011, Holt $23 (978-080509323-0). In 1987 Unferth and her boyfriend dropped out of college and went to join the revolutionaries in Central America, an idealistic journey that brought danger and disillusion; for mature readers. (Rev: BL 1/1/11) [921]

WALKER, JERALD

1502 Walker, Jerald. *Street Shadows: A Memoir of Race, Rebellion, and Redemption* (11–12). 2010, Bantam $25 (978-055380755-4). Alternately grim and inspiring, this memoir describes reconciling a gritty, violent past as an African American youth on the South Side of Chicago with an increasingly stable life as a writer and college professor. (Rev: BL 11/15/09) [921]

WELLS, JEFF

1503 Wells, Jeff. *All My Patients Have Tales: Favorite Stories from a Vet's Practice* (10–12). 2009, St. Martin's $24.95 (978-0-312-53739-5). Whether ministering to circus animals or the common house cat, this veterinarian recounts his adventures with humor and compassion. (Rev: BL 2/15/09; SLJ 9/09)

WILSON, G. WILLOW

1504 Wilson, G. Willow. *The Butterfly Mosque: A Young American Woman's Journey to Love and Islam* (10–12). 2010, Atlantic Monthly $24 (978-080211887-5). Wilson, daughter of two atheists, tells the story of her conversion to Islam, her move to Cairo, and her romance with an Egyptian teacher. ☺ (Rev: BL 5/15/10*) [921]

WOLFF, MISHNA

1505 Wolff, Mishna. *I'm Down* (10–12). Illus. 2009, St. Martin's $23.95 (978-031237855-4). Wolff writes of her confusing childhood as a white girl who could never fit in while living in a black neighborhood with a father who wanted to be black. ⌒ ☺ (Rev: BL 4/15/09; SLJ 6/09) [921]

WOODS, VANESSA

1506 Woods, Vanessa. *Bonobo Handshake: A Memoir of Love and Adventure in the Congo* (10–12). 2010, Gotham $26 (978-159240546-6). Woods tells the story of her and her husband's research in the Congo, trying to save the threatened bonobo ape as civil war boiled around them. ⌒ ☺ (Rev: BL 4/1//10) [921]

ZAILCKAS, KOREN

1507 Zailckas, Koren. *Fury* (11–12). 2010, Viking $25.95 (978-067002230-4). The author of the memoir *Smashed* (2005) follows up her bestseller by examining the source of her deep-seated anger, sharing both personal stories and the results of extensive reading and research; for mature readers. (Rev: BL 9/1/10) [921]

The Arts and Entertainment

General and Miscellaneous

1508 Robson, David. *The Black Arts Movement* (7–12). Series: Lucent Library of Black History. 2008, Gale/ Lucent $32.45 (978-1-4205-0053-0). Black nationalism, cultural influences, identity, and assimilation are all considered as factors in this overview of the movement that has had an impact in literature, music, and art. (Rev: SLJ 2/1/09) [700.89]

Architecture and Building

General and Miscellaneous

1509 Phillips, Cynthia, and Shana Priwer. *Ancient Monuments* (7–10). Illus. Series: Frameworks. 2008, Sharpe Focus LB $43.95 (978-076568123-2). A look at monuments in ancient Greece, Rome, China, Europe, and other regions, with discussion of the engineering feats involved as well as their beauty and significance. (Rev: BL 4/1/09; SLJ 9/09) [732]

Painting, Sculpture, and Photography

Europe

1510 Gunderson, Jessica. *Gothic Art* (5–10). Series: Movements in Art. 2008, Creative Education $32.80 (978-1-58341-610-5). With good reproductions and clear historical context, Gunderson looks at the era of Gothic art. Also use *Realism* and *Romanticism* (both 2008). (Rev: SLJ 12/08) [709.02]

Music

Jazz and Popular Music (Country, Rap, Rock, etc.)

1511 Bradley, Adam, and Andrew DuBois, eds. *The Anthology of Rap* (10–12). 2010, Yale $35 (978-030014190-0). An extensive anthology of rap lyrics, presented chronologically starting with "The Old School" (1978 to 1984). (Rev: BL 11/15/10) [782.421]

1512 Burns, Kate, ed. *Rap Music and Culture* (9–12). Series: Current Controversies. 2008, Gale/Greenhaven $36.20 (978-0-7377-3964-0); paper $24.95 (978-0-7377-3965-7). More than 20 essays consider various aspects of rapping, DJ-ing, break dancing, hip-hop, and graffiti and their contributions — as well as sometimes destructive messages — within African American culture. (Rev: SLJ 3/1/09) [306.4]

1513 Espejo, Roman, ed. *Should Music Lyrics Be Censored for Violence and Exploitation?* (9–12). Series: At Issue. 2008, Gale/Greenhaven LB $29.95 (978-0-7377-4064-6); paper $23.96 (978-0-7377-4065-3). Diverse articles present varying viewpoints on violent and negative lyrics and the harm they potentially cause. (Rev: SLJ 2/1/09) [303.3]

1514 Evans, Mike, ed. *Woodstock: Three Days That Rocked the World* (10–12). Illus. 2009, Sterling $35 (978-140276623-7). This pictorial tribute book features many photographs and recollections from fans and musicians who were at the famous concert. (Rev: BL 7/09) [781.66]

1515 Higgins, Dalton. *Hip Hop World* (9–12). 2009, Groundwood $18.95 (978-0-88899-910-8); paper $10 (978-0-88899-911-5). This exploration of the genre of hip-hop discusses prevalent themes in the music and explains how the art form, now less socially relevant in the West, is becoming an increasingly popular and effective means of self-expression and social commentary in regions as diverse as Asia and the Middle East. (Rev: BL 11/1/09; SLJ 11/09) [782.421]

1516 Lang, Michael, and Holly George-Warren. *The Road to Woodstock: From the Man Behind the Legendary Festival* (9–12). Illus. 2009, Ecco $29.99 (978-006157655-3). One of the organizers of the rock event describes the planning for the festival and the aspects that just didn't work out. (Rev: BL 7/09) [781.66]

1517 Marsalis, Wynton, and Geoffrey C. Ward. *Moving to Higher Ground: How Jazz Can Change Your Life* (10–12). Illus. 2008, Random $26.00 (978-1-4000-6078-8). Marsalis explains the important role jazz played and continues to play in his life, and discusses several genres of music in great detail. **e** (Rev: BL 8/08*) [781.65]

1518 Nichols, Travis. *Punk Rock Etiquette: The Ultimate How-To Guide for DIY, Punk, Indie and Underground Bands* (7–10). Illus. by author. 2008, Flash Point $10.95 (978-159643415-8). This irreverent guide delivers lots of laughs as well as some practical, sage advice. **e** (Rev: BL 9/1/08; SLJ 12/08; VOYA 10/08) [781.6]

1519 Pollock, Bruce. *By the Time We Got to Woodstock: The Great Rock 'n' Roll Revolution of 1969* (10–12). Illus. 2009, Backbeat paper $19.99 (978-087930979-4). Focusing mostly on 1969, Pollock discusses the impact of the music of the 1960s and the events he believes caused the end of that idealistic time. (Rev: BL 9/09) [781.6609]

1520 Whitehead, Kevin. *Why Jazz? A Concise Guide* (10–12). 2011, Oxford $17.95 (978-019973118-3). This very basic introduction to jazz provides a history of the genre from its beginnings to the modern period, as well as information on music theory and important figures in the jazz world. (Rev: BL 11/1/10) [781.65]

Theater, Dance, and Other Performing Arts

Motion Pictures

1521 Lace, William W. *Blacks in Film* (7–10). Illus. Series: Lucent Library of Black History. 2008, Gale/Greenhaven LB $32.45 (978-142050084-4). From the earliest appearances of African Americans in silent films through their roles in today's movies, this book covers how blacks have been depicted in the cinema; photographs add to the presentation. (Rev: BL 2/1/09; SLJ 2/1/09) [791.43089]

1522 Miller, Logan, and Noah Miller. *Either You're in or You're in the Way: Two Brothers, Twelve Months, and One Filmmaking Hell-Ride to Keep a Promise to Their Father* (10–12). 2009, Harper $26.99 (978-006176314-4). The Miller twins recount their winning struggle to honor their late father by making a motion picture despite having no prior experience. (Rev: BL 5/1/09) [791.43]

1523 Rinzler, J. W. *The Making of Star Wars: The Empire Strikes Back* (9–12). Illus. 2010, Del Rey $85 (978-034550961-1). Rinzler provides an exhaustive account of the making of *The Empire Strikes Back* — complete with photographs, newspaper clippings, interviews, and archival records — in this thoroughly researched guide. (Rev: BL 6/1–15/10*) [791.43]

Radio, Television, and Video

1524 Rushfield, Richard. *American Idol: The Untold Story* (10–12). 2011, Hyperion $24.99 (978-140132412-4). Fans of the popular TV show will appreciate this candid look behind the scenes, which includes a rundown of some of the scandals and criticisms surrounding its production. ❤ (Rev: BL 1/1/11) [791.45]

History and Geography

General History and Geography

Atlases, Maps, and Mapmaking

1525 Collinson, Claire, ed. *The First Civilizations to 500 BCE* (10–12). Series: Curriculum Connections: Atlas of World History. 2010, Black Rabbit LB $39.95 (978-1-933834-65-8). With extensive maps and concise text, this book covers the world from 2000 BCE to 500 BCE, looking at agriculture, the development of cities, the Bible lands, and the Bronze Age. Also by this editor:

The Classical World: 500 BCE to 600 CE (2010). (Rev: LMC 8–9/10) [930]

1526 Spilsbury, Louise, ed. *World Wars and Globalization: 1914–2010* (10–12). Series: Curriculum Connections: Atlas of World History. 2010, Black Rabbit LB $39.95 (978-1-933834-70-2). Useful, well-organized maps are accompanied by concise text and give students a clear view of global trends. (Rev: LMC 8–9/10) [909.82]

Paleontology

1527 Holmes, Thom. *Last of the Dinosaurs: The Cretaceous Period* (9–12). Illus. Series: Prehistoric Earth. 2009, Chelsea House $35.00 (978-081605962-1). Holmes provides a detailed discussion of our current knowledge about the dinosaurs that flourished during this time and what led to their extinction. (Rev: BL 3/15/09) [567]

Anthropology and Evolution

1528 Gibson, Phil, and Terri R. Gibson. *Natural Selection* (6–12). Series: Science Foundations. 2009, Chelsea House $35 (978-0-7910-9784-7). Following a review of Darwin and Mendel's importance in this field, this volume looks at artificial selection, natural selection, and sexual selection, and discusses objections to Darwin's theory. (Rev: LMC 11–12/09) [576.8]

1529 Gordon, Sherri Mabry. *The Evolution Debate: Darwinism vs. Intelligent Design* (8–12). Series: Issues in Focus Today. 2009, Enslow LB $31.93 (978-0-7660-2911-8). Gordon provides an unbiased look at the debate over the teaching of Darwinism and intelligent design in American schools. (Rev: SLJ 4/1/09) [576.8]

1530 Walker, Sally M. *Written in Bone: Buried Lives of Jamestown and Colonial Maryland* (7–11). Illus. 2009, Carolrhoda $22.95 (978-082257135-3). Walker explores how forensic anthropology has helped researchers to learn more about the hard realities of life in colonial America. Lexile NC1140L (Rev: BL 2/1/09; HB 5–6/09; LMC 10/09; SLJ 2/1/09*) [614]

Archaeology

1531 Huey, Lois Miner. *American Archaeology Uncovers the Dutch Colonies* (6–10). Series: American Archaeology. 2010, Marshall Cavendish LB $31.36 (978-0-7614-4263-9). Huey looks at archaeological discoveries that have given us insight into the lives of early Dutch settlers and describes the scientific process of digging down layer by layer, examining everything from garbage to building foundations. Other recommended titles in this series include *American Archaeology Uncovers the Earliest English Settlements* and *American Archaeology Uncovers the Vikings* (both 2009). (Rev: BL 10/1/09; LMC 3–4/10; SLJ 2/10) [974.7]

1532 Rubalcaba, Jill, and Peter Robertshaw. *Every Bone Tells a Story: Hominin Discoveries, Deductions, and Debates* (8–12). 2010, Charlesbridge $18.95 (978-1-58089-164-6). Rubalcaba and Robertshaw tell a compelling version of human prehistory by focusing on four landmark discoveries, and the questions they raised and answered. (Rev: BL 2/15/10; SLJ 3/10) [930.1]

1533 Ryan, Donald P. *Beneath the Sands of Egypt: Adventures of an Unconventional Archaeologist* (10–12). Illus. 2010, Morrow $26.99 (978-006173282-9). This real-life story of the discovery of Hatshepsut's tomb crackles with the enthusiasm of an archaeologist who's passionate about his work. ℮ (Rev: BL 6/1–15/10*) [932]

World History and Geography

General

1534 Arthus-Bertrand, Yann. *Our Living Earth: A Story of People, Ecology, and Preservation* (6–12). Illus. by David Giraudon. 2008, Abrams $24.95 (978-081097132-5). Eye-catching aerial photographs of locations around the world reveal how people live, work, and relate to nature; statistics on sustainability and disparities will open readers' eyes to issues that affect the lives of millions on Earth. Lexile 1060L (Rev: BL 2/15/09; SLJ 1/1/09*; VOYA 12/08) [779]

1535 Badcott, Nicholas. *Pocket Timeline of Islamic Civilizations* (7–12). 2009, Interlink $13.95 (978-1-56656-758-9). An informative, eye-catching guide to the various achievements of Islamic civilizations from the 7th to the 20th century; includes color photographs and a detachable timeline. (Rev: LMC 3–4/10; SLJ 9/09)

1536 Bouchard, Constance Brittain. *Knights in History and Legend* (10–12). 2009, Firefly $40 (978-1-55407-480-8). A large-format, highly illustrated guide to knights not only in Europe during the Middle Ages but also in Asia. (Rev: BL 12/15/09; LMC 5–6/10) [940.1]

1537 Galeano, Eduardo. *Mirrors: Stories of Almost Everyone* (11–12). Trans. by Mark Fried. Illus. 2009, Nation $25.95 (978-156858423-2). Using a variety of literary forms, Galeano tells stories of the world from the dawn of time to more current events and highlights both the beautiful and the horrific aspects of humanity. ℮ (Rev: BL 5/1/09*) [909]

1538 Gilkerson, William. *A Thousand Years of Pirates* (6–10). Illus. by author. 2009, Tundra $32.95 (978-0-88776-924-5). With interesting biographical sketches, maps, and beautiful illustrations, this is a sweeping survey of piratical activity across time and geography. (Rev: BL 12/15/09; SLJ 2/10; VOYA 2/10) [910.4]

1539 Gonick, Larry. *The Cartoon History of the Modern World: Part II, from the Bastille to Baghdad* (10–12). 2009, HarperCollins paper $18.99 (978-0-06-076008-3). This final installment in Gonick's epic graphic history covers the years from the French Revolution to the wars in Iraq and Afghanistan. (Rev: BL 10/15/09; LMC 5–6/10; SLJ 11/09) [909.08]

1540 Mason, Phil. *How George Washington Fleeced the Nation: And Other Little Secrets Airbrushed from History* (10–12). 2010, Skyhorse $22.95 (978-161608075-4). This well-documented book irreverently points out some of the foibles of key figures in history. (Rev: BLO 7/10) [902]

1541 Sanna, Ellyn. *Nature's Wrath: Survivors of Natural Disasters* (6–12). Series: Survivors — Ordinary People, Extraordinary Circumstances. 2009, Mason Crest LB $24.95 (978-1-4222-0454-2). Sanna discusses our relationship with our planet and describes the experiences of survivors of tsunamis, hurricanes, and volcanoes. (Rev: SLJ 9/09)

1542 Standage, Tom. *An Edible History of Humanity* (10–12). Illus. 2009, Walker $26 (978-080271588-3). Standage's overview explains how food supply has affected the evolution of civilization from ancient times to the present. ℮ (Rev: BL 5/1/09) [394.12]

Ancient History

General and Miscellaneous

1543 Leon, Vicki. *How to Mellify a Corpse and Other Human Stories of Ancient Science and Superstition* (9–12). 2010, Walker paper $17 (978-080271702-3). This funny, accessible book details fascinating, amazing, and often disturbing ancient-world trivia relating to politics, art, warfare, and science. (Rev: BL 6/1–15/10) [509.3]

1544 Strapp, James. *Science and Technology* (7–10). Illus. Series: Inside Ancient China. 2009, Sharpe Focus LB $31.45 (978-076568169-0). Strapp looks at ancient Chinese inventions and innovations ranging from gunpowder and the compass to *feng shui*; includes maps, photographs, timelines, and drawings. (Rev: BL 2/15/09; SLJ 6/1/09) [609.31]

Egypt and Mesopotamia

1545 Fletcher, Joann. *Exploring the Life, Myth, and Art of Ancient Egypt* (7–12). Series: Civilizations of the World. 2010, Rosen LB $39.95 (978-1-4358-5616-5). Daily life, mythology, arts, religion, and various aspects of preparing for the afterlife are covered in this well-designed book that includes illustrations and a list of Web sites. (Rev: BL 10/1/09; LMC 1–2/10)

1546 Nardo, Don. *Peoples and Empires of Ancient Mesopotamia* (8–12). Series: Lucent Library of Historical Eras. 2008, Gale/Lucent $32.45 (978-1-4205-0101-8). This informative, well-illustrated volume describes ancient Mesopotamian society and politics, looking at urban and rural life, early systems of writing, and the successive empires of the region. Also use *Arts and Literature in Ancient Mesopotamia, Life and Worship in Ancient Mesopotamia,* and *Science, Technology, and Warfare of Ancient Mesopotamia* (all 2009). (Rev: SLJ 5/1/09)

Rome

1547 Hinds, Kathryn. *Everyday Life in the Roman Empire* (7–10). 2009, Marshall Cavendish $29.95 (978-0-7614-4484-8). Hinds looks at society across the Roman Empire, examining in turn the court, the city, the countryside, and the church. (Rev: BL 4/1/10*; LMC 5–6/10; SLJ 12/09) [937]

1548 Matyszak, Philip. *Legionary: The Roman Soldier's Unofficial Manual* (10–12). Illus. 2009, Thames & Hudson $24.95 (978-0-500-25151-5). Intended to resemble a guidebook for prospective Roman legionnaires, this generously illustrated, meticulously researched volume outlines the expectations, duties, and martial tactics of those who devoted their lives to the protection of ancient Rome. (Rev: SLJ 11/09) [356.1]

Middle Ages Through the Renaissance (500–1700)

1549 Elgin, Kathy. *Elizabethan England* (6–12). Series: Costume and Fashion Source Books. 2009, Chelsea House $35 (978-1-60413-379-0). This volume looks at fashion and clothing in the Elizabethan area, describing

the garb of men and women at court, the middle classes and professions, urban and rural residents, soldiers and sailors, and children. (Rev: LMC 11–12/09; SLJ 10-09) [391]

1550 Elgin, Kathy. *The Medieval World* (6–12). Series: Costume and Fashion Source Books. 2009, Chelsea House $35 (978-1-60413-378-3). This volume looks at the attire of men and women of various different walks of life in the Middle Ages. (Rev: LMC 11–12/09; SLJ 10/09) [391]

1551 Hinds, Kathryn. *Everyday Life in the Renaissance* (7–10). 2010, Marshall Cavendish LB $42.79 (978-0-7614-4483-1). Hinds looks at society in the Renaissance, examining in turn the court, the city, the countryside, and the church. (Rev: LMC 5–6/10; SLJ 12/09) [940.21]

1552 Stark, Rodney. *God's Battalions: The Case for the Crusades* (10–12). Illus. 2009, HarperOne $24.99 (978-006158261-5). In lively fashion, Stark presents newly discovered information that indicates that the Crusaders were not the avaricious, merciless opportunists that popular opinion maintains, but in fact many sacrificed wealth and exhibited higher moral standards than their contemporaries. ∩ ℮ (Rev: BL 10/1/09*) [909.07]

1553 Zahler, Diane. *The Black Death* (8–12). Series: Pivotal Moments in History. 2009, Lerner LB $38.60 (978-0-8225-9076-7). Full-color illustrations and first-person accounts punctuate this well-written history of the 14th-century pandemic that killed nearly half of Europe's population. (Rev: SLJ 5/1/09) [614.5]

Eighteenth Through Nineteenth Centuries (1700–1900)

1554 Hicks, Peter. *Documenting the Industrial Revolution* (6–10). Series: Documenting History. 2010, Rosen LB $26.50 (978-1-4358-9670-3). Following an overview of Britain's position as the first industrial nation, this slim volume looks in turn at steam, coal, and iron; the factory system; the transport revolution and the importance of steam; urbanization; and the problems involved in such rapid progress; a rich variety of primary source materials add interest. ℮ (Rev: LMC 11–12/10) [330.941]

Twentieth Century

General and Miscellaneous

1555 Kaufman, Michael T. *1968* (7–12). Illus. 2009, Flash Point $22.95 (978-159643428-8). Drawing on *New York Times* articles, Kaufman chronicles the events of the tumultuous year that saw the escalation of the

Vietnam War, assassinations in the United States, uprisings in Europe, and first pictures of Earth from space. Lexile NC1310L (Rev: BL 11/15/08; HB 1–2/09; LMC 3–4/09; SLJ 12/08; VOYA 10/08) [909.82]

1556 McEvoy, Anne. *The 1920s and 1930s* (6–12). Series: Costume and Fashion Source Books. 2009, Chelsea House $35 (978-1-60413-383-7). This volume looks at the attire of men and women of various different walks of life in the 1920s and 1930s, examining in particular the casual wear and sportswear. (Rev: LMC 11–12/09; SLJ 10/09) [391]

1557 Milo, Paul. *Your Flying Car Awaits: Robot Butlers, Lunar Vacations, and Other Dead-Wrong Predictions of the Twentieth Century* (10–12). 2009, Harper paper $14.99 (978-006172460-2). Milo explains why many of the technological advances we expected never happened. ℮ (Rev: BLO 12/1/09) [909.82]

1558 Rooney, Anne. *The 1950s and 1960s* (6–12). Series: Costume and Fashion Source Books. 2009, Chelsea House $35 (978-1-60413-385-1). This volume looks at the attire of men and women of various different walks of life in the 1950s and 1960s, covering formal evening wear, leisure wear, work wear and uniforms, and accessories. (Rev: LMC 11–12/09; SLJ 10/09) [391]

1559 Steere, Deirdre Clancy. *The 1980s and 1990s* (6–12). Series: Costume and Fashion Source Books. 2009, Chelsea House $35 (978-1-60413-686-8). This volume looks at the attire of men and women of various different walks of life in the 1980s and 1990s, covering the new fashion trends, the clothing of average people, and the extreme fashions and celebrity culture. (Rev: LMC 11–12/09; SLJ 10/09) [391]

World War I

1560 Best, Nicholas. *The Greatest Day in History: How, on the Eleventh Hour of the Eleventh Day of the Eleventh Month, the First World War Finally Came to an End* (10–12). Illus. 2008, PublicAffairs $27.95 (978-158648640-2). Best interweaves personal accounts with profiles of the key figures involved in bringing World War I to its final end. ℮ (Rev: BL 7/08) [940.3]

1561 Freedman, Russell. *The War to End All Wars: World War I* (6–10). 2010, Clarion $22 (978-0-547-02686-2). Freedman's photo-essay combines analysis of the key events and personalities of World War I with maps and personal stories drawn from letters and diaries. ∩ ℮ Lexile 1220L (Rev: BL 3/1/10*; HB 7–8/10; LMC 10/10; SLJ 6/10) [940.3]

1562 Steele, Philip. *Documenting World War I* (6–10). Series: Documenting History. 2010, Rosen LB $26.50

(978-1-4358-9673-4). With many interesting primary source materials — posters, postage stamps, photographs, cartoons, quotations — this slim volume looks at the causes of the war, the strategies, the social impact, and the eventual peace. (Rev: LMC 11–12/10) [940.3]

1563 Stone, Norman. *World War One: A Short History* (10–12). Illus. 2009, Basic $25 (978-046501368-5). Stone offers a concise overview of World War I including the events leading to the war, the strategies employed by opposing sides, and the reasons for the failures. ℮ (Rev: BL 5/1/09) [940.3]

World War II and the Holocaust

1564 Brenner, Hannelore. *The Girls of Room 28: Friendship, Hope, and Survival in Theresienstadt* (10–12). Trans. by John E. Woods. Illus. 2009, Schocken $26 (978-080524244-7). Ten detailed survivor stories of girls who endured the horrors of the Nazi concentration camp. ∩ (Rev: BL 9/15/09) [940.53]

1565 Burgan, Michael. *Hiroshima: Birth of the Nuclear Age* (8–12). Series: Perspectives On. 2010, Marshall Cavendish LB $39.93 (978-0-7614-4023-9). Burgan provides a concise account of the developments that led up to the destruction of Hiroshima, and of the long aftermath; sidebars, photographs, and illustrations enhance the well-written text. (Rev: LMC 3–4/10; SLJ 2/10)

1566 Mara, Wil. *Kristallnacht: Nazi Persecution of the Jews in Europe* (8–12). Series: Perspectives On. 2010, Marshall Cavendish LB $39.93 (978-0-7614-4026-0). Mara provides a concise account of the developments that led up to Kristallnacht and the long and terrible events that ensued; sidebars, photographs, and illustrations enhance the well-written text. (Rev: LMC 3–4/10; SLJ 2/10) [940.531]

Modern World History (1945–)

Mills, Dan**1567** Mills, Dan. *Sniper One: On Scope and Under Siege with a Sniper Team in Iraq* (11–12). Illus. 2008, St. Martin's $25.95 (978-031253126-3). A compelling firsthand account of Mills's time in Iraq as a British sniper platoon commander in 2004; for mature readers. ℮ (Rev: BL 9/1/08) [956.7044]

1568 Sutherland, James. *The Ten-Year Century: Explaining the First Decade of the New Millennium* (7–10). 2010, Viking $18.99 (978-0-670-01223-7). An engaging overview of key events of the first decade of the 21st century, a time of great innovation and political change. ℮ (Rev: BL 11/15/10; HB 11–12/10; LMC 11–12/10; VOYA 10/10) [973.93]

Geographical Regions

Africa

North Africa

1569 Childress, Diana. *Omar al-Bashir's Sudan* (10–12). 2009, Lerner LB $38.60 (978-0-8225-9096-5). Sudan's history and current political situation are addressed clearly in this well-organized volume that includes maps, photographs, and helpful backmatter. (Rev: BL 10/15/09; LMC 11–12/09; SLJ 9/09) [962.404]

Southern Africa

1570 Cruden, Alex, and Dedria Bryfonski. *The End of Apartheid* (9–12). Series: Perspectives on Modern World History. 2010, Gale/Greenhaven $38.50 (978-0-7377-4557-3). Articles, speeches, and extracts — combined with maps, charts, and photographs — examine the history of apartheid and the controversies surrounding it; personal narratives add perspective. (Rev: LMC 10/10; SLJ 6/10) [968.06]

1571 Lapierre, Dominique. *A Rainbow in the Night: The Tumultuous Birth of South Africa* (10–12). Trans. by Kathryn Spink. 2009, Da Capo $26 (978-030681847-9). This epic overview of South Africa's turbulent history reads like a novel. 🎧 ℮ (Rev: BL 12/1/09) [968.]

Asia

China

1572 Gay, Kathlyn. *The Aftermath of the Chinese Nationalist Revolution* (7–10). Illus. 2008, Lerner LB $38.60 (978-082257601-3). A well-researched exploration of

the Chinese civil turmoil — and eventual transition to communism — after the 1911 Wuchang Rebellion led by Sun Yat-sen. (Rev: BL 10/15/08; LMC 3–4/09; SLJ 3/1/09) [951.04]

1573 Mah, Adeline Yen. *China: Land of Dragons and Emperors* (6–12). 2009, Delacorte $17.99 (978-0-385-73748-7); LB $20.99 (978-0-385-90669-2). An engaging history of China from ancient times to the present, with insight into the land's people, traditions, beliefs, and cultures. (Rev: LMC 10/09; SLJ 8/09) [951]

1574 Troost, J. Maarten. *Lost on Planet China: The Strange and True Story of One Man's Attempt to Understand the World's Most Mystifying Nation; or, How He Became Comfortable Eating Live Squid* (11–12). 2008, Broadway $22.95 (978-076792200-5). Troost recounts his explorations in China, seeking a suitable place to move his family and finding many interesting social and physical factors to consider. (Rev: BL 7/08) [915.104]

India, Pakistan, and Bangladesh

1575 Eraly, Abraham, and Yasmin Khan. *India* (9–12). Illus. 2008, DK $40.00 (978-075663977-8). The fascinating history of India features beautiful pictures of the land and insightful narratives of its people who have shaped the country. (Rev: BL 9/15/08) [954]

Other Asian Countries

1576 Ayub, Awista. *However Tall the Mountain: A Dream, Eight Girls, and a Journey Home* (10–12). 2009, Hyperion $23.99 (978-140132249-6). The story of eight Afghani girls who get an opportunity to play soccer in America and then must return home. (Rev: BL 7/09) [796.334]

1577 Guibert, Emmanuel, et al. *The Photographer: Into War-Torn Afghanistan with Doctors Without Borders* (10–12). Illus. 2009, First Second paper $29.95 (978-159643375-5). In this graphic-novel presentation, photographer Lefèvre, with artist Guibert, recreates his harrowing journey into Afghanistan in 1986 with the charitable medical organization Médecins sans Frontières and tells the story of his growing awareness of the political forces at play. (Rev: BL 4/15/09*; SLJ 7/09*) [741.5]

1578 Kummer, Patricia J. *North Korea* (7–12). Illus. Series: Enchantment of the World. 2008, Children's Press LB $37 (978-053118485-1). Kummer presents a well-researched portrayal of the culture, economy, sports, education, and religion of the troubled Asian country. Lexile 970L (Rev: BL 8/08) [951.93]

1579 Mortenson, Greg. *Stones into Schools: Promoting Peace with Books, Not Bombs, in Afghanistan and Pakistan* (10–12). Illus. 2009, Penguin $26.95 (978-067002115-4). Mortenson recounts how the Central Asia Institute braved multiple obstacles to build schools in Afghanistan to promote peace. ∩ ℮ (Rev: BL 12/1/09*) [371.823]

1580 Zahler, Diane. *Than Shwe's Burma* (9–12). Series: Dictatorships. 2009, Lerner LB $38.60 (978-0-8225-9097-2). With many first-person accounts and quotes from journalists, this riveting, revealing book portrays the devastation, heartbreak, and injustice rampant in Burma under the dictatorship of Than Shwe. (Rev: BL 10/15/09; LMC 11–12/09; SLJ 10/09) [959.105.]

Europe

Italy

1581 Grodin, Elissa D., and Mario M. Cuomo. *C Is for Ciao: An Italy Alphabet* (7–10). Illus. by Marco Ventura. 2009, Sleeping Bear $17.95 (978-158536361-2). Many areas of Italy's culture, history, and language are explored in this alphabet book for older readers. (Rev: BLO 2/9/09) [945]

Russia and Other Former Soviet Republics

1582 Davenport, John C. *The Bolshevik Revolution* (10–12). Series: Milestones in Modern World History. 2010, Chelsea House $35 (978-1-60413-279-3). Davenport describes the key events and characters of the 1917 revolution and explains its importance for the remainder of the 20th century. (Rev: LMC 8–9/10; SLJ 6/10) [947.084]

1583 Gay, Kathlyn. *The Aftermath of the Russian Revolution* (8–12). Series: Aftermath of History. 2009, Lerner LB $38.60 (978-0-8225-9092-7). Gay outlines how the Bolshevik revolution and the establishment of communism in Russia would shape the future not only of that country's people, but of world politics as well. (Rev: SLJ 4/1/09)

1584 Seierstad, Asne. *The Angel of Grozny: Orphans of a Forgotten War* (11–12). Trans. by Nadia Christensen. 2008, Basic $25.95 (978-0-465-01122-3). Freelance journalist Seierstad provides a gritty, unflinching look at the realities of life in Chechnya and profiles a woman named Hadijat who has provided services for many of the suffering children; for mature readers. (Rev: BL 6/1–15/08*) [947.5]

Middle East

General and Miscellaneous

1585 January, Brendan. *The Arab Conquests of the Middle East* (8–11). Series: Pivotal Moments in History. 2009, Lerner LB $38.60 (978-0-8225-8744-6). This volume traces the history of the Arab conquest of the Middle East and parts of Europe, and how the new religion of Islam impacted society in the region. (Rev: SLJ 4/1/09) [956.013]

Israel and Palestine

1586 Aronson, Marc. *Unsettled: The Problem of Loving Israel* (9–12). 2008, Simon & Schuster $18.99 (978-141691261-3). Anonson blends personal anecdotes and history in this challenging yet engaging and thought-provoking examination of Israel's status and the conflict with Palestine. (Rev: BL 11/15/08; HB 1–2/09; LMC 5–6/09; SLJ 12/08; VOYA 12/08) [956]

1587 Immell, Myra, ed. *The Creation of the State of Israel* (10–12). Series: Perspectives on Modern World History. 2010, Gale/Greenhaven $38.50 (978-0-7377-4556-6). Offering a variety of enlightening perspectives on the state of Israel today, this collection includes many thought-provoking narratives, excerpts, and essays. (Rev: SLJ 3/10)

1588 Nusseibeh, Sari. *What Is a Palestinian State Worth?* (11–12). 2011, Harvard $19.95 (978-067404873-7). The president of al-Quds University in Jerusalem examines the relationship between Israel and Palestine, arguing that there can be no two-state solution; for mature readers. (Rev: BL 1/1/11) [956.940]

1589 Sacco, Joe. *Footnotes in Gaza* (10–12). Illus. 2010, Holt/Metropolitan $29.95 (978-080507347-8). Using vividly imagined graphic novel illustrations, Sacco tells the story of two mass killings that took place in 1950s Gaza and documents the hardships of life in the Gaza Strip. (Rev: BLO 1/14/10*) [956.04]

Other Middle East Countries

1590 Fassihi, Farnaz. *Waiting for an Ordinary Day: The Unraveling of Life in Iraq* (10–12). 2008, PublicAffairs $26.00 (978-158648475-0). Journalist Fassihi interviews a cross-section of middle-class Iraqis for a balanced and honest report about the impact of the war on the Iraqi people. **e** (Rev: BL 9/1/08) [956.7]

1591 Levy, Janey. *Iran and the Shia* (8–12). Series: Understanding Iran. 2010, Rosen LB $30.60 (978-1-4358-5282-2). Levy discusses the history of the Shia community in Iran and its current importance in the political and daily life of the nation. (Rev: LMC 1–2/10; SLJ 12/09) [955.05]

1592 Maslin, Jamie. *Iranian Rappers and Persian Porn: A Hitchhiker's Adventures in the New Iran* (11–12). Illus. 2009, Skyhorse $24.95 (978-160239791-0). Against his friends' advice, Maslin takes a solo trip into Iran and is surprised by the warm welcome and willingness of the people to share their country and their political opinions with him; for mature readers. (Rev: BL 9/15/09) [955.06]

North and South America (excluding the United States)

Central America

1593 Kallen, Stuart A. *The Aftermath of the Sandinista Revolution* (8–12). Series: Aftermath of History. 2009, Lerner LB $38.60 (978-0-8225-9091-0). Kallen outlines how the overthrow of the Nicaraguan government by the Sandinistas in 1979 had an international impact as well as a domestic one, spreading new fears about Communism. (Rev: SLJ 4/1/09) [972.8]

Polar Regions

1594 Anderson, Harry S. *Exploring the Polar Regions. Rev. ed.* (8–11). Series: Discovery and Exploration. 2010, Chelsea House LB $35 (978-1-60413-190-1). An updated edition of Anderson's analytical history of polar exploration that looks at the motivations behind expeditions as well as the specifics of early and modern ventures into new terrain. (Rev: LMC 8–9/10) [910]

1595 Ehrlich, Gretel. *In the Empire of Ice: Encounters in a Changing Landscape* (10–12). 2010, National Geographic $28 (978-142620574-3). Ehrlich draws on her recent National Geographic Expeditions journey into the Arctic to present this dismal assessment of the environmental catastrophes that await us, with portraits

of the impact on the peoples of the region. (Rev: BL 4/1/10*) [910.911]

1596 Haas, Robert B. *Through the Eyes of the Vikings: An Aerial Vision of Arctic Lands* (10–12). Illus. 2010, National Geographic $50 (978-142620638-2). This stunning collection of aerial photographs shows the Arctic Circle in all its natural glory. (Rev: BL 9/15/10) [910]

United States

General History and Geography

1597 Campbell, Ballard C., ed. *Disasters, Accidents, and Crises in American History: A Reference Guide to the Nation's Most Catastrophic Events* (9–12). Illus. 2008, Facts on File $95 (978-081606603-2). Encompassing about 500 years of events, this book includes chronologically organized, informative accounts of natural disasters, epidemics, accidents, terrorist attacks, and so forth. (Rev: BL 9/15/08; LMC 11–12/08; SLJ 6/08) [363.34]

1598 Carlisle, Rodney P., ed. *The Great Depression and World War II: 1929 to 1949* (9–12). Series: Handbook to Life in America. 2009, Facts on File $50 (978-0-8160-7180-7). Compelling period photographs, maps, charts, and sidebars add impact to this well-researched book exploring the events, social issues, and key figures of the Great Depression and World War II. (Rev: SLJ 1/10)

1599 Flamming, Douglas. *African Americans in the West* (9–12). 2009, ABC-CLIO $65 (978-1-59884-002-5). The history of African Americans in the West is the focus of this wide-ranging book that covers everything from Revolutionary-era slavery to the NAACP and urban migration. (Rev: LMC 11–12/09; SLJ 10/09)

1600 Hemming, Heidi, and Julie Hemming Savage. *Women Making America* (6–12). 2009, Clotho $45.95 (978-0-9821271-1-7); paper $28.95 (978-0-9821271-0-0). Women's roles — domestic and professional — throughout American history are the focus of this well-laid out book, which employs numerous biographical sketches, period photographs, and compelling vignettes to engage readers. (Rev: BLO 7/27/09; SLJ 6/1/09) [900]

1601 Nugent, Walter. *Habits of Empire: A History of American Expansion* (11–12). Illus. 2008, Knopf $28.95 (978-140004292-0). From the Manifest Destiny to early 20th-century Imperialism, this book examines the phenomenon of American expansion and the altruistic philosophies American leaders employed to justify their actions. (Rev: BL 6/1–15/08) [970.01]

1602 Panchyk, Richard. *Keys to American History: Understanding Our Most Important Historic Documents*

(6–12). Illus. 2009, Chicago Review $24.95 (978-155652716-6); paper $19.95 (978-155652804-0). An anthology of 72 important documents in the history of the United States, from the Mayflower Compact to the Patriot Act. With explanatory notes, facsimiles, and maps. (Rev: BL 5/1/09; SLJ 2/1/09) [973]

Historical Periods

NATIVE AMERICANS

1603 Brehm, Victoria, ed. *Star Songs and Water Spirits: A Great Lakes Native Reader* (10–12). Illus. 2010, Ladyslipper paper $27.95 (978-098433400-1). This extensive volume collects historical accounts, songs, stories, and poems by the Native American peoples of the Great Lakes past and present. (Rev: BLO 1/26/11) [398.208997077]

1604 Marsico, Katie. *The Trail of Tears: The Tragedy of the American Indians* (8–10). 2009, Marshall Cavendish LB $27.95 (978-0-7614-4029-1). Marsico examines the historical context, heartbreak, and aftermath of the American Cherokee relocation program and provides photographs, illustrations, and engaging sidebars. (Rev: LMC 3–4/10; SLJ 1/10) [973.04]

1605 Williams, Maria Shaa Tlaa, ed. *The Alaska Native Reader: History, Culture, Politics* (10–12). Illus. 2009, Duke paper $25.95 (978-082234480-3). The history and current status of Alaska's Native peoples are fully explored in this well-researched collection of stories, poems, art, and essays. (Rev: BLO 7/09) [305.89]

COLONIAL PERIOD AND FRENCH AND INDIAN WARS

1606 Steere, Deirdre Clancy, and Amela Baksic. *Colonial America* (6–12). Series: Costume and Fashion Source Books. 2009, Chelsea House $35 (978-1-60413-380-6). This volume looks at the attire of men and women from various different walks of life in Colonial America. (Rev: LMC 11–12/09; SLJ 10/09) [391]

1607 Turner, Glennette Tilley. *Fort Mose: And the Story of the Man Who Built the First Free Black Settlement in Colonial America* (7–10). 2010, Abrams $18.95 (978-0-8109-4056-7). Documenting the first free black settlement in North America and the key role of a slave called Francisco Menendez, Turner provides a thorough look at the culture of the place, which blended African, Native American, and Spanish elements. (Rev: BL 10/15/10*; LMC 1–2/11; SLJ 10/1/10) [975.9]

CIVIL WAR (1861–1865)

1608 Allen, Thomas B., and Roger MacBride Allen. *Mr. Lincoln's High-Tech War: How the North Used the Telegraph, Railroads, Surveillance Balloons, Ironclads, High-Powered Weapons, and More to Win the Civil War* (6–10). Illus. 2008, National Geographic $18.95 (978-

1-4263-0379-1); LB $25.90 (978-1-4263-0380-7). The authors argue that Lincoln's enthusiasm for technology contributed directly to the Union's success in the Civil War. Lexile 1180L (Rev: BL 12/15/08*; LMC 5–6/09; SLJ 2/1/09*; VOYA 2/09) [973.7]

1609 McNeese, Tim. *Civil War Battles* (6–12). Series: Civil War: A Nation Divided. 2009, Chelsea House $35 (978-1-60413-034-8). Bull Run, Shiloh, Antietam, Fredericksburg, Chancellorsville, and Gettysburg are among the battles covered in this volume that looks at real-life stories and the cost of war. (Rev: LMC 11–12/09) [973.73]

1610 Murphy, Jim. *A Savage Thunder: Antietam and the Bloody Road to Freedom* (6–10). 2009, Simon & Schuster $17.99 (978-0-689-87633-2). The terrible battle of Antietam is chronicled here, with maps, firsthand accounts, and discussion of its importance to the overall war. ◯ (Rev: BL 8/09*; HB 9–10/09; LMC 10/09; SLJ 8/09) [973.7]

1611 Reis, Ronald A. *African Americans and the Civil War* (6–12). Series: Civil War: A Nation Divided. 2009, Chelsea House $35 (978-1-60413-038-6). Free blacks and ex-slaves fought in more than 400 battles but faced prejudice and were underpaid despite their contributions. (Rev: LMC 11–12/09) [973.73]

1612 Taschek, Karen. *The Civil War* (6–12). Series: Costume and Fashion Source Books. 2009, Chelsea House $35 (978-1-60413-381-3). This volume looks at the attire of men and women from various different walks of life in the years before and during the Civil War, including the uniforms of North and South. (Rev: LMC 11–12/09; SLJ 10/09) [391]

1613 Wagner, Heather Lehr. *Spies in the Civil War* (6–12). Series: Civil War: A Nation Divided. 2009, Chelsea House $35 (978-1-60413-039-3). Wagner tells the stories of the men and women who served as spies during the Civil War, examining their motivations and diverse backgrounds. (Rev: LMC 11–12/09) [973.73]

1614 Williams, David. *Bitterly Divided: The South's Inner Civil War* (11–12). Illus. 2008, New Press $27.95 (978-159558108-2). Williams deftly explains that, among other mistakes, the Confederacy defeated itself by pushing secession although the majority of southerners were against it, and by establishing rules of enlistment that favored wealthy planters. (Rev: BL 8/08*) [973.7]

WESTWARD EXPANSION AND PIONEER LIFE

1615 McEvoy, Anne. *The American West* (6–12). Series: Costume and Fashion Source Books. 2009, Chelsea House $35 (978-1-60413-382-0). This volume looks at the attire of men and women of various different walks of life in the American West, covering explorers, settlers, Native Americans, soldiers, cowboys, and outlaws and lawmen. (Rev: LMC 11–12/09; SLJ 10/09) [391]

1616 McNeese, Tim. *The Donner Party: A Doomed Journey* (8–10). Series: Milestones in American History. 2009, Chelsea House $35 (978-1-60413-025-6). The author does not shy away from describing exactly what happened to the Donner Party on its trek to California, and places the events in historical context, aiding in understanding of the journey. (Rev: SLJ 8/09) [979.4]

RECONSTRUCTION TO WORLD WAR I
(1865–1914)

1617 Marsico, Katie. *The Triangle Shirtwaist Factory Fire: Its Legacy of Labor Rights* (7–12). Series: Perspectives On. 2009, Marshall Cavendish LB $27.95 (978-0-7614-4027-7). With direct quotations and historical background, this volume offers different perspectives on the 1911 disaster and its causes and consequences. (Rev: LMC 3–4/10; SLJ 2/10) [974.7]

WORLD WAR I

1618 Barnes, Harper. *Never Been a Time: The 1917 Race Riot That Sparked the Civil Rights Movement* (10–12). 2008, Walker $25.99 (978-080271575-3). In this exploration of the 1917 race riots in East St. Louis, IL, a lesser-known event that precipitated the civil rights movement, Barnes provides a strong narrative set atop richly illustrated historical context. **e** (Rev: BL 7/08; SLJ 8/08) [977.3]

1619 Bausum, Ann. *Unraveling Freedom: The Battle for Democracy on the Home Front During World War I* (8–11). 2010, National Geographic $19.95 (978-1-4263-0702-7); LB $34 (978-1-4263-0703-4). Bausum provides a riveting overview of life in the United States from the sinking of the *Lusitania* to the end of the war, covering the public outrage, the restrictions imposed on free speech and German Americans, the spying, and so forth. (Rev: BL 12/15/10*; SLJ 12/1/10*) [940.3]

BETWEEN THE WARS AND THE GREAT
DEPRESSION (1918–1941)

1620 Geary, Rick. *The Lindbergh Child* (10–12). Illus. Series: Treasury of XXth Century Murder. 2008, NBM/ComicsLit $15.95 (978-156163529-0). Well-written and researched, this graphic-novel presentation describes in detail the Lindbergh baby's kidnapping, the ensuing media circus, and the trial and execution of the suspected killer. (Rev: BL 9/1/08; LMC 3–4/09; SLJ 11/08) [921]

WORLD WAR II

1621 Hillstrom, Laurie Collier. *The Attack on Pearl Harbor* (7–12). Series: Defining Moments. 2009, Omni-graphics $49 (978-0-7808-1069-3). Readers learn why the Japanese attack on Pearl Harbor triggered the U.S. entry into the Second World War; primary documents and biographical information on key figures are included. (Rev: SLJ 8/09; VOYA 10/09) [940.5426]

1622 Moye, J. Todd. *Freedom Flyers: The Airmen of Tuskegee in World War II* (10–12). 2010, Oxford $24.95 (978-019538655-4). Working from more than 800 interviews recorded for the National Park Service's Tuskegee Airmen Oral History Project, the author uses the African American pilots' own words to pen a compelling history of how they battled the enemy abroad and racism at home. (Rev: BL 2/1/10) [940.54]

POST WORLD WAR II UNITED STATES
(1945–)

1623 Bowers, Rick. *Spies of Mississippi: The True Story of the State-Run Spy Network That Tried to Destroy the Civil Rights Movement* (7–10). 2010, National Geographic LB $26.96 (978-1-4263-0596-2). The alarming story of a spy network established in Mississippi in the mid-1950s to support segregation and work against civil rights. ☊ **e** (Rev: BL 2/1/10*; HB 3–4/10; LMC 3–4/10; SLJ 2/10) [323.1196]

1624 Mara, Wil. *Civil Unrest in the 1960s: Riots and Their Aftermath* (8–12). Series: Perspectives On. 2009, Marshall Cavendish LB $27.95 (978-0-7614-4025-3). With excerpts from primary sources and many pertinent sidebars and images, this is a useful survey of the causes, key events, and significance of the civil unrest of the 1960s. (Rev: LMC 3–4/10; SLJ 2/10) [303.6]

1625 Schou, Nicholas. *Orange Sunshine: The Brotherhood of Eternal Love and Its Quest to Spread Peace, Love, and Acid to the World* (11–12). Illus. 2010, St. Martin's $24.99 (978-031255183-4). An in-depth look at a 1960s counterculture group that encouraged the use of LSD and other drugs, considered Timothy Leary a prophet, and eventually devolved into a criminal organization, with interviews of surviving members of the group; for mature readers. (Rev: BL 2/15/10) [973]

1626 Tracy, Kathleen. *The McCarthy Era* (7–10). Series: Monumental Milestones. 2009, Mitchell Lane LB $29.95 (978-1-58415-694-9). Historic and political factors pertaining to McCarthy's persecution of innocent Americans are the focus of this interesting and informative book. (Rev: SLJ 6/1/09) [973.91]

1627 Watson, Bruce. *Freedom Summer: The Savage Season That Made Mississippi Burn and Made America a Democracy* (10–12). 2010, Viking $27.95 (978-067002170-3). Watson blends the story of the violence of the summer of 1964 with first-person accounts by those who were there, who include Sidney Poitier, Pete

Seeger, Stokely Carmichael, and numerous volunteer students. 🎧 🅔 (Rev: BL 5/1/10) [323.1196]

KOREAN, VIETNAM, AND GULF WARS

1628 Lansford, Tom, ed. *The War in Iraq* (9–12). Series: Global Viewpoints. 2009, Gale/Greenhaven $36.20 (978-0-7377-4162-9); paper $24.95 (978-0-7377-4163-6). Essays reprinted from a variety of news media provide two opposing viewpoints on the contentious causes of the Iraq War. (Rev: BL 10/15/09; SLJ 10/09) [956.7044]

Regions

MOUNTAIN AND PLAINS STATES

1629 Forsberg, Michael, et al. *Great Plains: America's Lingering Wild* (10–12). Illus. 2009, Univ. of Chicago $45 (978-022625725-9). With stunning photographs, this sweeping look at the vast and varied area known as the Great Plains juxtaposes the harmony the Native peoples shared with the land and the devastation inflicted by those who later settled there, also describing contemporary efforts to restore the land to its previous grandeur. (Rev: BL 10/15/09) [917.80022]

139

Philosophy and Religion

World Religions and Holidays

General and Miscellaneous

1630 Eckel, Malcolm David. *Buddhism* (9–12). Series: Understanding Religions. 2010, Rosen LB $31.95 (978-1-4358-5619-6). Eckels explores the origins, beliefs, scriptures, key figures, festivals, and rituals of Buddhism in this bright and appealing volume. (Rev: LMC 1–2/10)

1631 Tutu, Desmond M., and Mpho A. Tutu. *Made for Goodness: And Why This Makes All the Difference* (10–12). 2010, HarperOne $25.99 (978-006170659-2). Tutu and his daughter, also a minister, address the importance of forgiveness by examining many difficult episodes in South African history, with a special focus on the role of young people. **e** (Rev: BL 3/1/10) [170]

1632 Wade, Nicholas. *The Faith Instinct: How Religion Evolved and Why It Endures* (11–12). 2009, Penguin $25.95 (978-159420228-5). In this theoretical exploration of the evolution of religion, the author draws on hard biological evidence, hypothesizing that human civilization is naturally predisposed towards faith. (Rev: BL 11/15/09) [201]

Islam

1633 Calvert, John. *Islamism: A Documentary and Reference Guide* (10–12). 2007, Greenwood $85.00 (978-0-313-33856-4). Primary sources written by Islamist authors and short informative notes about these sources are included in this collection that contains documents written about jihad, family, women, revolution in Iran, and so forth. (Rev: BL 8/08; LMC 10/08) [320.5]

1634 Hafiz, Dilara, and Yasmine Hafiz. *The American Muslim Teenager's Handbook* (7–12). Illus. 2009, Simon & Schuster paper $11.99 (978-141698578-5). Friendly tips for young Muslim Americans on how to stand up to stereotypes and how to discuss their faith are accompanied by facts about the religion that will be useful for all readers. Lexile 1260 (Rev: BL 4/1/09; LMC 10/09; SLJ 4/08) [297.5]

1635 Hazleton, Lesley. *After the Prophet: The Epic Story of the Shia-Sunni Split in Islam* (10–12). 2009, Doubleday $27 (978-038552393-6). Carefully extracting events from history and the written word of Islam, Hazleton explains the anguish and upheaval that caused the Shia/Sunni divide that has continued for centuries. **e** (Rev: BL 9/09) [297.8]

Society and the Individual

Government and Political Science

General and Miscellaneous

1636 Judson, Karen. *Religion and Government: Should They Mix?* (9–12). Series: Controversy! 2009, Marshall Cavendish $25.95 (978-0-7614-4235-6). A clear discussion of the principles of separation of church and state precedes examples of thinking and practice in American society and throughout the world. (Rev: BL 11/15/09; SLJ 12/09) [322]

1637 Laxer, James. *Democracy* (7–12). Series: Groundwork Guide. 2009, Groundwood $18.95 (978-0-88899-912-2); paper $11 (978-088899913-9). Laxer discusses the history, present status, and future of democracy in this clearly written volume. (Rev: BL 7/09; VOYA 2/10) [321.8]

International Relations, Peace, and War

1638 Aronson, Marc, and Patty Campbell, eds. *War Is . . . : Soldiers, Survivors, and Storytellers Talk About War* (10–12). 2008, Candlewick $17.99 (978-076363625-8). Offering insight into combat, recruitment, training, and the lasting effects of war on veterans, Aronson and Campbell present a collection of stories, interviews, letters home, and essays stretching from World War II to the present day. (Rev: BL 11/1/08; LMC 3–4/09; SLJ 11/1/08; VOYA 2/09) [810.8]

1639 Bradbury, Adrian, and Eric Walters. *When Elephants Fight: The Lives of Children in Conflict in Afghanistan, Bosnia, Sri Lanka, Sudan and Uganda* (6–12). Illus. 2008, Orca $19.95 (978-155143900-6). Each of five chapters provides a haunting, unflinching glimpse into the experience of one child in war

— whether as target, child soldier, or collateral damage. ℮ (Rev: BL 10/15/08; LMC 3–4/09; VOYA 4/09) [305.230]

1640 Dunson, Donald H. *Child, Victim, Soldier: The Loss of Innocence in Uganda* (8–12). Illus. 2008, Orbis paper $16.00 (978-157075799-0). The author, a Christian missionary in Uganda, describes the horrors of war and child abuse in that country. (Rev: BL 1/1–15/09) [261.8]

1641 Ellis, Deborah. *Children of War: Voices of Iraqi Refugees* (7–12). Illus. 2009, Groundwood $15.95 (978-088899907-8). Interviews with children who have fled Iraq bring to life the harsh realities of war. Lexile 860L (Rev: BL 3/1/09*; LMC 8–9/09; SLJ 4/1/09; VOYA 6/09) [305.23086]

1642 Ellis, Deborah. *Off to War: Voices of Soldiers' Children* (6–12). Illus. 2008, Groundwood $15.95 (978-088899894-1). Interviews with about 40 children of Canadian and American soldiers deployed in Afghanistan and Iraq reveal pride, anger, and frustration, and a desire for a "normal" life. (Rev: BL 10/15/08; HB 11–12/08; LMC 1–2/09; SLJ 10/1/08; VOYA 12/08) [303.6]

1643 Janeczko, Paul B. *The Dark Game: True Spy Stories* (6–10). 2010, Candlewick $16.99 (978-0-7636-2915-1). Famous spies from the Revolutionary War through the cold war are the focus of this volume that also looks at modern techniques including cryptology and at organizations like the CIA and FBI. (Rev: BL 9/15/10; LMC 11–12/10; SLJ 8/10; VOYA 10/10) [327.73]

1644 Margulies, Phillip. *America's Role in the World* (9–12). Series: Global Issues. 2009, Facts on File $45 (978-0-8160-7611-6). This frank examination of U.S. foreign policy and how the United States is viewed by other countries in the world provides facts and figures, excerpts from primary sources, information on key organizations, and an annotated bibliography. (Rev: LMC 1–2/10)

1645 Polner, Murray, and Thomas E. Woods, eds. *We Who Dared to Say No to War: American Antiwar Writing from 1812 to Now* (10–12). Illus. 2008, Basic paper $16.95 (978-156858385-3). This is a collection of essays, letters, speeches, and song lyrics that expresses anti-war sentiment. **e** (Rev: BL 9/1/08) [973]

1646 Stewart, Sheila, and Joyce Zoldak. *In Defense of Our Country: Survivors of Military Conflict* (6–12). Illus. Series: Survivors — Ordinary People, Extraordinary Circumstances. 2009, Mason Crest LB $24.95 (978-1-4222-0452-8). Wars in Eastern Europe, the Middle East, Africa, and Asia are the focus of this volume that features first-person accounts as well as sidebars with interesting information on nonmilitary aspects of warfare. (Rev: SLJ 9/09) [362.87]

1647 Suvanjieff, Ivan, and Dawn Gifford Engle. *PeaceJam: A Billion Simple Acts of Peace* (5–10). 2008, Puffin paper $16.99 (978-0-14-241234-3). This volume introduces the Nobel Peace laureates who are active in the work of the PeaceJam Foundation and describes their activism along with efforts by young people to support their causes. (Rev: SLJ 5/1/09; VOYA 12/08) [303.6]

1648 van Creveld, Martin. *The Culture of War* (11–12). 2008, Presidio $27.00 (978-034550540-8). An engrossing look at war as part of human society that encourages fighting, decorates the victors, and builds memorials to the fallen. (Rev: BL 8/08) [306.2]

1649 Winckelmann, Thom. *Genocide* (7–12). Series: Man's Inhumanities. 2008, Erickson LB $23.95 (978-160217975-2). For reluctant and struggling readers, this is a simple overview of recent genocides with discussion of the social implications. (Rev: BL 10/15/08; LMC 8–9/09) [364.15]

United States Government and Institutions

General and Miscellaneous

1650 Kalman, Maira. *And the Pursuit of Happiness* (10–12). 2010, Penguin $29.95 (978-159420267-4). Author/illustrator Kalman collects here her reflections on democracy in America, focusing on key individuals from George Washington to Barack Obama; these pieces were initially published as a blog in the *New York Times*. (Rev: BL 9/1/10) [170]

1651 Ventura, Jesse, and Dick Russell. *American Conspiracies: Lies, Lies, and More Dirty Lies That the Government Tells Us* (10–12). 2010, Skyhorse $24.95 (978-160239802-3). Ventura provides interesting and entertaining — although not always objective — analyses of various events in American history where government motivations and actions have come under suspicion. ∩ (Rev: BL 3/1/10) [364.1]

The Constitution

1652 Biscontini, Tracey Vasil. *Amendment XIII: Abolishing Slavery* (9–12). Series: Constitutional Amendments: Beyond the Bill of Rights. 2009, Gale/Greenhaven $33.70 (978-0-7377-4122-3). Examining the background and historical context of the 13th Amendment, this volume in a recommended series provides a well-researched look at the relevant issues, as well as a discussion of all the court cases that have tested it. (Rev: LMC 10/09)

The Presidency

1653 Thomas, Helen, and Craig Crawford. *Listen Up, Mr. President: Everything You Always Wanted Your President to Know and Do* (10–12). 2009, Scribner $24 (978-143914815-0). Famous journalist Thomas and colleague Crawford offer a history of the American presidency and provide commentary on the intense scrutiny faced by contemporary presidents as well as guidelines for future chief executives. **e** (Rev: BL 10/1/09) [352.23]

Libraries and Other Educational Institutions

1654 Fortey, Richard. *Dry Storeroom No. 1: The Secret Life of the Natural History Museum* (10–12). Illus. 2008, Knopf $27.50 (978-0-307-26362-9). Paleontologist Fortey describes the different departments of the Natural History Museum in London and tells many interesting stories about hoaxes and accidental discoveries that shed light on the scientists' methods. **e** (Rev: BL 8/08) [508]

1655 Myron, Vicki, and Bret Witter. *Dewey: The Small-Town Library Cat Who Touched the World* (10–12). 2008, Grand Central $19.99 (978-044640741-0). Both Vicki Myron and Dewey the cat are survivors in this inspiring story about economic struggles, small-town life, and animal-human relationships. ∩ (Rev: BL 8/08*) [636.809]

The Law and the Courts

1656 Krygier, Leora. *Juvenile Court: A Judge's Guide for Young Adults and Their Parents* (7–12). 2009, Scarecrow $29.95 (978-081086127-5). Written by a judge in the Los Angeles Superior Court, this book arms teens with advice and practical information about what goes on in juvenile court. **℮** (Rev: BL 3/15/09; SLJ 3/1/09; VOYA 2/09) [345.73]

1657 Margulies, Phillip, and Maxine Rosaler. *The Devil on Trial: Witches, Anarchists, Atheists, Communists, and Terrorists in America's Courtrooms* (8–12). Illus. 2008, Houghton $22.00 (978-061871717-0). The authors examine five key trials in American history: the Salem witch trials, the Haymarket bomb trial, the Scopes monkey trial, the trials of Alger Hiss, and the trials of Zacarias Moussaoui. (Rev: BL 11/15/08; SLJ 9/1/08; VOYA 8/08) [345.73]

Politics

GENERAL AND MISCELLANEOUS

1658 Conrad, Jessamyn. *What You Should Know About Politics . . . but Don't* (10–12). 2008, Arcade paper $15.95 (978-155970883-8). Conrad provides a clear and impartial look at politics in the United States, covering a wide range of issues from election procedures and foreign policy to the economy and abortion. (Rev: BL 8/08) [320.60973]

ELECTIONS

1659 Cohen, Michael A. *Live from the Campaign Trail: The Greatest Presidential Campaign Speeches of the Twentieth Century and How They Shaped Modern America* (10–12). 2008, Walker paper $16.99 (978-080271697-2). In a comprehensive journey from 1896 to 1992, Cohen presents and interprets some of the most successful and eloquent presidential speeches, providing an interesting cross-section of the evolution of American politics. (Rev: BL 6/1–15/08; SLJ 8/08) [324.97309]

1660 Lansford, Tom, ed. *Voting Rights* (7–12). Series: Opposing Viewpoints. 2008, Gale/Greenhaven $36.20 (978-073774014-1); paper $24.95 (978-073774015-8). Essays by experts address issues relating to voting in the United States and other countries. (Rev: BL 1/1–15/09) [324.6]

Citizenship and Civil Rights

Civil and Human Rights

1661 Aretha, David. *Montgomery Bus Boycott* (7–10). Illus. Series: Civil Rights Movement. 2008, Morgan Reynolds $28.95 (978-159935020-2). An examination of an important event in the civil rights movement, with letters, photographs, and personal accounts that add impact. (Rev: BL 2/1/09; LMC 5–6/09; SLJ 2/1/09) [323.1196]

1662 Bales, Kevin, and Becky Cornell. *Slavery Today* (10–12). Series: Groundwork Guides. 2008, Groundwood $18.95 (978-088899772-2); paper $10.00 (978-088899773-9). The grim reality of slavery today — about 27 million slaves worldwide — and the root causes are examined here; personal stories enhance the text. (Rev: BL 11/15/08; LMC 3–4/09) [306.3]

1663 Collins, Gail. *When Everything Changed: The Amazing Journey of American Women from 1960 to the Present* (9–12). 2009, Little, Brown $27.99 (978-031605954-1). This inspiring account details women's struggle for equality over the past five decades; beginning with the obstacles women faced in the 1950s and drawing parallels with the civil rights movement, it also addresses the difficulties women currently encounter in balancing their professional and personal lives. (Rev: BL 10/1/09) [305.409]

1664 Farrell, Courtney. *Children's Rights* (7–10). Series: Essential Issues. 2010, ABDO LB $32.79 (978-1-60453-952-3). Child labor, child trafficking, child sexual abuse, and child soldiers are all discussed in this volume that also looks specifically at the rights of children in the United States. (Rev: LMC 10/10; SLJ 4/1/10) [305.23086]

1665 Freedman, Jeri. *Women in the Workplace: Wages, Respect, and Equal Rights* (7–12). Series: A Young Woman's Guide to Contemporary Issues. 2010, Rosen LB $31.95 (978-1-4358-3541-2). A conversational discussion of the history of women in the workplace, the need for equal opportunity and pay, and the protections available to women today, with chapters on sexual harassment and women in the military. (Rev: LMC 10/10; SLJ 4/1/10) [331.4]

1666 Lewis, Andrew B. *The Shadows of Youth: The Remarkable Journey of the Civil Rights Generation* (10–12). 2009, Hill & Wang $28 (978-0-8090-8598-9). John Lewis, Julian Bond, and Stokely Carmichael are among the individuals profiled in this account of the formation of the Student Nonviolent Coordinating Committee and its importance in sparking public interest in civil rights. (Rev: BL 10/15/09; SLJ 2/10) [323.1196]

1667 Marantz, Steve. *The Rhythm Boys of Omaha Central: High School Basketball at the '68 Racial Divide* (10–12). Illus. 2011, Univ. of Nebraska paper $17.95 (978-080323434-5). Even as the integrated 1967–1968 Omaha Central High School basketball team charged to tournament victory, a visit from segregationist presidential candidate George Wallace ignited racial riots that left the star black player and his coach in jail. (Rev: BL 3/1–15/11) [796.323]

1668 Meany, John. *Has the Civil Rights Movement Been Successful?* (7–12). Series: What Do You Think? 2008, Heinemann Library LB $32.86 (978-1-4329-1675-6). After a history of the civil rights movement, this volume looks at legal reform, discrimination in popular culture, stereotyping, and national security, with a chapter discussing the circumstances revealed by Hurricane Katrina. (Rev: SLJ 1/1/09) [323.0973]

1669 Partridge, Elizabeth. *Marching for Freedom: Walk Together, Children, and Don't You Grow Weary* (6–12). 2009, Viking $19.99 (978-0-670-01189-6). Children and young adults' role in the civil rights movement is the focus of this moving photo-essay that features quotes from personal interviews and detailed photographs. ∩ (Rev: BL 8/09*; HB 11–12/09; LMC 11/09; SLJ 10/09; VOYA 10/09) [323.1196]

1670 Roberts, Terrence. *Simple, Not Easy: Reflections on Community, Social Responsibility, and Tolerance* (10–12). 2010, Parkhurst Brothers $24.95 (978-193516616-0). This collection of stirring and often humorous speeches reveals the philosophy of Roberts, a successful educator and businessman and one of the nine African American students integrated into Central High School in Little Rock, Arkansas, in 1957. (Rev: BL 2/1/10) [323]

1671 Steele, Philip. *Documenting Slavery and Civil Rights* (6–10). Series: Documenting History. 2010, Rosen LB $26.50 (978-1-4358-9671-0). With many interesting primary source materials — posters, postage stamps, photographs, cartoons, quotations — this slim volume discusses slavery from ancient times and the struggle to achieve civil rights. (Rev: LMC 11–12/10) [306.3]

Immigration

1672 Bacon, David. *Illegal People: How Globalization Creates Migration and Criminalizes Immigrants* (10–12). 2008, Beacon $25.95 (978-080704226-7). Focusing mainly on the United States, Bacon explains why the migration of workers occurs, and advocates for the fair treatment of these laborers. (Rev: BL 9/1/08) [331.6]

1673 Barbour, Scott. *Does Illegal Immigration Harm Society?* (8–12). Series: In Controversy. 2009, ReferencePoint LB $25.95 (978-1-60152-085-2). A timely discussion of immigration issues, answering questions such as "Does Illegal Immigration Harm the American Economy?" and "Does Illegal Immigration Lead to Increased Crime and Terrorism?" (Rev: BL 10/1/09; LMC 1–2/10)

1674 Bausum, Ann. *Denied, Detained, Deported: Stories from the Dark Side of American Immigration* (6–12). Illus. 2009, National Geographic $21.95 (978-142630332-6); LB $32.90 (978-142630333-3). The author discusses cases in which immigrants (Jews, Mexicans, Japanese, and others) have been mistreated by the U.S. government in the past; she also looks at some of today's issues surrounding immigration. Lexile 1170L (Rev: BL 4/15/09; SLJ 5/1/09*) [325.73]

1675 Lansford, Tom. *Immigration* (9–12). Series: Global Viewpoints. 2009, Gale/Greenhaven $36.20 (978-0-7377-4158-2). Taking a global view, this balanced book explores the issue of immigration along with its associated issues and implications through clear, concise pro/con discussions. (Rev: LMC 10/09)

1676 McCage, Crystal D. *U.S. Border Control* (9–12). Series: Compact Research. 2008, ReferencePoint LB $25.95 (978-1-60152-052-4). With facts, statistics, and quotations, this volume addresses measures to control American borders. (Rev: SLJ 2/1/09)

Ethnic Groups and Prejudice

General and Miscellaneous

1677 Bartoletti, Susan Campbell. *They Called Themselves the K.K.K.: The Birth of an American Terrorist Group* (7–12). 2010, Houghton $19 (978-0-618-44033-7). Today's young readers will be fascinated by this account of the rise of the Ku Klux Klan at the end of the Civil War and its continuing presence through much of the 20th century. ∩ (Rev: BL 8/10*; SLJ 8/10) [322.4]

Asian Americans

1678 Lee, Joann Faung Jean. *Asian Americans in the Twenty-first Century* (10–12). 2008, New Press $24.95 (978-159558152-5). Subtitled *Oral Histories of First-to Fourth-generation Americans from China, Japan, India, Korea, the Philippines, Vietnam, and Laos,* this volume contains nearly 30 interviews with Asian Americans that reveal concerns about cultural choices, assimilation, prejudice, differences between generations, and so forth. (Rev: BL 9/1/08) [920]

Jewish Americans

1679 Alphin, Elaine Marie. *An Unspeakable Crime: The Prosecution and Persecution of Leo Frank* (9–12). 2010, Carolrhoda LB $22.95 (978-0-8225-8944-0). A moving account of the fate of Leo Frank, a Jewish man who was falsely accused of murdering a 13-year-old girl and was lynched by a mob in Atlanta in 1913. Lexile 1210L (Rev: BL 11/1/10; LMC 8–9/10; SLJ 3/10) [364.152]

Native Americans

1680 Weitzman, David. *Skywalkers: Mohawk Ironworkers Build the City* (7–10). 2010, Flash Point $19.99 (978-1-59643-162-1). With a dramatic account of a bridge collapse in Quebec in 1907, this volume describes the central role Mohawk men have played in ironwork and bridge and skyscraper construction, discussing the hazards they faced and including primary sources. Lexile 1150L (Rev: BL 10/15/10*; HB 11–12/10; LMC 11–12/10; SLJ 10/1/10; VOYA 8/10) [690.092]

Other Ethnic Groups

1681 Bayoumi, Moustafa. *How Does It Feel to Be a Problem? Being Young and Arab in America* (11–12). 2008, Penguin $24.95 (978-1-59420-176-9). In this compelling book for mature readers, Bayoumi explores the post-9/11 experiences of seven young Arab Americans living in Brooklyn. (Rev: BL 6/1–15/08*) [305.892]

1682 Malek, Alia. *A Country Called Amreeka: A Chronicle of America as Lived by Arab-Americans* (10–12). 2009, Free Press $25 (978-141658972-3). Using interviews and background material, the author gives the reader a sense of the experiences of Arab Americans from the early 1960s to the present. ❁ (Rev: BL 9/09) [973]

Social Concerns and Problems

General and Miscellaneous

1683 Morrison, Adrian R. *An Odyssey with Animals: A Veterinarian's Reflections on the Animal Rights and Welfare Debate* (10–12). 2009, Oxford $29.95 (978-019537444-5). The case for testing animals in biomedical research, albeit in a humane way, is presented by a leading researcher. (Rev: BL 7/09) [610.72]

Environmental Issues

General and Miscellaneous

1684 Alley, Richard. *Earth: The Operators' Manual* (10–12). Illus. 2011, Norton $27.95 (978-039308109-1). Nobel Peace Prize-winner Alley examines the history of humans' use of different kinds of energy, from burning wood to fossil fuels; how we have compromised our environment; and what we can do to save it in the future. (Rev: BL 3/1–15/11) [621.04209]

1685 Bowden, Ro. *Building Homes for Tomorrow* (8–12). Series: Development Without Damage. 2010, Smart Apple Media LB $34.25 (978-1-59920-252-5). This is an informative and accessible introduction to the global housing crisis and solutions including sustainable housing, improved energy conservation, and new strategies in urban planning. A companion title explores *Food and Water* (2010). (Rev: LMC 5–6/10; SLJ 11/09) [728.047]

1686 Brand, Stewart. *Whole Earth Discipline: An Eco-pragmatist Manifesto* (10–12). 2009, Penguin $25.95 (978-067002121-5). Brand, an expert in the environmental field, challenges the usual arguments against nuclear power, cities, and genetic engineering. (Rev: BL 9/15/09) [304.2]

1687 Brune, Michael. *Coming Clean: Breaking America's Addiction to Oil and Coal* (10–12). 2008, Sierra Club paper $14.95 (978-157805149-6). Brune, of the Rainforest Action Network, uncovers corporate deceit and promotes his quest for clean energy. (Rev: BL 9/1/08) [333.79]

1688 Casper, Julie Kerr. *Climate Systems: Interactive Forces of Global Warming* (9–12). 2009, Facts on File $40 (978-0-8160-7260-6). The carbon cycle, atmospheric energy, orbital variations, and ocean currents are among the topics covered in this volume that stresses the urgent need for action against global warming. (Rev: LMC 3–4/10; SLJ 11/09) [863.4]

1689 Danson, Ted, and Michael D'Orso. *Oceana: Our Endangered Oceans and What We Can Do to Save Them* (10–12). Illus. 2011, Rodale $29.99 (978-160529262-5). Actor and activist Danson teams up with Pulitzer Prize-nominated author D'Orso to trace Danson's activist roots and provide real-world solutions to the problem of our dying oceans. (Rev: BL 3/1–15/11) [333.95]

1690 Earle, Sylvia A. *The World Is Blue: How Our Fate and the Ocean's Are One* (9–12). Illus. 2009, National Geographic $26 (978-142620541-5). Interspersing scientific data with personal experiences, oceanographer Earle explains the role healthy oceans play in sustaining all life on Earth and details the devastating impact of human activities. (Rev: BL 10/1/09)

1691 Farquharson, Vanessa. *Sleeping Naked Is Green: How an Eco-cynic Unplugged Her Fridge, Sold Her Car, and Found Love in 366 Days* (10–12). 2009, Houghton paper $13.95 (978-054707328-6). A funny account of Farquharson's efforts to live green for one year. **e** (Rev: BL 5/1/09) [333.72092]

1692 Fishman, Charles. *The Big Thirst: The Secret Life and Turbulent Future of Water* (10–12). 2011, Free Press $26.99 (978-143910207-7). An engrossing analysis of the world's water supply, how it plays a part in poverty and politics, and what will happen in the future as water becomes less and less available. (Rev: BL 3/1–15/11) [333.91]

1693 Flannery, Tim. *We Are the Weather Makers: The History of Climate Change* (7–12). Adapted by Sally M. Walker. 2009, Candlewick $17.99 (978-0-7636-3656-2). This succinct overview of the perils of global warming provides explanations of our scientific understanding of the problem as well as examples of steps we each can take to reduce carbon emissions. (Rev: BL 12/1/09; LMC 11–12/09; SLJ 12/09) [363.73874]

1694 Gore, Al. *Our Choice: A Plan to Solve the Climate Crisis* (10–12). Illus. 2009, Rodale paper $26.99 (978-159486734-7). With illuminating diagrams and photographs, Al Gore provides a practical guide to solving the climate change crisis by enlisting the emerging technologies of wind, solar, and geothermal energy. (Rev: BLO 11/15/09*) [363.738]

1695 Haugen, David M., ed. *Should Drilling Be Permitted in the Arctic National Wildlife Refuge?* (10–12). Series: At Issue: Environment. 2008, Gale/Greenhaven $29.95 (978-073773930-5); paper $23.96 (978-073773931-2). This collection of essays examines the environmental implications of drilling for oil in the arctic refuge — a valuable resource for research and debate projects. (Rev: BL 9/1/08) [333.95]

1696 Hawley, Steven. *Recovering a Lost River: Removing Dams, Rewilding Salmon, Revitalizing Communities* (10–12). 2011, Beacon $26.95 (978-080700471-5). A thoughtful examination of the damage dams have caused to our ecosystems, featuring the removal of dams on the Snake River and the impact this would have on both human and wildlife populations. (Rev: BL 3/1–15/11) [333.91]

1697 Hunter, Emily, ed. *The Next Eco Warriors: 20 Young Women and Men Who Are Saving the Planet* (10–12). Illus. 2011, Conari paper $19.95 (978-157324486-2). Hunter, daughter of the cofounders of Greenpeace, profiles 22 young people dedicated to spreading ecological awareness through often unconventional and imaginative means. (Rev: BL 3/1–15/11) [333.72]

1698 Johnson, Rebecca L. *Investigating Climate Change: Scientists' Search for Answers in a Warming World* (6–10). Illus. Series: Discovery! 2008, Lerner LB $30.60 (978-082256792-9). A compelling historical overview of climate change and its causes is presented in this book full of data, diagrams, photographs, charts, and maps. (Rev: BL 9/1/08; SLJ 1/1/09; VOYA 12/08) [551.6]

1699 Kaye, Cathryn Berger. *Going Blue: A Teen Guide to Saving Our Oceans, Lakes, Rivers, and Wetlands* (6–10). 2010, Free Spirit paper $14.99 (978-1-57542-348-7). Readers learn about the need to protect Earth's water supply in this volume that provides practical tips on water preservation and activism. (Rev: BL 12/1/10*; SLJ 12/1/10*) [333.91]

1700 Kostigen, Thomas M. *You Are Here: The Surprising Link Between What We Do and What That Does to Our Planet* (10–12). 2008, HarperOne $25.95 (978-006158036-9). Kostigen provides detailed examples of how the demands of modern life are currently destroying the planet. ☊ ℮ (Rev: BL 9/1/08) [363.7]

1701 Kusky, Timothy. *Climate Change: Shifting Glaciers, Deserts, and Climate Belts* (8–12). Series: The Hazardous Earth. 2009, Facts on File $39.50 (978-0-8160-6466-3). The many factors contributing to global warming — both natural and the result of human activities — are covered in this wide-ranging volume. (Rev: SLJ 3/1/09) [551.6]

1702 Lerner, Adrienne. *Climate Change* (9–12). Series: Global Viewpoints. 2009, Gale/Greenhaven $36.20 (978-0-7377-4156-8). Taking a global view, this balanced book explores the issue of climate change along with its associated issues and implications through clear, concise pro/con discussions. (Rev: LMC 10/09)

1703 Maathai, Wangari. *Replenishing the Earth: Spiritual Values for Healing Ourselves and the World* (10–12). 2010, Doubleday paper $13 (978-030759114-2). Nobel Peace Prize winner Maathai deftly combines practical science, religion, and philosophy into a study of how we live with the Earth and its resources. ℮ (Rev: BL 9/1/10) [261.8]

1704 McKibben, Bill. *Eaarth: Making a Life on a Tough New Planet* (10–12). 2010, Times $24 (978-080509056-7). Environmentalist McKibben looks back at the effects of global warming and forward at the ways in which mankind can mitigate and reverse some of them. ☊ ℮ (Rev: BL 12/1/09*) [304.2]

1705 Miller, Debra A., ed. *Global Warming* (9–12). Series: Current Controversies. 2008, Gale/Greenhaven LB $36.20 (978-0-7377-4070-7); paper $24.95 (978-0-7377-4071-4). A variety of writings from diverse sources present opposing viewpoints on the causes, threats, and potential solutions for global warming. (Rev: SLJ 2/1/09) [363.738]

1706 Nagle, Jeanne. *Living Green* (10–12). Illus. Series: In the News. 2009, Rosen LB $21.95 (978-143585037-8). Nagle covers why, how, and where people are "living green" and discusses sustainable living as a worldwide movement. (Rev: BL 4/15/09; SLJ 5/1/09) [10.333.72]

1707 Nagle, Jeanne. *Smart Shopping: Shopping Green* (9–12). Illus. Series: Your Carbon Footprint. 2008, Rosen LB $19.95 (978-140421775-1). This book urges older teens to think about the impact their lifestyle may be having on the environment, and offers suggestions on how to reduce one's carbon footprint and organize for change. (Rev: BL 12/1/08) [640]

1708 Porter, David L. *Hell on Earth: The Wildfire Pandemic* (10–12). 2008, Forge $24.95 (978-076531380-5). Porter, who lost his own home to a fire in 2003, provides a sometimes alarmist examination of the causes and consequences of wildfires. (Rev: BL 7/08) [363.37]

1709 Rae, Alison. *Oil, Plastics, and Power* (8–12). Series: Development Without Damage. 2010, Smart Apple Media LB $34.25 (978-1-59920-251-8). Oil, gas, nuclear, and alternative sources of power are all covered in this introduction to the environmental damage caused. (Rev: LMC 5–6/10; SLJ 11/09) [333.82]

1710 Rae, Alison. *Trees and Timber Products* (8–12). Series: Development Without Damage. 2010, Smart Apple Media LB $34.25 (978-1-59920-247-1). This is an informative and accessible introduction to the timber industry around the world, discussing deforestation, soil erosion, and pollution as well as opportunities for agroforestry. (Rev: LMC 5–6/10; SLJ 11/09)

1711 Rutter, John. *Mining, Minerals, and Metals* (8–12). Series: Development Without Damage. 2010, Smart Apple Media LB $34.25 (978-1-59920-249-5). Rutter reviews how we use coal, iron, and other ores, metals, and minerals and the impact on the environment, before exploring ways to mitigate this. (Rev: LMC 5–6/10; SLJ 11/09) [622.028]

1712 Sivertsen, Linda, and Tosh Sivertsen. *Generation Green: The Ultimate Teen Guide to Living an Eco-Friendly Life* (7–12). 2008, Simon & Schuster paper $9.99 (978-141697242-6). Sivertsen and her 18-year-old son Tosh explore various aspects of green living in this very accessible yet solidly informative guide. (Rev: BLO 10/30/08; SLJ 8/08) [363.73874]

1713 Smith, Rick, et al. *Slow Death by Rubber Duck: The Secret Danger of Everyday Things* (10–12). Illus. 2010, Counterpoint $25 (978-158243567-1). Smith and Lourie present a startlingly grim exposé of the chemicals present in our daily lives — in cookware, carpeting, even pajamas — and the very real and little-known health risks they present. ℮ (Rev: BL 1/1/10*) [615.9]

1714 Taudte, Jeca. *MySpace/OurPlanet* (8–11). Illus. 2008, HarperTeen paper $12.99 (978-006156204-4). This engaging guide to eco-savvy, online environmental community OurPlanet provides tips on such compelling, relevant topics as "eco-dating" and green room makeovers via posts from online forums. (Rev: BL 8/08) [363.73874]

1715 Von Ruhland, Catherine. *Living with the Planet: Making a Difference in a Time of Climate Change* (9–12). Illus. 2009, Lion Hudson paper $19.95 (978-0-7459-5255-0). This comprehensive, well-organized volume calls attention to the devastating effects that human consumption continues to have on the global climate and offers examples of climate-related changes occurring throughout the world. (Rev: SLJ 12/09) [363.7]

1716 Waterman, Jonathan. *Running Dry: A Journey from Source to Sea Down the Colorado River* (10–12). 2010, National Geographic $26 (978-142620505-7).

Waterman makes a compelling case for saving water as he explores the natural and anthropogenic factors that threaten the Colorado River. ℮ (Rev: BL 5/1/10*) [979.1]

Pollution

1717 Safina, Carl. *A Sea in Flames: The Deepwater Horizon Oil Blowout* (10–12). 2011, Crown $25 (978-030788735-1). Safina offers an in-depth look from all angles at the Deepwater Horizon oil disaster and its short- and long-term effects on the Gulf Coast community, marine life, and politics and "big oil." (Rev: BL 3/1–15/11) [363.738]

1718 Sanna, Emily. *Air Pollution and Health* (7–10). Illus. Series: Health and the Environment. 2008, Alpha-House LB $29.95 (978-193497035-5). This thought-provoking look at the impact of air pollution on human health discusses such topics as ozone depletion, smog, and acid rain. (Rev: BLO 2/2/09; LMC 3–4/09) [363.739]

Population Issues

General and Miscellaneous

1719 Lorinc, John. *Cities* (7–12). Series: Groundwork Guides. 2008, Groundwood $18.95 (978-088899820-0). A fast-paced, detailed look at urban history and the issues cities face, such as poverty, overcrowding, and transportation. (Rev: BL 12/1/08) [307.76]

Crime, Gangs, and Prisons

1720 Bell, Suzanne. *Fakes and Forgeries* (7–12). Illus. Series: Essentials of Forensic Science. 2008, Facts on File $35.00 (978-081605514-2). Covering examples of forgery dating from Mesopotamia to the present day, Bell provides a compelling, accessible portrait of the crime, discussing techniques used and methods of detection. (Rev: BL 10/15/08) [363.25]

1721 Chura, David. *I Don't Wish Nobody to Have a Life Like Mine: Tales of Kids in Adult Lockup* (11–12). 2010, Beacon $25.95 (978-080700064-9). This eye-opening true account, written by a teacher who worked with teen convicts in adult prisons, paints a riveting portrait of young men struggling to come to terms with violent home lives, addiction, poverty, and the failure of the juvenile criminal justice system. (Rev: BL 2/1/10) [371.93092]

1722 Fast, Jonathan. *Ceremonial Violence: A Psychological Explanation of School Shootings* (11–12). 2008, Overlook $25.95 (978-159020047-6). Drawing on years of research, this books offers some insight into the common threads that link these teenage killers and the decisions that lead to the violence; for mature readers. (Rev: BL 8/08) [364.1]

1723 Haugen, David M., and Susan Musser, eds. *Media Violence* (7–12). Series: Opposing Viewpoints. 2008, Gale/Greenhaven $37.40 (978-073774218-3); paper $25.95 (978-073774219-0). Readers explore many aspects of the debate over whether violence in the media encourages violence in society. (Rev: BL 4/1/09) [363.3]

1724 Kuklin, Susan. *No Choirboy: Murder, Violence, and Teenagers on Death Row* (10–12). Illus. 2008, Holt $16.95 (978-080507950-0). Drawing on the prisoners' own words, with amplifications by Kuklin and lawyers, this volume addresses the plight of individuals who were sentenced to death while still teenagers and explores the criminal justice system. (Rev: BL 9/15/08; HB 7–8/08; SLJ 9/1/08*; VOYA 10/08) [364.66092]

1725 Marcovitz, Hal. *Gangs* (7–10). Series: Essential Issues. 2010, ABDO LB $32.79 (978-1-60453-954-7). "Why do young people join gangs?" "How do communities respond to gangs?" "Is there life after gangs?" These and other questions are answered in this well-organized volume. (Rev: LMC 10/10; SLJ 4/1/10) [364.106]

1726 Mason, Paul. *Frauds and Counterfeits* (6–12). Series: Solve It with Science. 2010, Smart Apple Media LB $34.25 (978-1-59920-329-4). The books in this series explore different ways to catch criminals using crime scene clues. (Rev: LMC 1–2/10)

1727 Sekulich, Daniel. *Terror on the Seas: True Tales of Modern-Day Pirates* (10–12). 2009, Thomas Dunne Bks $24.95 (978-0-312-37582-9). Pirates past and present are the topic of this interesting survey that provides information on modern maritime law. (Rev: SLJ 9/09) [910.4]

Poverty, Homelessness, and Hunger

1728 Khan, Irene. *The Unheard Truth: Poverty and Human Rights* (10–12). Illus. 2009, Norton paper $19.95 (978-039333700-6). With particular focus on women's issues, Khan provides meticulous research coupled with real-life examples in this lucid outline of the devastating ways in which poverty hampers basic human rights the world over. (Rev: BL 10/15/09) [330]

1729 Lusted, Marcia Amidon. *Poverty* (7–10). Series: Essential Issues. 2010, ABDO LB $32.79 (978-1-60453-957-8). The causes, impact, and stigma of poverty are examined in this volume that also looks at effects including homelessness, lack of education, and lack of health care and at various efforts to alleviate poverty. (Rev: LMC 10/10; SLJ 4/1/10) [363]

1730 Wagner, Viqi, ed. *Poverty* (7–12). Series: Opposing Viewpoints. 2008, Gale/Greenhaven $36.20 (978-0-7377-3747-9); paper $24.95 (978-0-7377-3748-6). This anthology describes the causes of poverty in America and around the world and debates the possible solutions, ranging from migration to government intervention; a revision of the 2003 edition. (Rev: SLJ 2/1/09) [362.5]

1731 Wolny, Philip. *Food Supply Collapse* (7–10). Series: Doomsday Scenarios: Separating Fact from Fiction. 2010, Rosen LB $29.25 (978-1-4358-3563-4). Are we facing food supply doomsday? This volume describes the current situation and the threats that face nations around the world. (Rev: LMC 11–12/10) [363.8]

Public Morals

1732 Otfinoski, Steven. *Science Fiction and Fantasy* (9–12). Series: Our Freedom to Read. 2009, Chelsea House LB $40.00 (978-160413032-4). A discussion of science fiction and fantasy books, including *A Wrinkle in Time* and *Fahrenheit 451,* that have been "challenged" and why they have been controversial. (Rev: BL 4/1/09; LMC 8–9/09) [098]

Sex Roles

1733 Berg, Barbara J. *Sexism in America: Alive, Well, and Ruining Our Future* (10–12). 2009, Lawrence Hill $24.95 (978-155652776-0). Author Barbara Berg, a women's studies author and expert, cites many examples of why the women's movement has stalled in the 21st century. (Rev: BL 9/09) [305.42]

1734 Douglas, Susan J. *Enlightened Sexism: The Seductive Message that Feminism's Work Is Done* (11–12). 2010, Times $26 (978-080508326-2). This insightful examination into the ways women are negatively portrayed in our supposedly "post-feminist" society draws on examples from popular TV shows and ads, and urges young women to remain active in the fight against such stereotyping. (Rev: BL 2/15/10) [302.23082]

1735 Mills, J. Elizabeth. *Expectations for Women: Confronting Stereotypes* (7–12). Series: A Young Woman's Guide to Contemporary Issues. 2010, Rosen LB $31.95 (978-1-4358-3543-6). Growing up too fast, body image, plastic surgery, the need to balance home and work, and aging gracefully are all explored in an easy, conversational manner. (Rev: LMC 10/10; SLJ 4/1/10; VOYA 8/10) [305.235]

Social Action, Social Change, and Futurism

1736 Alsenas, Linas. *Gay America: Struggle for Equality* (7–12). Illus. 2008, Abrams $24.95 (978-081099487-4). Personal accounts of gays and lesbians are interspersed with historical information about their struggles for acceptance in the United States since the Victorian period. Lexile 1340L (Rev: BL 2/1/09; LMC 1–2/09; SLJ 7/08) [306.76]

1737 Newkirk, Ingrid E., and Jane Ratcliffe, eds. *One Can Make a Difference: How Simple Actions Can Change the World* (11–12). 2008, Adams Media paper $16.95 (978-159869629-5). A look at more than 50 good deeds that have made a difference. **e** (Rev: BLO 9/15/08) [363]

1738 Rubel, David. *If I Had a Hammer: Building Homes and Hope with Habitat for Humanity* (6–12). 2009, Candlewick $19.99 (978-0-7636-4701-8). With a foreword by Jimmy Carter, this account of the work of Habitat for Humanity covers everything from the organization's Christian foundation to how it chooses partner families and the various tools and techniques the volunteers use. ∩ Lexile 1150L (Rev: LMC 1–2/10; SLJ 11/09) [363.5]

1739 Smith, Wendy. *Give a Little: How Your Small Donations Can Transform Our World* (10–12). 2009, Hyperion paper $14.99 (978-140132340-0). This accessible guide to philanthropy provides information about various charitable organizations and emphasizes the considerable impact of modest donations. **e** (Rev: BL 10/15/09) [361.7]

1740 Tisch, Jonathan M., and Karl Weber. *Citizen You: Doing Your Part to Change the World* (10–12). 2010, Crown $24 (978-030758848-7). Tisch calls on young people to move beyond simple volunteerism and into more complex civic engagement by examining present-day examples of philanthropists and the positive changes they're enacting. **e** (Rev: BL 5/1/10) [361.2]

Social Customs and Holidays

1741 Denizet-Lewis, Benoit. *American Voyeur: Dispatches from the Far Reaches of Modern Life* (11–12). 2010, Simon & Schuster paper $15 (978-141653915-5). Journalist Denizet-Lewis immerses himself in the fringes of American life: from preteen extreme athletes to gay subcultures; first published in magazines such as *Spin* and *Slate,* these 16 articles are suitable for mature readers. **e** (Rev: BL 12/1/09) [306.70973]

Urban and Rural Life

1742 Dyer, Hadley. *Watch This Space: Designing, Defending and Sharing Public Spaces* (9–12). Illus. by Marc Ngui. 2010, Kids Can $18.95 (978-1-55453-293-3). An interesting and thought-provoking look at a topic that has been neglected at the high-school level. Readers will learn about public spaces and their functions around the world. Dyer presents an interesting survey of the nature of public space, its importance to society, and questions about privacy, urban beautification, and so forth; specific examples and colorful artwork add appeal. (Rev: BL 6/18/10; LMC 8–9/10; SLJ 5/10) [307.1]

157

Economics and Business

General and Miscellaneous

1743 Klein, Grady, and Yoram Bauman. *The Cartoon Introduction to Economics, Vol. 1: Microeconomics* (10–12). Illus. 2010, Hill & Wang paper $17.95 (978-080909481-3). Basic economic concepts are given fresh life in this appealing, comic-style book, where information is presented by a team of three lab-coated figures with clipboards. (Rev: BL 1/1/10) [338.5]

Employment and Jobs

1744 Ching, Jacqueline. *Outsourcing U.S. Jobs* (7–10). Illus. Series: In the News. 2009, Rosen LB $21.95 (978-143585039-2). A helpful resource for students exploring the effects of the global economy on U.S. and foreign workers; includes photographs and diagrams. (Rev: BL 4/15/09) [331.13]

Labor Unions and Labor Problems

1745 Blum, Howard. *American Lightning: Terror, Mystery, Movie-Making, and the Crime of the Century* (10–12). 2008, Crown $24.95 (978-030734694-0). A fascinating, detailed account of the investigation into the 1910 *Los Angeles Times* office explosion that brought an ongoing conflict between labor and management to a head. ∩ e (Rev: BL 8/08*) [364.152]

1746 Skurzynski, Gloria. *Sweat and Blood: A History of U.S. Labor Unions* (7–10). Illus. Series: People's History. 2008, Lerner LB $31.93 (978-082257594-8). Charting the course of workers' rights from Jamestown through industrialization to the present day, Skurzynski provides a detailed, historically grounded survey of the rights, rules, and governance of labor unions in America. (Rev: BL 10/1/08; SLJ 11/1/08) [331.880]

Marketing and Advertising

1747 Haugen, David M, ed. *How Does Advertising Impact Teen Behavior?* (9–12). Series: At Issue. 2008, Gale/Greenhaven LB $29.95 (978-0-7377-3922-0); paper $23.96 (978-0-7377-3923-7). Diverse articles present varying viewpoints on the connection between advertising and teen behavior. (Rev: SLJ 2/1/09) [659.10]

Guidance and Personal Development

Education and Schools

General and Miscellaneous

1748 Daniels, Peggy, ed. *Zero Tolerance Policies in Schools* (9–12). Illus. Series: Issues That Concern You. 2008, Gale/Greenhaven $33.70 (978-0-7377-4189-6). Articles consider various aspects of zero tolerance policies and the ways in which they impact students, teachers, and schools. (Rev: SLJ 3/1/09) [371.5]

Development of Academic Skills

Study Skills

1749 Greenberg, Michael. *Painless Study Techniques* (6–12). Illus. by Michele Earle-Bridges. 2009, Barron's paper $9.99 (978-0-7641-4059-4). Pop culture references will draw students into this guide that teaches skills in all aspects of study organization, including note taking, creating outlines, time management, and effective studying (includes charts and lists of Web sites). (Rev: SLJ 9/09)

Writing and Speaking Skills

1750 Friedman, Lauri S. *Oil* (9–12). Illus. Series: Writing the Critical Essay, An Opposing Viewpoints Guide. 2008, Gale/Greenhaven $29.95 (978-0-7377-4038-7). Articles presenting opposing views about petroleum and alternative fuels are juxtaposed with chapters explaining how to write your own analytical essay — creating an outline, presenting theories and conclusions, using quotations, finding and citing information, and so forth. (Rev: SLJ 1/1/09) [333.8]

1751 Friedman, Lauri S. *Self-Mutilation* (7–10). Illus. Series: Writing the Critical Essay: An Opposing Viewpoints Guide. 2008, Gale/Greenhaven $29.95 (978-073774266-4). After presenting six perspectives on various forms of self-mutilation (including plastic surgery and body art), this volume provides sample essays and exercises that help the student to create thoughtful, well-researched theses. (Rev: BLO 2/17/09) [616.85]

1752 Williams, Heidi, ed. *Plagiarism* (8–12). Series: Issues That Concern You. 2008, Gale/Greenhaven $33.70 (978-0-7377-4072-1). Twelve essays address the problem of plagiarism from various perspectives, discussing in particular the temptations of new technology and the services available to prevent plagiarism. (Rev: SLJ 2/1/09) [808]

Academic Guidance

Colleges and Universities

1753 Rooney, John F., and John F. Reardon. *Preparing for College: Practical Advice for Students and Their Families* (10–12). 2009, Ferguson LB $34.95 (978-0-8160-7377-1); paper $16.95 (978-0-8160-7378-8). With many sidebars, statistics, and Web sites, this comprehensive guide covers numerous aspects of preparing for college, from selecting the right one to how to apply, plus tips on choosing majors and advice for succeeding. (Rev: SLJ 9/09; VOYA 8/09) [378.1]

Careers and Occupational Guidance

Careers

General and Miscellaneous

1754 *Animal Careers* (9–12). Series: What Can I Do Now? 2010, Ferguson $32.95 (978-0-8160-8075-5). With an overview of the field, descriptions of ten career choices, accounts of a typical day, and details of necessary qualifications and training, this is an attractive and informative volume. (Rev: LMC 11–12/10)

1755 Brezina, Corona. *Jobs in Sustainable Energy* (7–10). Series: Green Careers. 2010, Rosen LB $30.60 (978-1-4358-3569-6). Following an overview of the field, this well-organized book looks at jobs in various sectors (solar, wind, geothermal, and so forth) and explains the necessary education and training and the job prospects and salaries. (Rev: LMC 10/10; SLJ 8/10) [621.042]

1756 Byers, Ann. *Jobs as Green Builders and Planners* (7–10). Series: Green Careers. 2010, Rosen LB $30.60 (978-1-4358-3566-5). This well-organized book looks at the kinds of jobs available and explains the necessary education and training and the job prospects and salaries. Part of a series that covers other "green" careers in law, tourism, and cleanup of hazardous spills. (Rev: LMC 10/10; SLJ 8/10) [690.023]

1757 *Environment. 2nd ed.* (9–12). Series: What Can I Do Now? 2010, Ferguson $32.95 (978-0-8160-8073-1). With an overview of the field, descriptions of ten career choices, accounts of a typical day, and details of necessary qualifications and training, this is an attractive and informative volume. (Rev: LMC 11–12/10)

1758 *Organization Skills* (8–12). Series: Career Skills Library. 2009, Ferguson $25.95 (978-0-8160-7774-8). Time management, avoiding procrastination, and organization of materials and schedules are emphasized in this easy-to-read book that includes quizzes and exercises. (Rev: LMC 3–4/10) [650.1]

1759 Scott, Jennifer Power. *Green Career$: You Can Make Money and Save the Planet* (8–12). 2010, Lobster paper $16.95 (978-1-897550-18-2). Students whose interests range from farming to architecture will find that they can use their talents in environmentally friendly ways. (Rev: BL 2/15/10; LMC 8–9/10; SLJ 4/10) [333.72]

1760 *Teamwork Skills* (7–12). Series: Career Skills Library. 2009, Ferguson $25.95 (978-0-8160-7771-7). The importance of working as a team and solving conflicts are emphasized in this easy-to-read book that includes quizzes and exercises. (Rev: LMC 3–4/10) [658.4022]

1761 *The Teen Vogue Handbook: An Insider's Guide to Careers in Fashion* (7–12). 2009, Penguin paper $24.95 (978-1-59514-261-0). Full of profiles and advice from top fashion-industry movers and shakers, this book provides a practical, authoritative guide to breaking into a career in fashion. (Rev: SLJ 1/10; VOYA 12/09) [746.9]

1762 *Travel and Tourism. 2nd ed.* (9–12). Series: What Can I Do Now? 2010, Ferguson $32.95 (978-0-8160-8078-6). With an overview of the field, descriptions of ten career choices, accounts of a typical day, and details of necessary qualifications and training, this is an attractive and informative volume. (Rev: LMC 11–12/10) [647.94]

Arts, Entertainment, and Sports

1763 Crouch, Tanja L. *100 Careers in the Music Business. 2nd ed.* (10–12). 2008, Barron's paper $16.99 (978-076413914-7). This well-organized volume lists 100 careers in 16 categories and includes the skills that might be needed for each one; it also provides information about music organizations and schools. (Rev: BLO 8/28/08) [780.23]

1764 *Film* (9–12). Series: What Can I Do Now? 2010, Ferguson $32.95 (978-0-8160-8076-2). With an overview of the field, descriptions of ten career choices, accounts of a typical day, and details of necessary qualifications and training, this is an attractive and informative volume. (Rev: LMC 11–12/10)

Education and Librarianship

1765 *Education* (9–12). Series: What Can I Do Now? 2010, Ferguson $32.95 (978-0-8160-8079-9). With an overview of the field, descriptions of ten career choices,

accounts of a typical day, and details of necessary qualifications and training, this is an attractive and informative volume. (Rev: LMC 11–12/10)

Law, Police, and Other Society-Oriented Careers

1766 Echaore-McDavid, Susan, and Richard A. McDavid. *Career Opportunities in Forensic Science* (10–12). 2008, Ferguson $49.50 (978-081606156-3); paper $18.95 (978-081606157-0). This text provides a wealth of information about opportunities in forensic science from job descriptions and salaries to education requirements and personalities best suited for specific jobs. (Rev: BLO 9/4/08) [363.25]

Personal Finances

Money-Making Ideas

1767 Bielagus, Peter G. *Quick Cash for Teens: Be Your Own Boss and Make Big Bucks* (7–12). Illus. 2009, Sterling paper $12.95 (978-140276038-9). Bielagus recommends 101 businesses suited for teens and provides step-by-step strategies for success with interesting anecdotes and sample worksheets. (Rev: BL 6/1–15/09) [658.1]

Managing Money

1768 Byers, Ann. *First Apartment Smarts* (8–12). Series: Get Smart With Your Money. 2010, Rosen LB $29.95 (978-1-4358-5272-3). Clearly written and practical, this volume covers planning, budgeting, apartment searching, and moving in, and living smart, asking readers to assess their preparedness frankly. (Rev: BL 10/1/09; LMC 1–2/10)

Health and the Human Body

General and Miscellaneous

1769 Carroll, Aaron E., and Rachel C. Vreeman. *Don't Swallow Your Gum! Myths, Half-Truths, and Outright Lies About Your Body and Health* (9–12). 2009, St. Martin's paper $13.95 (978-0-312-53387-8). Accessible, accurate, and entertaining, this conversational book debunks approximately 60 commonly held misconceptions about our bodies and healthful practices. (Rev: SLJ 9/09) [612]

1770 Clegg, Brian. *Upgrade Me: Our Amazing Journey to Human 2.0* (10–12). 2008, St. Martin's $24.95 (978-0-312-37157-9). Clegg discusses the age-old desire of humankind to improve itself physically, and considers the modern pros and cons of this pursuit of perfection, including discussion of such topics as gene therapy, cloning, bionics, and nanotechnology. (Rev: BLO 8/28/08) [599.93]

1771 O'Connor, Anahad. *Always Follow the Elephants: More Surprising Facts and Misleading Myths About Our Health and the World We Live In* (9–12). Illus. 2009, Times paper $14 (978-080509000-0). This amusing look at the scientific truths behind many commonly held beliefs concerning healthful behavior separates fact from fiction. e (Rev: BL 10/1/09) [613]

Aging and Death

1772 Marcovitz, Hal. *Suicide* (7–10). Series: Essential Issues. 2010, ABDO LB $32.79 (978-1-60453-958-5). After a history of suicide this volume looks at risk factors, the contribution of mental disorders, the right to die, and how to prevent these deaths. (Rev: LMC 10/10; SLJ 4/1/10) [362.2]

1773 Sharp, Anne Wallace. *The Right to Die* (9–12). Series: Hot Topics. 2009, Gale/Lucent LB $32.45 (978-1-59018-834-7). Euthanasia, assisted suicide, refusing medical treatment, and the withdrawal of life-sustaining treatments are all covered in this volume that also addresses brain death, organ transplants, and cryonics. (Rev: SLJ 1/10) [174]

1774 Strauss, Alix. *Death Becomes Them: Unearthing the Suicides of the Brilliant, the Famous, and the Notorious* (11–12). Illus. 2009, Harper paper $14.99 (978-006172856-3). Hitler, Sylvia Plath, Hemingway, Hunter Thompson, and Kurt Cobain are among the individuals featured in this survey of celebrity suicides; for mature readers. (Rev: BL 9/09) [362.28092]

Alcohol, Drugs, and Smoking

1775 Bjornlund, Lydia D. *Teen Smoking* (9–12). Series: Compact Research: Current Issues. 2010, ReferencePoint $25.95 (978-1-60152-098-2). This book on the causes and consequences of teen smoking includes straightforward factual information as well as compelling graphs, charts, and photos. (Rev: BLO 8/16/10; SLJ 3/10) [362.29]

1776 Goldstein, Margaret J. *Legalizing Drugs: Crime Stopper or Social Risk?* (7–10). Series: USA Today's Debate: Voices and Perspectives. 2010, Lerner LB $35.93 (978-0-7613-5116-0). After a history of the war on drugs (since Prohibition), this attractive volume draws on *USA Today* to discuss the effectiveness of this battle and review arguments for and against legalization. (Rev: BL 4/1/10; LMC 10/10; SLJ 6/10) [364.1]

1777 Gottfried, Ted, and Lisa Harkrader. *Marijuana* (6–12). Series: Benchmark Rockets. 2010, Marshall Cavendish LB $28.50 (978-0-7614-4351-3). With information about marijuana's history, the ways in which it is consumed, the dangers it poses, the legal problems involved in its use, and some sidebar accounts of teen usage, this title is useful for reports and for young people who have a more personal interest;. (Rev: LMC 3–4/10) [362.29]

1778 LeVert, Suzanne, and Jeff Hendricks. *Ecstasy* (6–12). Series: Benchmark Rockets. 2010, Marshall Cavendish LB $28.50 (978-0-7614-4349-0). With information about the history of this drug, the ways in which it is consumed, the dangers it poses, the legal problems involved in its use, and some sidebar accounts of teen usage, this title is useful for reports and for young people who have a more personal interest;. Also use *Steroids* (2010). (Rev: LMC 3–4/10) [362.29]

1779 Lyon, Joshua. *Pill Head: The Secret Life of a Painkiller Addict* (10–12). 2009, Hyperion $24.99 (978-1-4013-2298-4). Interviews and statistics add depth to this journalistic look at the startling availability of prescription pills and the devastating effects of addiction. (Rev: SLJ 11/09) [616.86]

1780 Menhard, Francha Roffe, and Lisa Harkrader. *Inhalants* (6–12). Series: Benchmark Rockets. 2010, Marshall Cavendish LB $28.50 (978-0-7614-4350-6). With information about inhalants' history, the ways in which they are consumed, the dangers posed, and the legal problems involved, plus some sidebar accounts of teen usage, this title is useful for reports and for young people who have a more personal interest;. (Rev: LMC 3–4/10) [362.29]

1781 Sherman, Jill. *Drug Trafficking* (7–10). Series: Essential Issues. 2010, ABDO LB $32.79 (978-1-60453-953-0). After a history of drug trafficking this volume looks at the issue from the perspectives of producers, smugglers, dealers, and users and discusses the various approaches to law enforcement. (Rev: LMC 10/10) [363.4]

1782 Tenaglia-Webster, Maria. *Drugs* (9–12). Series: Global Viewpoints. 2009, Gale/Greenhaven $36.20 (978-0-7377-4152-0). Taking a global view, this balanced book explores the global war on drugs and its associated implications through clear, concise pro/con discussions. (Rev: LMC 10/09)

Diseases and Illnesses

1783 Ambrose, Marylou. *Investigating Diabetes: Real Facts for Real Lives* (7–10). Series: Investigating Diseases. 2010, Enslow LB $34.60 (978-0-7660-3338-2). Symptoms, diagnosis, treatment, and current research are all covered in this book that also tells the stories of children coping with the disease and provides historical background. (Rev: LMC 10/10) [616.4]

1784 Ambrose, Marylou, and Veronica Deisler. *Investigating Eating Disorders (Anorexia, Bulimia and Binge Eating): Real Facts for Real Lives* (7–10). Series: Investigating Diseases. 2010, Enslow LB $34.60 (978-0-7660-3339-9). Symptoms, diagnosis, treatment, and current research are all covered in this book that also tells the stories of children coping with these problems and provides historical background. (Rev: LMC 10/10) [616.85]

1785 Bakewell, Lisa, and Karen Bellenir, eds. *Cancer Information for Teens: Health Tips About Cancer Awareness, Prevention, Diagnosis, and Treatment* (8–12). Series: Teen Health. 2009, Omnigraphics $69 (978-0-7808-1085-3). Provides current information on cancer's warning signs, risk factors, and treatment. (Rev: SLJ 3/10)

1786 Ballard, Carol. *Explaining Food Allergies* (7–12). Series: Explaining . . . . 2010, Smart Apple Media LB $34.25 (978-1-59920-316-4). Well designed and written, these books about common illnesses affecting children include ways to help kids cope with the various conditions (glossary, index). (Rev: LMC 1–2/10)

1787 Cunningham, Kevin. *Flu* (9–12). Series: Diseases in History. 2009, Morgan Reynolds LB $28.95 (978-1-59935-105-6). Cunningham explores the history of the flu virus in humans and the likelihood of future pandemics in this comprehensive volume. Lexile 1040 (Rev: BL 10/1/09; SLJ 9/09) [614.5]

1788 Cunningham, Kevin. *HIV/AIDS* (9–12). Series: Diseases in History. 2009, Morgan Reynolds LB $28.95 (978-1-59935-104-9). Cunningham examines the brief history of HIV/AIDS, the treatment and prevention of the virus, and society's reaction to this epidemic. (Rev: SLJ 1/10; VOYA 10/09) [616.97]

1789 Cunningham, Kevin. *Malaria* (9–12). Series: Diseases in History. 2009, Morgan Reynolds LB $28.95 (978-1-59935-103-2). An in-depth look at the history, transmission, treatment, and prevention of this disease. Also use *Plague* (2009). (Rev: SLJ 1/10) [614.532]

1790 Currie-McGhee, Leanne. *Sexually Transmitted Diseases* (6–12). Illus. Series: Compact Research. 2008, ReferencePoint $25.95 (978-160152045-6). Using a blend of text, diagrams, primary sources, and bullet points this volume delivers sobering information on a variety of STDs, including HPV. (Rev: BL 10/15/08; LMC 8–9/09) [614.5]

1791 Dahl, Ken. *Monsters* (11–12). Illus. 2009, Secret Acres paper $18 (978-097996094-9). Giant, intrusive talking herpes sores symbolize the author's feelings of doom and shame in this bitingly funny graphic-novel-style take on the realities of STDs. (Rev: BL 11/15/09) [616.95]

1792 Drisdelle, Rosemary. *Parasites: Tales of Humanity's Most Unwelcome Guests* (10–12). 2010, Univ. of California $27.50 (978-052025938-6). Everything you always wanted to know about the role parasites have played in human history, from the downfall of cities to their role in wartime. (Rev: BLO 1/24/11) [757]

1793 Goldsmith, Connie. *Battling Malaria: On the Front Line Against a Global Killer* (8–12). 2010, Lerner LB $37.27 (978-0-8225-8580-0). Goldsmith emphasizes the devastating impact of malaria on nations around the world and provides facts about its transmission, treatment, and methods of control; with personal stories and interesting sidebars. (Rev: LMC 11–12/10)

1794 Goldsmith, Connie. *Hepatitis* (7–12). Series: USA Today Health Reports: Diseases and Disorders. 2010, Lerner LB $34.60 (978-0-8225-6787-5). Hepatitis is not sufficiently recognized as a health problem, and this succinct and accessible volume discusses symptoms, transmission, prevention, treatment, and research. (Rev: BL 6/1/10; LMC 11–12/10) [616.3]

1795 Goldsmith, Connie. *Influenza* (7–12). Series: USA Today Health Reports: Diseases and Disorders. 2010, Lerner LB $34.60 (978-0-7613-5881-7). This succinct and accessible volume discusses symptoms, transmission, prevention, and treatment of influenza as well as outbreaks of bird flu and swine flu. (Rev: LMC 11–12/10) [616.2]

1796 Hardman, Lizabeth. *Plague* (6–10). Series: Diseases and Disorders. 2010, Lucent Books (Gale) $32.45 (978-1-4205-0145-2). With real-life examples and many illustrations, this book describes epidemics of plague through the centuries. (Rev: LMC 5–6/10) [616.9232]

1797 Landau, Elaine. *Food Poisoning and Foodborne Diseases* (7–12). Series: USA Today Health Reports: Diseases and Disorders. 2010, Lerner LB $34.60 (978-0-8225-7290-9). This succinct and accessible volume discusses symptoms, transmission, prevention, and treatment of illnesses caused by contaminated food and water. (Rev: LMC 11–12/10) [615.9]

1798 Marisco, Katie. *HIV/AIDS* (7–10). Series: Essential Issues. 2010, ABDO LB $32.79 (978-1-60453-955-4). After a history of this disease, readers learn about its global impact, the medications available, continuing research, and the misconceptions and prejudices that have contributed to its spread. (Rev: LMC 10/10) [362.196]

1799 Parks, Peggy J. *HPV* (7–12). Illus. Series: Compact Research: Diseases and Disorders. 2008, ReferencePoint LB $25.95 (978-160152070-8). Recent developments in the understanding and prevention of human papillomavirus (HPV) make this an interesting book on a hot health topic. (Rev: BL 4/1/09; SLJ 6/1/09) [362.196]

1800 Silverthorne, Elizabeth. *Anorexia and Bulimia* (6–10). Series: Diseases and Disorders. 2010, Lucent Books (Gale) $32.45 (978-1-4205-0141-4). With real-life examples and many illustrations, this book describes the causes, diagnosis, and treatment of these eating disorders. (Rev: LMC 5–6/10) [616.85]

1801 Taylor, Kate, ed. *Going Hungry: Writers on Desire, Self-Denial, and Overcoming Anorexia* (10–12). 2008, Anchor paper $14.95 (978-030727834-0). This volume offers 18 vivid personal accounts of grappling with anorexia. (Rev: BL 8/08) [616.85]

Doctors, Hospitals, and Medicine

1802 Boleyn-Fitzgerald, Miriam. *Ending and Extending Life* (9–12). Series: Contemporary Issues in Science. 2010, Facts on File $35 (978-0-8160-6205-8). Boleyn-Fitzgerald explores ethical questions raised by medical innovations, looking at specific cases such as Karen Quinlan and Theresa Schiavo, and at the technologies such as ventilators and tube feeding that may improve length but not quality of life. (Rev: LMC 10/10)

1803 Campbell, Andrew. *Cosmetic Surgery* (6–12). Series: Science in the News. 2010, Smart Apple Media LB $34.25 (978-1-59920-322-5). Consistent in writing and design, these books allow students to examine issues that are current and cutting-edge (glossary, Web sites, index). (Rev: LMC 1–2/10)

1804 Kelly, Kate. *Early Civilizations: Prehistoric Times to 500 C.E.* (9–12). Series: The History of Medicine. 2009, Facts on File $40 (978-0-8160-7205-7). From Egyptian mummies to Chinese medicine and Hippocrates, this volume explores early beliefs and practices and includes images of instruments used. Also recommended is *The Middle Ages: 500–1450* (2009). (Rev: LMC 3–4/10; SLJ 1/10) [610.938]

1805 Lusted, Marcia Amidon. *Cosmetic Surgery* (7–10). Illus. Series: Essential Viewpoints. 2009, ABDO/Essential Library LB $32.79 (978-1-60453-530-3). An informative discussion — drawing on published sources — of the origins, popularity, and pros and cons of cosmetic surgery. (Rev: BL) 10/27/09; SLJ 1/10) [617.9]

1806 Sommer, Alfred. *Getting What We Deserve: Health and Medical Care in America* (10–12). 2009, Johns Hopkins $21.95 (978-080189387-2). Dr. Sommer explains that, while modern medical advances have prolonged our lifespans, human behavior and market and economic forces prevent many from benefiting from them. ℮ (Rev: BL 12/1/09) [362.1]

Genetics

1807 Hodge, Russ. *The Molecules of Life: DNA, RNA, and Protein* (9–12). Series: Genetics and Evolution. 2009, Facts on File $39.50 (978-0-8160-6680-3). With many illustrations and clear text, this volume introduces the basics of molecular biology and goes on to discuss DNA and genes and to explain their importance in health, with information on the instruments used in this science. (Rev: LMC 3–4/10) [611]

1808 Kurpinski, Kyle, and Terry D. Johnson. *How to Defeat Your Own Clone and Other Tips for Surviving the Biotech Revolution* (10–12). 2010, Bantam paper $14 (978-055338578-6). This tongue-in-cheek overview examines the science and ethics of cloning. **e** (Rev: BLO 12/1/09) [660.6]

1809 Meany, John. *Is Genetic Research a Threat?* (7–12). Series: What Do You Think? 2008, Heinemann Library LB $32.86 (978-1-4329-1674-9). After an explanation of the nature of genetic research, this volume discusses the topic as it relates to the individual and to society at large, crime and the law, health, and nonhuman life. (Rev: SLJ 1/1/09) [174.957]

Grooming, Personal Appearance, and Dress

1810 Williams, Heidi, ed. *Body Image* (9–12). Illus. Series: Issues That Concern You. 2008, Gale/Greenhaven $33.70 (978-0-7377-4182-7). Articles consider various aspects of our perceptions of ourselves and the importance of heredity, diet, and media and social forces, along with options such as plastic surgery and weight-loss surgery. (Rev: SLJ 3/1/09) [306.4]

The Human Body

General and Miscellaneous

1811 Macaulay, David. *The Way We Work: Getting to Know the Amazing Human Body* (7–12). Illus. by author. 2008, Houghton $35.00 (978-061823378-6). Whimsically illustrated, this book provides a broad, accessible tour of the human body and the myriad complex systems that make it work. (Rev: BL 10/15/08; HB 9–10/08; LMC 5–6/09; SLJ 10/1/08*; VOYA 1008) [610]

1812 Weiss, Marisa C., and Isabel Friedman. *Taking Care of Your "Girls": A Breast Health Guide for Girls, Teens, and In-Betweens* (6–12). Illus. 2008, Three Rivers $15.95 (978-030740696-5). Health, beauty, fashion, and personal aspects of breasts and bras are discussed in a conversational tone. **e** (Rev: BLO 10/7/08) [618.1]

Digestive and Excretory Systems

1813 Magee, Elaine. *Tell Me What to Eat if I Have Irritable Bowel Syndrome* (8–12). 2008, Rosen LB $23.95 (978-140421836-9). This book provides a wealth of information — and debunks some pervasive IBS myths

— in an approachable, matter-of-fact manner. (Rev: BL 10/15/08) [616.3]

Respiratory System

1814 Whittemore, Susan. *The Respiratory System* (7–12). Series: The Human Body: How It Works. 2009, Chelsea House $35 (978-1-60413-375-2). The functioning of the respiratory system is clearly explained, and there is discussion of diseases affecting it. (Rev: LMC 5–6/10) [612.2]

Senses

1815 Gilbert, Avery. *What the Nose Knows: The Science of Scent in Everyday Life* (10–12). 2008, Crown $23.95 (978-140008234-6). In this surprisingly humorous volume, Gilbert explores the science of smells, from origins to commercial uses. **e** (Rev: BL 7/08; SLJ 2/09) [612.8]

1816 Light, Douglas B. *The Senses* (7–12). Series: The Human Body: How It Works. 2009, Chelsea House $35 (978-1-60413-362-2). Sight, smell, taste, touch, and hearing are all examined here, as well as thirst and hunger, with interesting factboxes and clear illustrations. (Rev: LMC 5–6/10) [612.8]

Mental Disorders and Emotional Problems

1817 Allman, Toney. *Autism* (6–10). Series: Diseases and Disorders. 2010, Lucent Books (Gale) $32.45 (978-1-4205-0143-8). With real-life examples and many illustrations, this book describes the causes, diagnosis, and treatment of autism and discusses the prospects of finding a cure. (Rev: LMC 5–6/10) [616.8]

1818 Farrell, Courtney. *Mental Disorders* (7–10). Series: Essential Issues. 2010, ABDO LB $32.79 (978-1-60453-956-1). The nature of mental disorders and their impact on society, treatment, and associated stigma are all discussed here along with the role of medical professionals and various key pieces of legislation. (Rev: LMC 10/10; SLJ 4/1/10) [362.2]

1819 Levin, Judith. *Anxiety and Panic Attacks* (7–10). Illus. Series: Teen Mental Health. 2008, Rosen LB $19.95 (978-140421797-3). Teens curious about — or perhaps afflicted by — anxiety disorders will find much practical, comforting advice and information in this helpful guide. (Rev: BL 10/15/08) [616.85]

1820 Marcovitz, Hal. *Bipolar Disorders* (6–10). Illus. Series: Compact Research. 2009, ReferencePoint $25.95 (978-1-60152-066-1). Marcovitz provides a thorough and readable guide to the causes, symptoms, and treatment of bipolar disorders. (Rev: SLJ 6/1/09) [516]

1821 Meisel, Abigail. *Investigating Depression and Bipolar Disorder: Real Facts for Real Lives* (7–10). Series: Investigating Diseases. 2010, Enslow LB $34.60 (978-0-7660-3340-5). Symptoms, diagnosis, treatment, and current research are all covered in this book that also tells the stories of children coping with these problems and provides historical background. (Rev: LMC 10/10) [616.85]

1822 Metcalf, Tom, and Gena Metcalf. *Phobias* (6–10). 2008, Gale/Greenhaven $34.95 (978-0-7377-4027-1). A collection of articles that discuss the symptoms, causes, and treatment of phobias, with interesting first-person accounts. (Rev: SLJ 2/1/09) [616.85]

1823 Nakaya, Andrea C. *ADHD* (7–12). Illus. Series: Compact Research: Diseases and Disorders. 2009, ReferencePoint LB $25.95 (978-160152062-3). A balanced overview of attention deficit hyperactivity disorder and its symptoms and treatment. (Rev: BL 4/1/09; SLJ 6/1/09) [618.92]

1824 Parks, Peggy J. *Alzheimer's Disease* (6–10). Illus. Series: Compact Research: Diseases and Disorders. 2009, ReferencePoint $25.95 (978-1-60152-061-6). This accessible, illustrated book provides a thorough and readable guide to the causes, symptoms, and treatment of Alzheimer's disease. (Rev: SLJ 6/1/09) [616.831]

1825 Parks, Peggy J. *Autism* (7–12). Illus. Series: Compact Research: Diseases and Disorders. 2008, ReferencePoint LB $25.95 (978-160152058-6). "What causes autism?" and "How effective are autism treatments?" are among the questions discussed in this thoughtful and attractive volume. (Rev: BL 4/1/09) [616.85]

1826 Parks, Peggy J. *Down Syndrome* (7–12). Series: Compact Research. 2009, ReferencePoint $25.95 (978-1-60152-065-4). In this broad overview of Down syndrome, Parks focuses on the genetic causes and ethical considerations surrounding the disorder, also discussing technology that may prevent it in the future. (Rev: SLJ 6/1/09) [362.1]

Nutrition and Diet

1827 Fredericks, Carrie. *Obesity* (6–12). Illus. Series: Compact Research: Current Issues. 2008, ReferencePoint LB $24.95 (978-160152040-1). This fact-filled volume examines the causes, dangers, and treatment of obesity, including a section on how personal choices influence health. (Rev: BL 8/08) [616.3]

1828 Gay, Kathlyn. *The Scoop on What to Eat: What You Should Know About Diet and Nutrition* (6–10). Illus.

Series: Issues in Focus Today. 2009, Enslow LB $23.95 (978-076603066-4). A realistic and readable approach to choosing healthy foods, with a chapter on exercise. (Rev: BL 4/15/09; SLJ 10/09) [613.2]

1829 Hamilton, Jill, ed. *Vegetarianism* (9–12). Illus. Series: Issues That Concern You. 2008, Gale/Greenhaven $33.70 (978-0-7377-4188-9). Articles consider various aspects of vegetarianism and the ways in which it benefits and limits its adherents, as well as the potential benefits to the environment. (Rev: SLJ 3/1/09) [613.2]

1830 Pollan, Michael. *The Omnivore's Dilemma: The Secrets Behind What You Eat* (6–10). Adapted by Richie Chevat. Illus. 2009, Dial $17.99 (978-0-8037-3415-9). For young adults, this condensed version of Pollan's groundbreaking work offers an attractive and accessible take on the importance of choosing your food carefully. (Rev: BL 10/15/09*; HB 11–12/09; LMC 11–12/09; SLJ 10/09) [338.10973.]

Physical Disabilities and Problems

1831 Laney, Dawn, ed. *People with Disabilities* (8–12). Series: History of Issues. 2008, Gale/Greenhaven $36.20 (978-0-7377-3972-5). Laney presents articles supporting and opposing issues relating to people with disabilities, addressing such topics as legal rights, education, and new technologies. (Rev: SLJ 2/1/09) [362.40973]

Reproduction and Child Care

1832 Fisanick, Christina, ed. *Childbirth* (8–12). Series: Opposing Viewpoints. 2008, Gale/Greenhaven LB $37.40. (978-0-7377-4196-4); paper $25.95 (978-0-7377-4197-1). A collection of articles showing various points of view on aspects of childbirth practices. (Rev: SLJ 5/1/09) [618.2]

1833 May, Elaine Tyler. *America and the Pill: A History of Promise, Peril, and Liberation* (10–12). 2010, Basic $25.95 (978-046501152-0). May provides a thorough, apolitical history of "the pill," from its origins in the 1960s to its role today. ℮ (Rev: BL 4/15/10)

1834 Rosenthal, Beth, ed. *Birth Control* (7–12). Series: Opposing Viewpoints. 2008, Gale/Greenhaven $37.40 (978-073774194-0); paper $25.95 (978-073774195-7). Questions such as "How does birth control affect society?" and "Who should control access to birth control?" are tackled in this collection of articles offering various perspectives. (Rev: BL 4/1/09; SLJ 5/1/09) [363.9]

1835 Zerucha, Ted. *Human Development* (7–12). Series: The Human Body: How It Works. 2009, Chelsea House

$35 (978-1-60413-371-4). Zerucha describes the development of a human being from the initial single cell. (Rev: LMC 5–6/10) [612.64]

Sex Education and Sexual Identity

1836 Bily, Cynthia A., ed. *Homosexuality* (7–12). Series: Opposing Viewpoints. 2008, Gale/Greenhaven $37.40 (978-073774214-5); paper $25.95 (978-073774215-2). Questions such as "Should gay men and women serve in the military?" and "Should same-sex couples be allowed to marry?" are tackled in this collection of articles offering various perspectives. (Rev: BL 4/1/09) [306.76]

1837 Goldstein, Andrew, et al. *When Sex Hurts: A Woman's Guide to Banishing Sexual Pain* (11–12). 2011, Da

Capo paper $16 (978-073821398-9). Chock full of ob/gyn advice and information on the conditions that can cause women pain while having sex, including bladder infections and skin conditions. (Rev: BLO 1/26/11) [618.17]

Sex Problems (Abuse, Harassment, etc.)

1838 Gordon, Sherri Mabry. *Beyond Bruises: The Truth About Teens and Abuse* (7–12). Series: Issues in Focus Today. 2009, Enslow LB $31.93 (978-0-7660-3064-0). This book explores the causes and consequences of various forms of abuse through firsthand accounts, photos, and concise sidebars. (Rev: BL 4/15/09; SLJ 10/09) [362.76083]

Human Development and Behavior

General and Miscellaneous

1839 Brizendine, Louann. *The Male Brain* (11–12). 2010, Broadway $24.99 (978-076792753-6). This fast-paced, provocative follow-up to the author's *The Female Brain* (2006) draws on the psychiatric clinician's case files to paint a picture of the development of the male brain and the differences between the behavior of men and women. ∩ (Rev: BL 2/1/10) [612.8]

1840 Isaacson, Walter, ed. *Profiles in Leadership: Historians on the Elusive Quality of Greatness* (10–12). 2010, Norton $26.95 (978-039307655-4). "What makes a great leader great?" With profiles of notable Americans by historians, professors, and other commentators, this volume looks at the essential qualities. ∩ ℮ (Rev: BL 9/1/10) [324.2]

1841 Shenk, David. *The Genius in All of Us: Why Everything You've Been Told About Genetics, Talent, and IQ Is Wrong* (10–12). Illus. 2010, Doubleday $26.95 (978-038552365-3). Journalist Shenk makes the case that hard work, parenting, and environment are just as important as genetics in shaping successful lives. ∩ (Rev: BL 3/1/10) [155.2]

1842 Smith, Larry, and Rachel Fershleiser, eds. *I Can't Keep My Own Secrets: Six-Word Memoirs by Teens Famous and Obscure* (6–10). Illus. 2009, HarperTeen paper $8.99 (978-006172684-2). A fascinating and moving collection of more than 600 six-word teen memoirs such as "Born 1992. Unhappy. Adopted 2007. Happy." and "You're the parent, act like one." Includes a subject index. (Rev: BL 7/09; SLJ 8/09) [808]

Psychology and Human Behavior

General and Miscellaneous

1843 Jarvis, Cheryl. *The Necklace: Thirteen Women and the Experiment That Transformed Their Lives* (11–12). Illus. 2008, Ballantine $24.00 (978-0-345-50071-7). This is a true account of the experiences of an unlikely club that is formed when a group of women jointly buy an expensive necklace. ∩ ℮ (Rev: BL 8/08) [302.3]

1844 Louv, Richard. *The Nature Principle: Human Restoration and the End of Nature-Deficit Disorder* (11–12). 2011, Algonquin $24.95 (978-156512581-0). Louv lays out his latest findings, culled from sources as varied as medical research and poetry, to argue that reconnecting in a meaningful way with nature can help our minds as well as our bodies, and strengthen our human connections. (Rev: BL 3/1–15/11) [155.4]

1845 Oliver, Neil. *Amazing Tales for Making Men out of Boys* (10–12). Illus. 2009, Morrow $25.99 (978-006176613-8). The author has collected true tales of bravery, persistence, and toughness from the warriors of Sparta to explorer Captain Scott to the soldiers who fought in Normandy and so forth. ℮ (Rev: BL 4/15/09) [170.81]

1846 Spilsbury, Louise. *Together As a Team!* (6–10). Series: Life Skills. 2008, Heinemann Library LB $32.86 (978-1-4329-1363-2). With practical tips and quizzes at the ends of chapters, this volume discusses the benefits of teamwork and how to achieve it. (Rev: SLJ 3/1/09)

172

1847 Tannen, Deborah. *You Were Always Mom's Favorite! Sisters in Conversation Throughout Their Lives* (11–12). 2009, Random $26 (978-140006632-2). Through interviews and her own experience, Tannen studies the connections and bonds between sisters and the lasting effects these bonds can have. ∩ (Rev: BL 9/09) [306.875]

Emotions and Emotional Behavior

1848 Spilsbury, Louise. *Cool That Anger!* (6–10). Series: Life Skills. 2008, Heinemann Library LB $32.86 (978-1-4329-1365-6). With tips on handling anger and quizzes at the ends of chapters, this volume discusses the causes of anger and physical reactions to it. (Rev: SLJ 3/1/09)

Personal Guidance

1849 Bezdecheck, Bethany. *Relationships: 21st-Century Roles* (9–12). Series: A Young Woman's Guide to Contemporary Issues. 2010, Rosen LB $31.95 (978-1-4358-3540-5). A conversational discussion of ways to ensure good relationships with relatives, friends, and boys, with a chapter on being your own best friend. (Rev: LMC 10/10; SLJ 4/1/10; VOYA 8/10)

1850 Burningham, Sarah O'Leary. *Boyology: A Crash Course in All Things Boy* (7–12). Illus. by Keri Smith. 2009, Chronicle paper $12.99 (978-0-8118-6436-7). This chatty, approachable book provides guidance on everything from making the boy friend–boyfriend transition to kissing and setting sexual boundaries. (Rev: SLJ 6/1/09; VOYA 4/10) [306.7]

1851 Burton, Bonnie. *Girls Against Girls: Why We Are Mean to Each Other and How We Can Change* (7–10). Illus. 2009, Zest paper $12.95 (978-097901736-0). The author calls on "mean girls" and their targets to understand why girls can be cruel and what can be done about it. Lexile 860L (Rev: BL 2/15/09; SLJ 5/1/09; VOYA 4/09) [300]

1852 Ensler, Eve. *I Am an Emotional Creature: The Secret Life of Girls Around the World* (11–12). 2010, Villard $20 (978-140006104-4). While explicit themes and language are found in the entries throughout this book, the message to young women that they can be strong and powerful is authentic and empowering. ℮ (Rev: BL 2/15/10) [155.43]

1853 Hantman, Clea. *30 Days to Finding and Keeping Sassy Sidekicks and BFFs: A Friendship Field Guide* (7–10). 2009, Delacorte paper $7.99 (978-038573623-7). An upbeat approach to making lifelong friends, with

practical tips and activities that will make the effort easier. (Rev: BL 7/09; VOYA 4/09) [158.2]

1854 Hugel, Bob. *I Did It Without Thinking: True Stories About Impulsive Decisions That Changed Lives* (6–10). Series: Scholastic Choices. 2008, Watts LB $27 (978-0-531-13868-7); paper $8.95 (978-0-531-20526-6). Teens share their own stories of impulsive behavior and how the results changed their lives. (Rev: SLJ 10/1/08; VOYA 12/08)

1855 Jacobs, Tom. *Teen Cyberbullying Investigated: Where Do Your Rights End and Consequences Begin?* (7–12). 2010, Free Spirit paper $15.99 (978-1-57542-339-5). Jacobs encourages teens to think critically and consider every situation from the perspective of victim, bystander, and perpetrator. (Rev: BL 3/1/10; SLJ 3/10; VOYA 8/10) [345.73]

1856 Ricciotti, Hope, and Monique Doyle Spencer. *The Real Life Body Book: A Young Woman's Complete Guide to Health and Wellness* (11–12). Illus. 2010, Celestial Arts paper $22 (978-158761357-9). This conversational book covers everything from acne to tattoo care to rape, with "Real Life Facts" and checklists. ℮ (Rev: BLO 5/25/10) [613]

1857 Weinstein, Bruce. *Is It Still Cheating if I Don't Get Caught?* (8–12). Illus. by Harriet Russell. 2009, Flash Point paper $9.95 (978-159643306-9). The author gives readers five "life principles" to help guide them in making ethical decisions: "Do no harm," "Make things better," "Respect others," "Be fair," and "Be loving." He then gives examples of times when teens may have to make tough decisions. Lexile 1080L (Rev: BL 4/1/09; LMC 10/09; SLJ 4/09; VOYA 6/09) [300]

Family and Family Problems

1858 Buscemi, Karen. *Split in Two: Keeping It Together When Your Parents Live Apart* (7–12). Illus. by Corinne Mucha. 2009, Zest paper $14.95 (978-098007321-8). For children of divorce, this is a practical guide to creating your own living space in both houses, synchronizing schedules, packing and hauling, and negotiating with two sets of adults. (Rev: BL 7/09; VOYA 8/09) [300]

1859 Fields, Julianna. *Foster Families* (6–12). Illus. Series: The Changing Face of Modern Families. 2009, Mason Crest $22.95 (978-142221497-8). Fields explores the history of foster care and the reasons why children end up in foster homes, with real-life examples and discussion of potential problems. Also use *Gay and Lesbian Parents, Kids Growing Up Without a Home,*

Multiracial Families, and *Teen Parents* (all 2009). (Rev: LMC 5–6/10; SLJ 2/10) [306.874]

1860 Lerner, Alicia. *Marriage* (9–12). Series: Global Viewpoints. 2009, Gale/Greenhaven $36.20 (978-0-7377-4160-5). Taking a global view, this balanced book explores various marriage customs and variations from generally recognized norms. (Rev: LMC 10/09)

1861 Winchester, Elizabeth Siris. *Sisters and Brothers: The Ultimate Guide to Understanding Your Siblings and Yourself* (6–10). Series: Scholastic Choices. 2008, Watts LB $27 (978-0-531-13870-0); paper $8.95 (978-0-531-20528-0). Teens share stories about coping with siblings, including topics such as birth order, step and foster siblings, and being an only child. (Rev: SLJ 10/1/08)

Youth Groups

1862 Townley, Alvin. *Spirit of Adventure: Eagle Scouts and the Making of America's Future* (9–12). 2009, Thomas Dunne Bks $24.95 (978-0-312-37898-1). Townley reviews the principles and history of scouting and provides a collection of anecdotes about the contributions and achievements of Eagle Scouts. (Rev: SLJ 12/09) [369.4]

Physical and Applied Sciences

General and Miscellaneous

1863 Chown, Marcus. *The Matchbox That Ate a Forty-Ton Truck: What Everyday Things Tell Us About the Universe* (10–12). 2010, Farrar $25 (978-086547922-7). Astronomer Chown emphasizes that simple observations of the world around us can teach us much about scientific principles and about our planet. ℮ (Rev: BL 4/1/10) [500]

Experiments and Projects

1864 Vickers, Tanya M. *Teen Science Fair Sourcebook: Winning School Science Fairs and National Competitions* (6–10). Illus. 2009, Enslow LB $25.95 (978-076602711-4). In chapters such as "The Research Plan and the Scientific Method," "The Rules: Safety, Originality, and Consent," and "The Project Notebook: A Scientist's Cookbook," Vickers lays out the various stages of project creation and provides useful tips. (Rev: BL 7/09; LMC 10/09) [507.8]

Astronomy and Space Science

General and Miscellaneous

1865 Plait, Philip. *Death from the Skies! These Are the Ways the World Will End* . . . (10–12). Illus. 2008, Viking $24.95 (978-067001997-7). Expert Philip Plait describes how Earth could be destroyed by a variety of cosmic disasters, the likelihood of that happening, and what we should be doing to prevent such a catastrophe; a fascinating book full of astronomical facts. (Rev: BL 9/1/08) [520]

1866 Zimmerman, Robert. *The Universe in a Mirror: The Saga of the Hubble Space Telescope and the Visionaries Who Built It* (10–12). Illus. 2008, Princeton $29.95 (978-069113297-6). This engrossing read chronicles the design and execution of the Hubble space telescope, from its rocky start to the triumph of the deep-space images it eventually transmitted. (Rev: BL 6/1–15/08*) [629.435]

Astronautics and Space Exploration

1867 Nelson, Craig. *Rocket Men: The Epic Story of the First Men on the Moon* (9–12). Illus. 2009, Viking $27.95 (978-067002103-1). This is a detailed account of the scientific and political reasons behind Apollo 11, the many people involved with the project, and the innumerable steps taken to ensure the success of the mission. ∩ ℮ (Rev: BL 5/1/09*) [629.45]

1868 Roach, Mary. *Packing for Mars: The Curious Science of Life in the Void* (10–12). Illus. 2010, Norton $25.95 (978-039306847-4). Covering everything from weightlessness-induced motion sickness to hygiene and toilet procedures, Roach applies her zeal for science and novel experiences to this intriguing book. ∩ ℮ (Rev: BL 7/10) [629.45]

Comets, Meteors, and Asteroids

1869 Smith, Caroline, et al. *Meteorites* (10–12). Illus. 2009, Firefly $24.95 (978-155407515-7). A thorough and heavily illustrated overview of meteorites and their significance from London's Natural History Museum. (Rev: BL 12/1/09) [523.51]

Universe

1870 Perricone, Mike. *The Big Bang* (6–12). Series: Science Foundations. 2009, Chelsea House $35 (978-1-60413-015-7). This volume covers the pioneering work of Hubble and other key scientists before discussing what we now know about the origins of the universe and the implications of the Big Bang. (Rev: LMC 11–12/09) [523.1]

Biological Sciences

Botany

Foods, Farms, and Ranches

GENERAL AND MISCELLANEOUS

1871 Foer, Jonathan Safran. *Eating Animals* (11–12). 2009, Little, Brown $25.99 (978-031606990-8). Foer takes a hard, critical look at the practice of factory farming (including fish), supplying copious detail about the miserable lives of feedlot animals along the way; for mature readers. (Rev: BL 11/15/09*) [641.3]

1872 Freedman, Jeri. *Genetically Modified Food: How Biotechnology Is Changing What We Eat* (7–12). 2009, Rosen LB $29.95 (978-1-4358-5025-5). This balanced, thorough book provides insight into the history, challenges, issues, and risks of genetic modification of the foods we eat. (Rev: LMC 10/09) [363.1]

1873 Hamilton, Lisa M. *Deeply Rooted: Unconventional Farmers in the Age of Agribusiness* (10–12). 2009, Counterpoint $25 (978-159376180-6). Hamilton presents farmers and ranchers who believe in doing what is best for the land and its people by eschewing big business farming practices. **e** (Rev: BL 5/1/09) [338.10973]

1874 Smith, Jeremy N. *Growing a Garden City* (10–12). Illus. 2010, Skyhorse $24.95 (978-161608108-9). The lengthy subtitle *How Farmers, First Graders, Counselors, Troubled Teens, Foodies, A Homeless Shelter Chef, Single Mothers, and More Are Transforming Themselves and Their Neighborhoods Through the Intersection of Local Agriculture and Community — and How You Can, Too* describes this profile of food programs in Missoula, Montana. **e** (Rev: BL 9/15/10*) [635.09786]

Forestry and Trees

1875 Bjornlund, Lydia D. *Deforestation* (7–12). Series: Compact Research. 2009, ReferencePoint LB $25.95 (978-1-60152-075-3). Answering questions including "What Are the Consequences of Deforestation?," Bjornlund describes how the world's forests are being destroyed and discusses sustainable solutions for the future. (Rev: LMC 1–2/10)

1876 Rodd, Tony, and Jennifer Stackhouse. *Trees: A Visual Guide* (10–12). Illus. 2008, Univ. of California $29.95 (978-052025650-7). This beautifully illustrated guide looks at trees' form and function, diversity and design, their importance in the ecosystem, and the ways in which we use them. (Rev: BL 9/15/08) [582.16]

1877 Wells, Diana. *Lives of the Trees: An Uncommon History* (9–12). Illus. 2009, Algonquin $19.95 (978-156512491-2). In this illustrated album with brief and informative essays, Wells introduces 100 varieties of trees and offers insight into their cultural, historical, and environmental value. (Rev: BL 11/15/09) [398.24]

Plants and Flowers

1878 Stuppy, Wolfgang, and Madeline Harley. *The Bizarre and Incredible World of Plants* (9–12). Ed. by Alexandra Papadakis. Illus. by Rob Kesseler. 2009, Firefly $29.95 (978-155407533-1). Illustrated with beautiful electron microscopy images, this is a handsome guide to the diversity of plants. (Rev: BL 12/1/09) [580]

Zoology

General and Miscellaneous

1879 Conniff, Richard. *Swimming with Piranhas at Feeding Time: My Life Doing Dumb Stuff with Animals* (10–12). 2009, Norton $25.95 (978-039306893-1). Conniff provides amusing and interesting anecdotes from his international travels through the animal kingdom. (Rev: BL 4/15/09) [590]

1880 Laufer, Peter. *Forbidden Creatures: Inside the World of Animal Smuggling and Exotic Pets* (10–12). 2010, Lyons $19.95 (978-159921926-4). Journalist Laufer provides a haunting glimpse into the criminal world of exotic animal smuggling, and the often catastrophic effects of escaped exotics outside their native habitat. (Rev: BLO 6/1–15/10) [364.1]

1881 *Mammal Anatomy: An Illustrated Guide* (8–12). 2010, Marshall Cavendish LB $99.80 (978-0-7614-7882-9). This detailed yet accessible volume (a repackaging of an earlier multivolume set) examines the anatomy and physiology of mammals including chimpanzees, dolphins, elephants, giraffes, gray whales, grizzly bears, kangaroos, lions, manatees, seals, squirrels, wolves, and zebras. (Rev: BLO 1/21/10; LMC 1–2/10) [571.3]

Amphibians and Reptiles

GENERAL AND MISCELLANEOUS

1882 Means, D. Bruce. *Stalking the Plumed Serpent and Other Adventures in Herpetology* (10–12). Illus. 2008, Pineapple $19.95 (978-1-56164-433-9). Respected herpetologist Means shares his adventures in the field and explains the curious habits and anatomy of many different kinds of reptiles and amphibians. (Rev: BL 8/08) [597.9]

SNAKES AND LIZARDS

1883 Coates, Jennifer. *Lizards* (7–12). Illus. Series: Our Best Friends. 2009, Eldorado Ink LB $26.95 (978-193290431-4). An in-depth review of the benefits and responsibilities of owning a lizard, covering choosing the best lizard, potential health problems, and how to make an attractive terrarium. (Rev: BL 6/1–15/09) [639.3]

Animal Behavior

GENERAL AND MISCELLANEOUS

1884 Berger, Joel. *The Better to Eat You With: Fear in the Animal World* (10–12). Illus. 2008, Univ. of Chi-

cago $29.00 (978-022604363-0). Joel Berger examines whether or not animals' survival instincts will resurface when natural predators that have been gone for many years are returned to the environment. e (Rev: BL 9/15/08) [591.5]

1885 Schutt, Bill. *Dark Banquet: Blood and the Curious Lives of Blood-Feeding Creatures* (11–12). Illus. 2008, Harmony $25.95 (978-030738112-5). Vampire bats, chiggers, ticks, bedbugs, and the history and importance of blood are discussed informally in this scientifically correct and accessible book. (Rev: BL 8/08) [591.5]

1886 Smith, Lewis. *Why the Cheetah Cheats and Other Mysteries of the Natural World* (10–12). Illus. 2009, Firefly paper $29.95 (978-155407534-8). Smith recounts multiple incidents of animal responses to natural and man-made encroachments on their environments in lively text with eye-catching photographs. (Rev: BL 12/1/09) [590]

HOMES

1887 MacNamara, Peggy, and John Bates. *Architecture by Birds and Insects: A Natural Art* (10–12). Illus. 2008, Univ. of Chicago $25.00 (978-022650097-3). The study of birds' and insects' nests and burrows is shown to have relevance to human architecture in this dynamic fusion of art and science. (Rev: BLO 7/30/08) [598.156]

REPRODUCTION AND BABIES

1888 Senson, Pat. *Nasty, Brutish and Short: The Quirks and Quarks Guide to Animal Sex and Other Weird Behavior* (10–12). 2010, McClelland & Stewart paper $18.95 (978-077107968-9). Tales of the weird and wacky sexual habits of fish and animals across the globe, gleaned from Canadian radio interviews of experts. e (Rev: BLO 1/24/11)

Animal Species

GENERAL AND MISCELLANEOUS

1889 Carson, Mary Kay. *The Bat Scientists* (7–10). Photos by Tom Uhlman. Series: Scientists in the Field. 2010, Houghton $18.99 (978-0-547-19956-6). A fascinating photo-filled overview of bats, the environmental challenges they face, and the ways in which scientists study them. (Rev: BL 10/15/10*; SLJ 11/1/10) [599.4]

1890 Gibson, Graeme. *The Bedside Book of Beasts: A Wildlife Miscellany* (10–12). Illus. 2009, Doubleday $35 (978-038552459-9). This eye-catching compendium of images and text ranging from folklore and poetry to the writings of naturalists explores the relationship between humans and the larger predatory beasts. (Rev: BL 10/15/09) [591.5]

1891 Irwin, Robert. *Camel* (10–12). Illus. 2010, Reaktion paper $19.95 (978-186189649-0). In addition to covering camels' physiology and characteristics, this well-illustrated book looks at their history, place in literature and art, relationship with humans, and modern uses; with tips on riding them and eating their meat. (Rev: BLO 1/18/11) [599.6362]

BEARS

1892 Ellis, Richard. *On Thin Ice: The Changing World of the Polar Bear* (10–12). 2009, Knopf $27.95 (978-030727059-7). A thorough history of the polar bear and its habitat and life cycle, with discussion of its importance to Inuits and the potentially devastating impact of climate change on its survival. (Rev: BL 10/15/09*) [599.786]

Birds

GENERAL AND MISCELLANEOUS

1893 Montgomery, Sy. *Birdology: Lessons Learned from a Pack of Hens, a Peck of Pigeons, Cantankerous Crows, Fierce Falcons, Hip Hop Parrots, Baby Hummingbirds, and One Murderously Big Cassowary* (10–12). Illus. 2010, Free Press $25 (978-141656984-8). Nature junkie Montgomery describes memorable encounters with birds large and small, providing smart, compelling insights into their behavior and the threats they face. (Rev: BL 3/1/10) [598]

1894 Tudge, Colin. *The Bird: A Natural History of Who Birds Are, Where They Came From, and How They Live* (10–12). Illus. 2009, Crown $30 (978-030734204-1). This illustrated guide focuses on birds: their unique physical adaptations, their classification, their life cycle, and their interactions with humans. (Rev: BL 11/15/09)

Environmental Protection and Endangered Species

1895 Jacobsen, Rowan. *The Living Shore: Rediscovering a Lost World* (10–12). Illus. 2009, Bloomsbury $20 (978-159691684-5). Using the Olympia oyster beds of British Columbia as a springboard, Jacobsen explains how people and the natural world can coexist. **e** (Rev: BL 9/09) [639.9]

1896 McLeish, Todd. *Basking with Humpbacks: Tracking Threatened Marine Life in New England Waters* (10–12). Illus. 2009, Univ. Press of New England $26.95 (978-158465676-0). In 11 fascinating essays based on interviews, McLeish writes vividly about the residents of New England's coastal waters — from

humpback whales to horseshoe crabs to leatherback turtles — and the ways in which their habitats are compromised. (Rev: BLO 9/09) [78.680974]

Insects and Arachnids

GENERAL AND MISCELLANEOUS

1897 Dourlot, Sonia. *Insect Museum* (9–12). Illus. 2009, Firefly $39.95 (978-155407483-9). This lavishly illustrated compendium of insects and spiders will delight (or horrify) the eye and spur further research. (Rev: BL 12/1/09) [595.7]

1898 Moffett, Mark W. *Adventures Among Ants: A Global Safari with a Cast of Trillions* (10–12). Illus. 2010, Univ. of California $29.95 (978-052026199-0). A world-traveling entomologist examines ants and their environments in this volume that includes excellent close-up photos of his subjects at work. (Rev: BLO 1/18/11) [595.796]

1899 Stewart, Amy. *Wicked Bugs: The Louse That Conquered Napoleon's Army and Other Diabolical Insects* (10–12). Illus. 2011, Algonquin $18.95 (978-156512960-3). Stewart provides an overview of our relationship with bugs of all kinds, from the annoying to the deadly, in this fascinating, often funny book full of intriguing illustrations. (Rev: BL 3/1–15/11) [632]

BEES AND WASPS

1900 Pundyk, Grace. *The Honey Trail: In Pursuit of Liquid Gold and Vanishing Bees* (10–12). 2010, St. Martin's $25.99 (978-031262981-6). All about honey, the bees that produce it, the resulting commerce around the world, and the myriad uses for this "liquid gold." **e** (Rev: BLO 1/24/11) [638.16]

1901 Seeley, Thomas D. *Honeybee Democracy* (10–12). 2010, Princeton $29.95 (978-069114721-5). This highly readable book describes bees' behavior and includes an in-depth look at the research process. **e** (Rev: BLO 1/24/11) [595.79]

BUTTERFLIES, MOTHS, AND CATERPILLARS

1902 Marent, Thomas, and Ben Morgan. *Butterfly* (10–12). Illus. by author. 2008, DK $30.00 (978-0-7566-3340-0). Details of butterfly life, such as egg-laying, feeding, migration, and metamorphosis, are described through clearly written captions in this beautifully photographed book. (Rev: BLO 6/16/08) [595.78]

Marine and Freshwater Life

GENERAL AND MISCELLANEOUS

1903 O'Neill, Michael Patrick. *Wild Waters Photo Journal* (6–12). 2010, Batfish Books $29.95 (978-0-9728653-6-4). A wonderful collection of color photographs and brief descriptions of marine life in ecosystems as varied as Komodo National Park, Bali, the Palm Beach coral reefs, and the Everglades. (Rev: LMC 11–12/10; SLJ 8/10) [591.77]

FISHES

1904 Greenberg, Paul. *Four Fish: The Future of the Last Wild Food* (10–12). 2010, Penguin $25.95 (978-159420256-8). Greenberg examines the sorry state of the world's fisheries by focusing on four fish — tuna, cod, sea bass, and salmon — and the natural and anthropogenic pressures on their habitat. (Rev: BL 7/10) [338.372]

1905 Scales, Helen. *Poseidon's Steed: The Story of Seahorses, from Myth to Reality* (10–12). Illus. 2009, Gotham $20 (978-159240474-2). Sea horses and their importance in cultures around the world and throughout history are examined in fascinating detail. (Rev: BLO 7/09) [597]

WHALES, DOLPHINS, AND OTHER SEA MAMMALS

1906 Dudzinski, Kathleen, and Toni Frohoff. *Dolphin Mysteries: Unlocking the Secrets of Communication* (10–12). Illus. 2008, Yale $30.00 (978-030012112-4). This book is set apart by its informal first-person accounts of dolphin interactions and what has been learned about these creatures. **e** (Rev: BL 9/15/08) [599.53]

Pets

GENERAL AND MISCELLANEOUS

1907 Katz, Jon. *Soul of a Dog: Reflections on the Spirits of the Animals of Bedlam Farm* (10–12). 2009, Villard $24 (978-1-4000-6629-2). Katz describes his relationships with the various animals on his farm and discusses their inner lives. (Rev: BL 7-09; SLJ 11/09) [636]

1908 Sullivant, Holly J. *Hamsters* (7–12). Illus. Series: Our Best Friends. 2009, Eldorado Ink LB $26.95 (978-193290430-7). Everything you need to know about caring for a pet hamster, with interesting sidebars and eye-catching images. (Rev: BL 6/1–15/09) [636.935]

DOGS

1909 Forbes, Harrison. *Dog Talk: Lessons Learned from a Life with Dogs* (10–12). 2008, St. Martin's $24.95 (978-031237873-8). Drawing on his wealth of experience as a police dog trainer, Forbes discusses his theories of dog behavior and explains how time spent observing a dog's reactions throughout the day will aid in training. (Rev: BL 8/08) [636.7]

1910 Hawkins, Barrie. *Tea and Dog Biscuits: Our First Topsy-Turvy Year Fostering Orphan Dogs* (10–12). 2010, Chicago Review paper $14.95 (978-156976341-4). A touching account of a man and his wife who foster abandoned, neglected, and abused dogs and rehabilitate them before matching them to new owners. (Rev: BLO 1/24/11) [636.7]

1911 Katz, Jon. *Izzy and Lenore: Two Dogs, an Unexpected Journey, and Me* (10–12). 2008, Villard $24.00 (978-1-4000-6630-8). An emotional story of a trainer and his two newly rescued dogs who have a talent for bringing comfort to the sick and dying. ∩ (Rev: BL 8/08) [636.737]

1912 Koontz, Dean. *A Big Little Life: A Memoir of a Joyful Dog* (10–12). Illus. 2009, Hyperion $24.99 (978-140132352-3). This well-written account of the life of a beloved golden retriever explores deeper philosophical questions about animal intelligence and the deep connection between humans and pets. ∩ **e** (Rev: BL 7/09*) [636.752]

1913 McTague, Tracey. *City Puppy: Finding, Training, and Loving Your Urban Dog* (10–12). 2010, Overlook paper $16.95 (978-159020260-9). A helpful guide to the selection and training of a dog suitable for limited living space and an urban environment. (Rev: BLO 1/24/11) [636]

1914 Trout, Nick. *Love Is the Best Medicine: What Two Dogs Taught One Veterinarian About Hope, Humility, and Everyday Miracles* (10–12). 2010, Broadway $23.99 (978-076793197-7). Two very different dogs — an abandoned cocker spaniel and a spoiled miniature pincher — intersect in the ER of a Boston animal hospital in this book that looks at the relationships between people and their pets. ∩ (Rev: BL 2/15/10) [636.7]

1915 Winn, Steven. *Come Back, Como: Winning the Heart of a Reluctant Dog* (9–12). 2009, Harper $23.99 (978-006180259-1). *San Francisco Chronicle* columnist Steve Winn's humorous and poignant memoir recounts his efforts to acclimate Como, the cantankerous canine his family rescued from a shelter, to family life. (Rev: BLO 10/15/09) [636.70887]

Zoos, Aquariums, and Animal Care

1916 Mee, Benjamin. *We Bought a Zoo: The Amazing True Story of a Young Family, a Broken Down Zoo, and the 200 Wild Animals That Changed Their Lives Forever* (10–12). 2008, Weinstein $24.95 (978-160286048-3). An appealing account of how Mee and his family bought a rundown zoo full of exotic animals in southwest England and their adventures bringing the operation back to viability. (Rev: BL 9/15/08) [590.73]

Chemistry

General and Miscellaneous

1917 Cobb, Allan B. *Earth Chemistry* (8–12). Illus. Series: Essential Chemistry. 2009, Chelsea House $35 (978-0-7910-9677-2). Colorful illustrations and informative sidebars punctuate this comprehensive book on the chemical interactions between the four spheres — the atmosphere, hydrosphere, lithosphere, and biosphere — of the Earth. (Rev: SLJ 5/1/09)

1918 Kean, Sam. *The Disappearing Spoon and Other True Tales of Madness, Love, and the History of the World from the Periodic Table of the Elements* (10–12). 2010, Little, Brown $24.99 (978-031605164-4). A fascinating collection of stories about the scientists who contributed to the creation of the periodic table. ∩ (Rev: BL 7/10) [546]

1919 Lew, Kristi. *Acids and Bases* (8–12). Illus. Series: Essential Chemistry. 2009, Chelsea House $35 (978-0-7910-9783-0). Colorful illustrations and informative sidebars punctuate this comprehensive book on acids and bases and their importance. (Rev: SLJ 5/1/09)

1920 Roston, Eric. *The Carbon Age: How Life's Core Element Has Become Civilization's Greatest Threat* (10–12). 2008, Walker $25.99 (978-0-8027-1557-9). Science journalist Roston provides a compelling glimpse into the life of a carbon atom by examining its structure, properties, and many uses — and pitfalls — for humans. ℮ (Rev: BL 6/1–15/08) [577.144]

Geology and Geography

Physical Geography

General and Miscellaneous

1921 Bass, Rick. *The Wild Marsh: Four Seasons at Home in Montana* (10–12). 2009, Houghton $26 (978-054705516-9). Nature writer Rick Bass takes the reader on a 12-month exploration of the seasonal beauty of Yaak Valley, Montana. ℮ (Rev: BL 5/1/09*) [508.786]

1922 Heinrichs, Ann. *Continents* (10–12). Series: Real World Math: Geography. 2010, Cherry Lake LB $27.07 (978-1-60279-490-0). Clearly written and filled with bright photographs, the volumes in this series provide lessons in science, geography and mathematics, making for an interdisciplinary learning experience. Also use *Islands* and *Oceans* (both 2010). (Rev: LMC 1–2/10)

Mathematics

General and Miscellaneous

1923 Diacu, Florin. *Megadisasters: The Science of Predicting the Next Catastrophe* (10–12). Illus. 2009, Princeton $24.95 (978-069113350-8). Diacu explains very simply how multiple disasters — from earthquakes to hurricanes to market crashes — can be predicted by mathematicians who hope to avoid them or at least to mitigate their effects. (Rev: BL 12/1/09) [904]

1924 Tattersall, Graham. *Geekspeak: How Life + Mathematics = Happiness* (10–12). 2008, HarperCollins $19.95 (978-0-06-162924-2). By using mathematical formulas in an engaging and accessible manner that will appeal to independent thinkers, Tattersall answers twenty-six different questions about the world around us; the real-world nature of the topics will appeal to teens. **℮** (Rev: BL 8/08) [510]

Algebra, Numbers, and Number Systems

1925 McKellar, Danica. *Hot X: Algebra Exposed* (10–12). 2010, Penguin $26.95 (978-159463070-5). Part tutorial, part girl-talk, McKellar's book provides an appealing tool for mathematically challenged young women to gain confidence and skills while having plenty of fun. (Rev: BL 7/10) [512]

1926 Wingard-Nelson, Rebecca. *Algebra Word Problems* (6–10). Series: Math Busters Word Problems. 2010, Enslow LB $27.93 (978-0-7660-3367-2). A step-by-step guide to understanding basic algebra concepts and how they can be applied in real-life situations. Also use *Fraction and Decimal Word Problems* (2010). (Rev: LMC 11–12/10) [512.0076]

Oceanography

General and Miscellaneous

1927 Prager, Ellen. *Chasing Science at Sea: Racing Hurricanes, Stalking Sharks, and Living Undersea with Ocean Experts* (11–12). Illus. 2008, Univ. of Chicago $22.50 (978-022667870-2). Exciting and informative, this book, which spotlights various marine scientists who describe their fieldwork and discoveries, will be useful for students considering careers in this field. (Rev: BL 9/1/08) [551.46]

1928 Ulanski, Stan. *The Gulf Stream: Tiny Plankton, Giant Bluefin, and the Amazing Story of the Powerful River in the Atlantic* (10–12). Illus. 2008, Univ. of North Carolina $28.00 (978-0-8078-3217-2). A clear and very interesting explanation of the nature of the Gulf Stream and its importance today and throughout history. (Rev: BL 8/08) [551.46]

Physics

General and Miscellaneous

1929 Gardner, Robert. *Easy Genius Science Projects with Light: Great Experiments and Ideas* (6–10). Illus. Series: Easy Genius Science Projects. 2008, Enslow LB $23.95 (978-076602926-2). Gardner provides fascinating physics experiments and mind-benders in this approachable, well-organized book. (Rev: BL 10/15/08) [537.078]

1930 Karam, P. Andrew, and Ben P. Stein. *Radioactivity* (6–12). Series: Science Foundations. 2009, Chelsea House $35 (978-1-60413-016-4). Providing an overview of radiation and its characteristics, this volume looks at its uses in warfare, medicine, and other areas. (Rev: LMC 11–12/09) [539.2]

1931 Muller, Richard A. *The Instant Physicist: An Illustrated Guide* (10–12). Illus. by Joey Manfre. 2010, Norton $16.95 (978-039307826-8). Physics prof Muller offers humorous and understandable explanations of various aspects of physics, from the greenhouse effect to the relative toxicity of plutonium to the alleged alien spacecraft crash in Roswell, New Mexico, all accompanied by amusing illustrations. (Rev: BL 11/1/10) [530]

1932 Orzel, Chad. *How to Teach Physics to Your Dog* (10–12). Illus. 2009, Scribner $24 (978-141657228-2). Orzel uses the unique (and humorous) approach of explaining physics principles to his dog to make the discipline approachable for all audiences. **e** (Rev: BL 12/1/09) [530.12]

1933 Wilczek, Frank. *The Lightness of Being: Mass, Ether, and the Unification of Forces* (11–12). 2008, Basic $26.95 (978-0-465-00321-1). This accessible book explains the nature of mass and gravity, quarks and gluons. **e** (Rev: BL 8/08) [539.7]

Energy and Motion

General and Miscellaneous

1934 Doeden, Matt. *Green Energy: Crucial Gains or Economic Strains?* (7–10). Series: USA Today's Debate: Voices and Perspectives. 2010, Lerner LB $35.93 (978-0-7613-5112-2). After a history of energy and a discussion of global warming, this attractive volume that draws on *USA Today* looks at nuclear, solar, and wind power as well as biomass and biofuel, and electric cars, hybrids, and fuel cells. (Rev: LMC 10/10; SLJ 6/10) [163.25]

1935 Morris, Neil. *Biomass Power* (7–12). 2010, Smart Apple Media LB $34.25 (978-1-59920-337-9). A look at the technology of biomass power, with discussion of economic and environmental factors. Also use *The Energy Mix, Fossil Fuels, Geothermal Power, Nuclear Power, Solar Power, Water Power,* and *Wind Power* (all 2010). (Rev: LMC 1–2/10) [333.95]

1936 Tabak, John. *Coal and Oil* (10–12). Illus. Series: Energy and the Environment. 2009, Facts on File $40 (978-0-8160-7083-1). Tabak provides thorough information on each fuel's history, use, associated dangers, and so forth in this fact-filled volume. (Rev: BL 2/15/09) [333.8]

Nuclear Energy

1937 Nelson, David Erik. *Chernobyl* (9–12). Series: Perspectives on Modern World History. 2010, Gale/Greenhaven $38.50 (978-0-7377-4555-9). Nelson pulls together articles from secondary sources that discuss the historical background of the disaster, the impact on population and environment, and the relative safety of nuclear energy; personal accounts are also included. (Rev: LMC 10/10; SLJ 4/10) [621.48]

Technology and Engineering

General Works and Miscellaneous Industries

1938 Benford, Gregory, et al. *The Wonderful Future That Never Was: Flying Cars, Mail Delivery by Parachute, and Other Predictions from the Past* (10–12). 2010, Sterling $24.95 (978-158816822-1). A fascinating and sometimes hilarious look at the predictions of past generations, including hovercraft cars and aluminum clothing, drawn from the archives of *Popular Mechanics*. (Rev: BL 9/15/10) [609]

1939 Brockman, John, ed. *This Will Change Everything: Ideas That Will Shape the Future* (10–12). 2010, HarperPerennial paper $14.99 (978-006189967-6). Scientists and authors offer their predictions of the technological developments that will radically change the world in their lifetimes. ℮ (Rev: BL 12/1/09) [500.01]

1940 Challoner, Jack, ed. *1001 Inventions That Changed the World* (10–12). Illus. 2009, Barron's $35 (978-076416136-0). An interesting and useful although incomplete look at inventions that have shaped how we live, ranging from stone tools to the locomotive and the World Wide Web. (Rev: BLO 4/30/09) [600]

1941 Klein, Maury. *The Power Makers: Steam, Electricity, and the Men Who Invented Modern America* (10–12). 2008, Bloomsbury $29.95 (978-159691412-4). Klein explores the inventors behind the names everyone knows — Edison, Fulton, Morse — and provides a compelling chronological glimpse into the American Industrial Revolution and era of innovation. (Rev: BL 6/1–15/08) [609.73]

1942 Ryles, Briony, and Derek Hall, eds. *Medieval Period and the Renaissance* (9–12). Series: Curriculum Connections: Technology Through the Ages. 2010, Black Rabbit LB $39.95 (978-1-933834-84-9). An attractive survey of the technological innovations during the Middle Ages and Renaissance, stretching from the abacus and early water systems to paper, clocks and watches, guns, printing, and so forth. Also by these authors are *The Ages of Steam and Electricity, The Early 20th Century,* and *The Modern World* (all 2010). (Rev: LMC 8–9/10) [609]

1943 Ryles, Briony, and Derek Hall, eds. *The Scientific Revolution* (9–12). Series: Curriculum Connections: Technology Through the Ages. 2010, Black Rabbit LB $39.95 (978-1-933834-85-6). From the time of Galileo through the invention of the barometer and navigation instruments, locks and keys, the steam engine, and electricity, this attractive volume introduces many fascinating innovations and innovators. (Rev: LMC 8–9/10) [609.03]

Building and Construction

1944 Priwer, Shana, and Cynthia Phillips. *Bridges and Spans* (9–12). Illus. 2009, Sharpe Focus $39.95 (978-0-7656-8120-1). This well-designed book focuses on the art and science of bridge design and looks at some of the better-known bridge failures. (Rev: SLJ 6/1/09) [624]

1945 Roberts, Russell. *Building the Panama Canal* (7–10). Series: Monumental Milestones. 2009, Mitchell Lane LB $29.95 (978-1-58415-692-5). Both interesting and informative, this book focuses on the historic and technological factors relevant to the construction of the Panama Canal. (Rev: SLJ 6/1/09) [386.44]

Computers, Automation, and the Internet

1946 Baker, Stephen. *The Numerati* (10–12). 2008, Houghton $26.00 (978-061878460-8). Here is an insightful look into the field of data mining — collecting the traces that we leave behind when we use technology such as cell phones and online services. ⌒ ℮ (Rev: BL 9/1/08) [303.48]

1947 Blascovich, Jim, and Jeremy Bailenson. *Infinite Reality: Avatars, Eternal Life, New Worlds, and the Dawn of the Virtual Revolution* (11–12). Illus. 2011, Morrow $27.99 (978-006180950-7). A fascinating, insightful look into the future of virtual reality technology and how it may affect our lives, from entertainment to education and medicine and beyond. (Rev: BL 3/1–15/11) [303.48]

Telecommunications

1948 Kling, Andrew A. *Cell Phones* (8–12). Series: Technology 360. 2009, Lucent Books (Gale) $32.45 (978-1-4205-0164-3). An attractive and informative look at cell phone technology with a glossary and lists of material for further research. ℮ (Rev: LMC 8–9/10; SLJ 1/1/11) [621.3845]

Transportation

Railroads

1949 Sandler, Martin W. *The Secret Subway: The Fascinating Tale of an Amazing Feat of Engineering* (6–12). Illus. 2009, National Geographic $17.95 (978-

142630462-0); LB $26.90 (978-142630463-7). Sandler tells the compelling story of engineer Alfred Beach who in the late 1860s hoped to build an air-powered subway system in New York City without the knowledge of Tammany Hall boss William Tweed. (Rev: BL 6/1–15/09) [388.4]

Ships and Boats

1950 Walker, Spike. *On the Edge of Survival: A Shipwreck, a Raging Storm, and the Harrowing Alaskan Rescue That Became a Legend* (10–12). Illus. 2010, St. Martin's $24.99 (978-031228634-7). Perfect for those who love man-against-nature survival stories, this book provides a tense, fast-paced account of the Coast Guard rescue of a ship-wrecked crew in the frigid waters of Alaska in 2004, including interviews with rescuers and survivors. ⌒ ℮ (Rev: BL 9/1/10)

Weapons, Submarines, and the Armed Forces

1951 Graham, Ian. *Military Technology* (7–10). Illus. Series: New Technology. 2008, Smart Apple Media LB $22.95 (978-159920165-8). Unmanned spy planes, body armor, lasers, robots, and many other kinds of high-tech military equipment are examined in this accessible volume that includes many illustrations and thought-provoking ("What's Next?") sidebars. (Rev: BL 10/15/08; LMC 5–6/09) [355]

1952 Marcovitz, Hal. *Biological and Chemical Warfare* (7–10). Series: Essential Issues. 2010, ABDO LB $32.79 (978-1-60453-951-6). The characteristics of biological, chemical, and radiological substances are explained here and there is discussion of their use as weapons and measures that can be taken to guard against this. (Rev: BL 10/1/10; LMC 10/10; SLJ 4/1/10) [358.3]

Recreation and Sports

Crafts, Hobbies, and Pastimes

Cooking

1953 Opie, Fredrick Douglass. *Hog and Hominy: Soul Food from Africa to America* (10–12). Illus. 2008, Columbia Univ. $24.95 (978-023114638-8). A historical look at African American cooking, this book reveals information about the origins of familiar recipes. (Rev: BL 9/1/08) [641.5]

1954 Webb, Lois Sinaiko, and Lindsay Grace Roten. *The Multicultural Cookbook for Students: Updated and Revised* (10–12). 2009, Greenwood paper $85 (978-1-313-37560-6). Organized in seven regions, this cookbook introduces each country with basic information on the culture and typical ingredients and provides at least two recipes; a revised and expanded edition of the book published in 1993. (Rev: LMC 3–4/10; SLJ 3/10) [641.59]

Costume and Jewelry Making, Dress, and Fashion

1955 Chermay-Debray, Isabelle. *Polymer Clay Beaded Jewellery: 35 Beautiful Designs* (10–12). 2009, Search paper $13.95 (978-1-84448-400-3). The process of making jewelry and accessories from polymer clay is presented through detailed descriptions and color photographs. (Rev: SLJ 11/09) [745.5]

1956 Mokona, and CLAMP. *Okimono Kimono* (10–12). Illus. by CLAMP. 2010, Dark Horse paper $12.99 (978-159582456-1). A celebration of the kimono by manga author and kimono designer Mokona. (Rev: BL 9/1/10) [391.00952]

1957 Webber, Carmen, and Carmia Marshall. *Chic Sweats: 22 Ways to Transform and Restyle Your Sweatshirts* (9–12). Illus. 2009, St. Martin's paper $21.95 (978-0-312-37861-5). This how-to book offers suggestions for repurposing the common sweatshirt as garments ranging from hoodies to dresses, and contains detailed instructions with illustrations. (Rev: SLJ 12/09) [746.9]

Dolls and Other Toys

1958 Stone, Tanya Lee. *The Good, the Bad, and the Barbie: A Doll's History and Her Impact on Us* (7–10). Illus. 2010, Viking $19.99 (978-067001187-2). Stone tells a fascinating story of a controversial doll and her evolution. Lexile 1120L (Rev: BL 11/15/10*; HB 11–12/10; SLJ 10/1/10*) [688.7]

Drawing and Painting

1959 Abel, Jessica, and Matt Madden. *Drawing Words and Writing Pictures — Making Comics: Manga, Graphic Novels, and Beyond* (9–12). Illus. 2008, First Second paper $29.95 (978-159643131-7). Abel and Madden provide skill-building exercises and inspiring activities in this accessible, well-written how-to. (Rev: BL 6/1–15/08) [741.5]

Mysteries, Curiosities, and Controversial Subjects

1960 Aaronovitch, David. *Voodoo Histories: The Role of the Conspiracy Theory in Shaping Modern History* (10–12). 2010, Riverhead $26.95 (978-159448895-5). Aaronovitch explores conspiracy theories and why they survive and thrive. ⌒ ℮ (Rev: BL 2/1/10) [909.08]

1961 Gibson, Marley, and Dave Schrader, et al. *The Other Side: A Teen's Guide to Ghost Hunting and the Paranormal* (7–10). Illus. 2009, Graphia paper $10.99 (978-0-547-25829-4). This concise, often witty guide doesn't glamorize ghost-hunting — the authors stress that it's a hobby, not a career — but it does contain much in the way of practical advice for teens interested in paranormal investigation. (Rev: SLJ 3/10; VOYA 2/10)

1962 Gray, Amy. *How to Be a Vampire: A Fangs-on Guide for the Newly Undead* (7–12). Illus. by Scott Erwert. 2009, Candlewick $14.99 (978-0-7636-4915-9). The ultimate guide to all things vampire, covering feeding, etiquette, fashion, pets, dating mortals, and so forth. Lexile 1070L (Rev: SLJ 1/10; VOYA 4/10) [398.4]

1963 Jack, Albert. *Loch Ness Monsters and Raining Frogs: The World's Most Puzzling Mysteries Solved* (9–12). Illus. 2009, Random paper $15 (978-0-8129-8005-9). This highly readable collection of short essays addresses a variety of popular mysteries from the past two centuries. (Rev: SLJ 8/09) [001.94]

1964 Kallen, Stuart A. *Communication with the Dead* (7–12). Series: The Library of Ghosts and Hauntings. 2010, ReferencePoint LB $31.19 (978-1-60152-089-0). Well-written and filled with sources and documentation, this book allows students to examine claims of the paranormal in a straightforward, scholarly way. (Rev: LMC 1–2/10)

1965 Maberry, Jonathan, and David F. Kramer. *They Bite: Endless Cravings of Supernatural Predators* (10–12). Illus. 2009, Citadel paper $16.95 (978-080652820-5). This book explains the genesis of werewolves, zombies, and other monsters and compares the old folktales with modern interpretations. (Rev: BL 9/09) [398.21]

1966 Olmsted, Larry. *Getting into Guinness: One Man's Longest, Fastest, Highest Journey Inside the World's Most Famous Record Book* (10–12). 2008, HarperCollins $24.95 (978-0-06-137348-0). Guinness world-record holder Olmsted tells fascinating stories about incredible records and offers advice on selecting a feat to perform; many of the records are serious, but a large percentage are totally wacky. (Rev: BL 8/08) [030]

1967 Regan, Sally. *The Vampire Book: The Legends, the Lore, the Allure* (7–12). 2009, DK $19.99 (978-0-7566-5551-8). Regan surveys the various myths and stories that exist about vampires and similar beings around the world and throughout history, with details of vampires in literature and on the screen; with eye-catching illustrations. (Rev: LMC 1–2/10; SLJ 12/09) [398.21]

1968 Roeper, Richard. *Debunked! Conspiracy Theories, Urban Legends, and Evil Plots of the 21st Century* (9–12). 2008, Chicago Review $19.95 (978-155652707-4). Roeper debunks myths surrounding recent events ranging from the collapse of the Twin Towers to the death of Princess Diana in this irreverent and often humorous book. (Rev: BL 6/1–15/08) [364.10973]

1969 Selzer, Adam. *Your Neighborhood Gives Me the Creeps: True Tales of an Accidental Ghost Hunter* (9–12). 2009, Llewellyn paper $15.95 (978-073871557-5). He says he's a skeptic, but the author gives ghost tours in the Chicago area and shares some of his favorite eerie stories. (Rev: BLO 7/09) [133.1]

1970 Steiger, Brad. *Real Vampires, Night Stalkers, and Creatures from the Darkside* (10-12). 2009, Visible Ink Press (Gale) paper $24.95 (978-1-57859-255-5). Steiger draws on news articles, historical accounts, and first-person interviews to provide a history of vampirism and includes thirty tales of real vampires. (Rev: LMC 3–4/10) [133.4]

Sports and Games

General and Miscellaneous

1971 Brenkus, John. *The Perfection Point: Sport Science Predicts the Fastest Man, the Highest Jump, and the Limits of Athletic Performance* (10–12). 2010, Harper $26.99 (978-006184545-1). How fast can a human run? What's the longest someone can hold his breath? This fascinating volume answers these and many other questions about our expanding sports abilities. ℮ (Rev: BL 9/15/10) [612.044]

1972 Morris, Neil. *Should Substance-Abusing Athletes Be Banned for Life?* (7–12). Series: What Do You Think? 2008, Heinemann Library LB $32.86 (978-1-4329-1676-3). After a discussion of the use of drugs in sports, this volume discusses drug tests, penalties for abuse, and so forth; it includes a case study that looks at the Tour de France. (Rev: SLJ 1/1/09) [362.29]

1973 Sokolove, Michael. *Warrior Girls: Protecting Our Daughters Against the Injury Epidemic in Women's Sports* (10–12). 2008, Simon & Schuster $25.00 (978-074329755-4). Sokolove discusses the physiology and psychology of injury in women's sports, and the sometimes-high cost of an athlete's quest for perfection. ℮ (Rev: BL 6/1–15/08) [796.083]

Baseball

1974 Hample, Zack. *The Baseball: Stunts, Scandals, and Secrets Beneath the Stitches* (10–12). Illus. 2011, Vintage paper $14.95 (978-030747545-9). Hample, a veteran collector of baseballs — many of them caught during games — shares personal anecdotes, tidbits about famous catches, tips on the best ways to catch a foul ball, and much more in this rousing tribute to the baseball. (Rev: BL 3/1–15/11) [796.357]

1975 Kreidler, Mark. *Six Good Innings: How One Small Town Became a Little League Giant* (10–12). 2008, Harper $25.95 (978-006147357-9). Sportswriter Kreidler offers a detailed yet compelling story about a hardworking team and the supportive parents and town that helped them achieve so much. ℮ (Rev: BL 9/1/08*) [796.357]

Basketball

1976 Peavy, Linda, and Ursula Smith. *Full-Court Quest: The Girls from Fort Shaw Indian School, Basketball Champions of the World* (10–12). Illus. 2008, Univ. of Oklahoma $29.95 (978-080613973-9). Written by two well-known historians, this is an interesting and lively account of the Native American girls' basketball team that won the title of World Champions in 1904. (Rev: BL 9/1/08; SLJ 1/09) [796.323]

1977 Simmons, Bill. *The Book of Basketball: The NBA According to the Sports Guy* (10–12). Illus. 2009, Ballantine $30 (978-034551176-8). ESPN commentator Simmons looks back on the history of the NBA and chronicles his own personal fandom with a funny, self-deprecating tone. (Rev: BL 11/15/09*) [796.323]

Football

1978 Billick, Brian, and Michael MacCambridge. *More Than a Game: The Glorious Present — and the Uncertain Future — of the NFL* (10–12). 2009, Scribner $26 (978-143910918-2). Billick, former coach of the Baltimore Ravens, covers the many aspects of coaching in a straightforward style and with reference to the methods of many other NFL coaches. (Rev: BL 9/09*) [796.332.]

1979 Drape, Joe. *Our Boys: A Perfect Season on the Plains with the Smith Center Redmen* (10–12). 2009, Times $25 (978-080508890-8). Drape tells the story of a Kansas high school football team's amazing successes. (Rev: BL 9/09) [796.33]

1980 Fatsis, Stefan. *A Few Seconds of Panic: A 5-Foot-8, 170-Pound, 43-Year-Old Sportswriter Plays in the NFL* (9–12). 2008, Penguin $25.95 (978-1-59420-178-3). Though out of shape and older than most players, sportswriter Fatsis tries out for the Denver Broncos in this entertaining, behind-the-scenes experiment in participatory journalism. ⌒ (Rev: BL 6/1–15/08) [070.44]

1981 Freedman, Lew. *Thunder on the Tundra: Football Above the Arctic Circle* (9–12). Illus. 2008, Alaska Northwest paper $14.95 (978-088240742-5). Despite many obstacles, a high school superintendent of a remote Alaskan town starts a football program with the hope of lowering teenage substance abuse and keeping the kids in school. (Rev: BL 9/1/08; SLJ 11/1/08) [796.332]

1982 Hopkins, Theron. *The 80-Yard Run: A Twenty-Week, Coast-to-Coast Quest for the Heart of High School Football* (10–12). 2008, Skyhorse $24.95 (978-160239284-7). Hopkins taught high school English and coached football before embarking on a journey across America to get the inside story about high school football programs. (Rev: BL 9/1/08) [796.332]

1983 Jennings, Jay. *Carry the Rock: Race, Football, and the Soul of an American City* (10–12). Illus. 2010, Rodale $25.99 (978-160529637-1). Football and civil rights are interwoven in this account of the 2007 football season at Central High School in Little Rock, Arkansas, where desegregation was a hot issue 50 years earlier. ℮ (Rev: BL 9/1/10) [796.332]

1984 Longman, Jere. *The Hurricanes: One High School Team's Homecoming after Katrina* (10–12). 2008, PublicAffairs $26.00 (978-158648673-0). South Plaquemines High School and its Hurricanes football team emerge from the wreckage caused by Katrina with a strong spirit and the ability to inspire. ℮ (Rev: BL 9/1/08; SLJ 11/08) [796.332]

Running and Jogging

1985 Robbins, Liz. *A Race Like No Other: 26.2 Miles Through the Streets of New York* (10–12). 2008, HarperCollins $24.95 (978-006137313-8). This inside look at the New York Marathon covers the top runners, details of the course, and the many people who work behind the scenes. ℮ (Rev: BL 9/15/08*) [796.42]

Skateboarding

1986 Stutt, Ryan. *The Skateboarding Field Manual* (7–12). 2009, Firefly $29.95 (978-1-55407-467-9); paper $19.95 (978-1-55407-362-7). Stutt focuses on various skateboarding tricks and skills in this irreverent, nicely illustrated book; safety warnings are included, but are not prominent. (Rev: SLJ 6/1/09) [796.22]

Author Index

Authors are arranged alphabetically by last name. Authors' and joint authors' names are followed by book titles — which are also arranged alphabetically — and the text entry number. Book titles may refer to those that appear as a main entry or as an internal entry mentioned in the text. Fiction titles are indicated by (F) following the entry number.

Goldman, Steven. *Two Parties, One Tux, and a Very Short Film About The Grapes of Wrath*, 316(F)
Goldsmith, Connie. *Battling Malaria*, 1793
Hepatitis, 1794
Influenza, 1795
Goldstein, Andrew, et al. *When Sex Hurts*, 1837
Goldstein, Margaret J. *Legalizing Drugs*, 1776
Goldsworthy, Anna. *Piano Lessons*, 1462
Golus, Carrie. *Tupac Shakur*, 1362
Golway, Terry (ed.). *Fellow Citizens*, 1300
Gomez, Iris. *Try to Remember*, 404(F)
Gonick, Larry. *The Cartoon History of the Modern World*, 1539
Gonzales, Laurence. *Lucy*, 1045(F)
Gonzalez, Ann. *Running for My Life*, 277(F)
Gonzalez, Christina Diaz. *The Red Umbrella*, 192(F)
Goodman, Alison. *Eon*, 499(F)
Goodman, Carol. *The Night Villa*, 1046(F)
Goodman, Shawn. *Something Like Hope*, 317(F)
Gordon, Sherri Mabry. *Beyond Bruises*, 1838
The Evolution Debate, 1529
Gordon, Victoria. *Wolf in Tiger's Stripes*, 1122(F)
Gordon-Smith, Dolores. *A Hundred Thousand Dragons*, 1047(F)
Gore, Al. *Our Choice*, 1694
Gore, Shawna (ed.). *Creepy Archives, Vol. 1*, 666(F)
Gormley, Beatrice. *Poisoned Honey*, 768(F)
Gorrell, Gena K. *Say What? The Weird and Mysterious Journey of the English Language*, 1313
Goto, Hiromi. *Half World*, 500(F)
Gottfried, Ted. *Marijuana*, 1777
Gourley, Catherine. *The Horrors of Andersonville*, 880(F)
Gourley, Susan. *The Keepers of Sulbreth*, 501(F)
Gower, Iris. *Bomber's Moon*, 922(F)
Goyer, Tricia. *The Swiss Courier*, 923(F)
Graham, Ian. *Military Technology*, 1951
Grahame-Smith, Seth. *Abraham Lincoln*, 953(F)
Pride and Prejudice and Zombies, 954(F)
Grange, Michael. *Basketball's Greatest Stars*, 1412
Grant, Helen. *The Vanishing of Katharina Linden*, 1048(F)
Grant, K. M. *Blue Flame*, 773(F)
White Heat, 502(F)
Grant, Steven. *Hamlet*, 734(F)
Grant, Vicki. *Comeback*, 228(F)

Gray, Amy. *How to Be a Vampire*, 1962(F)
Gray, Claudia. *Hourglass*, 503(F)
Stargazer, 955(F)
Gray, Keith. *Ostrich Boys*, 828(F)
Green, John. *Paper Towns*, 1049(F)
Will Grayson, Will Grayson, 318(F)
Greenberg, Arielle (ed.). *Starting Today*, 1291
Greenberg, Martin H. (ed.). *Future Americas*, 1212(F)
Greenberg, Michael. *Painless Study Techniques*, 1749
Greenberg, Paul. *Four Fish*, 1904
Greene, Brenda. *America's Girl*, 1424
Greene, Brian. *Icarus at the Edge of Time*, 89(F)
Greenfield, Jacquie. *Colorado Pride*, 1123(F)
Gregson, Julia. *Band of Angels*, 829(F)
Griffin, Adele. *The Julian Game*, 90(F)
Griffin, Jason. *My Name Is Jason. Mine Too*, 1287
Griffin, Paul. *The Orange Houses*, 91(F)
Griggs, Vanessa Davis. *Practicing What You Preach*, 1124(F)
Grodin, Elissa D. *C Is for Ciao*, 1581
Grogan, John. *The Longest Trip Home*, 1344
Gross, Peter. *Tommy Taylor and the Bogus Identity*, 649(F)
Gruen, Sara. *Ape House*, 92(F)
Gruner, Jessica. *The Lost Days*, 1085(F)
Stranger and Stranger, 1086(F)
Guest, Jacqueline. *War Games*, 405(F)
Guibert, Emmanuel, et al. *The Photographer*, 1577
Guidry, Jeff. *An Eagle Named Freedom*, 1463
Gunderson, Jessica. *Gothic Art*, 1510
Guo, Xiaolu. *Twenty Fragments of a Ravenous Youth*, 791(F)
Gwin, Minrose. *The Queen of Palmyra*, 907(F)

Haas, Robert B. *Through the Eyes of the Vikings*, 1596
Hafiz, Dilara. *The American Muslim Teenager's Handbook*, 1634
Hafiz, Yasmine. *The American Muslim Teenager's Handbook*, 1634
Haigh, Jennifer. *The Condition*, 229(F)
Haldeman, Joe. *Marsbound*, 1210(F)
Hale, Marian. *The Goodbye Season*, 890(F)
Hale, Shannon. *Forest Born*, 504(F)
Hall, Barbara. *Tempo Change*, 93(F)
Hall, Derek (ed.). *The Ages of Steam and Electricity*, 1942
The Early 20th Century, 1942
Medieval Period and the Renaissance, 1942
The Modern World, 1942

Philosophy, Invention, and Engineering, 1395
The Scientific Revolution, 1943
Halperin, David. *Journal of a UFO Investigator*, 94(F)
Halpern, Julie. *Into the Wild Nerd Yonder*, 319(F)
Halpin, Brendan. *Forever Changes*, 278(F)
Shutout, 1254(F)
Hamilton, Jill (ed.). *Vegetarianism*, 1829
Hamilton, Kersten. *Tyger Tyger*, 505(F)
Hamilton, Lisa M. *Deeply Rooted*, 1873
Hamilton, Ruth. *A Parallel Life*, 230(F)
Hample, Zack. *The Baseball*, 1974
Han, Jenny. *The Summer I Turned Pretty*, 1125(F)
Hand, Elizabeth. *Illyria*, 95(F)
Hantman, Clea. *30 Days to Finding and Keeping Sassy Sidekicks and BFFs*, 1853
Hardinge, Frances. *The Lost Conspiracy*, 506(F)
Hardman, Lizabeth. *Plague*, 1796
Hardy, Mark. *Nothing Pink*, 320(F)
Harkrader, Lisa. *Inhalants*, 1780
Marijuana, 1777
Harley, Madeline. *The Bizarre and Incredible World of Plants*, 1878
Harmon, Michael. *Brutal*, 321(F)
Harper, Karen. *Down River*, 1126(F)
Harper, Suzanne. *The Juliet Club*, 96(F)
Harris, Charlaine. *Dead and Gone*, 956(F)
Harris, Lisa. *Blood Ransom*, 1127(F)
Harris, Tony. *The Starman Omnibus 1*, 725(F)
Harrison, C. C. *Running from Strangers*, 1128(F)
Harrison, Cora. *Writ in Stone*, 1050(F)
Harrison, K. David. *The Last Speakers*, 1314
Harrison, Kim. *Once Dead, Twice Shy*, 957(F)
Harrison, Mette Ivie. *The Princess and the Bear*, 507(F)
Harrod-Eagles, Cynthia. *Fell Purpose*, 1051(F)
Hart, Carolyn. *Merry, Merry Ghost*, 1052(F)
Hartnett, Sonya. *The Ghost's Child*, 508(F)
Harvey, Alyxandra. *Hearts at Stake*, 958(F)
Harvey, Sarah N. *Plastic*, 97(F)
Hatcher, John. *The Black Death*, 774(F)
Hatcher, Robin Lee. *A Matter of Character*, 891(F)
Hauck, Rachel. *Dining with Joy*, 1129(F)
Hauge, Lesley. *Nomansland*, 1211(F)

Title Index

This index contains both main entry and internal titles cited in the entries. References are to entry numbers, not page numbers. All fiction titles are indicated by (F), following the entry number.

Subject/Grade Level Index

All entries are listed by subject and then according to grade level suitability (see the key at the foot of pages for grade level designations). Subjects are arranged alphabetically and subject heads may be subdivided into nonfiction (e.g., "Africa") and fiction (e.g. "Africa — Fiction"). References to entries are by entry number, not page number.

A

Aaron, Henry
S–Adult: 1414

Abolitionists — Biography
See also Slavery (U.S.)
JS: 1371

Abuse
JS: 1838

Accidents
JS: 1597

Accidents — Fiction
S: 81

Acting
JS: 1280

Acting — Biography
S–Adult: 1455

Acting — Fiction
JS: 41
S–Adult: 1071

Activism
See also Social action
JS: 1647

Activism — Fiction
JS: 411

Adoption — Fiction
See also Foster care
JS: 395, 930
S–Adult: 28

Adventure stories — Fiction
See also Mystery stories — Fiction; Sea stories — Fiction; Survival stories — Fiction
JS: 1–3, 6–7, 10–11, 750, 790
S: 8, 1027
S–Adult: 180

Adventurers and explorers — Biography
JS: 1325

Adventurers and explorers — Biography
S–Adult: 1322

Advertising
JS: 1747

Afghan War, 2001–
S–Adult: 1465

Afghanistan
S–Adult: 1576–77, 1579

Afghanistan — Fiction
JS: 405, 798
S–Adult: 785, 1103

Africa
See also specific countries and regions, e.g., Nigeria; West Africa

African Americans
See also Civil rights; Civil War (U.S.); Slavery; and names of individuals, e.g., Walker, Madam C. J.
JS: 1368, 1521, 1599, 1607, 1611
S–Adult: 1622, 1667, 1670

African Americans — Biography
JS: 1362, 1371–72, 1386, 1394, 1411
S–Adult: 1306, 1338, 1413–14, 1416, 1484, 1502

African Americans — Fiction
JS: 26, 195, 199, 317, 326, 350–51, 388, 390, 413, 884, 910, 914, 927, 982, 1255
S: 211, 227, 762
S–Adult: 47, 189, 907, 1357

African Americans — Folklore
JS: 1296

African Americans — Poetry
JS: 1288
S–Adult: 1285–86

Afzal-Khan, Fawzia
S–Adult: 1447

Aging — Fiction
See also Death
JS: 17
S: 663

Agriculture
See also Community-supported agriculture; Farms and farm life
S–Adult: 1542

AIDS
See also HIV (virus)
JS: 1788, 1798

AIDS — Fiction
JS: 292
S–Adult: 375

Air pollution
JS: 1718

Airplane pilots — Biography
JS: 1323

Airplane pilots — Fiction
JS: 927

Alabama — Fiction
JS: 393
S–Adult: 415

Alaska
S–Adult: 1605, 1950, 1981

Alaska — Fiction
S–Adult: 161, 1126

Alcohol and alcohol abuse — Biography
S–Adult: 1457

Alcohol and alcohol abuse — Fiction
JS: 210, 291, 368
S–Adult: 258

Alcott, Louisa May
JS: 1337

JS = Junior High/Senior High; S = Senior High; S–Adult = Senior High/Adult

Booth, John Wilkes — Fiction
S–Adult: 651

Border control
JS: 1676

Boy Scouts
S–Adult: 1862

Boyle, Brian
S–Adult: 1451

Brain and nervous system
S–Adult: 1839

Brain injury — Fiction
JS: 410

Breast cancer — Fiction
S: 141

Breasts
JS: 1812

Bridge (game) — Fiction
JS: 255

Bridges
JS: 1680, 1944

Brill, Leigh
S–Adult: 1452

Brontë family — Fiction
JS: 948

Bronx (NY) — Biography
S–Adult: 1490

Bronx (NY) — Fiction
JS: 390

Brooklyn (NY)
S: 1681

Brooklyn (NY) — Fiction
S–Adult: 641

Brotherhood of Eternal Love
S–Adult: 1625

Brothers and sisters — Fiction
JS: 59, 234, 252, 263, 393, 1031
S: 286, 933

Brown, Rita Mae
S–Adult: 1339

Buckley, Bryan
S–Adult: 1453

Buddhism — Biography
S–Adult: 1435

Buffett, Warren
JS: 1403

Building and construction
See also Architecture
JS: 1680, 1685, 1756

Bulimia
JS: 1800

Bulimia — Fiction
JS: 282

Bull-riding — Fiction
JS: 266

Bullies and bullying
See also Cyberbullying
JS: 1851

Bullies and bullying — Fiction
JS: 23, 72, 90, 98, 162, 280, 309, 321, 372, 391
S: 841
S–Adult: 1064

Buried treasure — Fiction
S–Adult: 1094

Burma
JS: 1580

Burress, Plaxico
S–Adult: 1416

Bus travel — Fiction
S–Adult: 358

Busby, Cylin and John
JS: 1454

Business — Biography
JS: 1403, 1411

Butterflies
S: 1902

C

Calcines, Eduardo F.
JS: 1440

California — Fiction
JS: 37, 101, 129, 132
S–Adult: 250, 1094

Cambodia — Biography
JS: 1468

Camels
S–Adult: 1891

Camps — Fiction
JS: 61, 122, 947

Canada — Fiction
JS: 295, 869

Canals
JS: 1945

Cancer
JS: 1785

Cancer — Biography
S–Adult: 1496

Cancer — Fiction
JS: 49, 59, 169, 216, 283, 911, 1012
S–Adult: 103

Capital punishment
S: 1724

Capotorto, Carl
S–Adult: 1455

Carbon
S: 1920

Careers
JS: 1754–57, 1759, 1761–62, 1764–65
S–Adult: 1763, 1766, 1914

Caribbean — Fiction
JS: 863

Carjacking — Fiction
JS: 1055

Carroll, Lewis — Fiction
S–Adult: 811

Carthage — Biography
JS: 1432

Catholicism — Biography
S–Adult: 1344

Cats — Fiction
JS: 655

Celebrity
S–Adult: 1774

Celebrity — Fiction
JS: 29, 41–42, 62
S–Adult: 1009, 1014

Cell phones
JS: 1948

Censorship
JS: 1732

Central America — Biography
S–Adult: 1501

Chaplin, Charlie
JS: 1354

Charities
S–Adult: 1739

Chaucer, Geoffrey — Adaptations
S–Adult: 16

Chechnya
S: 1584

Cheerleading — Fiction
JS: 1170

Chemistry
JS: 1917, 1919

Chernobyl nuclear disaster
JS: 1937

Cherokee Indians
JS: 1604

Cherry-Garrard, Apsley — Fiction
S: 870

Chess — Fiction
JS: 263

Chicago — Fiction
JS: 915

Child abuse — Fiction
JS: 163, 215

Child labor — Fiction
JS: 1218

JS = Junior High/Senior High; S = Senior High; S–Adult = Senior High/Adult

JS = Junior High/Senior High; S = Senior High; S–Adult = Senior High/Adult

F

Friendship — Fiction
JS: 24, 27, 42, 48, 56, 58, 61, 70, 73, 86, 90, 113, 121–22, 133, 157, 164, 167–69, 173, 179, 185, 208, 280, 283, 302, 319, 331–32, 335, 339, 343, 355, 380, 384–85, 392, 620, 781, 828, 908, 913, 1008, 1121, 1150, 1164, 1254, 1257
S: 25, 106, 118, 793
S–Adult: 109, 177, 296, 381, 896

Friendship — Poetry
JS: 1287

Frontier life (U.S.)
JS: 1615–16

Frontier life (U.S.) — Fiction
JS: 884–86
S–Adult: 887–88, 1152

G

Gambling — Fiction
JS: 151, 218

Gangs
JS: 1725

Gangs — Fiction
JS: 116, 143, 413, 915
S: 841

Gates, Bill
JS: 1404

Gates, Bill and Melinda
JS: 1405

Gay and lesbian parents
JS: 1859

Gay men and lesbians — Fiction
JS: 226, 362, 377, 535
S–Adult: 22, 155

Gay rights
JS: 1736

Geeks — Fiction
JS: 1265

Geisel, Theodor Seuss
S–Adult: 1343

Generals (U.S.) — Biography
JS: 1383
S–Adult: 1373

Genetic engineering
JS: 1809

Genetic engineering — Fiction
S–Adult: 1045

Genetically modified food
JS: 1872

Genetics
S–Adult: 1841

Genocide
JS: 1649

Genocide — Fiction
JS: 779

Geography
JS: 1534
S: 1922

Gerbils — Memoirs
S–Adult: 1489

Germany — Fiction
JS: 837
S–Adult: 812, 1048

Gettysburg, Battle of — Fiction
JS: 881

Ghana — Fiction
JS: 778
S–Adult: 213

Ghosts
JS: 1969

Ghosts — Fiction
JS: 354, 423, 645, 681, 859, 893, 938, 950, 960, 982, 988, 1003, 1075
S: 552
S–Adult: 570, 845, 1036

Giants — Fiction
S–Adult: 687

Global warming
JS: 1688, 1705
S–Adult: 1704

Global warming — Fiction
JS: 439

Goblins — Fiction
JS: 505

Goldsworthy, Anna
S–Adult: 1462

Golf — Biography
JS: 1425

Golf — Fiction
JS: 243

Gossip — Fiction
JS: 62

Government and politics
JS: 1624, 1636

Government and politics (U.S.)
JS: 1568
S–Adult: 1388–89

Government and politics (U.S.) — Biography
JS: 1379, 1382

Grandfathers — Fiction
JS: 243

Graphic novels — Fiction
JS: 15, 17–20, 639–40, 642, 645, 647, 650, 652–53, 655–56, 659, 664–65, 667, 671, 674, 677, 681–82, 684–85, 688, 690, 692–93, 695, 699–701, 706, 708–09, 713, 716, 718, 727–30, 735, 739–42, 746–50, 752, 754–55, 757, 759–60, 763, 766, 1316, 1959
S: 643, 648, 658, 661–63, 668, 670, 673, 676, 703–04, 717, 720, 724, 726, 737, 745, 751, 756, 761–62, 765, 767
S–Adult: 638, 641, 644, 646, 649, 654, 657, 660, 672, 675, 678, 680, 686–87, 694, 696, 702, 707, 711–12, 715, 722–23, 725, 736, 738, 758, 764, 1299

Graphic novels — Fiction
S–Adult: 697

Graphic novels — Mythology
JS: 669

Graphic novels — Plays
JS: 731–34

Great Britain — Fiction
JS: 520
S–Adult: 736, 1077

Great Depression
JS: 1598

Great Depression — Fiction
JS: 900

Great Plains
S–Adult: 1629

Greece — Fiction
JS: 432

Greece — Mythology
JS: 632, 669

Greene, Nathanael
S: 1381

Grief — Fiction
JS: 104, 119, 199, 247, 262, 287, 289, 322, 340, 380, 789, 1062, 1162
S–Adult: 109, 822, 845

Grogan, John
S–Adult: 1344

Group homes — Fiction
JS: 332

Growing up
See also Coming of age
S–Adult: 1487

Growing up — Fiction
JS: 67, 240, 366, 371, 1273

Guadeloupe — Fiction
JS: 640

Guatemala — Fiction
JS: 201

Guenevere, Queen — Fiction
JS: 776

Guidry, Jeff
S–Adult: 1463

Guilt — Fiction
JS: 291

Gulf Stream
S–Adult: 1928

Gymnastics — Fiction
S: 1251

H

Habitat for Humanity
JS: 1738

Hamlet — **Adaptations**
JS: 734

Hamlet (play) — **Fiction**
JS: 136

Hamsters
JS: 1908

Hannibal
JS: 1432

Harems — **Biography**
S–Adult: 1474

Hargreaves, Alice Liddell —
Fiction
S–Adult: 811

Hate crimes — **Fiction**
JS: 75

Haydn, Joseph — **Fiction**
JS: 824

Health and hygiene
JS: 1771
S–Adult: 1713, 1856

Hearing impaired — **Fiction**
S: 91

Hell — **Fiction**
JS: 14

Hemingway, Ernest
JS: 1345

Henry VIII, King of England —
Fiction
JS: 839

Hepatitis
JS: 1794

Heroes (U.S.) — **Biography**
S–Adult: 1366

Herpetology — **Biography**
S: 1402

Hersh, Kristin
S–Adult: 1356

High schools
S–Adult: 1981–82, 1984

High schools — **Fiction**
JS: 33, 38, 53, 73, 82, 84, 86, 98–99,
112, 114–15, 120, 125, 133, 162, 164,
181, 208, 275, 281, 319, 321, 327, 349,
361, 365, 382, 388, 390, 493, 592, 620,
1007, 1059, 1118, 1254–55, 1260
S: 32
S–Adult: 50, 66, 165, 177, 315, 348,
389

High schools —**Biography**
S–Adult: 1483

Hillary, Sir Edmund
JS: 1324

Hip hop
JS: 1515

Hip-hop (music)
JS: 1512

Hiroshima
JS: 1565

Hispanic American literature
S–Adult: 1302

Hispanic Americans —
Biography
JS: 1326, 1425
S–Adult: 1490

Hispanic Americans — **Fiction**
JS: 191, 198, 361

History (U.S.)
JS: 1597, 1602
S: 1601

HIV (virus)
JS: 1788, 1798

Hollywood — **Fiction**
JS: 41
S–Adult: 46, 65

Holocaust
JS: 1566
S–Adult: 1564

Holocaust — **Biography**
JS: 1438, 1473

Holocaust — **Fiction**
JS: 667, 730, 919–21, 925, 929

Homeless — **Biography**
S–Adult: 1482

Homeless — **Fiction**
JS: 64
S–Adult: 386

Homosexuality
JS: 1736, 1836

Homosexuality — **Fiction**
JS: 70, 120, 304, 318, 367, 369, 393,
408, 1008
S: 314, 320, 338, 356
S–Adult: 375

Honesty — **Fiction**
JS: 531

Honey
S–Adult: 1900

Honeybees
S–Adult: 1901

Horror stories — **Fiction**
JS: 5, 19, 742, 949, 964–65, 974, 980,
985, 989, 1199, 1275
S: 662
S–Adult: 666, 946, 953, 967, 969–71,
973, 977, 986, 990, 992, 997–98, 1004

Horse racing — **Fiction**
JS: 900

Horseback riding — **Fiction**
JS: 51

Horses
S–Adult: 1488

Horses — **Fiction**
S–Adult: 1136

Hospice care
S–Adult: 1911

Hotels — **Fiction**
JS: 111

Houston (TX) — **Fiction**
JS: 341

Howard, Catherine — **Fiction**
JS: 839

Hubble space telescope
S: 1866

Human behavior
S–Adult: 1844

Human body
See also specific parts and systems, e.g.,
Senses
JS: 1811

Human embryos — **Fiction**
S–Adult: 155

Human evolution
S–Adult: 1770

Human rights
S–Adult: 1728

Human rights — **Fiction**
S: 1262

Human trafficking
JS: 407

Human-animal relations
S–Adult: 1339

Human-animal relationships
S–Adult: 1907

Humor and satire
S–Adult: 1298

Humorous stories — **Fiction**
JS: 174, 306, 424, 1007, 1010
S: 1027
S–Adult: 127, 140, 587, 672, 711, 939,
978, 1009, 1011, 1013–14, 1204

Hungary — **Fiction**
JS: 862

Hurricane Katrina
S–Adult: 1481, 1984

Hurricane Katrina — **Fiction**
JS: 26

Hurricanes
JS: 1541

Hurston, Zora Neale —
Criticism
S–Adult: 1306

JS = Junior High/Senior High;   S = Senior High;   S–Adult = Senior High/Adult

I

Icarus (mythological character) — Fiction
S–Adult: 89

Ice hockey — Fiction
JS: 1256

Iceland — Fiction
JS: 599

Identity — Fiction
JS: 357

Illegal aliens
S–Adult: 1672

Illegal aliens — Fiction
JS: 132
S: 91
S–Adult: 404

Immigration
JS: 1641, 1675

Immigration — Biography
S–Adult: 1477

Immigration — Fiction
JS: 204, 748, 830

Immigration (Germany) — Fiction
S–Adult: 812

Immigration (U.S.)
JS: 1674, 1676
S–Adult: 1460

Immigration (U.S.) — Biography
S–Adult: 1495

Immigration (U.S.) — Fiction
JS: 162, 192, 201–02, 894, 897, 1010

Immigration (U.S.) — Fiction
S–Adult: 197

Immortality — Fiction
JS: 607

Imperialism (U.S.)
S: 1601

Incest — Fiction
S: 95

India
S–Adult: 1575

India — Biography
S–Adult: 1500

India — Fiction
JS: 563, 788
S–Adult: 235, 654, 786, 802, 1180

Indian (Asian) Americans — Fiction
JS: 200, 202
S–Adult: 71, 654

Indian (Asian) students
S–Adult: 235

Industrial Revolution
JS: 1554

Infanticide — Fiction
JS: 74

Inferno — Adaptations
JS: 14

Influenza
JS: 1787, 1795

Influenza epidemic, 1918 — Fiction
JS: 893

Inhalants
JS: 1780

Inheritance — Fiction
S–Adult: 261

Insects
JS: 1897
S: 1887
S–Adult: 1899

Insomnia — Fiction
S–Adult: 1057

Intelligence
S–Adult: 1841

Intelligent design
JS: 1529

Interstellar travel — Fiction
S–Adult: 89

Inventors and inventions
S–Adult: 1938, 1940

Inventors and inventions — Biography
JS: 1380

Iran
JS: 1591
S–Adult: 1592

Iran — Fiction
S–Adult: 857

Iranian Americans — Fiction
S–Adult: 79

Iraq — Fiction
S–Adult: 832

Iraq War, 2003–
JS: 1315, 1628, 1641
S–Adult: 1567, 1590

Iraq War, 2003– — Biography
S–Adult: 1453

Iraq War, 2003– — Fiction
JS: 326, 410, 805

Iraq War, 2003– — Memoirs
JS: 1494

Ireland — Fiction
JS: 537, 849, 859
S–Adult: 819, 1050, 1079

Irish — Fiction
S–Adult: 364

Irish Americans — Fiction
JS: 882

Irish potato famine — Fiction
JS: 849

Iron
JS: 1711

Irritable colon
JS: 1813

Islam
JS: 1535, 1585, 1591, 1634
S–Adult: 1633, 1635

Islam — Biography
S–Adult: 1504

Israel
JS: 1586
S: 1587

Israel — Fiction
JS: 838

Italian Americans — Biography
S–Adult: 1455

Italian Americans — Fiction
JS: 894

Italy
JS: 1581

Italy — Fiction
JS: 51, 96, 816, 851
S–Adult: 1046

Ivory Coast — Fiction
S–Adult: 638

J

Jackson, Andrew
S–Adult: 1373

Jackson, Michael
S–Adult: 1357

Jacobs, Jane
JS: 1387

Jamaica — Biography
S–Adult: 1361, 1456

James, LeBron
S–Adult: 1415

Jane Austen — Fiction
S–Adult: 1147

Jane Eyre — Adaptations
JS: 15

Japan — Fiction
S: 796

Japanese — Fiction
JS: 876

Jazz
S–Adult: 1517

Jenkins, Missy
JS: 1464

Jewelry
S–Adult: 1955

Jews — Fiction
JS: 31, 76, 150, 692, 782, 862, 897, 919–20
S–Adult: 212, 832

Jobs, Steve
JS: 1406

Johnstown Flood — Fiction
JS: 895

Jones, Marion
S–Adult: 1421

Joplin, Janis
JS: 1358

Journalism
JS: 1980
S–Adult: 1321

Journalism — Biography
S–Adult: 1350, 1391

Julius Caesar — Adaptations
JS: 731

Jundi, Sami al
S–Adult: 1436

Junger, Sebastian
S–Adult: 1465

Juvenile court
JS: 1656

Juvenile delinquents
S–Adult: 1721

Juvenile delinquents — Fiction
JS: 9, 317, 332, 351

K

Kamara, Mariatu
JS: 1466

Kambalu, Samson
S–Adult: 1332

Kantner, Seth
S: 1467

Karenina, Anna — Fiction
S–Adult: 1248

Keat, Nawuth
JS: 1468

Kenya — Fiction
JS: 781

Kerman, Piper
S–Adult: 1469

Kidnapping
S–Adult: 1620

Kidnapping — Fiction
JS: 143, 1030
S: 370, 762
S–Adult: 1065

Kimonos
S–Adult: 1956

King Arthur — Fiction
JS: 606

Kings and queens — Fiction
JS: 772

Kirby, Jack
S–Adult: 1333

Kirn, Walter
S–Adult: 1346

Klein, Stephanie
S–Adult: 1470

Knights
S: 1536

Knights Templar — Fiction
JS: 708, 945

Knitting — Fiction
JS: 108

Kohler, Dean Ellis
JS: 1471

Kopelman, Jay
JS: 1472

Kor, Eva Mozes
JS: 1473

Korea — Fiction
S: 673
S–Adult: 795

Ku Klux Klan
JS: 1677

L

Labor disputes — Fiction
JS: 916

Labor unions
JS: 1746
S–Adult: 1745

Lady of the Lake — Fiction
JS: 606

Lang, Lang
S: 1359

Languages
S–Adult: 1314

Laos — Fiction
S–Adult: 1032

Lauren, Jillian
S–Adult: 1474

Lauren, Ralph
JS: 1407

Leadership
S–Adult: 1840

Lebanon — Fiction
S–Adult: 804

Lee, Harper
JS: 1347

Lefevre, Didier
S–Adult: 1577

Leiber, Jerry
S–Adult: 1328

Lennon, John
S–Adult: 1360

Letters — Fiction
JS: 112
S–Adult: 924

Levi-Montalcini, Rita
JS: 1401

Lewis, Meriweather
JS: 1325

Libraries and librarians — Fiction
See also Books and reading

Lightning — Fiction
S–Adult: 397

Lincoln, Abraham — Fiction
S–Adult: 651, 953

Lincoln, Abraham and Mary Todd
JS: 1374

Lindbergh, Charles A.
S–Adult: 1620

Lizards
JS: 1883

London (England) — Fiction
JS: 129, 809, 833, 855
S–Adult: 400, 570

Lopez, Nancy
JS: 1425

Lord's Resistance Army
JS: 1640

Los Angeles (CA) — Fiction
JS: 58

Lou Gehrig's disease — Fiction
JS: 78

Louisville (KY) — Fiction
S–Adult: 906

Love — Fiction
S: 864
S–Adult: 34, 47, 242, 797, 802, 854, 972, 1165, 1168, 1178

Love — Poetry
JS: 1282

Lucas, Frank
S–Adult: 1475

Lukas, Christopher
S–Adult: 1476

Lynchings
JS: 1679

Lynchings — Fiction
JS: 910

M

Macbeth — Adaptations
JS: 732

Macbeth, King of Scotland — Fiction
JS: 835

Mafia — Fiction
S: 703

Magic and magicians — Fiction
JS: 420, 444, 448, 453, 464, 481
S–Adult: 462, 559

Malaria
JS: 1789, 1793

Malawi — Biography
S–Adult: 1332

Mali — Biography
JS: 1342

Mammals
JS: 1881

Mandela, Nelson
S–Adult: 1433

Manga
JS: 743

Manic depressive illness
See Bipolar disorder

Manjiro — Fiction
JS: 876

Manning, Peyton
JS: 1418

Maori (people) — Fiction
JS: 509

Mapplethorpe, Robert
S–Adult: 1363

Maric, Vesna
S–Adult: 1477

Marijuana
JS: 1777

Marine animals
JS: 1903

Marley, Bob
S–Adult: 1361

Marriage
JS: 1860

Martial arts — Fiction
JS: 214, 1139

Martin, Luther
S–Adult: 1388

Mary Magdalene — Fiction
JS: 768

Mass media
JS: 1747
S: 1319

Masters, Jarvis Jay
S–Adult: 1478

Mathematics
See also specific branches, e.g., Algebra
S–Adult: 1923–25

Mathematics — Fiction
JS: 1025

May-Treanor, Misty
S–Adult: 1426

Mayor, Mireya
S–Adult: 1479

McCarthy, Joseph
JS: 1382, 1626

McEnroe, Patrick
S–Adult: 1420

Meaning (philosophy) — Fiction
JS: 172

Medecins sans Frontieres
S–Adult: 1577

Media
JS: 1723
S–Adult: 1653

Medicine
JS: 1769, 1771, 1802, 1804
S–Adult: 1806

Medxican Americans — Fiction
JS: 143

Memoirs
JS: 1440, 1454, 1461, 1464, 1466, 1468, 1471–73, 1480, 1494
S: 1467, 1492
S–Adult: 1344, 1346, 1349–50, 1356, 1363, 1431, 1436, 1442–43, 1446–49, 1451–52, 1455, 1458–60, 1462–63, 1469–70, 1474–75, 1477–79, 1482–91, 1493, 1495–97, 1499–1505, 1507

Mental disabilities
JS: 1831

Mental illness
See also specific disorders, e.g., Bipolar disorder; Depression (mental state); Schizophrenia
JS: 1818

Mental illness — Fiction
JS: 270, 275, 285
S–Adult: 722

Merlin — Fiction
JS: 433

Mermaids and mermen — Fiction
JS: 549

Mesopotamia
JS: 1546

Meteorites
S–Adult: 1869

Mexican Americans — Fiction
JS: 194, 288, 327, 387
S–Adult: 187, 190

Mexico — Biography
JS: 1335

Mexico — Fiction
JS: 144

Meyer, Stephenie
JS: 1348

Michigan — Fiction
JS: 157

Middle Ages
JS: 1553, 1804, 1942
S: 1536

Middle Ages — Fiction
JS: 520, 772–73, 775, 851
S–Adult: 1028–29

Middle East
JS: 1535, 1585

Migrant workers
S–Adult: 1672

Migrant workers — Fiction
JS: 194

Military cadets — Fiction
JS: 303

Mills, Dan
S–Adult: 1567

Miracles — Fiction
JS: 219

Missing children — Fiction
JS: 125, 184
S–Adult: 1048

Missing persons — Fiction
JS: 178, 1024, 1189
S: 1078
S–Adult: 1017, 1098

Mississippi — Fiction
S–Adult: 907

Missoula (MT)
S–Adult: 1874

Missouri — Fiction
JS: 902

Mohawk Indians
JS: 1680

Molecular biology
JS: 1807

Monaque, Mathilde
JS: 1480

Monet, Claude
JS: 1334

Money-making ideas
JS: 1767

Mongolia — Biography
S–Adult: 1458

Monologues
JS: 1281

Monsters
See also Fantasy; Folklore; Mythology; Supernatural

JS = Junior High/Senior High; S = Senior High; S–Adult = Senior High/Adult

S–Adult: 94, 189, 907

1968
JS: 1555

1970s — Fiction
S–Adult: 912

1980s
JS: 1559

1980s — Biography
S–Adult: 1483

1980s — Fiction
JS: 48, 692
S–Adult: 375

1990s
JS: 1559

1990s — Fiction
JS: 915
S: 313

19th century — Fiction
JS: 807, 892
S: 878

Ninjas — Fiction
JS: 528, 652

Niven, Jennifer
S–Adult: 1483

Norris, Michele
S–Adult: 1484

North Korea
JS: 1578

Nova Scotia — Fiction
JS: 865

Nuclear power plants
JS: 1937

Nurses — Fiction
S–Adult: 829

Nutrition
JS: 1813, 1828, 1830, 1872

O

Obama, Barack
S–Adult: 1291

Obesity
JS: 1827

Obesity — Fiction
JS: 280

Obsessive compulsive disorder — Fiction
JS: 53
S: 268

Occult — Fiction
S–Adult: 1061

Oceanography
S–Adult: 1927

Oceans
JS: 1690
S–Adult: 1689

Odors
S: 1815

Ohno, Apolo Anton
JS: 1419

Oil
S: 1936

Oil drilling
S: 1695

Oil pollution
S–Adult: 1717

Oklahoma — Fiction
S–Adult: 138

Online games — Fiction
JS: 134

Oppenheimer, Mark
S–Adult: 1485

Oregon — Fiction
S–Adult: 128

Oregon Trail — Fiction
JS: 885

Organ donation — Fiction
JS: 77

Organ transplants — Fiction
JS: 36, 297

Orphans — Biography
S–Adult: 1446

Orphans — Fiction
JS: 816, 918

Overweight persons — Fiction
JS: 33, 1260

Oysters
S–Adult: 1895

P

Pakistan
S–Adult: 1579

Pakistan — Biography
S–Adult: 1447

Pakistani Americans — Fiction
JS: 196
S–Adult: 412

Palestinians — Biography
S–Adult: 1436

Palestinians — Fiction
JS: 815

Panama Canal
JS: 1945

Panama Canal — Fiction
S: 864

Panic attacks
JS: 1819

Papillomavirus
JS: 1799

Paris (France) — Fiction
JS: 176

Parisites (Biology)
S–Adult: 1792

Parkin, Joe
S–Adult: 1427

Parties — Fiction
JS: 337

Patton, George S.
JS: 1383

Peace
JS: 1647

Peace Corps — Biography
S–Adult: 1458

Pearl Harbor
JS: 1621

Pelosi, Nancy
JS: 1384

Pennsylvania — Fiction
S–Adult: 248

Periodic table
S–Adult: 1918

Persia — Fiction
JS: 918

Personal conduct
JS: 1851

Personal finance
JS: 1768

Personal guidance
JS: 1518, 1850, 1854, 1857, 1861
S–Adult: 1852, 1856

Personal problems — Fiction
JS: 284, 298–99, 311, 355, 1012
S: 323
S–Adult: 334

Peterson, Brenda
S–Adult: 1486

Petroleum
JS: 1750

Pets
See Cats; Dogs

Philadelphia (PA) — Fiction
JS: 385

Philadelphia Centennial Exhibition — Fiction
JS: 892

Philanthropy — Biography
JS: 1405

Phobias
JS: 1822

JS = Junior High/Senior High; S = Senior High; S–Adult = Senior High/Adult

JS = Junior High/Senior High; S = Senior High; S–Adult = Senior High/Adult

S

Saberi, Roxana
S–Adult: 1391

Sanchez, Ivan
S–Adult: 1490

Sandell, Laurie
S–Adult: 1350

Sarkozy, Nicolas
JS: 1439

Saudi Arabia — Fiction
S–Adult: 1038

Schizophrenia — Fiction
JS: 264, 274, 277, 290

School shootings
JS: 1464
S–Adult: 1722

School shootings — Fiction
JS: 401
S–Adult: 1064

Schools
See also Boarding schools; High schools; School shootings
JS: 1748

Schools — Fiction
JS: 9, 56, 72, 150, 172, 309, 353, 377, 391, 735, 820, 1189
S: 767

Science
JS: 1543, 1802–03
S–Adult: 1863, 1931, 1939

Science — Biography
JS: 1395, 1398–1401

Science — Experiments and projects
See also Human body — Experiments and projects; Physics — Experiments and projects; Sports — Experiments and projects
JS: 1864

Science — Experiments and projects — Fiction
JS: 33

Science fairs
JS: 1864

Science fiction
See also Fantasy; Supernatural; Time travel
JS: 10, 639, 695, 752, 1187, 1189–90, 1192, 1195, 1197, 1203, 1206–07, 1209, 1211, 1214–15, 1220–21, 1224, 1226–29, 1231–33, 1241, 1244–45
S: 648, 756, 1212, 1240, 1242
S–Adult: 94, 156, 702, 758, 764, 1184–86, 1188, 1191, 1193–94, 1200–02, 1204–05, 1208, 1210, 1213, 1216–17, 1219, 1222–23, 1225, 1230, 1234–38, 1246–48, 1250

Scopes trial (1925) — Fiction
JS: 898

Scotland — Fiction
JS: 1054
S–Adult: 806, 822, 834

Scott, Robert Falcon
S–Adult: 1322

Scott, Wendell
S–Adult: 1413

Screenwriting
S–Adult: 1320

Sculpture — Poetry
JS: 1288

Sea horses
S–Adult: 1905

Sea stories — Fiction
JS: 7, 760, 1179

Secrets — Fiction
JS: 104, 179, 1069
S: 118
S–Adult: 827, 1095

Segregation (U.S.)
S–Adult: 1667

Self-confidence — Fiction
JS: 23

Self-destructive behavior — Fiction
JS: 382

Self-esteem — Fiction
JS: 88, 300

Self-mutilation
JS: 1751

Self-mutilation — Fiction
JS: 362

Sellers, Heather
S–Adult: 1491

Senses
JS: 1816

September 11, 2001 — Fiction
JS: 408
S–Adult: 412

Service dogs — Biography
S–Adult: 1452

1700s — Fiction
JS: 873

1770s — Fiction
JS: 865

7th century — Fiction
JS: 769

Sex — Fiction
JS: 330, 344, 380

Sex education
S–Adult: 1837

Sex roles
S–Adult: 1734

Sex scandals — Fiction
S–Adult: 50, 165

Sexism (U.S.)
S–Adult: 1733

Sexual abuse — Fiction
JS: 253, 265, 288, 305, 362
S: 370
S–Adult: 312, 825

Sexual abuse— Fiction
JS: 215

Sexual orientation — Fiction
S: 32, 307

Sexually transmitted diseases
JS: 1790
S–Adult: 1791

Shakespeare, William
S–Adult: 1317

Shakespeare, William — Adaptations
JS: 731–34

Shakespeare, William — Fiction
JS: 96, 852

Shakur, Tupac
JS: 1362

Shapeshifting — Fiction
JS: 485

Sheba, Queen of
JS: 1437

Sheff, Nic
S: 1492

Ships and boats
See also Titanic (ship)

Shipwrecks — Fiction
JS: 790

Shootings — Fiction
JS: 27

Shoplifting — Fiction
JS: 100

Short stories — Fiction
JS: 271, 440, 442, 473, 532, 544, 614, 753, 965, 976, 999, 1265–66, 1269, 1271, 1273–75, 1295
S: 307, 474, 1212, 1240, 1262
S–Adult: 189, 434, 540, 610, 646, 712, 935, 971, 1184, 1191, 1216, 1261, 1263–64, 1267, 1270, 1272, 1277–79

Siblings
JS: 1861

Siena (Italy) — Fiction
S–Adult: 1119

Sierra Leone — Biography
JS: 1466

Silverwood family
S–Adult: 1445

Singers — Biography
JS: 1358
S–Adult: 1356

JS = Junior High/Senior High; S = Senior High; S–Adult = Senior High/Adult

JS = Junior High/Senior High; S = Senior High; S–Adult = Senior High/Adult

V

Vacations — Fiction
JS: 130, 366

Vampires
JS: 1962, 1967
S: 1970

Vampires – Fiction
S–Adult: 1276

Vampires – Poetry
S–Adult: 1276

Vampires — Fiction
JS: 465, 486, 493, 503, 517, 528, 551, 581, 592, 937, 941, 943, 955, 958, 962, 993–94, 1001
S–Adult: 455, 935, 944, 953, 956, 966, 978–79, 1155

Vampires —Fiction
S–Adult: 963

Van Gogh, Vincent
JS: 1336

Vegetarianism
JS: 1829
S–Adult: 1871

Venice — Fiction
JS: 843

Veterans — Fiction
S: 91

Veterinarians — Biography
S–Adult: 1503

Veterinarians — Careers
S–Adult: 1914

Victoria, Queen of England — Fiction
JS: 840

Victorian Age — Fiction
JS: 808–09, 1063

Vietnam — Fiction
JS: 794

Vietnam War
JS: 1471, 1624

Vietnam War — Fiction
JS: 690, 930
S–Adult: 931, 934

Vikings
JS: 1531

Violence
JS: 1723

Violence — Biography
JS: 1454

Violence — Fiction
JS: 121, 206

Virginity — Fiction
S: 363

Virtual reality
S–Adult: 1947

Virtual reality — Fiction
JS: 1196

Vocational guidance
JS: 1758, 1760

Volcanoes
JS: 1541

Volleyball — Biography
S–Adult: 1426

Volunteers
JS: 1738

Voting
JS: 1660

W

Wales — Fiction
S–Adult: 842, 1095

Walker, Jerald
S–Adult: 1502

Walker, Madam C. J.
JS: 1411

War
See also specific battles and wars, e.g., Antietam, Battle of; World War II
JS: 1639–40, 1642, 1646
S: 1638
S–Adult: 1645, 1648

War — Fiction
JS: 252, 801
S–Adult: 804

War widows — Fiction
S–Adult: 242

Washington (DC) — Fiction
S–Adult: 259

Water
JS: 1685, 1699
S–Adult: 1692

Water conservation
S–Adult: 1716

Weapons
JS: 1951

Weapons of mass destruction
JS: 1952

Weight loss — Biography
S–Adult: 1470

Wells, Jeff
S–Adult: 1503

Werewolves — Fiction
JS: 470, 479, 518, 609, 940, 947, 983, 996
S–Adult: 956, 972

West (U.S.) — Fiction
JS: 167

West Africa — Fiction
JS: 6

West Virginia — Fiction
JS: 394

Westerns — Fiction
S–Adult: 1175

Wharton, Edith
JS: 1352

Wheelchairs — Fiction
S: 793

Whitfield, Simon
JS: 1429

Wildfires
S: 1708

Wildfires — Fiction
JS: 132

Wildlife rehabilitation — Biography
S–Adult: 1463

Wilson, G. Willow
S–Adult: 1504

Wishes — Fiction
JS: 453, 591

Witchcraft trials — Salem — Fiction
JS: 872

Witches — Fiction
JS: 444, 513, 602
S–Adult: 530

Wolff, Mishna
S–Adult: 1505

Wolves — Fiction
JS: 12

Women
JS: 1600, 1735
S–Adult: 1733, 1976

Women — Authors
S–Adult: 1311

Women — Biography
JS: 1323, 1337, 1347–48, 1352, 1355, 1358, 1370, 1379, 1384, 1386–87, 1398, 1401, 1408–10, 1424–25, 1438, 1466, 1480
S–Adult: 1306, 1338, 1349, 1390–91, 1421, 1426, 1447–48, 1450, 1456, 1469–70, 1486, 1497, 1500

Women — Business
JS: 1411

Women — Fiction
JS: 851, 927
S: 810
S–Adult: 46, 175, 891, 1270

Women — Sports
S: 1973

Women executives (U.S.)
S–Adult: 1369

JS = Junior High/Senior High; S = Senior High; S–Adult = Senior High/Adult

About the Author

CATHERINE BARR is the author or coauthor of other volumes in the Best Books series (*Best Books for Children* and *Best Books for High School Readers*) and of *Popular Series Fiction for K–6 Readers, Popular Series Fiction for Middle School and Teen Readers,* and *High/Low Handbook: Best Books and Web Sites for Reluctant Teen Readers*, 4th Edition.